Great Restaurants of South Australia COOKBOOK

Featuring selected South Australian Wineries

WATERFORD CRYSTAL

Volume 2

The object of the cookbook has been to primarily focus on South Australian restaurants, local family wineries and other businesses who locally produce fine foods.

Also included are a number of national appliance companies who support the local market.

Our aim has been to focus on the food as presented by the Chefs, rather than featuring food dishes within landscape or background scenes.

Editorials in the back of the book (Pages 126, 132 & 135) provide some interesting information about the wineries, food and products featured.

For detailed information about the restaurants and wineries, please turn to pages 140 and 142.

A sommelier page, produced by Chloe's Restaurant discusses the cellaring of our fine local wines on page 126.

This book is available at all participating restaurants, wineries and retailers appearing within the book, as well as leading bookshops and newsagents.

PUBLISHER
Simon Atkinson
PO Box 483, Paris Creek SA 5201
Telephone: (08) 8536 4011   Facsimile: (08) 8536 4322

PHOTOGRAPHY & STYLING
Peter Hoare & Carolyn Vandeleur
Mobile: 0407 587 353

PROOFREADING
The Written Word Editing Service
13 Somerset Avenue, Redwood Park SA 5097
Telephone: (08) 8263 9764 Facsimile: (08) 8263 9764

PRE-PRESS
Admotion Media
6/394 Henley Beach Road, Lockleys SA 5032
Telephone: (08) 8354 0233 Facsimile: (08) 8354 0255

PRINTING
Graphic Print Group
10-14 Kingston Avenue, Richmond SA 5033
Telephone: (08) 8443 8011 Facsimile: (08) 8234 0226

COPYRIGHT:
No part of this publication may be reproduced in part or whole, by any process, without written permission from the publisher or his representative, apart from those purposes as permitted under the Copyright Act.
Every care has been taken in regard to the accuracy of the information given in this book.
The publisher accepts no responsibility for errors and omissions.

Stemware and China by **WATERFORD WEDGWOOD**

Natural Gas delivered by Envestra

WEDGWOOD

restaurant teams

Alphutte
Restaurateur - Leo Schadegg
Chefs - Gavin Stansfield, Darren Nielsen

Argentinian Grill
Restaurateur - Paul Bratovic
Chef - Beau Leonard

Beyond India
Restaurateurs - George Papatolis
(Robby Gupta & Benita Paukkunen - absent)
Chef - Sajid Mehmood

Blanc Seafood & Wine
Restaurateur - Barbara Derham   Chef - Nick Muhlack
Blanc Bistro
Restaurateur/Chef - Norman Thanakamonnun

Blues Restaurant
Restaurateurs
Tenney & Allister Parker
Chefs - Allister Parker & Louis Nikolic

Bracegirdles
Restaurateurs - Sue & Garry Bracegirdle
Chef - Sarah Neill

Brasserie Mousttache
Gerald Viergever
Gastronome-in-Residence

Capriccio Italian Restaurant
Restaurateurs - Ilario & Francesco Scuteri
Chef - Adriana Lombardi

Chloe's Restaurant
Restaurateur - Nick Papazahariakis
Chef - Johnny Triscari

Cork & Cleaver
Restaurateurs - Stratos Pouras & Jim Boutsis
Chefs - Greg Favretto, Nick Smith, Jarrad Coffey & Janet Fox

Dhaba at the Spice kitchen
Restaurateur - Ragini Dey
Chefs - Jon Stevens & Jag Chawla

Food editorials start on page 135

Restaurant guide starts on page 140

Find more information about other great products starting on page 132

Natural Gas delivered by Envestra

The Paul Bocuse by
ROSIÈRES

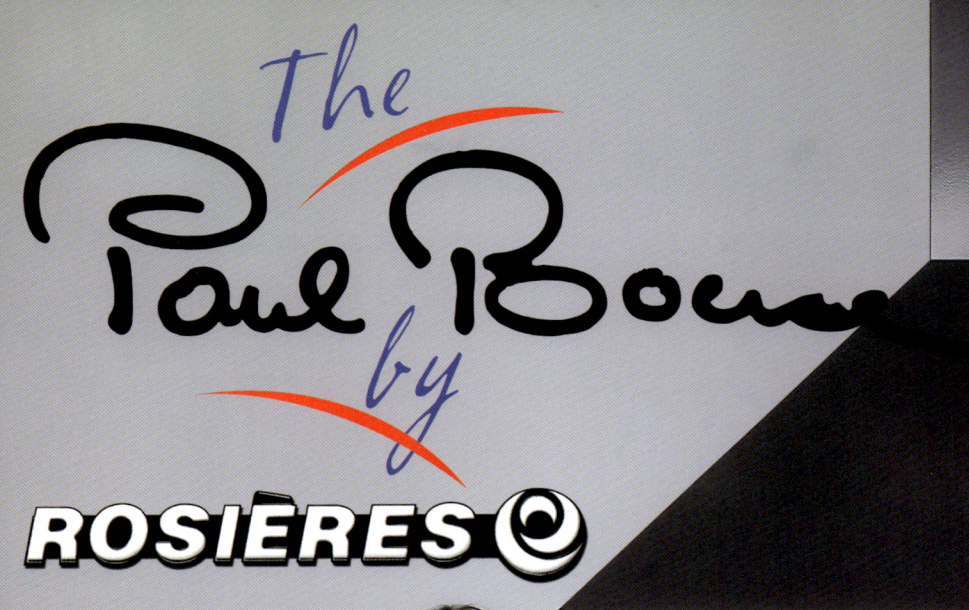

For a leaflet or further information contact Condari Pty Ltd on 1300 360 563

restaurant teams

Esca Restaurant
Restaurateur & Executive Chef - Peter DeMarco

Juergies Restaurant
Restaurateurs - Juergen & Venetta Leib
Chef - Juergen Leib

La Guillotine Restaurant
Restaurateurs - Jacques & Christine Naudin
Chefs - Jacques & Philippe Naudin

Sagarmatha Nepali Restaurant
Restaurateur - Deepak Bista
Chef - Nyingje (Sherpa) Lama

Seasons at the Bay
Restaurateurs - Mathew Tolson & Kristy Hastwell
Chefs - Mathew Tolson & Kelly McLoughney

Sevenhill Hotel
Restaurateur - Nedd Golding
Chef - Roger Graham

Star of Siam Thai Restaurant
Restaurateurs - Valeerat Ninkumvongs & Somchit Siow
Chef - Siriporn Obromwan

Sumo Station
Restaurateur - Patrick Lee
Chef - Larry Siu

The Greek Mezze
Restaurateurs - Ron Masullo & Christos Hronopolous
Chef - Bryan Montague

The Poplars at Chardonnay Lodge
Restaurateurs - James & Anne Yates
Chef - Richard Moretti

Treasury on King William
Restaurateur - Robert Parsons
Chef - Dan Nettlebeck

Wine editorials start on page 126

Winery guide starts on page 142

Sommelier editorial starts on page 124

Natural Gas delivered by Envestra

WEDGWOOD

LIVE LUXURY TODAY

Products featured: Wedgwood Night & Day Tableware, Reflections Cutlery and John Rocha at Waterford Crystal Trace White Wine Glasses.

Available in South Australia at selected Myer and David Jones Department Stores and selected retailers.
www.waterfordwedgwood.com.au Enquiries: 1300 852 022

Alphütte Restaurant

prosciutto lunganese
Serves 4

8 asparagus spears
1 tblspn basil pesto
olive oil
8 semi-dried tomatoes
2 medium tomatoes
4 bocconcini
balsamic vinegar
16 kalamata olives
4 leaves oak-leaf lettuce
200g finely sliced prosciutto

In a pot of boiling water, blanch asparagus for a few minutes until flexible. When done, place spears in iced water to cool. Drain and slice in half, diagonally.
Mix pesto with a small amount of olive oil to make a thin paste. Cut semi-dried tomatoes in half. Slice whole tomatoes into 8 even slices. Slice each bocconcini into 4 even slices. Drizzle olive oil, balsamic and pesto around the edge of a round plate (inside of the lip). Place 4 slices of tomato in the centre of each plate to form a square, with a piece of bocconcini on top of each. Arrange 4 halves of the asparagus in a cross over the tomato. In each of the 4 quarters created, place an olive and half a semi-dried tomato. Place the lettuce in the middle, with a quarter of the prosciutto rolled to form a floret on top.

chateau briand Serves 4

600g beef fillet
Dijon mustard
salt, pepper and paprika
oil
1 carrot, roughly chopped
1 onion, roughly chopped
1 celery stalk, roughly chopped

hollandaise sauce

60ml white wine vinegar
10g tarragon
500g butter
3 large egg yolks
lemon juice and pepper to taste

Trim sinew from meat, rub with mustard and sprinkle with salt, pepper and paprika. In a hot pan, add oil and brown meat on all sides. Place chopped vegetables in a baking tray and sit meat on top. Bake in a 300C oven and cook as desired, at least 30 mins for medium rare. Rest for 15 mins before slicing thinly, approx. ½ cm thick. (The closer you get to the centre, the rarer the meat will be).

sauce

Place vinegar and tarragon in a pan and reduce by half. When reduced, strain out tarragon. Melt butter in microwave until it separates, skim off the clear ghee and dispose of the milk solids. Have a small saucepan of water simmering. Place the egg yolks in a metal bowl larger than the pot of water, add the vinegar, and whisk over the simmering water until mixture begins to thicken. Remove from heat, place on a damp tea towel to stop the bowl from slipping. Slowly pour in the ghee, whisking continuously. When ½ is mixed in, add 1 tspn of hot water, and then add the remaining ghee. (Do not over-whisk, as it will cause the sauce to cool and split). Finish with a squeeze of lemon juice and pinch of pepper to taste. Serve the Chateau Briand with a red-wine demi glaze, herbed tomato and asparagus.

steak tuohy
Serves 4

4 x 180g fillet steaks
16 uncooked tiger prawns (shelled & cleaned)
mustard, salt and pepper
butter for frying
½ onion, finely chopped
30ml Irish Mist liqueur
30ml white wine
30ml red wine
40g blue vein cheese
½ tspn Dijon mustard
juice 1 orange
500ml gravy
pinch aromat seasoning
pepper to taste
50ml cream

With a paring knife, slice a small opening into the fillets and push 2 prawns into each.

Rub each steak with mustard and salt and pepper.

Cook as desired (if cooking to less than medium rare, you may need to remove prawns so that they cook, then return to pocket once they are cooked).

In a large pan, heat butter over a high heat and sauté onion. Add Irish mist and wines. Crumble in cheese and stir well.

Add mustard and juice and stir. Add gravy and reduce to a nice consistency. Season to taste. Just before serving, stir in cream.

In a small pot of simmering water, cook the remaining prawns, drain and serve with steak and sauce.

grand marnier parfait
Serves 8

1 small sponge cake
10 egg whites
250ml cream
2 tspn sugar
6 egg yolks
3 tspn Grand Marnier
80ml Limoncello
100g sugar
finely grated zest ¼ orange
1 tblspn water
125g sugar
juice of ¼ orange

Cut the sponge cake into 10mm slices then using a glass cut out rounds so that they fit the base of 8 individual moulds. Push the sponge down to fit and sprinkle with Limoncello. Whisk egg whites with about a quarter of the 100g of sugar. When nearly at peaks, add the remaining sugar. Place in fridge to cool. Whisk cream to medium peaks and place in fridge to cool. Add orange zest, 2 tspn sugar and water to pan, bring to the boil then strain off liquid. Whisk egg yolks with the 125g sugar, Grand Marnier, orange juice and zest over a water bath (simmering water) until thick and sugar has dissolved. Whisk regularly until cool. When cool, add to cream and mix in well. Fold in egg whites a little at a time. When well combined, gently pour into 8 individual moulds and freeze. Serve with fruit coulis or compote.

hedi's gleichschwer cake
Serves 8

150g butter (room temperature)
5 eggs, at room temperature
zest 1 lemon, finely chopped
1 tspn baking powder
4 plums, halved & stones removed
150g sugar
juice 1 lemon
pinch salt
160g plain flour

Separate eggs. Whip butter with ¾ of the sugar, egg yolks, lemon zest and juice until creamy. Whip egg whites, salt and remaining sugar until stiff peaks form. Mix baking powder and flour together. Carefully fold the flour and egg whites into the creamed mixture. Place mixture into a greased loaf tin. Push the plums evenly into the top of the mixture. Sprinkle a small amount of cream and sugar over the top and bake in a 180C oven for approximately 50 mins. Serve with creamy ice cream. Note: You can also use apples in place of the plums in this recipe.

AMADIO

WINE TO LIFT YOUR SPIRIT

Phone 8365 5988   www.movingjuice.com
Amadio family vineyards

moving juice — CELLAR DIRECT OUTLET

Argentinian Bar & Grill

zucchini flowers
Serves 2

stuffing
100g baby spinach
50g ricotta
salt and pepper
4 zucchini flowers
50g Queso Manchego cheese, grated

romanesco sauce
2 large capsicum, roasted
150ml tomato passata
60g almonds, toasted
60g hazelnuts, toasted
100ml sherry vinegar
100ml olive oil
125g dried breadcrumbs
salt and pepper

batter
125g SR flour
125g cornflour
1 egg
1 stubby sparkling ale
oil for frying
wedges of lemon to serve

filling
Cook spinach till wilted and mix with ricotta and Manchego cheeses. Season with salt and pepper. Remove stamen from the inside of flowers. Fill with filling and reshape.

romanesco sauce
Place all ingredients in a food processor and process until smooth.

batter
Whisk all ingredients together until it resembles the thickness of double cream.
Dip flowers in batter. Fry in hot oil till golden, by then the cheese would have melted. Serve with Romanesco sauce and lemon wedges.

lamb cutlets
Serves 4

jus
2 litres beef stock
500ml red wine
1 tblspn tomato paste

2 racks of 8 cutlets, frenched and fat scored
olive oil
salt and pepper
12 baby carrots,
1.5kg cocktail potatoes

Place all jus ingredients in a pan and bring to the boil. Lower heat and simmer till about 750ml remains.

to serve
Brush racks of lamb with oil and season with salt and pepper. Cook in a 220C oven for about 10 to 15 mins. Peel and blanch baby carrots. Steam the cocktail potatoes and allow to cool. Cut in half and deep fry till golden. Top with jus.

duck calvados
Serves 2

sauce
2 pig's trotters
10 apples
5 oranges
2 stalks celery
500g sugar
5 litres water
duck bones

size 20 duck
1 apple, halved
1 orange, halved
2 cloves
2 pimentos
salt and pepper
paprika

Place all the sauce ingredients into a large saucepan. Bring to the boil, lower heat and cook for 1 hour. Trim wingettes and excess fat from the cavity of the duck. Fill with apple, orange, cloves, pimento, salt and pepper. Using a skewer seal the cavity. Sprinkle duck with salt and paprika and steam for 90 mins or till the meat comes away from the legs. Cool duck. Using a pair of kitchen scissors, remove the spine. Using your hands remove the ribs and breast plate. To cook cover the duck with sauce and bake at 260C for 10 to 12 mins or till the skin is crisp.

manchego chicken
Serves 4

chicken stuffing
1 tblspn chopped, cooked spinach
1 tblspn grated Queso Manchego cheese
1 tblspn sultanas soaked in sugar syrup
1 tblspn pine nuts, toasted
4 chicken breast kievs, skin on

salad
8 asparagus spears, blanched   24 cherry tomatoes, halved
pitted olives as required

balsamic reduction
3 parts balsamic vinegar   one part sugar

Mix together the stuffing ingredients. Cut a small opening under the tenderloin of the chicken and fill with the stuffing. Fold tenderloin over the opening. Season chicken with salt and pepper and cook in a 220C oven for 25 mins or until cooked through.

salad - Cut asparagus spears into thirds. Heat the salad ingredients in a small amount of oil in a pan until warmed through.

balsamic reduction - Place sugar and balsamic in a small pan. Bring to the boil and reduce by half. Serve chicken and salad on a plate surrounded by a little of the balsamic reduction.

rapas selection
Serves 3

frittata
4 eggs   50ml cream
1 tspn chopped parsley   salt and pepper to taste
1 tblspn Queso Manchego cheese, grated
1 capsicum, roasted and diced

Mix ingredients together in a bowl. Pour into greased muffin tins and bake at 150C for 15 to 20 mins or till set.

oysters with champagne vinaigrette
3 parts olive oil   1 part champagne vinegar
3 oysters   coriander leaves to serve

Whisk oil and vinegar together. Pour 1 tablespoon over each oyster and garnish with fresh coriander leaves.

empanadas
dough
40g butter   400g plain flour
2 eggs, beaten   40g pig fat
2 tspn water   1 cup white wine
    1 tspn salt

Rub flour, butter and fat together until mixture resembles breadcrumbs. Mix other ingredients together. Knead the dough until it is smooth. Wrap in plastic wrap and rest for 20 minutes.

filling

1 large onion, diced
3 cloves garlic, crushed
salt
200g olives, pitted and chopped
250g minced pork
4 tblspn cumin
egg wash

Cook onion in a little oil until soft, add mince and cook till brown. Mix in remaining ingredients. Roll out dough on a lightly floured surface until 2mm thick. Cut out small circles using a pastry cutter. Brush dough with egg wash. Place one teaspoon filling on each circle. Fold the dough over and crimp closed like a pasty. Bake at 220C for 5 to 6 mins or till golden.

meatballs

1 onion, diced
1 tblspn crushed garlic
2 tblspn chopped parsley
60g dried breadcrumbs
chicken stock to cover fully
napoletana sauce to partly cover
200g minced beef
1 tblspn paprika
3 eggs, beaten
salt to taste

Cook onion in a little oil until softened. Add to remaining ingredients in a large bowl and mix well. Roll mixture into small balls and place in a baking dish. Cover with chicken stock and napoletana sauce. Cover dish with foil and bake at 220C for 45 minutes.

chicken croquettes

100g chicken thigh fillet
200g potato
2 tblspn plain flour
½ bunch spring onions, finely chopped
breadcrumbs
salt
3 tblspn béchamel sauce
egg wash

Poach chicken in water and salt until cooked thoroughly. Drain and puree in a food processor. Cook and mash potatoes. Add all ingredients except egg wash and breadcrumbs and mix together. Roll into small cylinder shapes. Flour then dip in egg wash, reshape. Flour lightly, reshape then dip in egg wash and roll in breadcrumbs. Deep fry in hot oil until golden.

crème caramel   Serves 2

red wine toffee

50ml water
100ml red wine reduced to 60ml
400g sugar

custard

2 cups milk
1 vanilla bean, split
100g sugar
6 eggs, beaten

cherry syrup

100ml cherry juice
1 cinnamon stick
200g cherries
1 clove
70g sugar

Place toffee ingredients in a pan and simmer till the liquid coats the back of a spoon. Keep stirring to a minimum. Pour toffee into the base of two 250ml dariole moulds.

custard

Heat milk, sugar and vanilla until sugar is dissolved. Add to eggs and whisk together. Sieve then pour on top of the toffee in the moulds. Bake in a 150C oven for 25 mins or until set. Once cooked place in fridge for approx. 3 hours or until firm and well chilled.

cherry syrup

Place all ingredients together in a pan and simmer on a medium heat for about 25 mins, stirring occasionally until liquid has reduced by half. Remove from heat and cool before serving. Drizzle the cherry syrup over the crème caramel and a little around the plate and place the cherries scattered to one side.

Invite a boutique
Barossan to dinner
www.balthazarbarossa.com

Beyond India Restaurant

varanasi vegetarian samosa
Makes about 16

7 to 8 potatoes
½ tsp cumin powder
1cm piece ginger, grated
¼ tspn turmeric
pinch chilli powder
¼ tspn pomegranate seed
2 tblspn lemon juice
½ cup mixed dried fruit
250g frozen peas, thawed and cooked
3 tblspn freshly chopped coriander
vegetable oil for frying
1 onion, finely chopped
½ tspn tomato paste
2 dried chillies
1 tspn crushed garlic
10 broken cashew nuts
vegetable stock
salt to taste

dough
1kg plain flour
2 tblspn ajwain seeds
200g ghee
water as required

samosa filling - mixture 1 - Cook potatoes in boiling water till tender. Cool, peel and slice potatoes.

mixture 2 - Heat oil in a wok until smoking. Add cumin and stir till mixed with the oil. Add onion, ginger, and sauté till golden brown. Add peas, tomato paste, turmeric, dried chillies, chilli powder, pomegranate seed, garlic and lemon juice. Add cashews and dried fruit. Adjust consistency by adding some vegetable stock. Add coriander and adjust salt seasoning to taste. Once cooked, remove from the heat and allow to cool. Fold the two mixtures together using gloved hands to ensure less potato breakage.

dough
Mix flour with ghee and ajwain seeds, using fingers to aerate. Add water and knead into a dough. Consistency should be that of plasticine. Form dough into a log shape. Cut into 2.5cm square pieces. Set aside for 30 mins, covered with a damp cloth. Press to flatten, dust with flour, using a rolling pin to flatten, turn, and roll again. Make dough into an oval shape then cut each piece in half. Moisten edges and form into a cone shape. Place filling inside the cone shape, moisten edges with water, press together, and fold under to form a triangular shape. Heat oil in a wok or deep fryer to 180C and cook until golden brown.

rack of lamb

Serves 4

1 tblspn lemon juice
2 tblspn French mustard
1 tspn minced ginger
4 racks of lamb or 8 half racks
1 tspn ground cumin
½ tspn salt
1 tspn turmeric
1½ tspn garam masala

2 tblspn white vinegar
2 tspn mustard oil
1 tspn crushed garlic
¼ tspn ground fenugreek
1½ tspn ground coriander
¼ tspn white pepper
½ tspn chilli powder

In a bowl, mix lemon juice, vinegar, mustard, mustard oil, ginger and garlic. Coat lamb racks with the mixture. Mix all dried spices together. Using your hands pat this mixture onto the lamb racks. If mixture is too dry, add a little extra lemon juice or vinegar. Place the racks, covered in the fridge for 3 to 4 hours. Cook in a 150 - 180C oven for approximately 25 mins. Serve with rice and kuchumber salad.

prawn masala

Serves 1

2 onions, finely chopped
¼ tspn chopped garlic
¼ tspn chopped green chilli
6 to 8 fresh curry leaves
¼ tspn brown mustard seed
2 tspn tomato paste
6 large tiger prawns
45ml chicken or veg. stock
¼ tspn white urad dal, peeled and washed
¼ tspn chopped ginger
100-120ml vegetable oil
¼ tspn fenugreek
¼ tspn cumin
¼ tspn turmeric
30ml tamarind pulp
salt to taste
30ml coconut milk

Mix onions, ginger, garlic and chilli together and set aside. In a pan, heat the oil until almost smoking and sizzle half the curry leaves, ensuring they do not lose their colour. Add fenugreek, mustard seed, cumin and white urad dal and cook for a few mins. Add onion mixture and cook until mixture has almost caramelised and reduced to about one quarter. Add turmeric, tomato paste, tamarind pulp and salt to taste. (This mixture can be kept in the fridge for up to 4 to 5 days). Heat some oil in a pan until almost smoking. Add remaining curry leaves and cook until sizzling. Add prawns, continually stirring and tossing for 20 to 30 seconds. Add stock. Add two teaspoons of the seafood sauce mixture. Deglaze the pan with the coconut milk. Serve with a timbale of rice.

simla mirch alu channa

Makes 6

2 tblspn vegetable oil
1 tblspn minced ginger
1 small onion, finely chopped
¾ tspn chilli powder
1 tspn garam masala
1 cup chickpeas, soaked overnight
6 large red or green capsicums
2 cups cooked potato, roughly cut into cubes
2 tblspn mustard seeds
1 tblspn crushed garlic
½ cup water
1 tspn salt

Heat oil in a pan until almost smoking. Add mustard seeds, stirring for 1 to 2 mins. Add ginger and garlic, then add onion and cook until starting to brown. Add potato, chickpeas, stirring together with the water. Add chilli, garam masala and salt. Cut capsicum in half and remove the seeds. Fill capsicum with potato mixture and bake in a 125 - 150C oven for around 8 to 10 mins.

fish tikka
Makes 20 pieces

20 x 3 to 4cm cubes barramundi fillet
3 to 4 curry leaves, shredded (optional)
1 tblspn minced ginger   1 tblspn crushed garlic
½ tspn chilli powder   ½ tspn turmeric
1 tblspn garam masala   salt to taste
1 tspn mustard oil   2 tblspn natural yogurt

Coat fish pieces with ginger and garlic and stand in a bowl about 3 mins. Add chilli, turmeric, garam masala, salt and curry leaves if using. Mix to combine. Add mustard oil, coat, and then add yogurt, coating all pieces. Allow to stand covered in the fridge for 2 to 3 hours. Remove from the fridge and bake in a 150 - 180C oven for about 10 - 12 mins or cook on a barbeque hot plate for around 2 mins each side. Serve on skewers.

mango chicken
Serves 4

4 pieces chicken (Kiev cut) with skin removed
2 fresh mangoes or equivalent in canned mango
4 - 5 curry leaves, shredded   salt to taste
½ tspn mustard oil   2 tblspn vegetable oil
1 tspn mustard seeds   ¼ tspn asafoetida
1 cup mango puree   2 tblspn cream

Rub chicken pieces lightly with mustard oil. Make a 5cm incision halfway through the fillet, making a pocket. Fill the pocket with either fresh or canned mango. Bake in 150C oven for 15 mins or until cooked. Set aside and keep warm.

mango sauce
Heat oil in a wide-based pan until almost smoking. Add mustard seeds, curry leaves and asafoetida. Add mango puree and stirring constantly cook over a high heat for about 2 mins. Fold in cream to make a smooth consistency and season to taste with salt. To serve spread the sauce on a plate. Place chicken fillet in the centre. Spoon a couple of tablespoons of sauce over the chicken to moisten and serve with a timbale of rice.

Natural Gas
delivered by Envestra

21

CAPE JAFFA

From humble beginnings great wines are grown

Blanc

Blanc Seafood & Wine

Blanc Bistro

carpaccio of kingfish and atlantic salmon with pickled marron and citrus dressing.

Serves 4

160g kingfish, finely sliced
160g Atlantic salmon, finely sliced
4 × 120g live marron

for the pickle
zest and juice of 2 lemons
1 red onion, finely sliced
½ head garlic, peeled and smashed
salt and freshly ground black pepper
½ bunch coriander
100ml olive oil

for the dressing
1 ruby red grapefruit
1 lime
75ml white wine
150ml olive oil
1 orange
150ml water
6 sprigs lemon thyme
salt to taste

for the salad
½ punnet baby purple basil
½ punnet baby watercress
½ punnet Tatsoi

Blanch marron in boiling water and refresh in iced water. Remove the head and soft shell on the underside of the tail with scissors. Chop all ingredients of the pickling mix except onion and toss together in a bowl with the marron tails. Cover and leave in the fridge overnight to infuse flavours. Peel citrus fruits with a knife, removing all pith. Segment and reserve the membranes and any juices. Reserve segments for garnish. Place water, wine, lemon thyme, membranes and citrus juices in a pan. Bring to the boil and reduce by half. Remove from heat and cool completely. Pour into a food processor and process until smooth.

Slowly add oil in a fine stream with the motor running until the dressing thickens slightly (like thin mayonnaise). Season with salt. Lay alternate layers of kingfish and salmon on a plate. Arrange marron alongside. In a bowl, toss salad greens with citrus segments and a little dressing. Place on top of marron. Drizzle a little dressing over the fish and finish with a little cracked pepper.

chilli bug tails with basil pesto and taglierini
Serves 4

16 bug tails

for the pesto
1 clove garlic, finely chopped
100g fresh basil leaves
1 tblspn roasted pine nuts
juice of 1 lemon
60ml olive oil
3 tspn finely grated parmesan cheese

for the sauce
1 large onion, finely diced
2 cloves garlic, finely diced
1 chilli, seeded and diced
1 tblspn chilli jam
1 tblspn Nam Prik Pow
75ml white wine
250ml Napoletana sauce
salt & chilli flakes to taste
15 basil leaves, finely sliced

for the pasta
400g taglierini (fine egg pasta)
20g unsalted butter
dried chilli flakes
8 basil leaves, finely sliced
salt

Using scissors trim away the membrane or soft shell under each bug.

pesto - Place all the ingredients into a food processor and process until it forms a thin paste. Season with salt.

sauce - Fry onion, garlic and chilli in a hot pan until it begins to colour. Add chilli jam and nam prik pow and continue cooking for 1 min. Add white wine, reduce slightly, and then add napoletana sauce. Continue reducing, stirring occasionally until sauce becomes thicker and darker (about ¾ original volume). Season with salt and chilli flakes to taste. Add basil. Fry bug tails flesh side down in a pan until they begin to colour. Add to the sauce to finish them. Cook pasta in boiling salted water until al dente. Strain and toss in a pan with butter, chilli flakes, salt and basil. Twist pasta to form a nest in the centre of each plate. Arrange bugs around the pasta and drizzle with pesto. Note: Nam Prik Pow can be found in most Asian grocery stores. Chilli jam can be found in gourmet food stores, or you can substitute sweet chilli sauce with a little extra fresh chilli and a dash of vinegar.

seared salmon with masala curry and scallops
Serves 4

4 x 180g Atlantic salmon
8 half-shell scallops
½ bunch coriander
oil for frying
pickled veg and yogurt for garnish

for the curry
30g coriander seeds
20g cumin seeds
2 cinnamon sticks
5 cardamom pods
8 cloves
2 star anise
4 medium onions
10 cloves garlic
25g ginger
2 small tomatoes
1 tblspn oil
½ bunch curry leaves
25g dried chilli powder
100ml natural yogurt
250ml fish stock
100g raisins
extra tomato to serve
100ml cream

for rice cake
500g jasmine rice
2 cloves garlic
20g ginger
1 chilli
7 mint leaves
salt
150g dry breadcrumbs
2 eggs

curry paste
Dry roast coriander, cumin, cinnamon, cardamom, cloves and star anise in a pan over medium heat until spices become aromatic. Remove from heat and grind to a powder in a mortar and pestle Place onion, garlic, ginger and tomato into a food processor and puree. In pot heat oil until very hot, add onion/tomato puree stirring quickly to avoid sticking and burning. Cook over high heat until it begins to colour. Add spices, curry leaves, chilli powder and yogurt. Reduce heat to low and cook for 1 to 2 hours, stirring occasionally until paste is quite dry.

rice cakes
Cook rice in a rice cooker or by absorption method. Finely mince garlic, ginger and chilli and slice mint. While rice is still hot, place in a bowl with onion, garlic, chilli, mint and a few pinches of salt. Form rice into logs. Wrap tightly in a few layers of plastic wrap. Place in fridge for a few hours to cool and set.

to serve
Heat a small amount of oil in a pan and fry off 50g of curry paste for a minute then add fish stock, bring to a simmer, then add raisins, 1 diced tomato and cream and continue to simmer until curry thickens slightly. Season with salt and sugar. Whisk eggs in a bowl. Cut the rice cake logs into 7cm long lengths. Remove plastic wrap, dip in eggs and breadcrumbs. Fry in oil until golden brown. Place in a 180C oven for 5 mins to warm through. Fry salmon skin side down until skin is crispy. Turn over and finish in the curry sauce. Fry scallops and finish in the sauce as well. Arrange on a plate and top with a little yogurt and garnish with pickled vegetables and coriander. Note: Pickled vegetables available from most gourmet food stores.

semolina gnocchi with grilled shellfish and bisque sauce   Serves 4

for the gnocchi
600ml milk
pinch nutmeg
salt and pepper
175g fine semolina
50g unsalted butter
2 eggs
60g finely grated parmesan cheese

bisque sauce
600g lobster shells
1 onion
5 cloves garlic
1 celery stalk
4 tblspn tomato paste
90ml brandy
pinch saffron
1 litre fish stock
120ml cream
16 black mussels
4 cooked marron
8 scallops
100g vongole (baby clams)
4 whole king prawns
olive oil
lemon juice

gnocchi - Place milk in a pot with nutmeg and a little salt and pepper.

Gently bring to boil then stir in semolina with a wooden spoon, continue stirring until mixture thickens.

Add butter and parmesan, stirring until butter is melted and incorporated. Remove from heat, stir in eggs until well mixed.

Pour mix into a tray or square cake tin and press flat. Place in fridge, chill, and set (min. 3 hours).

bisque - Roast the shells until they become fragrant, and then smash them with a mallet or rolling pin. Fry off the onion, garlic and celery in a pot, add tomato paste and cook 2 mins. Deglaze with brandy.

Add the shells and saffron, cover with fish stock. Bring to the boil and simmer 2 hours.

Remove from heat, strain through muslin, then reduce by half. Add cream and adjust seasoning with salt and pepper. Brush seafood with olive oil and lemon juice and chargrill.

Dice gnocchi and fry in a pan until golden. Arrange seafood and gnocchi on a plate and drizzle with bisque sauce.

crispy skin snapper fillet with gumbo broth, jalapeño and olive salsa
Serves 4

for the salsa
150g pitted kalamata olives
1 large ripe tomato
3 cloves garlic
1 small red onion
1 jalapeno pepper
zest of 1 lemon
30ml olive oil

for the broth
1 small onion
200g okra
700ml good quality fish stock
salt
1 tspn Tabasco sauce
1 corn on cob
1 small red capsicum, finely diced
20 black mussels
200g vongole (baby clams)
4 x 200g snapper fillet
½ bunch coriander for garnish

salsa - Cut tomato into quarters and discard the pulp. Roughly chop all ingredients and place in a food processor.

Pulse a few times so that the mixture is still chunky.

broth - Roughly chop onion and 50g okra. Place in a pot with stock and bring to the boil. Reduce slightly to about 500ml.

Season with a little salt and Tabasco. Pass through a sieve; discard the onion and okra.

Cut the kernels off the cob with a knife. Slice the rest of the okra, place in a pot with the capsicum and broth.

Bring to a simmer, add the mussels and vongole and simmer for 1 min. until they pop open.

Seal the snapper on both sides in a pan.

Finish under the grill to give a crispy skin. Divide the broth and shellfish into 4 bowls; place the snapper in the centre of each, top with a spoonful of salsa and garnish with coriander.

CERAVOLO

THE CERAVOLO VINEYARDS ARE ON HIGHLY PRIZED TERRA ROSSA RED SOILS OVER LIMESTONE ON THE FERTILE ADELAIDE PLAINS IN SOUTH AUSTRALIA. FIFTY YEARS AGO, THE CERAVOLO FAMILY MIGRATED FROM CALABRIA IN THE 35°N. PARALLEL IN THE SOUTH OF ITALY TO A NEW LIFE IN THE 35°S. PARALLEL IN AUSTRALIA. OLD WORLD TRADITION MEETS NEW WORLD WINEMAKING EXPERTISE.

www.ceravolo.com.au

Blues Restaurant

bug and beast

Serves 4

4 × med. Coliban potatoes
salt & cracked black pepper

sauce
1 med. brown onion, finely diced
3 cloves garlic, crushed
8 × prawn tails, shelled
1 tspn hot English mustard
2 tblspn grated parmesan cheese
4 × 200g venison topside
300g button mushrooms, quartered

extra virgin olive oil

4 tblspn olive oil
3 tblspn plain flour
60ml thick cream
300ml full cream milk
60ml white wine
4 × bug tails, shelled

Boil potatoes whole with their skins on until soft. Drain and set aside. Place on a baking tray and squash slightly using the palm of your hand. Drizzle with oil and season with salt and pepper. Bake in 180 – 200C oven for 15-20 mins or until crisp and golden.

sauce

In a heavy-based pan, heat oil and cook onions until clear. Add garlic and mushrooms and cook for 2 mins. Add mustard and flour to form a roux – do not allow to colour. Add wine and milk mixing well to make a sauce. Cook over a gentle heat until sauce thickens about 15 mins. Add cream, parmesan cheese and season to taste. Check consistency, you can thin down with cream, milk, water or stock if required. Heat a pan with a teaspoon of oil. Season venison – drizzle with oil, pepper and salt. Sear for 1 min on each side and transfer to a warm ovenproof dish and roast at 190C for 8-10 mins. It will come out deliciously rare! Remove from oven, cover with foil, and allow to rest for a few minutes.

Season the bug and prawn tails and steam till cooked. Make a deep cut in each of the pieces of venison and insert two prawn tails and a bug tail. Place a potato on each plate, place the venison on top of the potato and spoon the sauce over. Garnish with a sprig of fresh herbs.

grilled kangarilla marron on herb risotto
Serves 4

½ small onion, finely diced
2 tblspn olive oil
1 clove garlic
220g Arborio rice
300ml white wine
1 litre fish stock
4 tblspn olive oil
salt and pepper
100g parmesan cheese, grated
½ bunch mixed herbs, chervil, chives, basil

garlic butter
½ bunch parsley, roughly chopped
½ onion
5 cloves garlic
250g butter

8 x 120g baby marron
1 lemon
4 black peppercorns
2 bay leaves

risotto
Heat oil in a pan, add onion and cook until clear. Add garlic and rice and cook for 1 min. Add wine then slowly add fish stock a ladle at a time until rice is nearly cooked, cover with greaseproof paper and allow to steam. You may not need all the stock it depends what consistency you like your risotto. Process the mixed herbs with oil, salt, and pepper in a food processor. At the last minute stir the parmesan cheese and herb oil into risotto and adjust seasoning.

garlic butter
Place onion in a food processor and pulse until like a paste. Drain excess water from the onion and return to food processor with garlic, butter and parsley. Process until smooth.

marron
To humanely kill marron place marron in freezer. Bring a pot of water with half a lemon, bay leaves and peppercorns to the boil. Add marron and cook for 2 mins. Remove from the water and allow to cool. Split lengthways into two and remove the intestinal tract. Heat some oil in a pan and place marron shell-side up in the pan.

Allow to colour then turn placing one teaspoon of garlic butter on each half. Place in oven and cook until butter melts. Remove from oven, arrange on top of risotto, and drizzle with extra virgin olive oil. Serve with lemon wedges.

red onion and goat's cheese tartlet
Serves 4

sour cream pastry
500g plain flour
300ml sour cream
400g butter

red onion confit
5 large red onions
50g butter
125ml red wine
100g caster sugar
125ml balsamic vinegar
½ tspn ground cinnamon or Chinese five spice

sticky balsamic
150g caster sugar
200ml red wine
200ml balsamic vinegar
100g rocket for garnish
sticky balsamic for garnish
1 round goat's milk cheese, sliced

Place flour, butter and sour cream into a food processor and pulse until they combine. Remove and knead lightly on a floured surface. Refrigerate for 30 mins before using. Roll pastry until ½ cm thick and cut out 12cm rounds using a pastry cutter.

Drape pastry rounds over dariole moulds or the back of a muffin tin to form tartlet cases. Bake at 180C until golden about 10 mins.

red onion confit
Peel and slice onions. Melt butter in a pan, add onions and cook over low heat until soft. Add red wine, vinegar, spice and sugar and continue to cook until most of the liquid has cooked off. Set aside to cool.

seared coorong mulloway with panzanella and lemon-infused olive oil
Serves 4

1 ciabatta bread, one day old is better
2 tblspn salted capers, rinsed
salt and cracked pepper
24 kalamata olives, pitted
4 vine-ripened tomatoes, peeled, seeded & chopped
4 x 250gm Coorong mulloway fillets, skin scored
100ml lemon-infused olive oil
lemon wedges to serve
1 large capsicum
150ml olive oil
8 large basil leaves

Roast capsicum in a hot oven until it collapses, place in a bowl and cover with plastic wrap. Allow to cool, remove skin and seeds. Cut into strips. Remove crust from bread and drizzle with oil and season with salt and pepper. Grill bread on chargrill, grill pan or BBQ. Break the bread into bite-sized bits. In a bowl, mix the olives, capers, tomatoes, basil (torn not chopped), capsicum and bread. Drizzle with oil and season with cracked pepper. Divide the salad into four and place in the centre of each plate. Sear the mulloway fillets skin-side down for 3 mins in a hot pan, turn over and cook a further 3 mins. Place fish on salad and drizzle with the lemon-infused olive oil. Serve with fresh lemon wedges.

sticky balsamic
Put sugar, red wine and balsamic into a pan and bring to the boil. Reduce heat and simmer until volume has reduced by half. Set aside to cool.

to serve
Assemble the tartlets by placing a spoonful of confit into each pastry case and top with a few slices of goat's cheese. Return the tartlets to a hot oven and bake till the cheese colours and they are warmed through.

Dress the rocket leaves with olive oil and place them in the centre of the plates. Place a tartlet onto each plate and drizzle with the reserved sticky balsamic.

pear tarte tatin with red wine ice cream   Serves 4

tarte tatin
2 firm pears (cut in half, seeds removed)
50g butter
300g puff pastry
200g sugar
½ tspn cinnamon butter

red wine ice cream
1400ml red wine
2 cinnamon sticks
12 egg yolks
650g unsalted butter
6 cloves
2 vanilla pods
400g caster sugar

red wine ice cream - Boil one litre of the red wine with the cloves, cinnamon and vanilla pods. Allow to reduce in volume by half. Add remaining red wine and bring to the boil. In a large bowl, mix the egg yolks with the sugar and butter. Add the wine gradually, a little at a time and blend with a stab mixer. Return mixture to a double boiler and cook until it coats the back of a spoon. Strain through a fine sieve and cool for 2 hours. Churn in an ice cream machine until set. Store in freezer until ready to use.

tarte tatin - Melt butter and sugar in an ovenproof pan (with ovenproof handles) and allow to colour to a sandy caramel colour. Place pears flat side down onto the sugar mixture and sprinkle with cinnamon and dot with a knob of butter on each pear. Cover with rounds of puff pastry.

Or you can make one big one instead of individual sized ones, in which case you cover with a whole piece of pastry. Bake in an 180C oven until pastry is golden. Remove from the oven and allow to cool for 1-2 mins, then cover pan with a large heatproof tray. Using a tea towel to protect against the heat, hold the tray firmly against the pan and with one swift movement invert the pan to allow the tarts to drop onto the tray along with the syrup. Leave in a warm place until ready to serve. Place a tarte in the centre of each serving plate accompanied by a scoop of red wine ice cream.

blueberry crème brulee   Serves 4

½ vanilla pod
1 egg
50g caster sugar
300ml thickened cream
2 egg yolks
blueberries

Split the vanilla pod lengthwise and put it into a saucepan, add cream and heat slowly to infuse the vanilla. In a large bowl, whisk the eggs, yolks and sugar. Whisk the hot cream slowly into the eggs. Strain mixture through a fine sieve. Whisk continually over a double boiler until the custard has thickened. Place a few blueberries into 6 individual 5cm wide ramekins and pour in the custard. Refrigerate until custard has set (2 to 4 hours). Dust the top of each brulee with sugar and caramelise with a blowtorch or under a very hot griller. Serve garnished with remaining blueberries.

CHAIN OF PONDS

"Meet a new Australian with an Italian Accent"

CHAIN OF PONDS WINES PTY LTD
Main Adelaide to Mannum Rd, Gumeracha SA 5233
08 8389 1415
winery@chainofponds.com.au
www.chainofponds.com.au

Tasting Room - Open 7 days a week

Adelaide Hills Wine Region

Bracegirdles

pure indulgence
Serves 4

250g butter, softened
125g granulated sugar
125g perle sugar or sugar cubes, coarsely crushed
4 eggs
250g plain flour
50g vanilla sugar
3 tspn olive oil

Warm the butter until almost melted.

Mix in the sugars then whisk in eggs one at a time.

Mix the flour and vanilla sugar and add to mixture, stirring vigorously, add oil and mix well.

Heat and grease a waffle iron pour in 2 tblspn of the mixture and bake until golden brown.

Serve with liquid Belgian chocolate, fresh strawberries and vanilla ice cream.

hot chocolate with chilli
Serves 1

¼ tspn ground chilli
¼ tspn ground cinnamon
100g dark Belgian chocolate buttons
250ml milk
cocoa powder
marshmallow

Mix chilli and cinnamon powders together. Melt chocolate to blood temperature in large mug. Stir chilli mixture into melted chocolate.

Heat milk and froth if possible. Slowly stir the milk into the chocolate mixture until completely dissolved.

Decorate with cocoa powder and marshmallow.

chocolate affair
Serves 4

250g fine Belgian chocolate
oranges
bananas
pineapple
strawberries
chocolate fondue set

Melt chocolate gently in a bowl over a saucepan quarter-filled with water.

Do not allow water to boil or come over the edge of the bowl.

When chocolate has melted, transfer to fondue bowl and light candle. Wash all the fruit and dry well.

Cut oranges, bananas and pineapple into portions. Arrange on a serving plate with fondue and enjoy!

bailey's seduction
Serves 4

160g dark Belgian chocolate
2/3 cup thickened cream
2 tblspn sugar
3 egg yolks
3 egg whites
25ml Bailey's Irish Crème
chocolate cone shape made with Belgian chocolate
fresh strawberries

Melt the chocolate. Whip cream until soft peaks form. Whip half the sugar with egg yolks until thick and fluffy.

Add remaining sugar to egg whites and whip to stiff peaks.

Mix Baileys into melted chocolate.

Fold 1/3 of whipped cream into melted chocolate.

Fold whipped egg yolk mixture into chocolate mix.

Alternatively, fold in the remaining cream, then whipped egg whites to the chocolate mixture until smooth and glossy.

Pipe mixture into pre-made cone shape chocolate and decorate with fresh strawberries.

chocolate bomb
Serves 4

100g milk chocolate almonds
1 litre quality vanilla ice cream
Baileys to taste
melted Belgian milk chocolate

Gently crush almonds in blender. Place ice cream in mixing bowl, add Baileys slowly, and mix well.

Add crushed almonds and stir in well. Put in freezer.

To serve put 2 scoops in a large sundae dessert dish and accompany with a small bowl of melted chocolate.

good morning muesli
Serves 1

toasted muesli with fruit and nuts
organic yogurt with vanilla bean and honey
freshly cut strawberries
freshly cut bananas

In a tall sundae glass, layer one tablespoon of muesli, one tablespoon of yogurt and a layer of cut strawberries and bananas.

Repeat finishing with a layer of fruit.

Serve with good coffee.

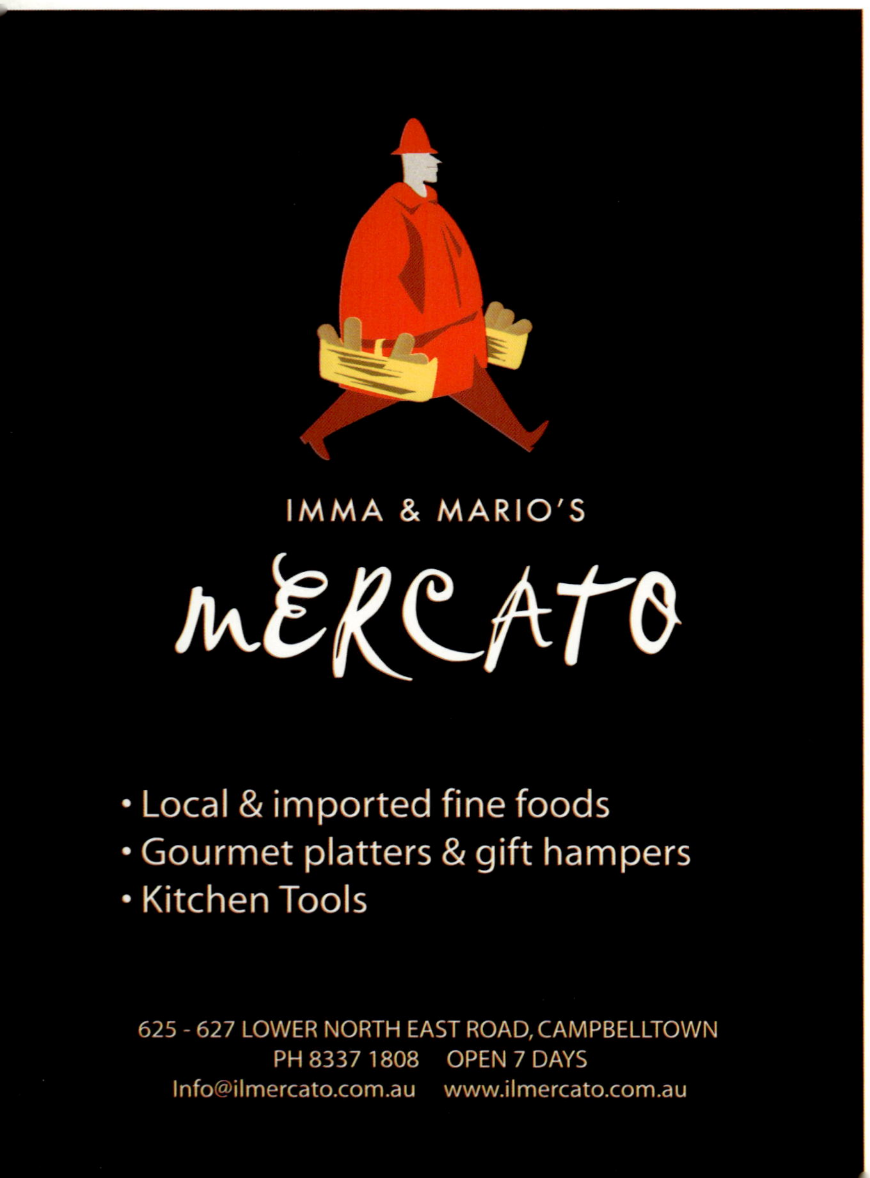

IMMA & MARIO'S
mercato

- Local & imported fine foods
- Gourmet platters & gift hampers
- Kitchen Tools

625 - 627 LOWER NORTH EAST ROAD, CAMPBELLTOWN
PH 8337 1808   OPEN 7 DAYS
Info@ilmercato.com.au   www.ilmercato.com.au

WEDGWOOD

The three elements of chocolate excellence

Fruit from the orchards of the Riverland

The very best chocolate

Hand crafted perfection

THE FINEST AUSTRALIAN
HAVENHAND
HANDMADE
FRUIT CHOCOLATES

22 Peake Terrace, Waikerie
Phone: 08 8541 2134
See editorial on page 135

Perfection from the Barossa, naturally handmade by Charles Cimicky

Brasserie Moustache

mussels as enjoyed at moustache
Serves 4

500g mussels, cleaned & de-bearded
2 tblspn unsalted butter
2 tblspn Eden Valley olive oil
(or other quality oil)
4 eschalots, peeled and finely sliced
½ tspn sea salt
1 tspn curry powder or paste
250ml Herschke "Joseph Hill"
(or other quality Gewurztraminer)
½ cup cream
pepper
1 cup sliced Italian parsley
1 French sourdough baguette, sliced

Rinse and allow cleaned mussels to dry. In a large deep saucepan, add butter and oil, melt slowly over a medium heat. Add eschalots and salt, sweat slowly for 3 - 4 mins. Add curry powder and wine. Bring to the boil and reduce by half, this takes 5 - 6 mins. Add mussels and cream, season with the pepper and stir. Cover and cook for about 3 - 5 mins. Check and stir occasionally. Do not overcook. When mussels have opened, transfer to warm bowls and sprinkle with the parsley. Pour broth over mussels and serve with sliced baguette.

keyneton pistou
Serves 4

the beans
500g fresh small white beans, shelled
or 250g dried white kidney beans (soaked overnight)
500g borlotti beans in the pod, shelled
or 250g dried borlotti beans (soaked overnight)
3 tblspn extra virgin olive oil
3 cloves garlic, finely chopped
fresh bay leaves and several sprigs of thyme
(tied together with string - bouquet garni)
2 litres water or homemade chicken stock
sea salt to taste

the soup
125ml extra virgin olive oil
2 leeks, white and tender green parts finely sliced
2 onions, coarsely chopped
10 cloves garlic, cut into ¼ lengthwise
200g small carrots, peeled and trimmed
500g potatoes, peeled and cubed
fresh bay leaves and several sprigs of thyme
(tied together with string - bouquet garni)
200g zucchini, halved lengthwise and cut into 'half moons'
250g tomatoes, peeled, cored and chopped
250g green beans, trimmed and ¼
sea salt to taste
1 qty of pistou
150g parmesan, freshly grated
150g gruyere cheese, grated

pistou
4 cloves garlic
sea salt to taste
2 large bunches basil
125ml extra virgin olive oil

Drain and rinse the beans if using dried. In a large heavy-based pan, combine the oil, garlic and bouquet garni. Cook over a moderate heat until the garlic is soft and fragrant, about 2 mins.

Add beans; stir for 1 min, until well coated with oil. Add water and stir. Cover, bring to a simmer for 5 mins for fresh beans or 30 mins for dried. Season lightly with salt. Add extra water or stock if needed.

soup
In a 10-litre stockpot, combine oil, leeks, onions and garlic over a low heat and sweat for about 2 - 3 mins, stirring from time to time.

Add the carrots, potatoes and bouquet garni and soften over moderate heat, stirring frequently. Remove and discard the bouquet garni from the beans. Add the beans and their cooking liquid to the vegetables in the stockpot. Add zucchini, tomatoes and green beans, along with 2 litres of cold water.

Simmer gently, uncovered until the beans are very tender, about 20 mins. Add extra water if the soup becomes too thick. Taste and adjust the seasoning. Serve the soup very hot with the pistou and cheeses to stir through.

pistou
Place the garlic, salt and basil into a food processor and process to a paste. Add the oil, process again. Taste for seasoning. Stir well just before serving.

Note: Pistou, unlike the Italian Pesto does not contain pine nuts or cheese.

cassoulet
Serves 4

duck confit
4 duck legs
450g duck fat
4 sprigs fresh thyme
1 clove garlic
sea salt
black pepper
1 sprig fresh rosemary

cassoulet
1.1kg dried white beans, soaked overnight
2 onions, roughly chopped
2 large carrots, roughly chopped
sea salt and coarse ground pepper
900g pork belly
1 dried bay leaf or 3 fresh
12 cloves garlic or to taste
6 thin pork sausages
450g pork rind
2 sprigs thyme
60g duck fat
3 onions, thinly sliced

Rub the duck generously with salt, place in a shallow dish and cover with plastic wrap. Refrigerate overnight. Preheat oven to 190C. Melt duck fat in a pan until it is clear. Season the duck legs with pepper and place in an ovenproof casserole. Place thyme, rosemary and garlic amongst the duck legs, pour the duck fat over the legs so they are just covered. Cover the dish with foil and cook in the oven for about 1 hour. Duck is cooked when the shin comes away from the ankle and the meat comes away easily from the leg. Meat should be tender.

Cool and place as it is in the fridge, sealed under the fat. They will keep this way until you are ready to use them. Drain and rinse the beans. Bring a large pot of water to the boil, add beans and cook for about 5 mins. Add pork belly, onions, carrot, bay leaves and thyme. Add 150g of the pork rind. Pour in enough water to cover the beans by about 4cm. Add salt and pepper and bring back to the boil. Leave the mixture to simmer until beans are tender about one hour. Cool for about 20 mins.

Remove the vegetables and herbs. A trick is to loosely tie in a piece of cheesecloth all the ingredients that need to be removed, then you can just lift out the whole bundle. Remove the pork belly and cut into 5cm squares, and set aside. Strain the beans and the rind and set aside, keeping the cooking liquid separate. Cut the rind into 2cm squares. In a saucepan, heat all but one tablespoon of the duck fat over a medium heat until it goes all shimmery and transparent. Carefully add the sausages and brown on all sides. Remove and drain on paper towel.

In the same pan, brown the onion, garlic and reserved squares of pork rind. Remove and put into a blender or food processor. Add the reserved tablespoon duck fat and puree until smooth. Set aside. Preheat oven to 180C. Place the uncooked pork rind in the bottom of a deep earthenware ovenproof dish. Arrange all the ingredients in alternate layers, beginning with a layer of beans, then the coarsely sliced sausages, more beans, then pork belly, beans, duck confit and finally more beans, between each layer add some of the onion/pork rind puree. Add enough of the bean cooking liquid to just cover the top layer of the beans, reserving about 1 cup in the fridge for later use.

Cook the cassoulet in the oven for 1 hour, reduce heat to 130C and cook for a further hour. Remove from the oven and cool. Refrigerate overnight. Next day, preheat oven to 180C. Cook the cassoulet for one hour. Break the crust on the top with a spoon and add 60ml of the reserved bean cooking liquid. Reduce the heat to 130C and cook for 15 mins, and then serve.

tartelettes aux pommes lionel poilane
Serves 4

pastry
175g plain flour
100g unsalted butter
2 tspn sugar
pinch salt
3 tblspn iced water

filling
4 Golden Delicious or Granny Smith apples (about 750g)
60g unsalted butter
50g granulated sugar
1 egg, beaten
1 tblspn light brown sugar

Place 150g of the flour, butter, sugar and salt into a food processor. Process no more than 10 seconds, just so that the mixture looks like coarse crumbs. Add water and pulse, until the pastry begins to hold together, (about 6 to 8 pulses). Do not allow to form a ball. Transfer the pastry to some waxed paper; flatten the dough into a round disc.

If the dough seems sticky, sprinkle it with a tablespoon at a time of the remaining flour and work in. Wrap the pastry in waxed paper and put in the fridge for at least 1 hour. Preheat oven to 220C. Divide the dough into four equal portions. On a floured surface, roll out to 15cm circles. Place on an oiled baking sheet and put in the fridge until ready to bake. Peel and core the apples, cut each apple into 12 even wedges. In a large heavy-based frying pan, melt the butter over medium heat until hot but not smoking. Add apples and sprinkle with the sugar, sauté until lightly brown, about 15 mins. Remove the pastry from the fridge and place 12 wedges of apple in the centre of each pastry disc. Fold the edges over the fruit to form a square of about 10cm x 10cm. Brush the border with beaten egg. Bake until golden, about 20 mins. Sprinkle the apple tartelettes with brown sugar and serve warm or cold with cream and fresh berries.

- Winery Restaurant open for Lunch & Dinner

Restaurant

- Garden Ceremonies

- Wedding Receptions & Functions

Accommodation

- Luxury spa villas

- Local Produce & Wine tasting & Sales

Cellar Door

- Open 7 days

Currency Creek Estate Wines

Winery Rd, Currency Creek, South Australia 5214
www.currencycreekwines.com.au

Phone: 08 8555 4069
enquiries@currencycreekwines.com.au

Capriccio Italian Restaurant

penne con prosciutto
Serves 4

100ml olive oil
1 onion, finely diced
200g mushrooms, thinly sliced
2 cloves garlic, chopped
100g semi-sundried tomatoes
500g prosciutto, sliced
100ml white wine
4 tomatoes, chopped
½ bunch basil, chopped
salt and pepper
1kg penne, cooked
1 tspn chopped parsley

Heat 50ml oil in frypan.

Add onion, mushrooms, garlic, sundried tomatoes and prosciutto.

Cook until prosciutto changes colour.

Add wine, tomatoes, basil and salt and pepper to taste.

Toss the pasta through, adding rest of the oil.

To serve, sprinkle with parsley.

fillet steak poivere
Serves 4

300g fillet steak
400ml thickened cream
50ml white wine
100g green peppercorns
salt and pepper
1 tspn chopped parsley
60ml olive oil
6 large potatoes
2 red capsicums
1 clove garlic
1 large zucchini

Chargrill steak to your liking. Add 300ml cream, wine and peppercorns to a frypan.

Reduce sauce on high heat then reduce to a simmer. If sauce splits, add 2-3 tspn hot water.

Add rest of cream and season to taste with salt and pepper. Pour sauce over the top of steak and sprinkle with parsley.

Serve with vegetables as below. Heat oil in frypan until oil smokes. Add finely sliced potatoes, capsicum, garlic and zucchini and cook until tender.

Add salt and pepper to taste. Serve vegetables on the side.

spaghetti amatriciana
Serves 4

4 cans whole peeled tomatoes
50ml olive oil
3 onions, chopped
3 cloves garlic, finely chopped
½ bunch parsley, finely chopped
1 bunch basil, finely chopped
salt and pepper
1kg pkt spaghetti
50g butter
1 tspn chilli powder
200g bacon, thinly sliced
30ml white wine
4 tomatoes, diced

Blend the canned tomatoes in a blender or food processor. Heat oil in a saucepan; add 1 onion, 1 clove garlic and cook lightly. Add tomatoes, bring to the boil, reduce heat and simmer for about 1 hour.

Add 1 teaspoon of parsley and half the basil and season to taste with salt and pepper. Meanwhile, cook pasta according to directions on the back of the packet.

Place butter into a large frying pan. When melted, add remaining onions, chilli, bacon and garlic. Sauté until bacon and onion are cooked.

Drain excess fat, add wine and diced tomatoes. Allow the flavours to interact then add basil, parsley and napoletana sauce.

Toss the pasta through and serve.

osso bucco milanese
Serves 4

4 cans peeled tomatoes
1.5kg osso bucco
50g plain flour
100ml vegetable oil
salt and white pepper
100ml white wine
1 onion, finely chopped
1 red capsicum, finely chopped
100g black kalamata olives
1 tspn chopped parsley
5-6 large potatoes
50ml milk
40g butter
50ml olive oil
2 carrots
100g mushrooms
2 zucchinis
1 clove garlic, chopped
1 tspn parsley

Preheat oven to 180-200C. Blend the canned tomatoes. Heat a large tray over the stovetop or you can use a large frypan. Lightly coat the osso bucco with flour. Heat oil either on the tray or in frypan and sear both sides of the osso bucco. Add salt, pepper and wine, wait a few moments, then add onion, capsicum, olives, parsley and tomatoes. Allow flavours to blend for about 5 mins. Cover with foil and cook for 2 hours in the oven. Boil potatoes, mash adding salt, pepper, milk and butter. Heat olive oil in a frying pan. Sauté sliced vegetables, adding garlic, salt and pepper. Place mashed potato on bottom of plate adding the osso bucco over the top. Serve with the vegetables and sprinkle with parsley.

Dennis
OF McLAREN VALE

WINES OF DISTINCTION

Chloe's Restaurant

roasted gawler river quail on white truffle-scented noodles and salted mushroom
Serves 1

½ cup flour
2 egg yolks
1 tspn olive oil
a pinch salt
1 extra large quail
2 oyster mushrooms, sliced
2 enoki mushrooms, sliced
1 shitake mushroom, sliced
1 spring onion, cut into thin strips
2 sprigs parsley
6 snow pea sprouts
1 sprig dill
4 sprigs chervil
2 tspn butter
1 tspn truffle oil
1 tomato, diced
salt and pepper

Make pasta dough by mixing flour, eggs, oil and salt. Using a pasta machine, pass through on no. 7 then through linguini cutter. Season and roast quail in a 180C oven for 10 minutes. Rest for 7 mins.

Fry mushrooms until golden. Remove from heat; add herbs, butter, truffle, tomato, salt, and pepper.

Cook pasta in boiling, salted water for 3 mins then add to mushroom mixture. Serve quail on top of pasta. Spoon juices from tray over the top and sprinkle with some crispy fried mushrooms. Season well.

garfish, scallop and crispy duck skin salad with ginger shallot caramel

Serves 1

1 leaf butter lettuce
6 rocket leaves
2 sprigs coriander
2 sprigs mint
6 snow pea sprouts
100ml sesame oil
1 spring onion, cut into thin strips
4 sprigs chervil
1 mild chilli, cut into thin strips
1 sprig dill
2 shallots, sliced
½ cup caster sugar
1 tblspn Mitsukan vinegar
1g ginger, grated
1 tspn fish sauce
juice 2 limes
1 piece duck skin
50g tempura flour
2 garfish fillets
2 fresh scallops

Wash lettuce and herbs in cold water. Drain and pick lettuce and herbs until very small.

Mix in the spring onion and chilli and set aside. In a small pot fry shallots in sesame oil until golden brown.

Add sugar and cook till a toffee forms. Add ginger, vinegar, fish sauce, lime juice. Bring to the boil then remove from heat and cool. Fry duck skin slowly till crisp.

Flour and pan-fry garfish and scallops. Assemble salad, drizzle with caramel and finish with crushed duck skin.

topless chocolate pastry, armagnac & prune ice cream & macerated muscatels
Serves 1

1 sheet puff pastry

ice cream
500ml cream
300g sugar
50g prunes, chopped
100ml sugar syrup
1 cinnamon stick
6 egg yolks
100ml Armagnac
pinch cinnamon
1 star anise
50g muscatels, chopped

chocolate filling
40g plain flour
20g icing sugar
100g chocolate calabaut, melted
40g almond meal
40g butter, melted
4 egg whites

Using a round cutter, cut a round of pastry. With the off cuts, cut a strip to place on the edge of the round. Set aside in fridge.

ice cream - Cook prunes in Armagnac for 30 secs. Add cream and bring to 65C. Add egg yolks and sugar, whisking vigorously for 30 sec. Churn in an ice cream machine to its specifications. Freeze. In a pot, simmer sugar syrup, star anise, cinnamon and muscatels for 3 mins. Cover and set aside.

chocolate filling - Mix flour, almond meal, icing sugar. Add chocolate, butter and egg whites and beat for 3 mins on low. Place in fridge. Serve with a small scoop of the chocolate in centre of cold pastry. Bake 180C for 10 mins. Spoon muscatels on one side of plate and top with a scoop of ice cream. Place hot pastry on plate and dust with icing sugar.

lasagne of woodside edith ash & caramelised pumpkin
Serves 1

pasta
200g plain flour
1 whole egg
300g butternut pumpkin
50g brown sugar
100g Woodside Edith goat's cheese
3 egg yolks
1 tspn olive oil
pinch salt
10 baby spinach leaves

sabayon
1 tspr Chardonnay vinegar
1 tspn chicken stock
pinch salt and pepper
finely grated parmesan cheese
1 egg
1 sprig thyme
1 tspn truffle essence

salad
1 spring onion, cut into thin strips
2 roma tomatoes, diced
10 baby rocket leaves
8 snow pea sprouts

Prepare pasta by mixing flour, eggs, oil and salt till smooth. Rest 20 mins. Slice 1cm square pieces from the solid part of the pumpkin. Place on a tray lined with greaseproof. Season with salt, pepper, and sprinkle with brown sugar. Roast in 180C oven for 5 mins. Slice goat's cheese and put in fridge. Using a pasta machine, roll out to no. 7 and cut three 8cm x 8cm pieces. Cook in boiling, salted water. Prepare sabayon by whisking in a bowl over boiling water until thick. Assemble goat's cheese, pumpkin and spinach in a stack. Mask with sabayon and grated parmesan. Garnish with a salad of snow pea sprouts, spring onion, tomato and rocket.

poached rhubarb with spiced savarin and homemade yogurt sorbet

Serves 1

2 rhubarb stalks
200ml double sugar syrup
1 vanilla pod, split lengthwise
1 tblspn Cointreau

savarin dough
50ml milk
1 egg
2 tspn sugar
10g yeast
200g plain flour
80g butter, softened

soaking syrup
1 lemon grass stalk
1 star anise
200ml single sugar syrup
1 cinnamon stick

sorbet
200ml sugar
200ml water
2 tspn lemon juice
100ml yogurt

Peel rhubarb and cut into 10cm lengths. Place in a saucepan with sugar syrup, cointreau and vanilla. Bring to a simmer for 3 min then remove from heat and steep for 1 hour.

savarin
Mix milk, egg, sugar and yeast together in an electric mixer on low. Add flour and mix. Add softened butter to dough. Work for 2 mins.

Place in fridge to prove overnight. Take out and form into baking moulds. Prove then bake in 160C oven for 10 mins. Turn out to cool.

soaking Syrup
Bring all ingredients to the boil and allow to steep for 10 mins. Pour over the savarin.

sorbet
Bring sugar, water and lemon juice to the boil. Then chill. In an ice cream machine, proceed to churn according to the manufacturer's directions.

Add yogurt about halfway through the process then freeze.

Place the rhubarb on serving plate, top with the savarin and sorbet.

Drizzle with the rhubarb syrup.

DiGiorgio

FAMILY WINES

COONAWARRA

Available at leading restaurants and independent retail outlets throughout South Australia

DiGiorgio Family Wines
Riddoch Highway, Coonawarra

Cellar door open for tasting daily from 10am to 5pm.

Ph 08 8736 3222
Fax 08 8736 3233
dfw@digiorgio.com.au

DiGiorgio Family Wines
LUCINDALE · COONAWARRA · SOUTH AUSTRALIA
www.digiorgio.com.au

Cork & Cleaver

oyster duo florentine / manhattan
Serves 4

florentine
1 large brown onion, finely chopped
oil for frying
2 cloves garlic, finely chopped
350g baby spinach, washed
250g grated parmesan cheese
48 oysters in the shell
400g bacon, finely sliced
200g roasted pine nuts
salt and pepper
300ml cream
2 eggs

Heat oil in a frying pan, add onion, garlic and bacon, and cook until golden brown in colour. Drain and add spinach, pine nuts, parmesan cheese and salt and pepper to taste. Cook until spinach wilts. Allow to cool. In a separate bowl, beat eggs and cream together. Transfer cooled spinach mixture to chopping board and chop finely. Add to cream and eggs and mix thoroughly. Warm oysters under the griller and top with the spinach mixture. Cook under grill until lightly browned.

manhattan
Serves 4

3 very ripe tomatoes, pulp removed
1 small red onion, chopped
100ml olive oil
300g bacon, finely chopped
300ml Worcestershire sauce
1 bunch chives, chopped
25ml red wine vinegar
48 oysters in the shell
lemon or lime wedges

Place onion, tomatoes and chives into a small bowl. Add oil and vinegar and mix to combine. Set aside.

Sprinkle tops of oysters with bacon and drizzle with Worcestershire sauce. Cook under griller until bacon is browned. Remove and top with a little of the reserved tomato salsa mixture. Return to the grill and heat for a moment. Serve with lime or lemon wedges.

louisiana crab cakes
Serves 8

beer batter
375ml bottle Cooper's ale
1 tspn turmeric
300g plain flour
1 tspn baking powder
salt and pepper

crab cakes
1.5kg crabmeat
500g firm white fish fillets
2 corn cobs, steamed and kernels removed
2 chillies
2 eggs
1 cup dry breadcrumbs
150ml mayonnaise
1 bunch chives, chopped
100ml chilli sauce
salt to taste
1 litre oil for frying
flour for dusting
julienned vegetables for serving
300ml sweet chilli sauce for dipping

beer batter
Combine all ingredients in a food processor and set aside.

crab cakes
Process crab and fish in a food processor. Chop corn and chillies, combine remaining crab cake ingredients and processed fish in a bowl and mix well.

Divide mixture into 80g portions and form into balls. Heat oil; meanwhile dust the fish balls with flour.

Dip into beer batter allowing excess to drip off and cook in hot oil until golden brown.

Serve on a bed of julienned vegetables with a sweet chilli dipping sauce.

prime rib off the bone with creamed spinach and red wine sauce
Serves 4

3 bunches spinach, stalks removed
2 cloves garlic, finely chopped
250g grated parmesan cheese
sweet potatoes to serve
50g butter
500ml cream
salt & pepper to taste

red wine sauce
50g chopped shallots
1 litre demi-glace (see note)
500ml red wine Shiraz

Blanch spinach and refresh in iced water. Drain and squeeze dry; process in a food processor. In a frying pan, melt butter and sauté garlic lightly. Add spinach and cream and heat through. Add parmesan cheese and season to taste with salt and pepper.

red wine sauce - Place shallots and red wine into a small saucepan. Bring to the boil, lower heat and reduce by 2/3. Add demi-glace and simmer gently until a coating consistency. Strain. Cook steaks to your liking, then rest. To serve pour sauce over steaks with creamed spinach on the side. Garnish with some fried sweet potato.
Note: Demi-glace is a rich glossy brown sauce from which the liquid has been partly evaporated.

steak tartar (classic)
Serves 1 or 4 as an entrée

200g beef tenderloin
1 tspn chopped capers
1 tspn chopped dill gherkin
1 tspn chopped red onion
1 tspn salt
1 tspn horseradish

dry ingredients
1 tspn chopped parsley
1 tspn paprika
1 tspn chopped anchovies
1 tspn pepper
1 tspn chopped green peppercorns

to serve
2 tblspn brandy
1 tspn Tabasco sauce
1 egg yolk
2 tblspn Worcestershire sauce
2 cloves minced garlic
4 slices toasted Turkish bread

Chop or process the tenderloin, being very careful to keep the mince that little bit coarse. Remove any fat or sinew at this point. On a separate plate, arrange the dry ingredients around the plate. Form the minced tenderloin into a ball. Place in the centre of the plate so dry ingredients are surrounding it. Using an egg, form a depression in the centre of the mince. Place the brandy, sauces and garlic in the depression and top with the egg yolk. Serve with slices of toasted Turkish bread.

sticky date pudding
Serves 8

375g dates, finely chopped
600ml water
150g butter
5 eggs
vanilla ice cream for serving

1 tspn vanilla essence
30g bi-carb soda
330g sugar
450g SR flour, sifted

butterscotch sauce
200g butter
200ml cream
200g brown sugar

Preheat oven to 180C. Line a large baking dish with baking paper. In a pan place dates, vanilla essence and water. Bring to the boil, add bi-carb and cool. Cream butter until it turns white, add sugar, and then add eggs one at a time beating well between each addition. Add flour to the butter mixture. Add date mixture and mix to combine. Pour mixture into baking dish and bake for approx. 45 minutes or until a skewer inserted in the centre comes out clean. Serve with butterscotch sauce and ice cream.

butterscotch sauce
Melt butter over a low heat. Whisk in brown sugar. Add cream being careful not to overheat.

scotch fillet tower
Serves 4

4 x 200g aged scotch fillet steaks
1 large eggplant, barbecued and sliced
1 zucchini, barbecued and sliced
2 red capsicums, roasted and sliced
4 slices good quality melting cheese
6 tspn basil pesto
100ml balsamic vinegar
100ml extra virgin olive oil

Cook steaks to your liking and set aside to rest. Using the eggplant as the base, place a slice of eggplant, top with zucchini and capsicum and finish with cheese. Grill until cheese has melted.

Place vegetable tower on top of each steak and finish with some basil pesto. To serve, drizzle with combined balsamic vinegar and olive oil.

ELDREDGE
Vineyards

One of the best kept secrets of the Clare Valley

Dhaba
at the Spice kitchen

prawns with vegetables and 5 spice
Serves 4

1 tspn panch phoron (see note)
2 fresh green chillies, split
2 tblspn ginger paste
1 tspn turmeric powder
500g green prawns, shelled and deveined
1 cup thinly sliced vegetables (cauliflower, peas, capsicum, cabbage etc.)
1 tblspn oil
1 cup sliced onion
2 tblspn garlic paste
salt to taste

Heat oil in a pan; add panch phoron, chillies, then the onion and prawns with the ginger, garlic, turmeric and salt. Cook for 2 minutes on a high heat. Add the vegetables, cover and finish cooking on a low heat. Note: Panch phoron or Indian 5 spice is a mixture of fenugreek, black and yellow mustard seeds, onion seeds and fennel seeds.

mixed vegetable coconut sambar
Serves 4

½ cup red lentils, washed and drained
2 cups diced vegetables
(eggplant, cauliflower, green beans, capsicum, tomato)
1 tblspn tamarind pulp
1 tspn turmeric
¼ cup chopped onion
chopped coriander leaves to garnish

sambar paste
¼ tspn powdered fenugreek seeds
1 tspn red chilli powder
1 tspn powdered cumin
2 tblspn powdered coriander
5 tblspn desiccated coconut
2 tblspn powdered yellow split peas

tempering
½ tspn brown mustard seeds
2 tblspn ghee
1 tspn cumin seeds
¼ tspn fenugreek
2 dry red chillies
few curry leaves

Cook red lentils in boiling water until soft. Mix the sambar paste ingredients together with the tamarind pulp and turmeric and add to the lentils along with the vegetables. Cook for a further 15 minutes. Season to taste. In a separate frying pan, heat the ghee and add the tempering ingredients. When they crackle, add onions and sauté till clear. Pour the tempering over the sambar. Garnish with chopped coriander & serve with boiled rice.

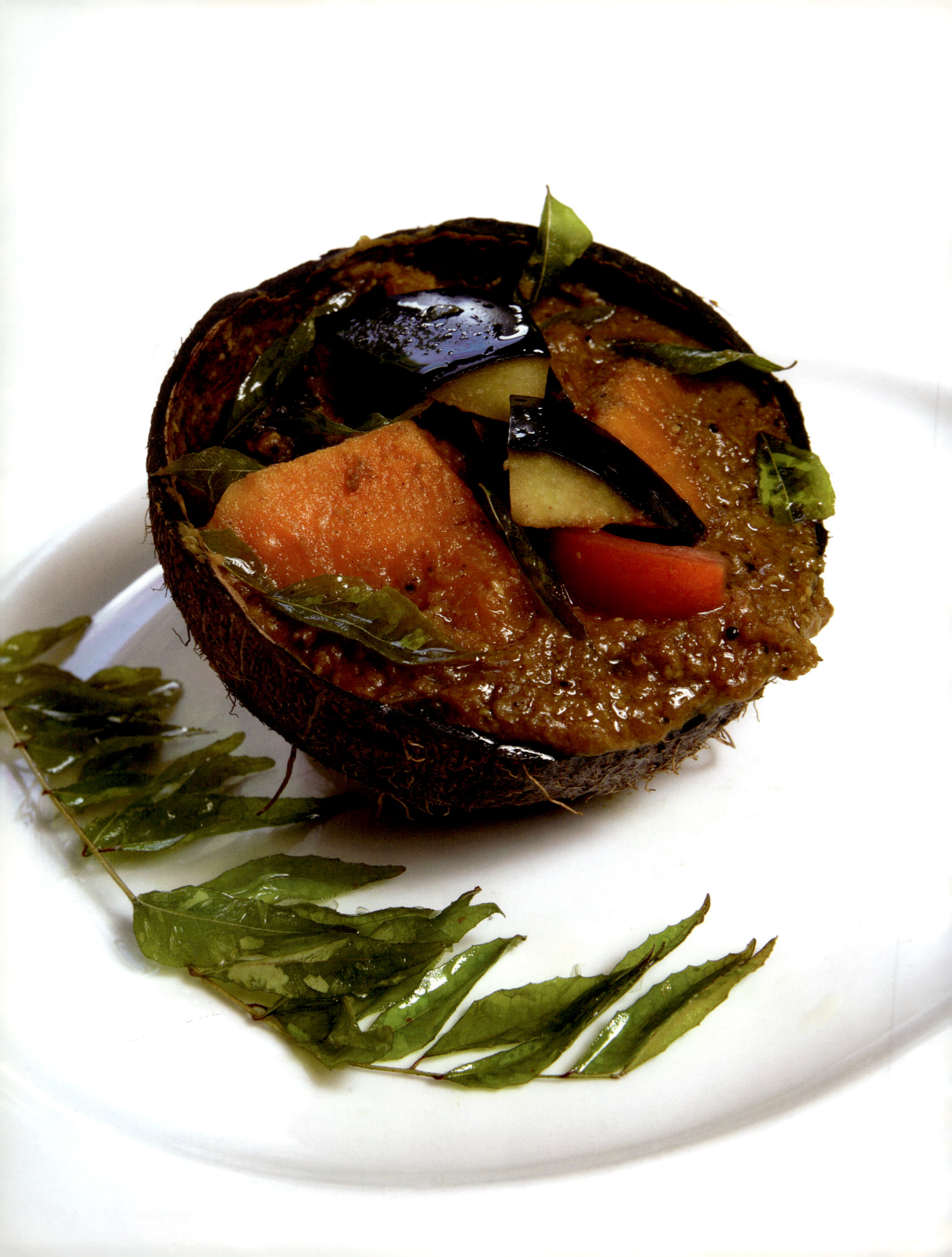

saffron chicken korma
Serves 4

30g ghee/30ml oil
3 whole cloves
4 green cardamom pods
½ cup chopped onion
3 tspn garlic paste
2 tspn coriander powder
salt to taste
½ cup dried almond meal
dried nuts and sultanas to garnish
1kg chicken thigh fillets, cut into 4 to 6 pieces
1 dry red chilli
2.5cm piece cinnamon stick
½ tspn whole mace
1 tblspn ginger paste
½ tspn turmeric powder
½ cup yogurt
½ tspn saffron threads
½ cup cream

Heat ghee in a pan, add chilli, cloves, cinnamon stick, mace and onion, and cook until a light brown colour. Add ginger and garlic pastes and cook for about 2 minutes. Add turmeric and coriander; moisten with yogurt and season with salt to taste. Add chicken and stir. Cover and cook on a low heat until chicken is thoroughly cooked. Infuse the saffron in a little warm water and add to the korma with cream and almond meal. Allow the korma to thicken for about 5 minutes. Garnish with dried nuts and sultanas.

boneless lamb shanks masala
Serves 4

1 tblspn cumin seeds
1 tblspn coriander seeds
1 tspn fenugreek seeds

1 kg boneless lamb shanks
salt to taste
4 black cardamon pods
2 cups sliced onion
1 tblspn ginger paste
2 tblspn desiccated coconut
1 tspn red chilli powder
1 tblspn kewra water (see note)
1 cup yogurt
60ml oil
4 whole cloves
2 bay leaves
1 tblspn garlic paste
½ tspn mace flakes
¾ cup water
30ml rum

Roast cumin, coriander and fenugreek seeds, grind to a powder. Butterfly lamb shanks and make small slits along its length. Marinate in yogurt and salt for about 20 minutes. Roll in foil and bake in 180C oven in a little water for 1 to 1½ hours. Meanwhile, heat oil in a pan. Add cloves, cardamom, bay leaves and onion. Cook till brown, add ginger and garlic pastes and cook one min. Add mace, ground spices, coconut and chilli powder with water. Bring to simmer and cook for at least 15 minutes before adding the cooked lamb, rum and kewra water, including any juices from the lamb. Allow the lamb to cook in the gravy for another hour before serving. Note: Kewra water is an extract distilled from pandanus flowers.

duck mulligatawny soup — Serves 4

2½cm piece cinnamon stick
¼ tspn cumin seeds
¼ tspn coriander seeds
¼ tspn fenugreek seeds
¼ tspn fennel seeds

3 tspn oil
2 tblspn finely chopped onion
½ tspn ginger paste
½ tspn garlic paste
6 cups duck stock
2 cups diced tomatoes
½ tspn turmeric powder
1 cup coconut milk
salt to taste
sprig curry leaves
1 lime, juiced
boiled rice and fried onion to serve

Roast spices and grind to a powder. Heat oil in a deep pan. Add onion and cook until clear. Add ginger and garlic pastes then the duck stock and tomatoes. Add turmeric, ground spices, coconut milk, salt and curry leaves. Bring to a simmer and cook for 20 minutes. Flavour with lime juice. Serve hot garnished with rice and crispy fried onion.

tomato fish curry — Serves 4

1kg fish cutlets or fillets, cut into 5cm pieces
100ml oil
salt to taste
1 tspn panch phoron
1 tblspn garlic paste
½ tspn red chilli powder
¼ cup chopped tomatoes
boiled rice to serve
2 tspn turmeric
2 dried whole red chillies
1 tblspn ginger paste
2 tblspn tomato paste
2 fresh green chillies, split
coriander to garnish

Heat oil in a pan. Coat the fish pieces with turmeric and salt and fry till lightly golden. Remove and keep aside. In the same oil, add red chillies and panch phoron, then the ginger and garlic pastes, red chilli powder and green chillies. Cook about one min. then add tomato paste and fresh tomatoes. Season to taste. Add a little water (about ½ cup). Bring to the boil, lower the heat and simmer for 10 minutes. Add fish pieces and cook a further 5 minutes. Garnish with coriander and serve with boiled rice.

Natural Gas
delivered by Envestra

In 1889, Amos Howard discovered subterranean clover growing on his small farm in the Adelaide Hills. Making a major contribution to the increase in pasture productivity, the 'Mt. Barker' clover became widespread throughout rural Australia. Howard Vineyard now stands on the site of this discovery.

Amos William Howard

PHOTOGRAPH COURTESY OF THE STATE LIBRARY OF SOUTH AUSTRALIA B 13311

History in the Making

HOWARD VINEYARD
ADELAIDE HILLS

We encourage you to visit our newly opened Cellar Door for a complimentary tasting of our range of wines. Or just come to relax and enjoy the beautiful views. Cellar door open 7 days, see website for opening times.

Visit our website for current prices, special offers and delivery throughout Australia, and join our mailing list.

WWW.HOWARDVINEYARD.COM

CELLAR DOOR PHONE: 08 8188 0203
LOT 1 BALD HILLS ROAD, NAIRNE
(SE FREEWAY, MT BARKER EXIT TO NAIRNE)

Esca Restaurant

seafood risotto
Serves 4

500g Arborio rice
250g crushed tomatoes
4 cloves garlic, finely chopped
50ml extra virgin olive oil
extra olive oil for frying
chilli to taste
200g cleaned calamari
12 green tiger prawns
200g cockles
200g mussels
100g crabmeat
cockle stock
100g butter
¼ bunch parsley, chopped
½ bunch basil, chopped
salt and pepper to taste

Cook rice as per instructions on the packet. Combine tomatoes, 2 cloves garlic and oil in a pan and cook over a low heat for 30 mins.

In a deep heavy-based saucepan, heat some oil with remaining garlic and chilli to taste. Add seafood and cook stirring and shaking the pan until almost cooked. Mix a little cockle stock into the tomato mixture, add to the seafood with the rice, and heat through for 5 mins. Finish with butter, parsley, basil and season to taste with salt and pepper. Serve immediately.

chargrilled beef fillet with potato and rice crochette, roasted field mushrooms, caramelised shallots and cherry tomatoes

Serves 4

1kg beef fillet, cut into medallions
2 cloves garlic, finely chopped
120ml extra virgin olive oil
2 tblspn chopped parsley
2 tblspn chopped rosemary
4 open field mushrooms
10 cherry tomatoes
10 shallots
2 potatoes, cooked with skin on
100g Parmesan cheese, finely grated
2 eggs
2 cups cocked rice
100g plain flour
oil for frying
beef glaze

Marinate beef in half the garlic, olive oil, parsley and rosemary. Marinate mushrooms, tomatoes and shallots in remaining garlic, olive oil, parsley and rosemary.

Cook mushrooms and shallots for 10 mins, add tomatoes and cook further 10 mins. Grate potatoes and combine with parmesan, eggs and rice.

Mould into shapes, roll in the flour to cover. Heat some oil and shallow fry until golden brown on both sides.

Chargrill beef to desired doneness. Rest for one minute before serving with the mushrooms, tomato, shallots and crochette. Dress with beef glaze and serve.

pressed chicken thigh with lardo, potato fritti and salted eggplant
Serves 4

salt
1 eggplant, thinly sliced
1 tblspn plain flour
8 chicken Maryland (with bone in)
100g lardo (cured Italian bacon), finely chopped
2 capsicums, roasted and chopped
juice of 1 lemon
4 potatoes, sliced and blanched
1 tblspn extra virgin olive oil
1 tblspn chopped rosemary
1 tblspn crushed garlic
salt and pepper to taste

Sprinkle slices of eggplant with salt and set aside for 1 hour. Wash off and dry with paper towel. Toss lightly in flour. Using a heavy cast iron pan, grill chicken skin-side down until brown. Turn and brown the other side then finish cooking in a 180C oven. Using the same pan, add lardo, capsicum and lemon juice to make a sauce. Deep fry the potatoes and then toss with rosemary, garlic and salt and pepper to taste. Cook eggplant in some hot oil till golden. To serve assemble dish to look like the picture.

chargrilled quail with potato and egg salsina
Serves 4

4 whole quails, boned and cleaned
2 cloves garlic, crushed
1 tblspn chopped rosemary
¼ bunch parsley, chopped
juice of ½ lemon
30ml extra virgin olive oil
2 potatoes, cooked with skin on
2 eggs, hard-boiled
2 shallots, finely chopped
100ml mayonnaise
50g gherkins, chopped
1 tblspn Dijon mustard
30g capers
baby beetroot leaves for garnish

Marinate quail in garlic, rosemary, half of the parsley, lemon juice and olive oil for 1 hour. Peel and chop potatoes and cut eggs into cubes. Combine with shallots, mayonnaise, gherkins, mustard, capers and the remaining parsley. Chargrill the quail until cooked to your liking. To serve, place ½ quail on each plate next to the salsina and garnish with baby beetroot leaves.

marsala zabaglione with almond biscotti
Serves 4

zabaglione
10 egg yolks
250g caster sugar
150ml Marsala

biscotti
60g caster sugar
60g plain flour
zest of 1 orange
2 egg whites
75g butter, melted
flaked almonds

zabaglione
Whisk egg yolks, sugar and Marsala in a heatproof bowl. Place bowl over a double boiler and cook stirring continuously until thickened.

Serve in martini glasses.

biscotti
In a bowl, combine sugar, flour and orange zest. Add egg whites and mix thoroughly. Fold in butter.

Rest in fridge for 30 mins. Place mixture in a piping bag. Pipe mixture into long strips on a baking tray.

Scatter with almonds and cook for 5 - 6 mins in a 150C oven.

Mould into shape while still warm.

PURE SUFFOLK
Pure Taste

coorong angus beef
SOUTH AUSTRALIA'S FINEST

Feast! FINE FOODS

Great recipes deserve great produce
Meat direct from the farm as used by Adelaides best restaurants

coorong angus beef • Maylands Farm • Angus Beef • PURE SUFFOLK • PATCHAWARRA Free Range Beef • Hay Valley Lamb

Feast @ David Jones 83053210 • Feast @ The Market 82314700 • Feast @ Norwood 83322538

IMMA & MARIO'S mERCATO

Large selection of Kitchen Tools:

- Utensils
- Chinaware
- Bakeware
- Servingware
- Cookbooks
- Cookware
- Chef's Uniforms
- Cutlery
- Glassware
- Bar Accessories

625 - 627 LOWER NORTH EAST ROAD, CAMPBELLTOWN
PH 8337 1808   OPEN 7 DAYS
Info@ilmercato.com.au   www.ilmercato.com.au

ASCOT TEAK

Indoor & Outdoor Teak Furniture Of Exceptional Value

From our factory to your home, today
60 The Parade, Norwood
Ph: 8363 7911   Fax: 8362 3341
Email: ascotteak@chariot.com.au
www.ascotteak.com

KILIKANOON

Raw Materials.
Rich History.
Rare Beauty.

"This is one of the most brilliantly run wineries in Australia"

ROBERT PARKER JNR.

Kilikanoon winery.

Kilikanoon Cellar Door.

TASTINGS & SALES

*11am - 5pm Thursday to Sunday,
Public Holidays and by Appointment*

Penna Lane, Skillogallee Valley, Penworthan, South Australia

Ph: 08 8843 4377

CELLARDOOR@KILIKANOON.COM.AU
WWW.KILIKANOON.COM.AU

Juergies Restaurant

kangaroo tail soup
Serves 6

1kg kangaroo tail, cut into small pieces
75ml vegetable oil
60g tomato paste
pinch salt
1 small bay leaf, chopped
¼ tspn mixed herbs
2 juniper berries, crushed
1 bouquet garni
1 small onion, diced
1 small carrot, diced
1 small parsnip, diced
½ clove garlic, crushed
50ml dry red wine
30ml sherry
½ beef stock cube
salt and pepper

Heat 50ml of the oil in a large frypan add kangaroo and brown. Add tomato paste stir, and simmer 2 mins. Remove from heat and transfer to a large stockpot. Add 5 litres water, salt, bay leaf, mixed herbs, juniper berries and bouquet garni. Bring to boil, then simmer for approx. 1½ hours. Strain through a fine sieve. You should have about 1 litre of stock. Heat remaining oil in a large pan, sauté onion, carrot and parsnip then add garlic followed by wine, sherry and stock. Bring to the boil, add stock cube, salt and pepper to taste. Clean meat from tail bones and add to soup.

barramundi and mango salad
Serves 6

200g mixed gourmet lettuce
1 iceberg lettuce
900g Barramundi fillets
salt and pepper
1 Spanish onion, sliced into rings
1 lemon
2 ripe mangoes, peeled and sliced
1 punnet cherry tomatoes, halved

dressing
100ml balsamic vinegar
50ml extra virgin olive oil
3 basil leaves, finely chopped
2 chive spears, finely chopped

Wash and dry all lettuce thoroughly. Break iceberg lettuce into bowl and mix with gourmet lettuce.

Season fish with lemon, salt and pepper to taste. Line grill tray with foil, place fish on top and grill at 240C, depending on thickness 3 to 5 mins.

Divide lettuce onto plates; arrange fish in long strips over lettuce, top with mango slices, tomatoes and several onion rings.

dressing
Mix balsamic, oil, basil and chives in blender. Drizzle dressing over fish and salad and serve with a wedge of lemon.

Can also be topped with lemon or cracked pepper depending on individual taste.

garlic prawns and avocado
Serves 4

4 large ripe avocadoes
20 large raw prawns
1 white onion, finely chopped
400ml cream
200g rice, cooked
virgin olive oil
2 cloves garlic, crushed
50ml dry white wine
salt and pepper
1 lemon

Cut avocado lengthwise touching centre stone as you go around, gently turn the two halves in opposite directions until they come apart. Remove stone, scoop out one half with a teaspoon, place flesh in a bowl. Gently peel the other half without removing the darker green flesh and cut into slices. Devein and butterfly-cut prawns, dry with paper towel. Heat 30ml oil in a frying pan, when hot place 10 prawns in pan, sear both sides and remove. Place on plate with paper towel, clean pan and repeat with remaining prawns. Clean pan, add 50ml oil, add onion and when glazed and shiny, add garlic. Stir using a wooden spoon then add prawns. Stir, when hot pour in wine and reduce. Stir in avocado and cream, reducing to a thick consistency. Add salt and pepper to taste. Spoon rice onto plates, place avocado shell on top. Divide mixture between each shell. Decorate with avocado slices and a twist of lemon.

venison pie with sweet potato mash
Serves 4

500g venison shoulder (cut into 2cm cubes)
100ml vegetable oil
1 medium carrot, diced
¼ bay leaf
¼ tspn mixed herbs
50g tomato paste
30ml port
30g marmalade
salt and pepper
1 medium onion, diced
1 medium parsnip, diced
¼ tspn caraway seeds
1 clove garlic, crushed
50ml dry red wine
2 juniper berries, crushed
½ chicken stock cube
2 sheets puff pastry
(30cm x 30cm)

sweet potato
1 large sweet potato
½ clove garlic, crushed
salt & pepper
15g butter

Pan-fry venison in 50ml hot oil until brown. Heat 50ml oil in large saucepan, sauté onion, carrot, parsnip, bay leaf, caraway seeds, herbs and garlic. Add meat, tomato paste, stir, then add wine, port, juniper berries and marmalade. Cook until tender. Add stock cube and salt and pepper to taste. Lightly grease a 20cm pie dish. Line dish using 1 sheet pastry for base and sides. Fill with pie mixture, cover with second sheet of pastry, trim edges, slightly moisten edges to crimp together. Make 3 slits in the top and bake in preheated 220C oven until golden brown.

sweet potato
Peel and cut into large chunks. Place in a saucepan, cover with water, add pinch salt and bring to boil, simmer until soft, strain, mash with butter, garlic, salt and pepper to taste.

artichoke and pork boulangere
Serves 4

4 large artichokes
1 small lemon, sliced
1 onion, finely diced
¼ tspn chopped parsley
50ml double cream
½ chicken stock cube
1 sheet puff pastry (30cm x 30cm)
3 tspn salt
100g butter
1 clove garlic, crushed
250g pork mince
1 egg yolk
salt and pepper
30ml milk

salsa
1 onion, finely chopped
2 oregano leaves, chopped
juice of 1 small lemon
2 large tomatoes, skinned, seeded and diced
30ml olive oil
3 tspn brown sugar
30ml dry white wine

Wash artichokes, cut stem at base so they stand straight and firm. Remove old outside leaves shorten tips with scissors. Fill a large pan with hot water; add salt, lemon and artichokes. Bring to boil and simmer covered 30 mins. Remove, drain by turning upside down and allow to cool. Pull out centre leaves and remove the hairy 'choke' with a spoon. Heat butter in frying pan, sauté onions until transparent, add garlic, stir and take off heat. Add parsley, mince, egg yolk, cream, stock cube, salt and pepper to taste, mix and allow to cool. Fill artichokes with pork mixture. Cut pastry into 4 squares, place artichokes in the centre, bring corners to top and pinch together, making sure stuffed artichoke is fully enclosed. Brush with milk. Place on greased tray and bake 180C (fan forced) for 20 mins or 220C (conventional) oven.

salsa
Heat oil in frying pan, add onions cook till transparent, add brown sugar then oregano, tomatoes, lemon juice and wine. Stir and simmer for one min. Spoon salsa onto plate and place boulangere in centre. Garnish and serve.

75 Natural Gas delivered by Envestra

wild berries and chocolate brownie parfait
Serves 6

90g dark chocolate
90g unsalted butter
150g caster sugar
100g toasted nut mix, chopped
90g plain flour, sifted
1 large egg
1 tspn vanilla essence
10ml dark rum

ice cream
½ vanilla pod, split lengthwise (or 3 tspn vanilla essence)
80g caster sugar
150ml whipping cream
3 egg yolks
100g mixed berry halves

coulis
300ml double cream
50ml raspberry syrup

brownie - Preheat oven 180C. Grease 15cm x 30cm baking tray. Melt chocolate and butter in large bowl over pan of simmering water. Lift off, whisk in egg, sugar and vanilla essence, fold in nuts, rum and flour. Pour mixture into tray and bake 20 mins. Cool then refrigerate.

ice cream - Stir sugar with vanilla pod and 75ml water in a heavy pan over low heat until dissolved. Raise heat to medium and boil for 10 mins without stirring. Beat yolks until light and creamy with electric mixer on high speed. With beater still running, slowly pour in hot syrup and continue beating until cool. Whip cream to form stiff peaks, fold in egg mixture and raspberries. To assemble: Line a 15cm round springform cake tin with baking paper. Cut brownie in half; fit one snugly in base of tin. Pour over half of ice cream and freeze. Refrigerate remaining ice cream. When first ice cream layer is firm, fit second brownie layer, pour over remaining ice cream and freeze.

coulis - Drizzle cream around each serve, dot with raspberry syrup and pattern with a toothpick.

KIRRIHILL
WINES

a passion shared

www.kirrihillwines.com.au

La Guillotine Restaurant

bouillabaisse des pecheurs
Serves 6

24 mussels
1kg fish (flathead, boarfish)
3 cloves garlic, crushed
3 onions, finely chopped
4 tomatoes, finely chopped
2 potatoes, finely chopped
½ capsicum, finely chopped
1 orange, finely chopped
2 tspn finely chopped nutmeg
2 tblspn finely chopped parsley
2 tspn finely chopped fennel

12 scallops
12 medium prawns
2 leeks, finely chopped
4 tblspn olive oil
crab stock or water
salt and pepper
1 bay leaf
pinch saffron

Heat oil in a large pan and sauté for 3 mins. Add onions, leeks and sauté for 5 - 7 mins. Add tomatoes, potatoes, capsicum and orange and cook for a further 15 mins. Add 500g of the fish. Add enough crab stock or water to cover. Add fennel, nutmeg, bay leaf, salt, pepper, and saffron. Cook for 40 mins over a medium heat, stirring occasionally. Remove from heat and cool a little.

Using a stick mixer, blend until smooth. Pass mixture through a strainer and place into a separate saucepan. Add remaining fish and shellfish and cook over a low heat for 10 - 15 mins or until cooked. Serve with long croutons of toasted baguette covered with aioli and shavings of Gruyere cheese and fresh parsley.

Note: You can use several different types of fish in this recipe but avoid oily fish. Aioli is a garlic flavoured mayonnaise/sauce.

crevettes a i'ail
Serves 4

24 medium prawns
1 tblspn finely chopped parsley
1 tblspn finely chopped basil
1 tblspn finely chopped dill
1 tblspn finely chopped sage
1 bunch chives, chopped
salt and pepper
1 medium onion
1 clove garlic, crushed
1 small leek
2 sticks celery
200g butter

Place herbs and garlic in a food processor and process until finely chopped or chop very finely by hand. Dice the onion, celery and leek into very small pieces. Melt butter in a large frying pan. When butter is hot, reduce the heat to medium and sauté the prepared herbs and vegetables for 10 mins, stirring occasionally. Season with salt and pepper. Add the prawns so that they lay flat along the base of the pan. Cook for 2 - 3 mins on one side, turn and cook for an additional 2 - 3 mins or until cooked. Serve with chives sprinkled over the top of the dish.

petit chevre chaud
Serves 4

1 egg
4 tblspn butter
400g goat's cheese
1 capsicum, roasted and cut into strips
2 tblspn roughly chopped basil
½ bunch chives, chopped
100ml milk
1 lettuce
breadcrumbs

Mix egg and milk together in a small container. Place 100g of the goat's cheese in the egg and milk mixture then toss in breadcrumbs, coating well. Repeat process for remaining 3 portions and set aside. Heat butter in a frying pan over a medium to high heat, when hot add the cheese portions and cook for 1 minute on each side. Remove from heat. Prepare a bed of lettuce on or inside 4 dishes and lay over strips of the roasted capsicum in each one. Carefully place the goat's cheese portions on top of each and drizzle with a little butter. Serve with chopped basil and chives sprinkled over the top of each dish.
Note: A hard goat's cheese is preferable for this recipe. To present the goat's cheese in circular portions, place a sheet of plastic wrap over a plastic egg ring. Push the goat's cheese into the ring and fill it. Wrap the plastic wrap around the cheese and refrigerate for 30 mins before use.

cervelle au beurre-noir
Serves 4

1 carrot
1 medium onion
8 lamb's brains
4 tblspn capers
2 tblspn finely chopped parsley
2 sticks celery
4 tblspn olive oil
4 tblspn butter, melted
4 tblspn balsamic vinegar
1 lemon, quartered

Roughly cut carrot, celery and onion and place in a saucepan. Add olive oil and sauté over a medium to high heat for 10 - 15 mins. Add sufficient water to cover brains in saucepan and bring to the boil. Add brains and cook for 10 mins. Strain and discard the vegetables. Put the butter, brains and capers in a frying pan over a medium to high heat and cook for 5 mins, turn brains and cook for an additional 3 mins. Add the balsamic vinegar and the parsley. Serve with a lemon wedge.

moules mariniere
Serves 4

1 tblspn chopped basil
1 tblspn chopped parsley
1 clove garlic, crushed
2 sticks celery
salt and pepper to taste
200g butter
70ml thickened cream
1 bunch chives, chopped
1 tblspn chopped sage
1 tblspn chopped dill
1 medium onion
1 small leek
300ml white wine
2kg mussels
juice of 4 lemons

Place herbs and garlic together in a food processor and process until finely chopped or you can chop very finely by hand. Dice the onion, celery and leek into very small pieces. Melt butter in a very large pot. When the butter is hot, reduce the heat to medium and sauté the prepared herbs and vegetables for 10 mins, stirring occasionally. Season to taste with salt and pepper. Add the white wine, cream and bring to the boil over a high heat. Add mussels and cover. Cook for 6 mins turning the mussels occasionally whilst cooking. Shake the pot from side to side knocking the mussels. Remove from heat and check that all the mussels are open. If not, stir and return to heat for an additional minute. Check again and discard any unopened mussels. Add the lemon juice. Just before serving, sprinkle chives over the top of the pot.

crème brulee   Serves 5

250ml thickened cream
1 tblspn vanilla essence
8 egg yolks
60g sugar
extra 3 tblspn sugar
250ml milk

Place the milk, cream and vanilla essence into a pan and bring to the boil. Whisk egg yolks and sugar in a bowl until smooth. Add milk and cream mixture and stir until liquid is smooth. Strain mixture into another bowl. Pour about 150ml mixture into 5 individual bowls. Put the bowls in a deep baking tray and place in a 150C oven. Fill the baking tray with water so that it comes halfway up the sides of the brulee bowls (bain-marie). Cook for 50 mins and remove carefully. Slide a skewer or thin-bladed knife in the centre of the brulee dishes and if it comes out clean it is cooked, but if a little creamy, cook an additional 10 mins. Remove from the oven and from the bain-marie and leave to cool. Refrigerate. When cool, remove from the fridge. Dry any excess condensation from the top with some paper towel and spread each dish evenly with about 3 teaspoons of sugar. Using a blowtorch or a griller, melt the sugar to form a hard toffee lid on the top of the brulee. Serve with fresh fruit and biscuits of langue de chat. Note: There are many versions to this dish. This is the traditional style but you can infuse such flavours as lavender, aniseed etc. The simplest method is to slowly infuse the flavours while boiling milk, and then continue the recipe as normal.

Langmeil

The home of the Barossa & Australia's oldest surviving vineyard;

The 1843 Freedom Shiraz

Sagarmatha
Nepali Restaurant

kheer (nepali-style rice pudding)
Serves 4

1 cup rice
1 cinnamon stick
2 to 3 cardamom pods
3 cups milk
4 tblspn sugar
2 tblspn thickened cream
mixed nuts and fruit (cashew nuts and raisins)

Wash rice thoroughly and drain well. Add cinnamon and cardamom to the milk. Bring to the boil for a few minutes. Add rice to the milk and stir constantly until it thickens. Add sugar and cream and cook for 2 to 3 minutes. Sprinkle with mixed nuts before serving.

sel roti
Makes 6

1 tblspn ghee
pinch baking powder
3 tspn sugar
½ banana, peeled & mashed
2 cups rice flour
1 cup milk
2 cups vegetable oil for deep-frying

In a bowl, add ghee, banana, baking powder, rice flour and sugar and mix well. Add milk and make a batter. Heat oil in a deep pan, making sure the oil is not too hot. Take a handful of the mixture and pour into the oil making a donut-like shape. Once it comes to the surface, turn it over and cook for one minute on the other side. Remove from the oil and place on paper towel until you are ready to serve.

kukhkurako tihun (chicken curry)
Serves 3 to 4

2 tblspn vegetable oil
2 bay leaves
½ tspn crushed fresh ginger
2 cloves garlic, finely diced
2 onions, finely diced
1 tspn ground coriander
1 tspn curry powder
½ tspn ground turmeric
½ tspn salt
500g chicken thigh fillets, cut into bite-size pieces
2 tomatoes, diced
4 sprigs coriander leaves, finely chopped

Heat oil, add bay leaves, ginger and garlic and cook for a minute. Add onions and cook until golden brown. Add remaining spices, salt, and mix well. Cook for 2 to 3 minutes. Add chicken pieces and mix thoroughly. Cook for 5 to 6 minutes. Add tomatoes and if mixture is too dry, add some water. Reduce the heat to low and continue cooking until the chicken is tender. Just before serving, sprinkle with freshly chopped coriander. This dish can be served with rice and bread.

misayeko tarkari (mixed vegetable curry)
Serves 4

1 tspn ghee
2 bay leaves
2 cloves garlic, finely chopped
1 tspn crushed ginger
2 medium potatoes, diced
½ cup green peas
1 tspn ground coriander
½ cauliflower, separated into florets
1 bunch fresh coriander

1 tspn vegetable oil
1 tspn cumin seeds
2 onions, diced
2 small carrots, diced
1 tspn ground turmeric
3 tomatoes, diced
1 tspn salt

Heat ghee and oil together in a pan, add bay leaves and cumin seeds and cook until golden brown. Add garlic, ginger and onion and cook until the onions are soft. Add potatoes and carrot and cook until the vegetables are soft. Add turmeric, cauliflower, peas, tomatoes, coriander and salt and mix well. If needed, add half a cup of water and cook for 3 to 4 minutes. Serve with steamed rice or roti.

alu bodi tamako tarkari
Serves 3 to 4

½ cup black-eyed beans
3 tblspn vegetable oil
1 tspn finely crushed ginger
1 tspn finely crushed garlic
1 onion, finely diced
2 potatoes, peeled and diced
½ tspn ground turmeric
1 cup bamboo shoots
½ tspn ground cumin
½ tspn salt

Place beans in a pan and fill with enough water to cover. Bring to the boil, reduce heat and simmer until the beans are soft. Drain and set aside. Heat oil, add ginger, garlic and onion, and cook for at least 3 to 4 minutes. Add potatoes, turmeric and cook until the potatoes are tender. Add bamboo shoots, pre-cooked beans, cumin and salt. Cook for 4 to 5 minutes. Serve with rice and bread.

poleko lamb (charcoal barbecued lamb cutlets)
Serves 3

9 French-cut lamb racks (cut into 3 pieces)
1 cup natural yogurt
1 tspn crushed garlic
1 tspn crushed ginger
1 tspn garam masala
1 tspn salt
½ tspn chilli powder
½ tspn Tandoori colour (saffron)
½ tspn white pepper

to serve
mint sauce
mixed salad

Mix all the ingredients together in a mixing bowl. Place the lamb cutlets in the bowl and coat well.

(Use a marinade container with lid if you have one).

Cover the mixing bowl with plastic wrap and marinate overnight in the fridge.

The next day, remove the marinated lamb cutlets from the fridge.

Thread three pieces of lamb onto each skewer.

Cook in a preheated Tandoori oven (charcoal-fired clay oven) for 5 to 6 minutes or until cooked to your liking.

Remove lamb cutlets from the skewers place on a serving plate.

Serve hot with mint sauce and your choice of mixed salad.

Parish Hill
NEBBIOLO
ADELAIDE HILLS
Piccadilly Valley
2004

Fresh FRAGRANT & ZIPPY

2006 SAUVIGNON BLANC
ADELAIDE HILLS
AUSTRALIA
750ml

NEPENTHE

NEPENTHE IS THE ADELAIDE HILLS

Seasons at the Bay Restaurant

seasons' dukkah with turkish bread
Serves 6

100g sesame seeds, toasted
75g coriander seeds, toasted
50g almonds or hazelnuts, toasted and skins removed
Turkish bread, toasted
salt to taste
black pepper to taste

Blend each ingredient separately and then combine. Can be left coarse or ground finely according to your preference (we grind fine to medium). Keep sealed in an airtight jar until required. It is best used quickly so that the natural seed and nut oils don't go rancid. Serve with olive oil and toasted Turkish bread pieces. Can be sprinkled over salads and meats after cooking as a dry rub.

seafood paella
Serves 4

500g Ferron rice
(Arborio if you can't find it)
pinch saffron, soaked in 1 tblspn water
1.5 litres seafood or vegetable stock
16 large green prawns, peeled and deveined
2 large squid tubes, cleaned and sliced
¼ cup chopped flat leaf parsley
¼ cup olive oil
1 large red onion, diced
1 cup sliced chorizo
8 large cloves garlic, sliced
2 tblspn smokey paprika
1 cup dry white wine
salt and pepper to taste
500g black lip mussels
16 scallops
1 lemon, cut into wedges

Preheat oven to 180C or heat large frypan. Add oil and sauté onions and chorizo for 2 mins. Do not allow to burn. Add rice, stir for a minute to coat the rice with oil. Add garlic, saffron, paprika and stir to combine. Add wine, reduce then add stock and salt and pepper to taste. Cook covered for 10 mins over a low heat. Add seafood, stir and return to stove or oven. Add more liquid if you feel it is too dry. Cook for 10 - 15 mins until rice is just cooked and seafood is cooked. Allow to stand before serving. Sprinkle with parsley and serve with lemon wedges.

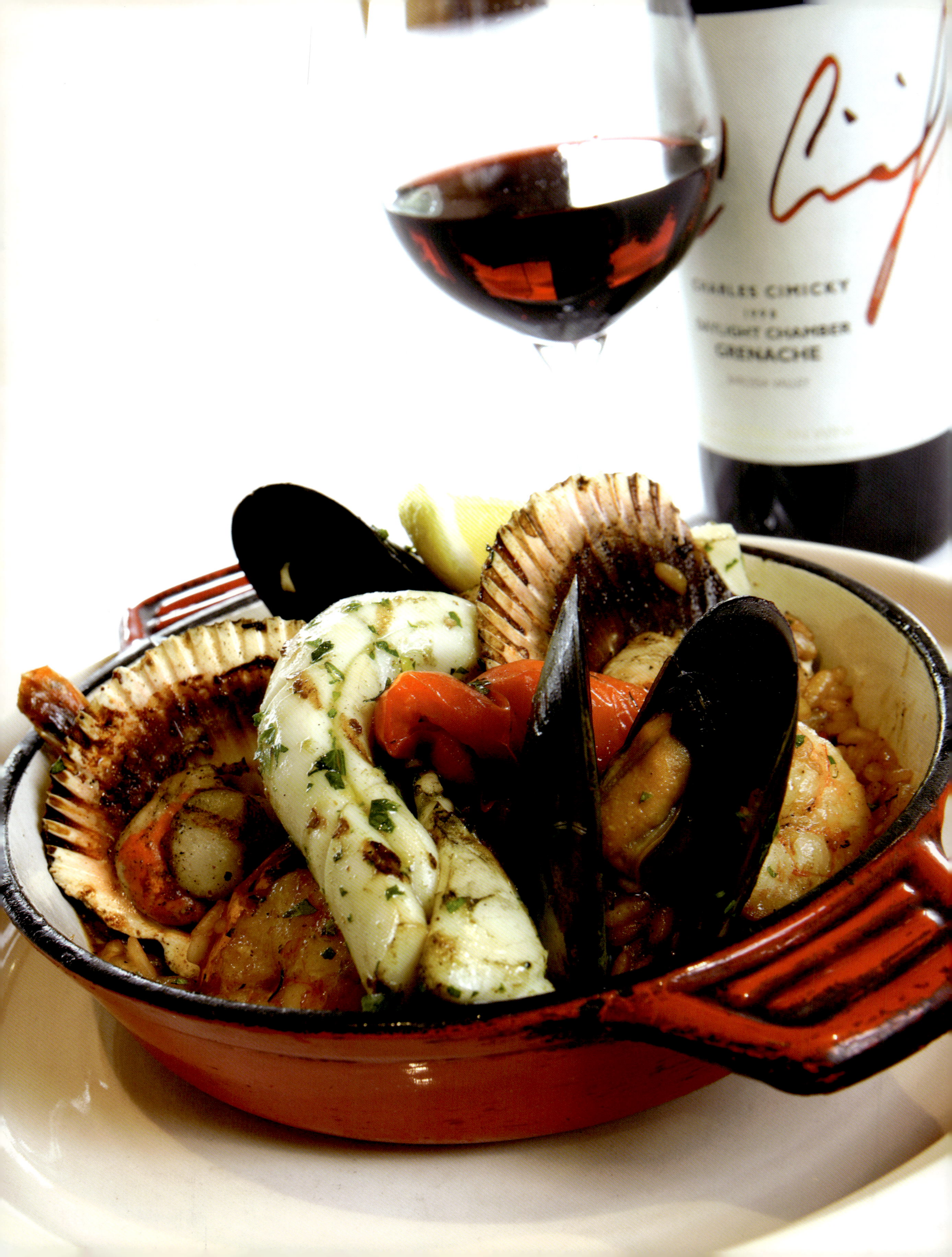
GRENACHE

charmoula chicken
Serves 6

4 bunches coriander
½ bunch flat leaf parsley
zest of 2 lemons
10 bird's eye chillies
½ tspn turmeric, toasted
2 cups vegetable oil
½ tspn salt
½ tspn pepper
½ tspn ground cumin, toasted
6 chicken breasts/pieces
1 tspn ground coriander, toasted

Blend herbs and spices to form a smooth marinade. Cook chicken pieces to your liking. The marinade can be used for basting or simply marinating for grilling, roasting or barbecuing. Store in the fridge in an airtight container for up to a week. Use on fish, chicken and meats.

grilled atlantic salmon with semi-sundried tomatoes and preserved lemon dressing
Serves 1

250g semi-sundried tomatoes
2 preserved lemons, seeded
1 tblspn ground black pepper
220g Atlantic salmon
125ml red wine (lighter red)
2 cups basil leaves
salt to taste
2 tspn saffron threads
125ml balsamic vinegar
500ml olive oil

In a food processor or blender, combine tomatoes, lemons, basil, pepper, salt, saffron and blend until smooth. Add the balsamic, red wine and oil in small amounts alternately. Process until you have a smooth dressing. This will store in a jar in the fridge for approx. 2 months. Spoon over salmon portion and bake until done to your liking in a 170C oven or this can be used with extra oil as a salad dressing and the fish left plain.

lamb shank tagine
Serves 6

2 lamb shanks, cleaned and trimmed of tough fat
2 tblspn ras el al hanoute spice mix
 (or bought Moroccan spice blend)
6 pitted prunes, soaked in warm water
¼ preserved lemon, sliced-skin only
¼ cup toasted sesame seeds
1 large brown onion, chopped
1 tblspn chopped garlic
1 tblspn clear honey
salt and ground black pepper
¼ cup natural yogurt
1 tblspn chopped ginger
2 cups water
1 pkt couscous
¼ cup olive oil

Rub lamb shanks with the spice mix, cover with plastic wrap and put in fridge overnight. Heat oil in a heavy-based saucepan, add lamb shanks and brown on a medium to high heat. Remove once sealed. Brown onions, ginger and garlic in the same pan. Add shanks, lemon, water (enough to cover shanks) to a saucepan, cover, and simmer for 45 mins to 1 hour until shanks are nearly tender. Add prunes, honey, and season to taste with salt and pepper and cook for another 15 mins until shanks are tender. Remove from heat and allow to stand for 5 mins. Transfer shanks to a tagine and serve with couscous that has been cooked according to the directions on the packet. Serve with yogurt and toasted sesame seeds. A tagine is a clay pot used to cook in and can be purchased at Seasons at the Bay. Shanks can be cooked in the tagine for a more traditional effect. The tagine is designed to self-baste itself, so only add enough water to make it moist (2cm up from the base of the tagine).

soft-centred chocolate pudding
Serves 5

250g dark cooking chocolate (curvature if possible)
200g unsalted butter, softened   80g SR flour
4 eggs, room temperature   250g caster sugar

sauce
250g dark cooking chocolate (curvature if possible)
100ml cream

Grease with butter and sprinkle with sugar, five 200ml baking moulds or muffin tins. Preheat oven to 200C. Melt 250g of chocolate and butter over a bain-marie or in short, sharp bursts in the microwave. Beat eggs and sugar until pale and thick. Add warm chocolate. Sift flour over the mixture and stir to combine. Pour evenly into moulds. Bake in oven for 20 - 25 mins or until tops crack. Stand in moulds for 5 mins, loosen gently and turn out onto baking paper.

sauce
Melt chocolate and cream together, stir until smooth. Do this either over a bain-marie or in the microwave.

Parish Hill

Australian wines from Italian vines in the Adelaide Hills

Taste the difference!

www.parishhill.com.au

Sevenhill Restaurant

dukkah and marinated olive plate with crusty bread
Serves 4

250g kalamata olives
2 tblspn chilli paste
5 cloves garlic, finely chopped
400ml olive oil
2 tblspn assorted herbs
250g green olives
grated zest of 1 lemon
1 tblspn finely chopped rosemary
100g dukkah (ready-made)
Ready-made quince paste
1 loaf crusty bread

Combine kalamata olives, chilli paste, 3 cloves chopped garlic, 100ml olive oil and assorted herbs into a jar. Marinate overnight. Combine green olives, lemon zest, 2 cloves chopped garlic, 100ml olive oil and rosemary into a jar and marinate, at least overnight. Just before serving, spoon portions of the kalamata olives, green olives, dukkah, remaining 200ml olive oil and quince paste into individual dishes. Heat bread in a hot oven until it is crusty. Remove from oven and slice. Place all on a plate and serve while bread is still warm.

balsamic chicken breast served on pea and corn frittata with gremolata
Serves 8

balsamic chicken breast
8 skinless chicken breasts
100ml olive oil
50ml balsamic vinegar
1 red onion, sliced
½ cup chopped oregano
1 clove garlic, finely chopped

pea and corn frittata
250g peas (can use frozen)
250g corn kernels (can use frozen)
3 spring onions, finely sliced
2 eggs, lightly beaten
50g plain flour
salt and pepper

gremolata
2 cups chopped parsley
grated zest of 2 lemons
2 cloves garlic
salt and pepper to taste
olive oil as required

chicken breasts
Place chicken breasts on a baking tray. Combine oil, balsamic, onion, oregano and garlic and then pour over the chicken.

Place tray in the fridge for 1 to 2 hours. Place chicken in a preheated 180C oven for 15 minutes until they are just cooked through.

pea and corn frittata
Preheat oven to 180C. Line a small tray (approx 30cm squared) with baking paper and put to one side.

Combine peas, corn, spring onion and lightly beaten eggs in a bowl and mix together. Slowly add flour, mixing in as you go. Season with salt and pepper to taste. Pour into prepared tray and bake for 15 minutes.

Cut into slices and serve under the chicken breast.

gremolata
This can be made in advance. Combine parsley, lemon zest, garlic, salt and pepper in a food processor. Then add olive oil to get desired consistency.

Serve drizzled over the chicken and frittata.

salt and pepper squid with sweet chilli sauce
Serves 4

2 tblspn cracked pepper
oil for deep-frying
4 tblspn sweet chilli sauce
1 continental cucumber, sliced into ribbons
150g plain flour
500g squid tubes

Combine pepper and flour in a bowl and put to one side. Heat oil in deep fryer. Meanwhile, cut a vertical line down each squid tube so that it can be opened out to lay flat on a board. Score the flesh diagonally in a criss-cross pattern so that it looks like the skin of a pineapple. Be careful not to cut all the way through. Cut the squid into approximately 3cm x 3cm pieces and coat with the flour mix. Deep-fry squid in the hot oil for 2 to 3 minutes then remove from oil. Season with salt and pepper and place squid on a bed of cucumber ribbons with the sweet chilli sauce drizzled around it. Note: a deep fryer will be needed for this recipe.

zucchini, potato and bacon soup
Serves 8

100g butter
100g bacon, sliced
2 litres chicken stock
salt and pepper
2 onions, sliced
2 large potatoes, peeled & diced
6 zucchinis, chopped
100ml cream, optional
1 cup of optional herbs, either coriander, dill, chervil or basil, chopped

Melt butter in a pan and fry onion until golden brown. Add bacon and potato and continue to fry for ten minutes. Add chicken stock and zucchini and bring to the boil. Simmer until potato is soft, which will take approximately 20 minutes. Turn off heat and add chosen herb, blending until smooth. Season to taste with salt and pepper. Serve hot with the option of adding a dollop of cream to each bowl, if you wish.

blyth plains' mutton backstrap with ratatouille and basil pesto
Serves 4

100ml olive oil
3 tblspn tomato paste
100g eggplant, diced
150g mushrooms, diced
4 x 180g mutton backstrap
2 medium red capsicums, diced
1 small brown onion, diced
2 cloves garlic, crushed
250g zucchini, diced
salt and pepper
4 tblspn basil pesto

Turn BBQ on high to heat plate. Heat olive oil in a medium-sized saucepan and fry onion until it is a dark golden colour. Add tomato paste and garlic and fry for 5 minutes. Add eggplant, zucchini, capsicum and mushrooms and cook until soft. Season with salt and pepper. Remove from the heat. Place mutton backstrap on heated BBQ plate and cook for 4 minutes each side for medium or until desired doneness. Slice into approximately 5 pieces and serve on a mound of ratatouille. Place a tablespoon of basil pesto over each serve of meat.

thai prawn salad
Serves 4

100ml sweet soy sauce
1 tspn chilli paste
1 tspn grated ginger
1 tspn crushed garlic
juice of 2 limes
2 tblspn water
20 medium-sized prawn tails
1 medium Lebanese cucumber, sliced into ribbons
100g snow pea sprouts
1 spring onion, finely sliced
¼ cup fresh coriander, roughly chopped
8 blanched snow peas, thinly sliced
2 kaffir lime leaves, very thinly sliced

Combine soy sauce, chilli paste, ginger, garlic, lime juice and water in a jug. Set aside. In four separate bowls, evenly distribute prawns, cucumber, sprouts, spring onion, coriander, snow peas and lime leaves. Mix ingredients together. Stack bowl contents into a mound on each serving plate. Spoon sauce evenly over each mound.

PARRI ESTATE
PARRI ESTATE
SALMON BRUT
Pinot Noir Chardonnay
Southern Fleurieu
Bottle Fermented
PARRI ESTATE

Star of Siam Restaurant

tom-kha-gai (chicken in coconut milk soup)
Serves 4

250g chicken breast, sliced in small pieces
2 stalks lemongrass, cut into 2.5cm lengths
5 fresh kaffir lime leaves
1 tspn fish sauce
1 small red chilli, chopped
500ml coconut milk
6 thin slices of young galangal
5 tspn lime juice
1 tspn sugar
¼ cup coriander leaves

Pour half of the coconut milk into a saucepan with the galangal, lemongrass and lime leaves and bring to the boil. Add chicken and cook until the chicken is cooked through. Add the remaining coconut milk, lime juice, fish sauce, sugar, chilli and heat until it is just boiling. Put coriander on top before serving.

kaeng-dang gai
Serves 4

2 cups bamboo shoots
2 tblspn red curry paste
2 tblspn cooking oil
600ml coconut milk
250g chicken, sliced
3 kaffir leaves, halved
1 tblspn fish sauce
1½ tspn sugar
½ cup sweet basil leaves
1 red chilli, sliced

Slice bamboo shoots and rinse in boiling water for 2 to 3 minutes. Fry the red curry paste with the cooking oil until fragrant. Reduce the heat and add half of the coconut milk. Stir until the coconut milk appears to have an oily sheen.

Add the chicken and cook until the chicken is semi-cooked, then add the remaining coconut milk. Once the curry is boiling, add the kaffir lime leaves, bamboo shoots, fish sauce and sugar, season to taste. Add the basil and chilli and it is ready to serve.

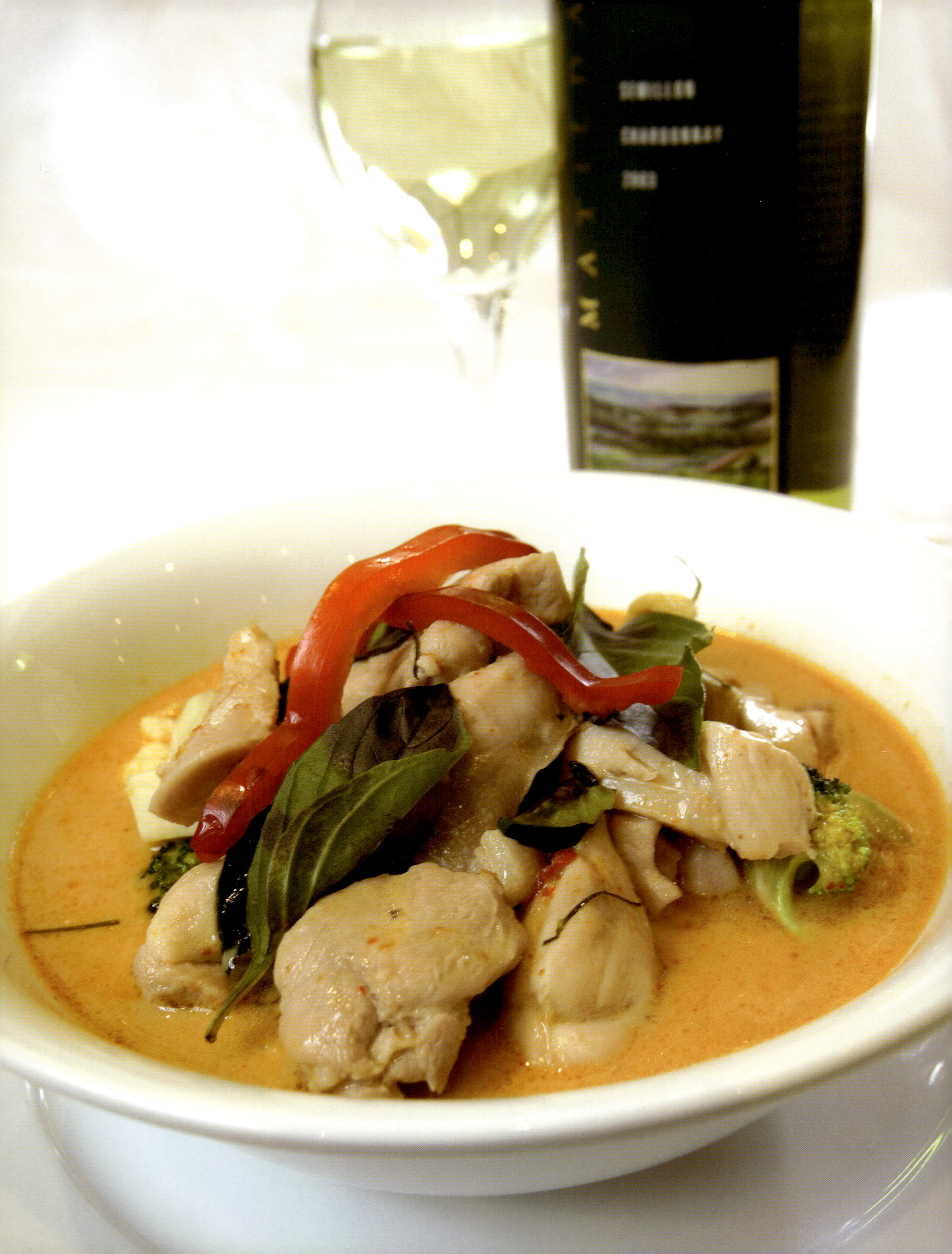

pad-thai

Serves 4

50g soybean curd, cut into small pieces
5 tblspn cooking oil
100g prawn meat
300g thin rice noodles
3 eggs
50g pickled white radish
3 tblspn dried shrimp
3 tblspn sugar
3 tblspn tamarind juice
3 tblspn fish sauce
3 tblspn ground roasted peanuts
500g bean sprouts
50g chopped chives

Heat 3 tablespoons of the cooking oil in a frying pan, add soybean curd. When it has yellowed, add prawn meat and noodles with just enough water to soften them. Fry turning constantly to prevent sticking. Then move the noodles to one side of the pan. Put the remaining oil in pan, break eggs into the pan, and spread in a thin layer to cover the base of the pan. When set, turn the noodles on top and add pickled radish, shrimp, sugar, tamarind juice, fish sauce and mix together. Cook until well mixed, add ground peanuts, bean sprouts and chives, and toss them together. Ready to serve.

larb chicken

Serves 4

200g chicken mince
4 tblspn lemon juice
2 tblspn fish sauce
1 tblspn sugar
¼ tspn chilli powder
¼ cup sliced shallots
1 tblspn chopped spring onion
1 tblspn mint
1 tblspn chopped coriander
1 tblspn ground roasted jasmine rice

Cook the minced chicken in hot boiling water until the chicken is cooked. Drain. Add the lemon juice, fish sauce, sugar and chilli powder to taste. Add the shallot, spring onion, coriander, mint and ground jasmine rice. Toss them all together and serve.

tod-mon pla (fish cake)
Serves 4

500g minced white fish
1 egg
1 tspn salt
3 tblspn chopped kaffir lime leaves
vegetable oil for frying
1 tblspn red curry paste
½ cup finely sliced fresh beans
1 tspn sugar

cucumber chilli sauce
cucumber
sweet chilli sauce
freshly ground peanuts

Place all the ingredients in a large bowl and mix well using your hands. Spoon 2 tablespoons of the mixture and shape into small patties about 3cm in diameter. Deep fry in vegetable oil until golden brown. Serve with cucumber chilli sauce.

cucumber chilli sauce
Slice cucumber into small pieces top with sweet chilli sauce and freshly ground peanuts.

sweet sticky rice with mango
Serves 4

2 cups sticky rice
250ml coconut milk
½ cup sugar
pinch salt
2 mangoes

Soak the sticky rice in water overnight. Drain the rice and place into a steamer that has been lined with cheesecloth to prevent the rice from falling through the holes. Steam the rice on high heat for 15 minutes. In a bowl, mix the coconut milk with the sugar and salt. Stir until well mixed. Transfer the rice into the coconut milk in the bowl. Stir and cover the bowl with a lid. Leave for 30 minutes. It is then ready to serve with the mango. Peel the mangoes carefully so as not to bruise the fruit. Slice in half as close to the seed as possible, then slice each half into 1cm slices.

monjava
COFFEE

Premium beans selected from around the globe, hand roasted in Adelaide to perfection, delivered fresh to your door the next working day

www.monjava.com.au

New showroom now open at 57 King William Street, Kent Town
p: 8362 9899 e: info@monjava.com.au

RED EARTH

Australia's mysterious outback, its red centre, the last frontier, recognised with this wine for those who enjoy new experiences

www.redearthwines.com.au

Sumo Station

chawamushi

Serves 4

4 eggs
½ tspn salt
120ml water
½ tspn dashi water

to serve
4 prawns
shitake mushrooms, shredded
crabstick
fish cake

Mix eggs, water, salt and dashi water together. Strain out the bubbles created during mixing. Pour into 4 cups. In each cup place a prawn, some shredded shitake mushrooms, fish cake and crabstick. Seal the cup with a lid or plastic wrap, steam in a pan of boiling water for 8 - 10 minutes. Serve garnished with lemon zest.

sushi combination

cooking japanese rice.
Wash the rice thoroughly in cold water, changing the water several times until the water runs clear. Drain rice in a fine strainer and set aside for 1 hour. Put the rice into a deep pan; add enough cold water so that the water level is not more than one third from the base of the pan. Cover the pan, place over a high heat and bring to the boil. Reduce the heat to the lowest setting and simmer for 10 - 15 minutes or until the water has been absorbed. Remove pan from the heat and set aside still covered for 10 - 15 minutes before serving. The most efficient way to cook rice is to use an electric rice cooker preparing as per the first 2 steps.

making sushi rice
Sushi vinegar is the base for all kinds of sushi and it is essential to cook the rice correctly. To make hoso-maki (nori-rolled sushi) use 120g short grain rice. When rice is cooked, mix with the sushi vinegar. This makes 3 rolls (about 18 pieces) enough to serve 2 people.

making sushi vinegar
45ml Japanese rice vinegar
40ml sugar
2 tspn salt

Place rice vinegar into a saucepan and bring to the boil. Turn off the heat and add sugar and salt, stir well until dissolved.

nori-rolled sushi (hoso-maki)
Makes 24

50g very fresh salmon
1 qty sushi rice
2 nori sheets, cut in ½ crosswise
3 tblspn wasabi mixed with 2 tblspn water
1 cucumber, cut into 1cm strips
1 tblspn toasted sesame seeds

filling
Cut salmon with the grain into 1cm wide strips. Place the sushi-map on a flat work surface. Put a nori sheet on the sushi-map horizontally, rough sides facing upwards. Put the sushi rice on the nori sheet, leaving a 1cm edge on the side furthest from you. Press firmly to smooth the surface. Spread a little wasabi paste across the rice and arrange some of the salmon strips in a row across the middle. Hold sushi-map with both hands and carefully roll it away from you. Hold rolled sushi-map with both hands and squeeze gently to firm the hoso-maki. Slowly unwrap the sushi-map, remove the rolled salmon and set aside to allow the shape to settle. Repeat the same process with your favourite ingredients like cucumber, toasted sesame seeds, oshingo, tuna, prawns, avocado etc. To serve cut each hoso-maki roll into 6 pieces using a very sharp knife. Wipe knife with a damp towel before you cut it. Tip – Fill a small bowl with water; use this to wet your hands to prevent the rice sticking when you are rolling the sushi.

sukiyaki
Serves 4

500g eye fillet or scotch fillet
4 shallots
125g tofu
½ bok choy, well washed
100g Inoki mushrooms
50g konyukoo noodles (rice noodles)
½ Japanese cabbage
1 carrot
3 mushrooms
1 egg
100g oyster mushrooms

sauce
1 cup soy sauce
½ cup sugar
¼ cup mirin
¼ cup dashi-no-moto

Thinly slice the beef fillet. Slice the cabbage into 5cm pieces, cut shallots into 7.5cm lengths, cut carrots into fine shreds and the tofu into 2.5cm squares. Soak the konyukoo in a bowl of warm water for 30 minutes or until tender.

sauce
Combine all the sauce ingredients in a small pan and warm over a low heat for 30 minutes. To serve sukiyaki, place beaten egg in a bowl for dipping the sukiyaki pieces into. Place mushrooms and vegetables near the egg. Sukiyaki is served from the pot into small bowls.

tempura prawns and vegetables
Serves 4

3 tspn lemon juice
½ sweet potato
½ eggplant
½ carrot
½ lotus root
3 prawns
1 onion, sliced into 5mm rings
1 red capsicum, seeded & cut lengthwise into 2.5cm strips

condiment
200g daikon (white radish)
100g fresh root ginger

batter
200ml iced water
1 egg, beaten
90g tempura flour
2 to 3 ice cubes

dipping sauce
400ml dashi stock
100ml shoyu
100ml mirin

Fill a bowl with cold water and add lemon juice. Peel the sweet potato and cut into 5mm thick slices.

Plunge the pieces into the bowl immediately to prevent discolouring. Just before frying, drain and pat dry with paper towel. Follow the same procedure for eggplant, carrot and lotus root.

condiment
Peel and grate the daikon and ginger separately. Lightly squeeze out the excess liquid from both the daikon and the ginger.

batter
Pour the ice-cold water into a mixing bowl, add the beaten egg and mix well. Add the tempura flour and very roughly fold in with a pair of chopsticks.

The batter should be quite lumpy, then add some ice cubes. Pour in enough oil to come halfway up the sides of a wok or deep fryer and heat to 175C.

To check the temperature of the oil without a thermometer, drop a little batter into the oil, if the batter sinks to the bottom and immediately rises to the surface, the oil is hot enough.

Holding a prawn in your hand, lightly run it across the surface of the batter mix, coating the prawn with the mixture. Repeat with remaining prawns.

Gently slip the prawns into the oil and cook until they go crisp and golden brown. Drain on paper towel. Repeat this process for all of the vegetables.

Divide the warm dipping sauce between 4 bowls. Place bowls near the condiment. Arrange the tempura on a large plate and serve immediately. Mix the condiment into the sauce and then dip in the tempura as you eat.

agedashi tofu
Serves 4

250g pkt fresh tofu
vegetable oil for deep-frying
2 tblspn plain flour

sauce
50ml shoyu
50ml mirin
pinch salt
300ml dashi stock or 300ml water & 7.5ml dashi-no-moto

garnish
2.5cm fresh root ginger, peeled and finely grated
60ml finely chopped chives
spring onion
bonito flakes

Drain the water from the tofu, leave for 15 minutes for the excess liquid to be absorbed by the paper towel.

sauce
Place all the sauce ingredients into a small pan over a medium heat. Mix well and cook for 5 minutes. Set aside. Squeeze the grated ginger and make into a ball shape. Set aside for later. Cut the tofu block into squares about 2.5cm x 2.5cm. Heat the oil to about 190C. Dust the tofu with the flour and slide into the hot oil. Deep fry until golden brown. Drain well on paper towel. Serve the tofu in 4 bowls. Reheat the sauce and gently pour from the side of the bowl. Try not to splash over the tofu. Put the ginger ball on the tofu and sprinkle with chives, spring onion and bonito flakes.

yakitori (skewered chicken)
Serves 2

300g chicken thigh fillets, cut into 2.5cm pieces
leeks cut crosswise into 2.5cm lengths
bamboo skewers (soak in water 20 minutes prior to use)
seven-spice mixture

yakitori sauce
6 tblspn sake
200ml dark soy sauce
3 tblspn mirin
2 tblspn sugar

Thread the chicken and leeks onto the prepared skewers. Grill over a high heat or coals, turning occasionally until the juices begin to flow from the foods. Brush with yakitori sauce and continue grilling, allowing excess sauce to drip into a pot, so that the coals do not flare up. Season with seven-spice mixture. Do not overcook or the chicken will be dry.

sauce
Combine all sauce ingredients together in a saucepan and bring to the boil to burn off the alcohol.

Rusticana
wines

...at Langhorne Creek

The Greek Mezze

kangaroo island yabby and black mussel saganaki with pistachio and lemon pilaf rice
Serves 4

pilaf
olive oil for frying
500g long grain rice
zest of 2 lemons
juice of 2 lemons
salt and pepper
1 white onion, finely diced
650ml hot vegetable stock
200g pistachio nuts
olive oil

saganaki
½ tspn salt
olive oil for frying
1 red onion, sliced
50ml red wine
10 yabbies
2 cloves garlic, finely chopped
1kg black mussels, cleaned
1 litre rich napoletana sauce
½ cup chopped flat leaf parsley
200g good feta cheese, cut into cubes
salt and pepper

In a saucepan heat olive oil, add onion and sauté for 2 mins being careful not to brown. Add rice and fold through the onion so that the rice is coated with oil. Add hot stock and bring to a simmer. Cover saucepan with foil and place in 180C oven for about 35 mins.

Once rice is cooked, fold in lemon zest, pistachios, lemon juice, a little olive oil and salt and pepper to finish. Bring a pot of water to the boil, add salt and yabbies and cook about 5 - 8 mins.

Tip yabbies into a strainer and leave while you prepare saganaki. In a large frying pan, heat some oil. Add garlic and onion and sauté till soft.

Add mussels and red wine; cover and steam for about 3 mins. Uncover and remove the mussels that have not opened and discard. Add napoletana sauce, yabbies and half the parsley. Simmer for 5 mins. Add feta and toss through the sauce. Season with salt and pepper and serve garnished with remaining parsley.

kleftiko of saltbush goat with roasted root vegetables Serves 4

vegetables
4 parsnips, peeled and cut into 10cm pieces
4 medium carrots, cut into 10cm pieces
2kg saltbush goat (cut for braising)
500g cocktail potatoes   250g pickling onions
4 cloves garlic   1 bunch rosemary
salt and pepper   flour for coating
2 large white onions, diced   5 medium carrots, diced
½ bunch celery, diced   2 litres hot beef stock
5 cloves garlic, finely chopped 3 bay leaves
2 chillies, seeded and chopped salt and pepper
250g whole peeled tomatoes, crushed
1 bunch fresh thyme, chopped

Place all vegetables for roasting into a deep baking tray with olive oil, garlic, picked rosemary and salt and pepper. Mix thoroughly and place into a 180 – 200C oven for 1 hour to roast. Take out after 30 mins and toss. Return to oven. Coat goat pieces with flour and brown in a frying pan. Once browned, place in a deep roasting dish. Sauté onion, carrot, celery, garlic and chilli in a frying pan and tip over the browned goat. Add tomatoes and pour in hot stock. Add sprigs of thyme and bay leaves. Cover with foil and braise in a 180 – 200C oven for 1 hour and 40 mins. Once cooked, season with salt and pepper. Serve with the roasted vegetables.

youvarlakia soup
Serves 4

500g minced beef
100g raw rice
1 medium onion, pureed
1 egg
salt and pepper
125ml olive oil
4 litres chicken stock
1 bunch parsley, finely chopped

egg and lemon sauce
2 eggs
juice 2 lemons

Place beef, rice, onion, egg, salt, and pepper into a bowl, mix together thoroughly. Shape mixture into small balls. Bring chicken stock to the boil in a saucepan. Add oil and carefully add meatballs one at a time. Simmer for about 30 minutes.

Take 2 cups of the liquid from the meatballs and place in a bowl. In a separate bowl, whisk egg whites until they come to a peak. Whisk the yolks, stock and lemon juice together and add to the egg whites. Add this mixture to the soup folding through carefully. Season with salt and black pepper, add parsley and serve.

grain-fed t-bone with 3 cheese polenta and mithos beer batter prawns

Serves 4

polenta
2 litres chicken stock
280g fine polenta
100g Kefalogravera cheese, crumbled
50g grated parmesan cheese
100g SA blue cheese, crumbled
50g unsalted butter
salt and white pepper

beer batter
200g plain flour
50g cornflour
1 x 330ml bottle mithos beer
salt and white pepper

seasonal greens
1 bunch medium green asparagus
200g snow peas
1 bunch broccolini
100g baby spinach
100g flaked almonds
1 clove garlic, finely chopped
2 tblspn olive oil
salt and white pepper
4 x 500g grain-fed American T-Bones
12 green prawns, peeled with tails on
4 litres vegetable oil

polenta
Place stock into a saucepan and bring to the boil. Reduce heat to low and whisk while slowly adding the polenta. Continue stirring and cook for about 4 mins. Add one cheese at a time while whisking all the time. Whisk in butter and season to taste with salt and pepper. Cover with plastic wrap and set aside.

beer batter
Sift both flours into a bowl; make a well in the centre. Pour the beer slowly into the well and mix well. Season with salt and pepper. If too thick, add a little cold water. Cover with plastic wrap and place in the fridge.

seasonal greens
Cut asparagus into 7.5cm pieces. Discard the bottom sections, as they are generally woody and unpleasant to eat.

Prepare snow peas by removing their stems. Cut broccolini into 10cm pieces, also discarding the bottom stem sections.

To finish, cook T-Bones on a hot chargrill or BBQ to your liking. Meanwhile, heat oil in a saucepan. Bring 5 litres of water in another pot to the boil for blanching the vegetables. Place all vegies except spinach into the boiling water for 1 min.

In a frying pan, heat olive oil, add garlic, spinach, drained vegies, almonds, and sauté. Coat prawns in plain flour. Tap off excess flour and place in batter. Lift each prawn out individually from batter allowing excess to drip off. Carefully place in hot oil and cook until light golden colour.

To serve place polenta on the plate, top with T-Bone and place the prawns along the side of steak and polenta.

loukoumades
Serves 4

1kg plain flour
1 tspn sugar
honey
sesame seeds

30g fresh yeast
oil for frying
cinnamon
fresh fruit for garnish

Place 250g flour, yeast, sugar and a little water into a bowl and knead thoroughly to form a smooth dough. Cover bowl with a tea towel, place in a warm place and allow dough to double in size. Work in remaining flour adding a little water if needed, to form a workable dough. Cover bowl, leave in a warm place and allow to rise again for about 1 hour or until no bubbles are visible on the surface. Heat some oil in a deep-fryer or deep saucepan. Using two spoons scoop small balls of the mixture from the bowl and place into hot oil to cook until golden brown. Once cooked, remove from oil and drain on paper towel. Place loukoumades onto serving plates and cover generously with honey, cinnamon and sesame seeds. Garnish with your choice of fresh fruit and serve.

lightly floured zucchini flowers stuffed with braised leek, goat's cheese and pine nuts with a raspberry vinaigrette.
Serves 4

olive oil for frying
salt and pepper
50g pine nuts
150ml good quality olive oil
1 bunch chives

1 leek, finely chopped
200g soft goat's cheese
300g frozen raspberries
8 zucchini flowers

Heat a small amount of oil in a frying pan. Add leeks, a little salt and pepper and sauté until soft. In a bowl put goat's cheese, pine nuts, leek, and mix together. Place raspberries into a saucepan with a little water and bring to a simmer. Blend cooked raspberries in a food processor. Pass raspberries through a fine sieve or a piece of cheesecloth to remove all seeds and remaining flesh. Place the raspberry couli into a bowl and whisk in olive oil and salt and pepper to make a vinaigrette. Using a teaspoon, stuff zucchini flowers with cheese mixture being careful not to rip the flowers. Tie the tops of the stuffed flowers with chives. Coat the flowers with flour and fry until golden. Serve with raspberry vinaigrette.

Natural Gas
delivered by Envestra

TAPESTRY

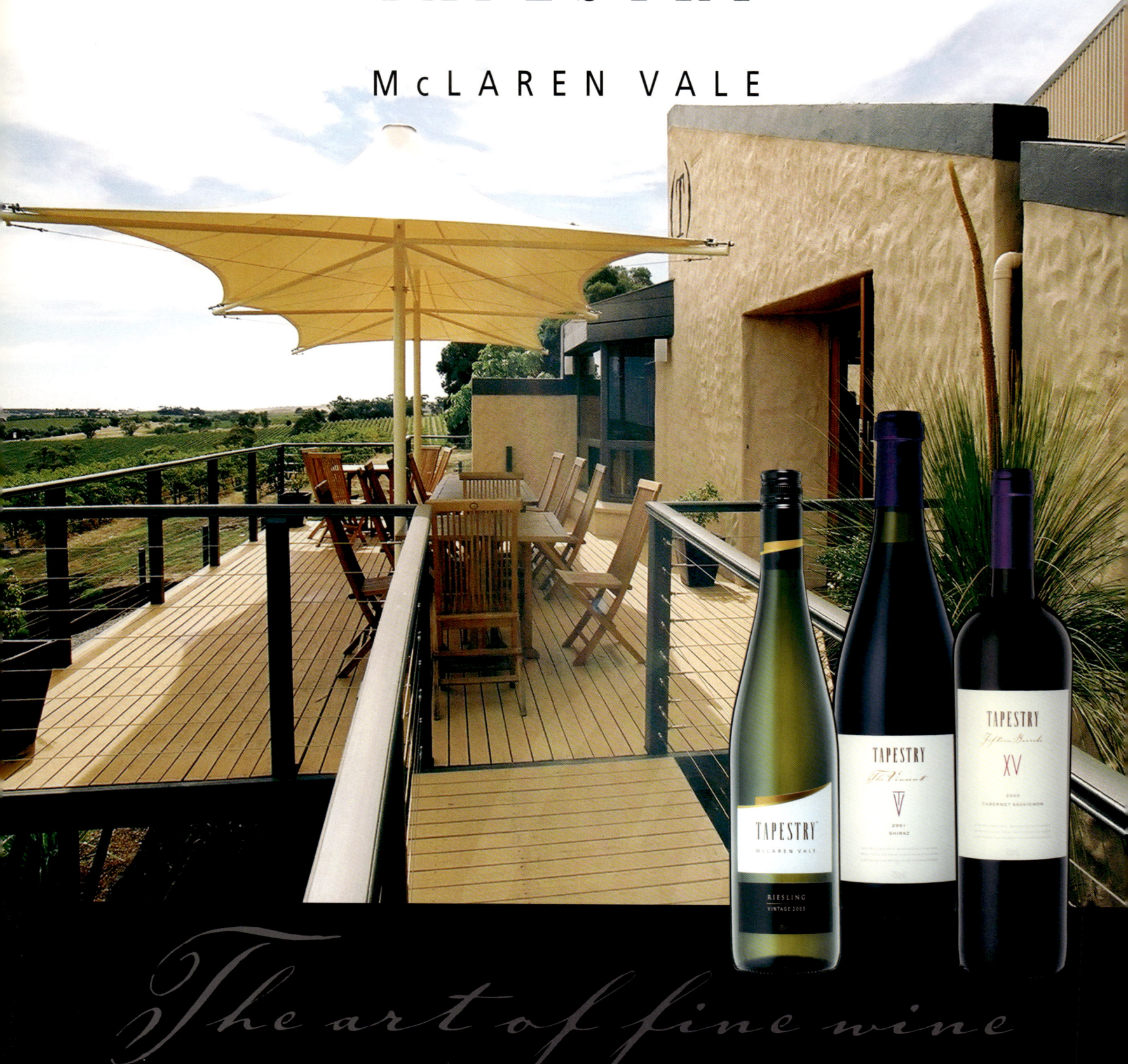

McLAREN VALE

The art of fine wine

Open daily 11am to 5pm.
Telephone: (08) 8323 9196
Olivers Rd, McLaren Vale

Chardonnay Lodge

The Poplars Restaurant

garfish paupiettes served with lime and rockmelon salad

Serves 4

8 medium garfish fillets
salt and pepper for seasoning
100g caster sugar
200g diced rockmelon
200g rocket leaves
1 punnet cherry tomatoes, cut in halves
8 strips prosciutto
50g butter, melted
150ml lime juice
125ml water

Cut garfish fillets in half along the spine to remove any fins or bone matter. Layer the fillets tail to tail and roll.

Wrap the fish in prosciutto and use a skewer to hold in place. Drizzle with melted butter and season with salt and pepper. Bake in a 175C oven for ten minutes just prior to being served. In a heavy-based saucepan place the sugar, lime juice, water and bring to the boil. Simmer for about 10 mins. Turn off the heat and allow to cool slightly. Add the rockmelon and cool completely. In a mixing bowl, place the rocket, cherry tomatoes and the rockmelon together using a small amount of the liquid for the dressing. Portion out the salad on the plates and place the cooked garfish on the salad and dress with the liquid.

terra rossa rib eye steak on pesto mash topped with steamed asparagus and béarnaise sauce

Serves 4

500g Coliban potatoes, peeled and diced
100g butter
salt and pepper to taste
Basil Pesto (250g)

béarnaise sauce (250g)

2 egg yolks
200g melted butter
½ bunch fresh tarragon
4 rib eye steaks
1 tspn vinegar
juice of 1 lemon
salt and pepper to taste
2 bunches asparagus

In a pan of cold water place potatoes and bring to the boil. Cook until al dente. Drain completely and place back into the pot and mash, using the butter and season to taste with the salt and pepper. Add pesto, mix together, and keep warm. Whilst potatoes are cooking, place egg yolks into a stainless steel bowl and place over a pan of boiling water. Add vinegar and whisk, being careful not to make scrambled eggs.

Remove from the heat and slowly add the melted butter, whisk until a creamy sauce is formed. Add the lemon juice, tarragon and season to taste. In the pan of water, steam the asparagus until tender. Grill the steaks to medium rare and rest for a few minutes. Portion out the mashed potato evenly, place the steak on top, drizzle with the béarnaise and top with the asparagus.

pork fillet and caramelised pear salad with blue cheese dressing and roasted walnuts
Serves 4

3 pears, peeled, cored and thinly sliced
200g Tarago River Blue Orchid cheese, melted
2 tomatoes, cut into wedges
caster sugar
125g mayonnaise
3 pork fillets
200g mixed lettuce leaves
walnut halves, roasted

Place the pears and tomatoes on a baking tray and sprinkle with some caster sugar. Cook in a 120C oven until semi-dry then allow to cool. Mix melted blue cheese with the mayonnaise. Cook pork fillets on the grill until just cooked, and then slice thinly. Toss the pears, tomatoes, lettuce, walnuts and pork in a bowl and serve drizzled with the dressing.

lemon myrtle and sweet chilli scallops with soused vegetable salad
Serves 4

300g carrot, cut into long ribbons with a peeler
300g cucumber, cut into long ribbons with a peeler
1 onion, thinly sliced
24 scallops in the shell
olive oil for frying
2 tspn chopped fresh ginger
1 clove garlic, chopped
125ml white wine
100ml sweet chilli sauce
10 lemon myrtle leaves
200g rocket

pickling solution
500ml water
250ml vinegar
125g sugar
8 peppercorns

In a pan place the pickling solution ingredients and bring to the boil. Cool slightly and add the vegetables. This will cook them slightly and give them a sharp flavour. Remove the scallops from their shells; put the shells aside for serving. Heat a little oil in a frying pan and sauté the scallops. Add garlic and ginger and deglaze the pan with the wine when the scallops are close to being cooked. Add sweet chilli sauce, lemon myrtle leaves and simmer until the scallops finish cooking. Place scallops back in their shells to serve and drizzle with the sauce. Serve with the pickled vegetables that have been mixed with the rocket.

the poplars' jaffa ice cream and candied orange cups
Serves 4

500ml full cream milk
125g caster sugar
200ml cointreau
zest of 2 oranges
4 cinnamon sticks
2 litres water

550ml double cream
8 egg yolks
150g dark chocolate
4 oranges
500ml orange juice

Mix milk, cream and two thirds of the sugar in a saucepan, bring to boiling point. Cool slightly. In a large bowl place the rest of the sugar and the egg yolks and whisk until well combined. Slowly add milk mixture, whisking constantly. Place back into the pan with the cointreau, chocolate and orange zest. Heat gently, stirring until mixture thickens and coats the back of a spoon. Be careful not to overcook it or it will become scrambled eggs. Pour into a container and put in the freezer. Approximately every 20 mins, take out of the freezer and whisk until it becomes light and silky. Whilst it is freezing, place the oranges into a pot with the cinnamon, orange juice and water and poach until the skin becomes soft. Cool the oranges cut the tops off and gently scoop out the pulp. Fill the orange shells with the ice cream and allow to set in the freezer. Serve with your favourite biscotti and dessert sauces if desired.

wattle seed pavlova with double cream
Serves 4

4 egg whites
250g caster sugar
2 tspn vinegar
few drops vanilla essence
125ml water
300ml double cream, firmly whipped
pinch salt
2 tspn cornflour
2 × 50g wattle seed
200g caster sugar

Preheat oven to 180C and line a baking tray with baking paper. Beat egg whites and salt in a mixer until soft peaks form. Add sugar, a third at a time and beat until stiff and shiny. Fold in cornflour, vinegar, half the wattle seed and vanilla. Spread mixture evenly on the tray and place into the oven, reduce the temperature to 150C and cook until a soft crust forms. Turn out onto a tea towel and roll up gently. Allow to cool. Place wattle seed, sugar and water in a saucepan and bring to the boil. This creates a wattle seed essence with a coffee-like aroma. Allow to cool. Mix a small amount of the essence with the cream. Cut the pavlova roll in half crosswise and fill with the cream. Decorate the plate by drizzling over the remaining essence. This pavlova can be served with fresh citrus fruits and spun toffee.

The Poplars
COONAWARRA

Introducing our new label, The Poplars Reserve, warranted only for the finest examples of Coonawarra wine.

The Poplars 2003 Reserve Cabernet Sauvignon is one of four new releases from The Poplars Winery, located in the heart of Coonawarra.

Wines available at Cellar door, Winery café, Chardonnay Lodge and via mail order.

Fine wines from the Australia's *Other* Red Centre.

Chardonnay Lodge
Riddoch Highway, Coonawarra
Cellar door open every day
from 9am until 5.30pm
Telephone: 08 8736 3309
www.chardonnaylodge.com.au

The Treasury Restaurant

chanterelle risotto with steamed asparagus and truffled parmesan
Serves 4

15g dried Chanterelle mushrooms
500ml hot water
1 litre vegetable stock
120g unsalted butter
1 small onion, finely diced
½ small leek, finely diced
1 clove garlic, crushed
500g Arborio rice
250ml white wine
50g parmesan cheese, grated
asparagus spears, blanched
100g truffled parmesan, shaved with a peeler

Soak chanterelles in the hot water for 20 minutes. Drain the liquid into the vegetable stock. Chop the mushrooms finely. Heat the stock in a saucepan. In a wide-based pan, melt half the butter and sauté the onion, leek and garlic until opaque. Add the rice and stir until the rice is coated with butter.

Add white wine and cook a few minutes to allow the alcohol to cook off. Add stock one cup at a time making sure it is absorbed slowly, so that the rice is firm but tender. Stir in remaining butter and the grated parmesan. Serve with blanched asparagus spears and shaved truffled parmesan.

Note: Chanterelles can be replaced with other mushroom varieties and truffled parmesan can be replaced with plain parmesan.

beetroot-cured atlantic salmon with seaweed and wasabi

Serves 4 to 5

2 large beetroot bulbs
200ml rice wine vinegar
200ml water
200g white sugar
500g Atlantic salmon, skin removed
salt to taste
wakami (seaweed salad)
wasabi

day 1

Cook beetroot in a pan of boiling water until tender. Allow to cool and rub off the skin. Cut into cubes approx. 2cm x 2cm. Place vinegar, water and sugar in a pan and bring to the boil.

Allow to cool and add the beetroot. Allow to pickle overnight.

Alternatively, use canned pickles, drained beetroot and add a little rice wine vinegar.

day 2

Drain beetroot and puree in a food processor or use a stick blender. Season to taste with salt if required.

Smear over the salmon fillet. Cover with plastic wrap and cure overnight in the fridge.

day 3

Wipe excess beetroot from the fish. Slice thinly and serve with wakami and wasabi (seasoned to taste).

seared kangaroo with mango chutney, mustard greens and yogurt and cucumber
Serves 5

marinade
50ml lemon juice
50g ginger, sliced
2 cloves garlic, sliced
1 long red chilli, seeded and sliced
50ml oil
2 tspn ground coriander
2 tspn ground cumin
2 tspn turmeric
1 tspn garam masala

green mango chutney
2 tspn chilli flakes
salt to taste
6 green mangoes, peeled and grated
2 tspn crushed mustard seeds
1 tblspn whole mustard seeds
½ cup oil
6 green chillies, sliced
2 cloves garlic, sliced
1 cup vinegar
1kg kangaroo loin

Mix the marinade ingredients together and marinate the kangaroo for at least 4 hours.

green mango chutney
Mix chilli flakes, salt, grated mango, crushed mustard and half of the whole mustard in a large bowl. Heat oil in a medium-sized frying pan and cook the green chillies slowly until light brown. Add garlic and soften. Add remaining mustard seeds. When the seeds stop crackling, add vinegar. Add to mango mixture and store in the fridge. Sear the marinated kangaroo in a large pan, a few pieces at a time. When they are all browned, place in 220C oven and cook for a further 5 minutes or until medium rare. Serve with steamed basmati rice, steamed mustard greens and yogurt mixed with coriander.

pan-seared veal kidneys with witlof, celery heart, walnut and mustard dressing
Serves 4

dressing
1 tblspn Dijon mustard
3 tblspn white vinegar
2 tspn white sugar
extra virgin olive oil

salad
witlof leaves
½ cup walnuts, roasted
50ml oil
celery heart, sliced
300g veal kidney

Whisk the dressing ingredients together and slowly add olive oil until the dressing becomes thick. This should be a good coating consistency for the witlof leaves and sliced celery heart. Slice the kidney across the lobe into 1cm portions. Place on paper towel to drain. Heat oil in a heavy-based pan and seal kidney until medium rare. Remove kidney, season and place on paper towels to drain. Serve warm with the salad and walnuts and an extra good drizzle of the dressing.

red roast duck legs with tandoori glaze
Serves 4

½ tspn chopped chilli
1 tblspn grated ginger
½ cup char sui sauce
1 litre stock
1 bunch coriander roots & stalks
5 tblspn sweet soy sauce
3 cloves garlic, crushed
12 duck legs
2 tblspn tandoori paste

cucumber salsa
1 continental cucumber
1 bunch garlic chives
4 tblspn olive oil
8 roma tomatoes
juice and zest of 1 lemon
salt and pepper

Combine chilli, soy, ginger, garlic, char sui sauce, and rub into the duck legs. Marinate in the fridge overnight. Add remaining ingredients and place in a deep baking dish. Cover with foil and cook in an 180C oven for 1½ hours. Remove foil and liquid and return to oven, cook uncovered for a further 30 minutes or until a rich red/brown colour. Allow stock to sit for 10 minutes and remove the duck fat that separates and comes to the top. Reduce the stock by half and use as a sauce. Serve the duck with salsa, rice and coriander leaves.

salsa
Remove the seeds from the cucumber and tomatoes and dice, chop the chives and add remaining ingredients, mixing to combine. Allow to sit for 15 minutes before serving.

blessed cheese

150 Main Road
McLaren Vale
Phone 8323 7958

WEDGWOOD

MERCATO
ON THE ROAD

- Large range of exclusive products, local and imported fine foods.
- Accessible to businesses, caterers, restaurants and cafes.
- Next day delivery, 7 days per week.

625 - 627 LOWER NORTH EAST ROAD, CAMPBELLTOWN
PH 8337 1808   OPEN 7 DAYS
Info@ilmercato.com.au   www.ilmercato.com.au

Wirra Wirra Vineyards
Rich rewards for those who venture "amongst the gums"

As its aboriginal name infers, Wirra Wirra is nestled "amongst the gums", in McLaren Vale, an historic ironstone winery that bears testament to the unique vision of its founder, the late Greg Trott.

A man of big ideas and grand gestures, Trott's pioneering spirit and sense of fun is on display for all to enjoy at the cellar door. From the call of the Angelus bell atop the winery, to the massive post and rail fence (sculpture?) known as "Woodhenge" that welcomes visitors, Wirra Wirra offers a unique and memorable winery experience.

Of course, none of this would matter if the wines didn't deliver. But deliver they do, with Winemaker Samantha Connew producing an eclectic range that showcases classic grape varietals from the pick of South Australia's regions. Be it Riesling, Chardonnay and Sauvignon Blanc from the Adelaide Hills or the rich Shiraz that has made the region famous, Wirra Wirra's reputation as a world class winery continues to grow.

Naturally it wouldn't be Wirra Wirra without something a little different. Cellar Door visitors who make their pilgrimage to try the latest vintage of the famous "Church Block", can expect to discover some of Samantha's more interesting experiments. Arneis or Moscato anyone? The Trott spirit lives on…

WIRRA WIRRA

The Sommelier at Chloe's

There are two main reasons for decanting wine. The most obvious reason is to separate the clear wine from the sediment. The second is to aerate the wine and a third reason, which might be just as important to the consumer, is the visual-added value to its service and presentation.

Almost all wines benefit from a little aeration before drinking, particularly those that have been in a bottle for several years. A mature wine can "come alive" remarkably by being poured into a glass from a little height so that it splashes and bubbles momentarily. Red wines are customarily decanted with the same object, added to the essential one of pouring them clear from the sediment. Whether wines benefit from being decanted an hour before being served is frequently debated.

The conventional French view is that early decanting dissipates precious aromas; the British view that time in the decanter softens and smooths a wine. There is no surprise in this - the French by tradition will drink their wines younger, enjoying their crispness and vigour, the British have traditionally appreciated maturity, gentleness and the beginning of decadence. Decant a very good vintage port approaching maturity at say, 15 years old. Taste it straight away it will be aggressively full flavoured.

A simple experiment demonstrates the effect of very long aeration on vigorous wine. Decant a very good vintage port approaching maturity at say, 15-years-old. Taste it straight away and it will be aggressively full flavoured, gripping your taste buds and invigorating your palate. Taste it 24 hours later, its power to shock will be slightly less, but you will find more subtleties in the smell and taste. To a lesser extent, that is the effect of decanting on all wines in their prime or before it. Wines beginning to tire with age can support correspondingly less aeration. Certain old burgundies never smell so ethereally sweet as immediately on opening – to miss that moment by delaying drinking them would be a shame. The decanting machine was invented for them – a device that allows the bottle to be tipped so gradually and steadily that one glass after another can be poured without disturbing the sediment and without resorting to a decanter.

Temperature of the wine

There are hundreds, perhaps thousands, of compounds which make up the aroma and flavour of a wine, and different groups are released from the surface of the wine at different temperatures. Aromatic, fragrant aromas are released at lower temperatures, while the more complex compounds evaporate at higher temperatures. The temperature of the wine also affects the perception of basic tastes and mouth-feel sensations. The lower the temperature, the less the perception of sweetness, and the wine can appear to be more acidic and refreshing. At lower temperatures, the bitter and astringent sensations can be accentuated. At higher temperatures the hotness of alcohol can be more apparent.

Generally speaking, wines that should be drunk chilled are usually too cold and those that must be consumed at room temperature (chambré) are too warm. In fact, the term chambré has become somewhat redundant now that homes are centrally heated to as much as 24 degrees C in winter, very much warmer than our grandparents' dining-rooms, which never went over 17 or 18 degrees C. Each type of wine of course needs an optimum tasting temperature, although this is always relative since a glass of wine at 18 degrees C will taste different according to the season and outside conditions. Most white wines should be chilled, but this does not mean 'frozen', and anything much below 8 degrees C is below the taste threshold.

While there are no set rules, there is general agreement regarding the optimal range at which to drink wines. The table provided below is a guide to the temperature range at which to serve different wine styles.

Wine   (Degrees Celsius)
Sparkling white   6-8
Fino   6-8
Amontillado   10-12
Light-bodied dry white   8-10
Med & full-bodied white   10-14
Semi-sweet & sweet white 8-10
Rosé   8-12
Light-bodied red   12-16
Medium & full-bodied red 16-20
Sparkling red   6-8
Oloroso and tawny   12-14
Muscat and tokay   12-14
Vintage fortified   16-20

Red wine service procedure

A bottle of wine should be brought up from the cellar at least one hour before the meal. A young wine should be carried and uncorked in the upright position, while an older vintage likely to throw off a deposit, should be placed gently in serving basket and poured from this near-horizontal position.

Cut the foil capsule under the lower lip of the bottle. Remove the top of the capsule and then wipe the top of the bottle with a clean, damp cloth to remove any sediment and/or pieces of

Decanting Wine

capsule. Insert the tip of the corkscrew into the centre of the cork with the corkscrew at an angle, so that you do not push the cork in when inserting it. Straighten the corkscrew and twist it in a clockwise direction until it is inserted almost fully into the cork, with about one or two turns visible above the cork. Place the end of the lever on the lip of the bottle. Be careful with old, crumbly corks and proceed cautiously when inserting the corkscrew. If the cork breaks during the extraction and crumbles, it is best to decant the wine through a funnel with a metal filter, to remove the pieces of cork prior to serving.

To remove the cork, pull the handle of the corkscrew up with a gentle, even pressure. Change the pivotal contact point of the lever on the lip of the bottle during cork extraction so that the cork is removed vertically. As you are raising the handle it also helps to hold the bottom of the lever in place on the lip of the bottle with the fingers of the other hand.

The cork from an old bottle of wine is often presented to the consumer on a small plate or appropriate salver. This is done to demonstrate the condition of the cork and thus, the condition of the wine.

Before serving wine, it is customary to allow the host or the person ordering the wine to sample it. This is done by pouring approximately 30 mls into the host's glass, or even better using a glass being provided for that purpose.

Red wine with sediment can be prepared for decanting in two ways. With sufficient foresight it can be taken from its rack and stood upright for long enough for the sediment to fall from the side of the bottle to the bottom. Sediment in certain wines is so fine that it can take two or three days. Without this preparation the bottle must be moved from its rack directly into a cradle or basket that holds it tilted just enough for the cork to be drawn. This device allows the bottle to be tipped gradually and pour the wine steadily into a decanter.

The wine bottle may also be lifted from (rather than in) the cradle or basket and poured gradually and steadily into a decanter. A torch or candle is needed to throw light through the bottle so that the sediment can be seen approaching the neck and pouring stopped in time.

To some people wine means fun, enjoyment, the good life; to some it is a serious and consuming passion and to others a relentless quest for perfection. I am content to let each individual justify their position as they see fit.

As a restaurateur/sommelier how do you establish and maintain a wine philosophy that will at least please people most of the time?

Surely the starting point is that our clients join us in our restaurant to have an enjoyable evening and experience a range of tastes in good company and surroundings.

We aim to exceed their expectations and provide a memorable experience and to that end I try to direct and advise clients to enjoy the difference on offer and to experience something new.

I love recommending a wine that I have discovered and having the customer fall in love with it!

Cheers
Nick Papazahariakis

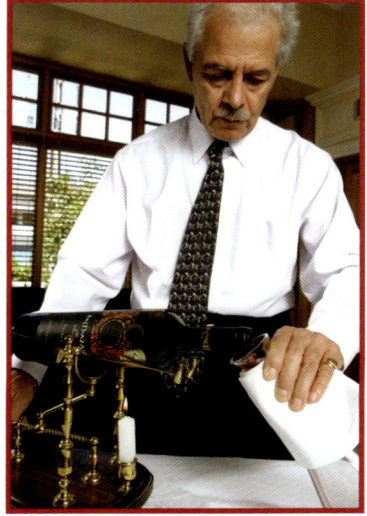

famous winemakers of South Australia

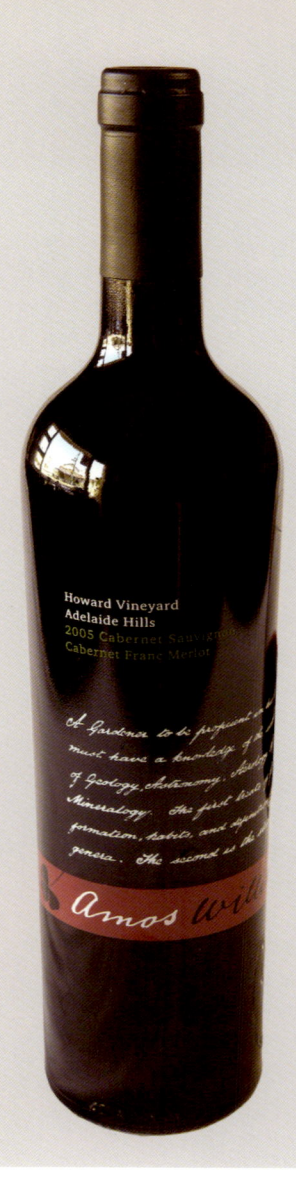

Incorporating family owned wineries to promote the different wine growing regions within South Australia

Check the table on page 142 for full tabulated details about the individual wineries - where they are - distance from Adelaide - buying on line - cellar door times - etc.

Amadio Wines

The AMADIO label - arguably represents the best value, premium Australian range of wines. The unparalleled value for quality derives from Danniel Amadio's (owner/winemaker), passionate determination to maintain his "We grow the vines, make the wine, and sell direct to you" - production process. Danniel confidently challenges "I personally guarantee, you cannot buy such consistent premium quality wines – for our prices, anywhere else". A winemaking family, the AMADIO name first commercially registered wine in 1936 - and in more recent years Danniel's parents, Caj and Genny - successfully developed the most awarded boutique winery in Australia. Consequently, Danniel experienced 'hands on' vineyard management and concise winemaking,

The AMADIO family vineyards – nestled in the Adelaide Hills, are perfectly positioned to benefit from long warm days, and crisp cool nights, with the soil analysis ideal for the various grape varieties planted. Danniel says; "For me, the natural fruit characters of our vineyards, really help me to qualify the precise way I will approach making each vintage. I believe the basic quality and nature of the fruit makes up to seventy per cent of the winemaking". Danniel's experienced, successful approach is self evident, with a host of industry awards and accolades – most recently a Gold Medal - Reserve Block 2A 04 Shiraz, Shanghai International Wine and Spirits Fair (only Aussie Gold awarded). Only available in South Australia from the Moving Juice outlet - (visit and 'try before you buy'), or online www.movingjuice.com.au

Balthazar Barossa

Anita Bowen's boutique wine brand burst from obscurity at the 2005 Barossa Wine Show when her 2002 Balthazar Barossa Shiraz won a coveted gold medal and two trophies. Anita made her first wine at Mudgee in 1986, before heading to McLaren Vale then Barossa Valley, where she undertook wine studies at Roseworthy Agricultural College.

After a brief absence in New Zealand and Sydney, Anita returned to the Barossa Valley to develop the family's vineyard at Stonewell Road, Marananga, situated on the Barossa's western slopes – a celebrated shiraz microcosm. The land, an original 19th Century vineyard was replanted in the 1990s with vines painstakingly sourced from one of the oldest shiraz vineyards in the Barossa and nurtured using biological farming practices to produce premium quality, low yielding wine grapes.

From 2001 Anita began to choose the best grapes from her vineyard to make a limited amount of premium, single vineyard shiraz wine under the Balthazar Barossa label. Balthazar is named after a 6th Century BC Babylonian King, famous for holding a great feast for 100 of his court at which he commanded the drinking of wine from holy gold and silver chalices taken from the Temple of Jerusalem. This blasphemous act secured Balthazar's fate and he perished that night at the hands of the invading Persians thus bringing an end to the Babylonian Empire.

For Further information about the wineries see the Info section on page 142

famous winemakers of SA

Cape Jaffa

Derek Hooper and his family moved to Cape Jaffa some 15 years ago to become the founding winery in the Mount Benson region. A bold move at the time, Derek's father Kym, recognised a red tinge on the sheep's wool, revealing the presence of 'terra rossa' soil in the area. This along with Derek's observation of the surf break down the road cemented the Hooper family's decision to plant vines in the area. The winery's unique location alongside South Australia's spectacular Limestone Coast also happens to be home to one of the country's best lobster fishing industries, the historic town of Robe - established 150 years ago and picturesque Coastal Parks and Lakes.

The Cape Jaffa philosophy is one of low impact winemaking, environmental sustainability and creating wines that are both regional and varietal distinction. After establishment of the vineyard, Derek began to experiment with organic and biodynamic growing techniques to increase quality. The results were impressive! Cape Jaffa will be a fully certified biodynamic producer in 2008. Biodynamic farming is more of a spiritual than scientific method of farming based on the lectures of Rudolf Steiner. 'At Cape Jaffa, we see our farm as a living system and are able to substitute the use of chemicals by maintaining natural balance from soil to vine'. Although many of the philosophies cannot be scientifically proven, the effect on quality and uniqueness in wines has been proven. Cape Jaffa produces fruit (rather than oak) driven wines with deliberation to compliment, rather than dominate, accompanied cuisine.

Chain of Ponds

A taste of Tuscany in the Adelaide Hills, Chain of Ponds is located amidst the rolling hills and vineyards surrounding the old township of Gumeracha on the banks of the River Torrens, just a short forty minute drive from the city of Adelaide. The "Chain of Ponds" story started in 1985 with the planting of a small pilot vineyard to test the suitability of several exciting different grape varieties in the newly emerging cool climate Adelaide Hills wine region, which has now established a global reputation for high quality wines with a style of their own.

In the years since the first release of two white and one red wine in 1995, the Chain of Ponds label has enjoyed continual recognition and accolades for the creation of innovative wine styles endorsed by a succession of show awards. Our highly regarded "Novello" family of "Rosso" (rosé), "Nero" (red) and "Bianco" (white) wines has been created as an everyday accompaniment to informal dining. A visit to our Tasting Room offers visitors an opportunity to experience cool climate wines in a range of varieties and styles – our family ranges from Italianate Sangiovese, Nebbiolo and Pinot Grigio to the traditional and classical Chardonnay, Shiraz and Cabernet Sauvignon together with refreshing Sauvignon Blanc. Call by and meet our family! Tasting Room – Open Monday to Friday 9.30 – 4.30; Weekends 10.00 – 4.30. Tuscan platters and regional cheese plates with wood oven ciabatta bread and home-made olive oil available all day every day.

Charles Cimicky

A prestigious and picturesque winery near Lyndoch, gateway to the Barossa Valley, Charles Cimicky Wines is doing its utmost to promote our wine-growing region as the best in the country. Winemaker Charles Cimicky has achieved an impressive total of 12 gold medals and 6 trophies over a two year period. Long recognized as premium producers of red wine, Charle's area of specialization, the family owned and operated winery displays a total dedication to quality, which is revealed by their consistent success at the national wine shows. Three time winner of the coveted Barossa Wine Grape Council Trophy adds further emphasis.

Within the imposing Tuscan-style building, a mecca for overseas tourists, state-of-the-art technology is combined with traditional methods of winemaking. Unlike many other small concerns, Cimicky wines is a genuine producing winery, handling all aspects of winemaking from specialized, organic viticulture, through to crushing, maturation, bottling and packaging.

Although many of the grapes are estate-grown and managed, Charles is supported by a loyal group of expert Barossa growers who take much pleasure in having the opportunity to ultimately taste the fruits of their labours. This support, combined with that of devoted staff members, renders Charles Cimicky Wines a charming Barossa enterprise committed to the region.

Currency Creek Estate

Situated in close proximity to Lake Alexandrina and the Southern Ocean, our vines thrive in this mild maritime climate. Early bud burst, together with a prolonged ripening period, result in fruit of exceptional complexity. This allows veteran winemaker, John Loxton, to produce consistently elegant, fruit driven wines. Our wines are made from estate grown fruit, with the premium range consisting of single vineyard parcels – the best selected from each vintage. As well as an extensive range of award winning wines, Currency Creek Estate offers so much more.

Our restaurant, with cosy open fires in the winter, overlooks picturesque gardens with a back drop of rural views. You can enjoy coffee any time of the day, with a great range of tempting cakes from which to choose. We cater for weddings and functions, host art exhibitions and our cellar door incorporates the "Producers' Pantry" offering local produce, delicacies and artifacts.

For nature enthusiasts the Black Swamp Walking Trail wanders around this heritage listed swamp, offering glimpses of local flora and fauna and spectacular photographic opportunities. Our six luxury spa villas are situated within walking distance opposite the restaurant, allowing you to indulge in all we have to offer to your heart's content! Quality wine - great food – luxury accommodation – all in a picturesque setting.

For Further information about the wineries see the Info section on page 142

famous winemakers of SA

Dennis Wines

In 1968, Egerton Dennis initiated the emergence of Dennis Wines with the object of converting the high quality grapes produced at his McLaren Flat estate into premium wine.

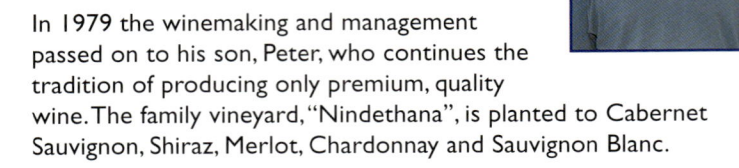

In 1979 the winemaking and management passed on to his son, Peter, who continues the tradition of producing only premium, quality wine. The family vineyard, "Nindethana", is planted to Cabernet Sauvignon, Shiraz, Merlot, Chardonnay and Sauvignon Blanc.

The property is beautifully situated at McLaren Flat at the base of the Mount Lofty Ranges where the soil, climate and rainfall are ideal for the purpose. Pioneered at the winery in the early seventies is the production of Mead, made from fermented honey, the oldest alcoholic beverage in recorded history (the wine of the Vikings, King Arthur, Robin Hood etc.)

The ancient Romans regarded Mead as an aphrodisiac and therefore, the honeymoon beverage. Mead has an enormous following. As well as the Dan Murphy Trophy and Bushing King awards (twice) for the best wine in the McLaren Vale Winemakers' Exhibition, Dennis Wines have won over two hundred medals at Australian, European, North American and Asian capital city wine shows.

DiGiorgio Wines

The DiGiorgio family acquired the Coonawarra vineyard and winery in early 2002, in addition to the original vineyard planted by the family on their Lucindale property in 1989. The vineyards and winery are managed by Frank DiGiorgio, with legendary Coonawarra winemaker Peter Douglas in charge of production. Three ranges of wine are produced and sold under the DiGiorgio family name. The 'Coonawarra' range comprises a Cabernet Sauvignon, Shiraz, Emporio (blend of Merlot, Cabernet Sauvignon and Cabernet Franc) and a bottle fermented sparkling Pinot Noir. All wines in the 'Coonawarra' range are made from fruit grown on the famous 'terra rossa' soils surrounding the winery. In late 1989, the DiGiorgio family set aside 4 hectares on their Lucindale farm for vines. Following the success of these first plantings the total area under vine at Lucindale is now 126 hectares. The 'Lucindale' range of wines consists of a sparkling Pinot Noir/Chardonnay, Sauvignon Blanc, Chardonnay, Merlot, Cabernet Sauvignon, 'Francesco Reserve' Cabernet Sauvignon and sparkling Merlot. The Lucindale property is named 'Sterita' after Stefano and Rita DiGiorgio. The 'Sterita' range includes a Semillon/Sauvignon Blanc, Unoaked Chardonnay, Shiraz and Cabernet/Merlot. The wines capture the essential fruit flavours of each grape variety, and are made to be fresh, lively and approachable. Throughout the year events such as the "Vintage Stomp" enable visitors to enjoy the family's passion for food, wine and fun. The family regularly conduct winery tours and the cellar door welcomes both individuals and group bookings.

Eldredge Vineyards

Eldredge Vineyards cellar door and restaurant operations began in December 1994 after many months of renovating an 80-year-old stone cottage.

Situated on the Spring Gully scenic drive route it has, over the years, become one of the best kept secrets of the Clare Valley due to not only its unique location, but also the superb classic and contemporary food served with National & International award winning wines.

Located directly west of Sevenhill, we are on the boundary of the Clare Valley at 440 metres above sea level overlooking the Blyth Plains, with the vineyard rising to 530 metres at its highest point. It is an excellent tourist destination and vineyard site which is beginning to produce high quality Shiraz, Cabernet Sauvignon, Sangiovese, Merlot, Malbec and Riesling. Our range includes the following – Riesling, Semillon/Sauvignon Blanc, Late Harvest Riesling, Mourvedre/Grenache/Shiraz blend, Sangiovese/Cabernet Sauvignon blend, Shiraz and Cabernet Sauvignon.

Our wines are produced from 100% Clare Valley fruit, our focus being to create affordable wines of premium high quality that reflect not only our character, but also that of the wonderfully unique Clare Valley

Howard Vineyard

"Come up for air" to the scenic Adelaide Hills – an undulating mosaic of farms, orchards, vineyards, forests and historic towns. Enjoy fine wine, local produce and good food in picturesque surroundings.

Howard Vineyard Cellar Door offers a rustic ambiance for enjoying an extensive, award-winning range of white and red wines within a stunning vineyard setting, including picnic grounds lined by native ghost gums.

Our white wines reflect the region's distinctive cool climate with full and complex flavours. Think contemporary styles: fruity, zing and zest! Varieties include Sauvignon Blanc, Riesling, Semillon, Chardonnay and Viognier.

Red varieties include Cabernet Sauvignon, Cabernet Franc and Shiraz, all nurtured at low yields to ensure full flavour development. These elegant wines are aromatic, fruity and melded by subtle use of oak.

Platters are available on weekends or by arrangement to accompany informal or formal wine tastings. The hosting of private parties, events and corporate functions is also offered in conjunction with catering by local chefs.

Please visit and enjoy the Howard Vineyard experience!

famous winemakers of SA

Kilikanoon

Winemaker Kevin Mitchell purchased the Kilikanoon property in late 1997 with a vision of creating his own brand. After months of extensive renovation the cellar door opened in April 1998 coinciding with the release of the 1997 vintage wines. The Penna Lane family arrived in Clare from Cornwall in the 1850s. They had worked at an estate in Cornwall called Killa-goon which has an enigmatic translation of 'sloping nut tree grove'. Our cellar door is the original farmhouse which dates from 1860s to 1870s.

The name has evolved over time to Kilikanoon and was retained when the wine brand was conceived. Kevin was born and raised in the Clare Valley spending most of his free time in the vineyard with his father Mort Mitchell. Mort has always enjoyed a reputation as one of the Clare Valley's more meticulous and experienced grape growers. This dedication has resulted in premium quality signature brands such as the 'Mort's Block' Riesling, 'Blocks Road' Cabernet Sauvignon, the 'Oracle' and 'Covenant' Shiraz.

The winery and range of wines has continued to grow at a rapid rate from a 2000 case production in 1997 to over 25,000 in 2005. We are currently extending our winery and barrel storage at the Kilikanoon Leasingham site, which will be finished in time for the 2007 vintage. The Kilikanoon range of wines continues to grow and has been further enhanced by the release of the 'Attunga 1865', a single vineyard wine, hand made from Shiraz planted in 1865. Certainly our most opulent and premium Shiraz to date.

Kirrihill Wines

Kirrihill Wines is located in the premium winegrowing region of the Clare Valley on the banks of the Hill River, surrounded by the beautiful hills of the prestigious valley. The winery was founded on a passion for wine and a desire to produce super-premium wines equal to any in the world. With this as the benchmark, the Kirrihill Wines team has drawn on centuries of winemaking tradition while embracing innovation and technology to produce wine of great varietal flavour and quality. All the wines are made on site at Kirrihill Wines. The $10 million 'winery without walls' development is set on a sloping site to take advantage of gravity in the production process. An innovative, cantilevered roof and sails provide natural light and shade with plenty of open space and room to expand.

Designed for ease of use, the layout has an emphasis on environmentally sound practices, including reusing waste water and the recycling of grape marc into organic mulch for the vineyards, which now surround the winery. In addition to exceptional fruit, vital to the process of creating high quality wines at Kirrihill Wines is the employment of the best equipment and resources such as new stainless steel fermenters, the very best cultured and wild yeasts, and quality French, American and Russian oak.

This inspiring winery environment gives the winemaking team the space, flexibility and support required to turn their passion for making good wine into Kirrihill Wines exceptional super-premium range, Kirrihill Estates and premium Kirrihill Companions' range.

Langmeil

The Long Mile - Langmeil Winery is a small, family owned business which was established in 1996 by three friends, Richard Lindner, Chris Bitter and Carl Lindner, all fourth generation Barossans. The property was originally settled by Christian Auricht, a German migrant who established the estate as the main trading area of the original Langmeil village.

Langmeil Winery ensured that the old ironstone buildings which housed the butcher, cobbler's shop, blacksmith and baker were restored and they are maintained. In the 1840s Christian Auricht planted Shiraz vines on this estate which still exist today. They produce a single vineyard wine called "The 1843 Freedom Shiraz". This vineyard is recognised as the oldest known surviving Shiraz vineyard in Australia and possibly the world. Paul Lindner is the head winemaker at Langmeil Winery. His aim is to produce wines which are distinctly from the Barossa but have his own individual style.

Vineyard selection and grower education help to maintain the quality of all Langmeil's fruit, which is reflected in the wines. Paul uses traditional methods to make the wine, including open fermentation and basket pressing. With minimal handling and filtration techniques, he ensures that the full potential of the fruit is captured and the essence of the varietal and regional characters are enhanced in all Langmeil's wines. Langmeil Winery was given 5 stars in James Halliday's Australian Wine Companion.

Nepenthe

In 1994 the Tweddell family purchased a premium property in the subregion of Lenswood in the Adelaide Hills, spurred on by the passion for wine shared by James and his father Ed, the patriarch of Nepenthe. Over the subsequent years Nepenthe has enjoyed significant growth and recognition in Australia and overseas.

Situated in the rolling hills between the two villages of Hahndorf and Balhannah, the Nepenthe cellar door is the perfect spot to escape to. Enjoy stunning views of the Mt Lofty ranges while sampling the award winning range of Nepenthe wines. Indulge in the delectable selection of goodies on the regional cheese platter and be tempted by the aroma of great coffee.

Nepenthe specialises in the traditional cool climate varieties of Sauvignon Blanc, Pinot Noir and Chardonnay. Try these elegant wines at the cellar door and why not explore something a little different, such as the Nepenthe Pinot Gris, Tempranillo, Zinfandel and eclectic Tryst Blends; Tryst White, a zesty combo of Sauvignon Blanc, Semillon and Pinot Gris and Tryst Red, an enticing blend of Cabernet Sauvignon, Tempranillo and Zinfandel.

The Nepenthe cellar door is open daily, come and escape!

For Further information about the wineries see the Info section on page 142

famous winemakers of SA

Parish Hill

Parish Hill Wines is one of the smallest wineries in the Adelaide Hills, with only 1.6 hectares of vineyard. It is also one of the bravest, daring to be different by growing and making only Italian varieties – Dolcetto, Nebbiolo, Negro Amaro, Arneis, Moscato Giallo, Pinot Grigio and Vermentino.

Andrew Cottell who is both the viticulturist and winemaker believes that great wines start with great grapes in the vineyard. The environmentally friendly vineyard overlooks the Piccadilly Valley on a warm west facing hill making it the ideal site for growing the Italian varietals.

Licensed to crush only 15 tonnes of grapes each year, a very small quantity of each wine is made and because of this the wines cannot be entered into most of the wine shows. However, they have been tasted by many wine writers and received very favourable reviews.

Parish Hill Wines are only available by mail order and tastings can be arranged. Telephone 08 8390 3927 or visit the website at www.ParishHill.com.au for more information.

Parri Estate

Alice, Peter and John Phillips established Parri Estate winery in 1998 on an 82-acre vineyard located between Mount Compass and Victor Harbor. In 2004 the modern cellar door, located on Ingoldby Road, McLaren Flat was purchased incorporating a modern warehouse and function area and premium 45-year-old vineyards planted with Shiraz, Grenache and Cabernet Sauvignon. Parri Estate produces a diverse range of premium wines, as well as offering innovative wine education activities for people to experience and enjoy. On a daily basis, you can sniff the aroma bottles to help you understand the scent of different wine varieties and recognise their various characteristics. French and American oak samples are also available to help educate your palate, as is a fault kit, which can be used to detect corked or oxidized wine. In conjunction with this, Parri Estate conduct fully-accredited Understanding Wines and More About Wine courses. Special theme nights are held at the cellar door throughout the year.

A large all-weather pergola is used as an outdoor entertaining area and is available to book your next function. In December of last year, the Mount Compass cellar door was opened. Currency Creek runs through the 82-acre property and in time, the area will be developed to include walking trails and interesting plant life. Vineyard tours are available by appointment and bus tours are encouraged to enjoy a wine tasting at Ingoldby Road and then continue on to the Mount Compass site for a vineyard tour.

Rusticana Wines

The vineyard was established in the early 90s on the rich alluvial flood plains in Langhorne Creek and the first Rusticana Wines were produced in 2003. While most of the fruit is sold, about 25% is retained for the Rusticana Label.

There are two ranges, a White Label range and a Premium Black Label range. Along with the Cabernet and Shiraz, two new varieties Durif and Zinfandel will be harvested for the first time in 2007.

A Sauvignon Blanc and a Rosé are part of the White Label range and go very well with our platters on hot summer days.

A new cellar door was opened in 2006 and with its wonderful elevated deck and views over the property has been an outstanding success, offering light lunches, tastings, local produce, coffee and the Newmans Horseradish range.

The logo for Rusticana Wines is an amazing burnt out Red Gum Stump standing 5 metres high and located at the ramp entrance to the cellar door.

The name chosen for the wines comes from "Amoracia Rusticana" which is the botanical name for Horseradish, and gives a connection between the two businesses.

Tapestry Wines

School holidays were spent labouring, developing a passion and starting to learn the practical side of wine grape growing at an Uncle's Springton Vineyard in the Hills above the Barossa Valley. Winemaker (and licensed commercial pilot), Jonathan Ketley was Adelaide born and educated.

In 1986, after completing his studies, Jonathan began his career with the Penfolds Wine Group at Loxton, in South Australia's Riverland. In 1991, he transferred to the Penfolds Nuriootpa Winery, then to Seppeltsfield Winery where he remained for eight years. During this time he was involved in the production of Fortifieds premium red and white table wines. Jonathan then headed offshore to California in 1999 for the vintage at Southcorp's Californian joint venture, Seven Peaks.

Jon was reluctantly drawn back to Australia and in 2001 left Southcorp to join Merrivale (now Tapestry Wines), a small unknown yet promising venture with little or no market presence at the time, but two fantastic, reputable old vineyards (Oliver's Road and Bakers Gully). Both vineyards, located in key subregions of McLaren Vale, are old, very low yielding, and produce fruit and wines with intense flavour and concentration. It is Tapestry's creed to produce the highest quality table wines using fruit harvested primarily from those two, long established vineyards. For further information about the winery see the information section on page 142.

For Further information about the wineries see the Info section on page 142

famous winemakers of SA

Wirra Wirra

Wirra Wirra Vineyards was originally established in McLaren Vale in 1894 by known South Australian eccentric and State cricketer, Robert Strangways Wigley. The winery prospered in its early days, producing many wines including a much acclaimed Shiraz, which was exported to England and the Empire until Wigley's death in 1925. It ran into disrepair in the pursuant years and was eventually abandoned.

Fast forward to 1969 and local farmer Greg Trott is looking for a suitable location to follow his dream of establishing a winery. He finds the ruins of the old Wirra Wirra practically on his doorstep and assisted by his cousin Roger, rebuilds the winery from the remnants of two walls and some slate fermenting tanks.

As with all subsequent Trott endeavours, it was the sheer magnitude and unlikeliness of the project that made it so attractive. Following Trott's passing in 2005, Wirra Wirra continues to showcase its wines at the very same site in a stunning cellar door built from local Kangarilla ironstone.

From the 3/4 tonne Angelus bell atop the winery, to the massive post and rail fence dubbed "Woodhenge", the winery is a popular destination for visitors to the region and carries the unmistakable stamp of Trott's vision and unique take on life. Wirra Wirra has developed a strong following for intense, beautifully-crafted red wines and expressive whites, forging an enviable reputation as one of Australia's most recognizable and leading wineries.

IMMA & MARIO'S Mercato

Cooking demonstration classes now at Imma and Mario's Mercato featuring talented Adelaide Chefs, and wine tasting by various SA wineries. Learn traditional and authentic yet different Italian cookery.

Email: maria@ilmercato.com.au to register your interest with name and contact details

625 - 627 LOWER NORTH EAST ROAD, CAMPBELLTOWN
PH 8337 1808   OPEN 7 DAYS
Info@ilmercato.com.au   www.ilmercato.com.au

CERAVOLO ESTATE   ReD EARTH   Adelaide Plains - Adelaide Hills

The Ceravolo family came to Australia from Italy over fifty years ago from the 35 N Parallel in Southern Italy, in the old world, to the 35 S Parallel in South Australia, in a new world. They brought with them their age old traditions of growing grapes, making wine and olive oil, and planted vineyards and an olive grove on the rich red fertile soils on the Adelaide Plains.

New World Wine – Old World Tradition

Joe and Heather Ceravolo, with their son Antony, are building on the traditions of their Italian heritage, and the reputation of the grapes from their estate that previously went into other wineries' award-winning wines. They now produce under their own distinctive award-winning labels contemporary fine Australian wines.

The Best of Both Worlds

Joe is the passionate vigneron and wine producer, Heather looks after marketing and Antony represents them in Europe and America.

"It is a way of life for us ... growing the best grapes, producing the best wines ... and enjoying what we do! It gives us enormous pleasure to know that someone, somewhere in the world enjoys our beautiful wine ... we hope with good food and good conversation."

Enjoy!   Joe, Heather and Antony Ceravolo

CERAVOLO ESTATE Single varieties from single vineyards. These wines highlight the different styles of warm climate and cool climate wines. Luscious, richly coloured, full-flavoured wines from the Mediterranean maritime climate of the sunny Adelaide Plains – Shiraz, Merlot, Cabernet Sauvignon, Petit Verdot, Sangiovese, Chardonnay, Sangiovese Rosé ... and classic sleek wines - an Italian-inspired Pinot Grigio, Sauvignon Blanc and Sparkling Pinot Chardonnay - from the cooler climes of the beautiful Adelaide Hills.

ReD EARTH Youthful and vibrant wines with an easy drinking style. Shiraz, Merlot, Cabernet Sauvignon, Chardonnay and N.V. Brut Cuvee. Medium-bodied, soft flavours and full of character.

For Further information about the wineries see the Info section on page 142

ASCOT TEAK

Ascot Teak is an international manufacturing & trading company with its main factory and supply source in Java, Indonesia. Ascot Teak runs an enlightened business where our concerns about our staff's harmony and welfare are only matched by our commitment and dedication to product quality.

Ascot Teak is proud to be able to make furniture that the whole world can enjoy. We manufacture from an extensive range of selected teak and only teak that is certified as coming from Government controlled plantation forests is used.

After aging and proper Kiln-drying we construct our teak furniture using only pegged mortise and tenon joinery and solid brass fittings. These quality benchmarks mean that all Ascot Teak furniture is maintenance free (if you choose), imperious to water damage and guaranteed against rotting or warping.

Because we manufacture, wholesale and retail one of the most extensive, exclusive and diverse ranges of teak furniture, we are able to offer our customers a 12 month limited guarantee on any purchase. Everything from folding tables, fixed and extension tables, benches, folding chairs, armchairs, pool lounges, steamers, planters, indoor flooring, outdoor decking and Bali Huts to suit any home, made to your size requirement.

IMMA & MARIO'S MERCATO

WOOD OVEN TAFER
Made in Italy

This stainless steel cooking chamber allows you to cook bread, sweets, pizza, roasts and so much more.

Come into Imma and Mario's Mercato to find out more

625 - 627 LOWER NORTH EAST ROAD, CAMPBELLTOWN
PH 8337 1808   OPEN 7 DAYS
Info@ilmercato.com.au   www.ilmercato.com.au

Breville

It was on Melbourne Cup Day 1932 that Bill O'Brien, a radio salesman and Harry Norville, an engineer, founded "Breville Radio". Breville is a derivative from the names O'Brien and Norville.

In an era when the radio was the centre of family entertainment, the fledgling company was a near-instant success.

During World War Two Breville's focus turned to the war effort manufacturing mine detectors. Post war, the radio market boomed, sensing the impact of television, the radio business was sold and Brevile's focus turned to small appliances.

John O'Brien was charged with the task of sourcing small appliance agencies for Breville and therefore introduced brands such as Braun, Pifco and Friedland into Australia.

He then became passionately involved in the small appliance business and as a result founded the Breville Research and Development centre.

In 1974 the Breville Snack'n'Sandwich Toaster was released, selling 400,000 in a year - one of the most successful product launches in Australian history. Three years later came Australia's first food processor, the Breville Kitchen Wizz. A product that is still an icon in kitchens today.

As more women joined the workforce, saving time became a priority. Fast food boomed. Breville's range expanded to bring new levels of convenience, with blenders, dairy bars, yogurt makers and waffle irons. The major success story was the Kitchen Wizz, the first Australian food processor. By now, Breville had established an office in Hong Kong, and was exporting products to 15 countries.

The 90s brought with it an awareness of healthy, low fat cooking and the acceptance of Mediterranean and Asian cooking.

Breville responded by developing high performance electric woks and health grills, and brought the 'Café Culture' into the home through the invention of the Sandwich Press and world-acclaimed Juice Fountain™.

World-leading design innovations such as the Breville Electric Wok, Sandwich Press and Moda Blender were recognised by Australian Engineering Design Awards and other accolades, with the Breville Juice Fountain being awarded an Australian Design Award. The Juice Fountain is on display in Sydney's Powerhouse Museum as a showpiece of Australian design skill.

In 2001 Housewares International, an Australian listed company, acquired Breville and has demonstrated its commitment to Breville's culture of innovation and design by supporting the expansion of Breville's Centre of Design Excellence in Botany, Sydney.

Through HWI owned distribution companies in Los Angeles and Montreal, Breville branded products will be launched into the North American markets this year.

Natural Gas delivered by Envestra

The chef's best friend. Whenever great culinary creations are being prepared, master chefs insist on Natural Gas. Cooking with Natural Gas is easy, clean, quick and economical.

Chosen by professional chefs the world over, Natural Gas provides instant, clean and visible heat that gives you complete control over whatever recipe you might be preparing.

From elegant entrees to sumptuous seafood, sizzling steaks and vegetable dishes, not to mention a mouth-watering array of delicious desserts. Natural Gas is the ideal way to cook those special dishes that delight the tastebuds.

Natural Gas is perfectly controllable and ideal for frying, simmering, chargrilling, baking and roasting. In fact, just about any cooking method currently in use in both restaurant and domestic kitchens across the nation.

Natural Gas is such a versatile and economical fuel and when it comes to throwing a shrimp on the barbie, Natural Gas will be there with you. It's easy to see why Natural Gas is the natural choice and the chef's best friend.

WEDGWOOD

Wedgwood tableware is made to be enjoyed everyday.

Wedgwood tableware is completely versatile and allows you to express your individual style.

Simply take a base pattern and use your creativity to intermix with other Wedgwood patterns and accessories to create various tabletop looks for different meal and entertaining occasions.

Contrary to common misconceptions, Wedgwood Fine Bone China is in fact the strongest tableware on the market.

Its strength and resilience means it's too good to save only for a special occasion so there's no excuse for locking it away in a display cabinet.

Make everyday more special. Enjoy Wedgwood today. Available in South Australia at selected department stores and specialty retailers.

ROSIERES

QASAIR Rangehoods have been manufactured in Melbourne for over 40 years. Originally designed and made by Helmut Goertz a German engineer, his background provided the foundation for the excellent performance, which QASAIR is well-known. The range from QASAIR reveals the latest designs in the most modern styling. Boasting an array of sensual lines, which create a striking presence while still retaining a purposeful ability to function over all cooking appliances on the Australian market today. QASAIR Rangehoods are designed to work efficiently over all domestic and commercial cookware or high heat cookers that are becoming popular in domestic kitchens. Australia is a true multicultural society with an abundance of cultures and a great array of cuisine. Walk down any main shopping street in Australia and count the number of different eating places offering food from the four corners of the globe. Options and variations now available to home chefs are limited only by their imagination. The explosion of celebrity chefs on television, cooking schools and the fact that Australians buy more cookbooks than any other English speaking country has led to a greater demand for more exotic and top quality cooking equipment. With the introduction of indoor barbecues, fish burners and high-speed gas burners a huge amount of smoke, heat and odour is generated in the kitchen. This must be removed quickly and quietly. QASAIR low noise rangehoods do this efficiently because of the high air movement resulting in a quiet, clean odour free kitchen.

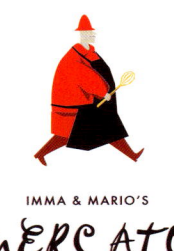

IMMA & MARIO'S MERCATO

At Imma and Mario's Mercato we believe the old Italian proverb "A tavola nessuno diventa vecchio" translated to "At the table no one grows old" so much so that we have dedicated ourselves to providing the best selection of local and imported fine foods to our customers, many of which are exclusive to us. A family business with over 35 years of experience, our store stocks a huge selection of cheeses and antipasto, a wide range of oils and vinegars, a sumptuous selection of imported biscuits, chocolates and torrone and an assortment of organic and gluten free foods. We also have wood oven tafers, made in Italy to cook pizzas, roasts, fish, sweets and of course home-made fresh bread, just to name a few. There is also a large selection of fabulous kitchenware to accompany your food selection, from glassware, utensils, cutlery, bakeware to chinaware and servingware. We can also provide a platter of the very best cheeses and antipasto for all your entertainment needs or you can choose from an exciting selection of lavish hampers perfectly suited for any occasion. New to Imma and Mario's Mercato in 2007 are our cooking class demonstrations. We will be featuring talented Adelaide Chefs who will cook up a storm right in front of your eyes using various combinations of Mercato products to prepare traditional and authentic, yet different Italian dishes. For information or to register your interest please email maria@ilmercato.com.au with your name and contact details.

B.-d. Farm Paris Creek

organic *biodynamic*

Dairy Produce

The Healthy Choice...

New!

Try our range of exciting, award winning dairy products, full of natural goodness for today's health conscious consumers.

B.-d Farm Paris Creek, for enquiries phone (08) 8388 3339 or visit www.bdfarmpariscreek.com.au

B.-d. Farm Paris Creek

organic DAIRY PRODUCTS FRESH FROM OUR FARM

The Healthy Choice...

B.-d. Farm Paris Creek is situated between Fleurieu Peninsula and the Adelaide Hills at Meadows. Not only do the owners run an environmentally friendly biodynamic dairy farm, but Ulli and Helmut Spranz are also producers of extremely popular genuine biodynamic/organic dairy products such as milks (including flavours such as Strawberry-Delight, Choco-Lat, Café-Latte), various Yogurts (Swiss, Low-Fat, Bush-Honey-Vanilla, Blueberry, Raspberry, Apricot, Strawberry, Mango) and Quarks (European version of cottage cheese). Originally milking 40 dairy cows, B.-d. Farm now uses milk from another 3 biodynamic suppliers with another 4 in conversion to biodynamic status. All other ingredients such as fruit, honey, sugar, vanilla are sourced from certified, predominantly Australian producers. Biodynamic farming is the only way of farming, where we can get the optimal goodness in products without the use of any chemical input. It is the most environmentally friendly way of farming, scientifically proven with the least water-usage, optimum carbon building and optimising the nutritional value of food with no use of chemicals. The secret is to enhance the micro-organisms in the soil to optimise the activity of the soil-food-web. Use of fertilisers, pesticides, fungicides, hormones, antibiotics or anything artificial is avoided. Purchasing B.-d. Farm Paris Creek's multi award winning dairy products (all products have won at least Gold or Silver in one of the most prestigious dairy competitions), consumers do not only buy premium food and get the healthiest value out of dairy products, but they also support the environment.

HAVENHAND
THE FINEST AUSTRALIAN HANDMADE FRUIT CHOCOLATES

Havenhand Chocolates is a family owned business with its heart in South Australia's premium fruit growing region of the Riverland. Built on the talents of our European trained Chocolatier Janet, Daniel & Dean Grosse have never swayed from our original concept of "Blending the luxury of hand-crafted chocolates with the unique tastes of Riverland fruit". The three basic elements of premium fruit, excellence in craftsmanship and the addition of quality chocolate from the Belgian chocolate maker, Barry Callebeaut, have all led to our success. Our Apricot Gems won "Silver" in 2005 and our Apricot & Almond Bars won "Gold" at the 2006 Royal Adelaide Show. Ever ready to diversify, we have developed a line of truffles which also led to "Top Gold" for our Chai, "Gold" for both Strawberry and Jaffa and "Silver" for our Chilli Redback truffles in Adelaide 2006. Our range of chocolate novelties needs to be seen. We supply many retailers including South Australia's and Victoria's leading dried fruit shops, also quality gift basket providers and the new "Bracegirdle's House of Fine Chocolates" shops within Adelaide. Overlooking the majestic River Murray, our current retail shop is to become a unique tourist destination at Waikerie later in 2007. Just two hours from much of Adelaide, we will offer an expanded range including a selection from the emerging Riverland gourmet fruits, chocolate-covered desserts, fondues and rich chocolate drinks from our shaded decking. A true chocolate experience. 22 Peake Terrace, Waikerie. Phone: 08 8541 2134 Fax: 08 8541 2134 Email: info@havenhandchocolates.com

Monjava Coffee are local roasters of premium gourmet coffees selected from around the globe from some of the finest estate plantations. Monjava ensures flawless results every time. Hand roasted twice a week you are guaranteed to find a blend you like, and fresh, like it should be! As well as coffee, Monjava specialise in top of the range espresso machines for both commercial and domestic use. In addition to their range of espresso machines Monjava also stock accessories to suit your coffee making requirements such as tampers, dump tubes, thermometers and a range of cups to name a few. Retail coffee sales are also available to the general public via the Monjava showroom at 57 King William Street, Kent Town. Taste testing is available upon request. Monjava are the only South Australian Roaster who offers a website order process with same day delivery to home or office and also support small boutique South Australian businesses. Monjava have a range of blends and straight coffees, including our unique blended Monjava which has an earthy and slightly spicy flavour, our Costalumbian for a strong clean cup with a soft mellow and buttery finish. Monjava also stock a number of single origin coffees such as Guatemala, Kenya AA, Skybury (Australian Plantation) as well as two certified organic coffees Peruvian and Mexican. As well as single origin coffees, Monjava also stock Colombian Swiss Water processed decaffeinated coffee 100% chemical free, roasted dark to produce a strong cup with a soft finish.

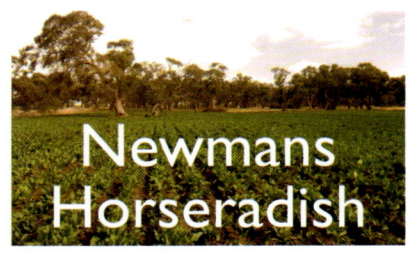

Newmans Horseradish

Grown at Langhorne Creek on the rich alluvial flood plains Newmans Horseradish has been sold in South Australia for over 80 years and owned by the Meakins family since 1947.

The range incudes the Original Red Label Horseradish, a Horseradish Dip, Beetroot and Horseradish Relish and the Horseradish Mustard.

The Beetroot Relish and the Horseradish Mustard were awarded bronze and silver medals respectively in 2006 Sydney Fine Food Show.

The 25 acres of Horseradish grow alongside the vineyard and next to a wonderful Red Gum swamp area, all of which can be enjoyed from the deck of the cellar door with a food platter and a glass of wine or a coffee.

Blessed Cheese

The South Australian artisan cheesemaking industry is on the rise, driven by a renewed consumer enthusiasm for high quality, hand-made produce, and the passion of a small group of skilled souls who transform milk into art. Over the last twenty years, the Australian wine industry has transformed itself into a world leader. In doing so, it has revolutionized the Australian palate, teaching our consumers that quality food and drink can be enjoyed at a deeper level, encouraging them to employ all of the senses as they embrace the offerings of our producers. This natural evolution of consumer education has allowed the cheese industry to reinvent itself, with consumers discovering that there is more to cheese than the range of products in the supermarket. Cheese is a living product, the ultimate in slow food. Whether presented integrated within a meal, or as a stand-alone item, cheese offers such a rich and layered experience to the consumer, which has only just begun to be appreciated. Our cheesemakers, through innovation, experimentation and education, have brought themselves to the National fore. Many of our producers have drawn on experiences and skills developed in the wine industry, redefining themselves and highlighting the synergies between the fields. As our wine has taken the World in hand, so too will our cheese. As artisan cheese continues to evolve and be redefined, and as our consumer base continues their education, I wait with excitement for this evolution overflow into the restaurant fraternity, redefining the position of the cheese trolley as a pivotal part of any meal.

Willunga Farmers Market

The Willunga Farmers Market was the first farmers market in South Australia. Established by a group of local producers and regional food enthusiasts, the Willunga Farmers Market was officially launched by world-renowned environmental scientist, Dr David Suzuki in February 2002. Each Saturday the Willunga Farmers Market attracts hundreds of shoppers to Willunga. The Market is a showcase for fresh, regional and seasonal produce including dairy products, venison, gourmet rabbit, organic sausages, fresh fruit and vegetables (organic & minimal spray), organic herbs, fresh & smoked fish, organic vegetable seedlings, potted herbs and plants, fresh flowers, chutneys, tapinades, pastes, dips, pate, dukkah, sauces, oils, local almonds, baked goods, wine, free range eggs plus much, much more! Farmers and producers alike sell their goods direct to the public and everyone benefits. Consumers have access to freshly harvested fruit and vegetables and quality locally made products at affordable prices. Producers are able to maximize their profits by selling direct while receiving instant feedback from customers and increasing brand awareness. Farmers markets breathe new life into country and regional areas. In Willunga, several stallholders who needed access to a commercial kitchen got together to establish the Community Kitchen. But the benefits don't stop there! This popular event helps raise the profile of Willunga and the entire Fleurieu Peninsula as an attractive place to visit and to live. What could be more appealing than a country address that has access to a wealth of quality, food less than an hour drive from Adelaide?

JASPER CONRAN AT WEDGWOOD

Hahndorf Venison

As a leading supplier of Venison to the Australian foodservice industry for over 25 years, we know and understand venison, its virtues and limitations. Hahndorf Venison Supply has now introduced the new benchmark in Venison quality. "VIANDE" grade venison is a multiple award winning trade marked product distinguishing it as the finest venison produced in Australia. Viande, Australia's only graded 'quality specified, no compromise' Venison where eating quality is guaranteed. Produced under strict documented quality controls, the grading features bring together "on farm" controls, processing evaluation and final assessment before the Viande label can be applied. With improved cutting lines of uninterrupted individual muscle structure and "super trimming", Viande is the ultimate choice.

Our traditional product, Hahndorf Venison is the timeless favourite among many of our clients. Offered in standard restaurant cutting lines, catering packs and to customer specification. Available all year round. Hahndorf Venison process a limited number of North American Elk each year. The Elk are bred and raised on our own farm and maintained in prime condition for that special occasion when something unique is needed. Elk will make an excellent meat dish choice to compliment food & wine matching banquets, exclusive functions and reserved vintage releases. For more information about elk and its features, contact our office.

Richard Gunner Beef

Beef and Lamb a layman's guide

Australia is fortunate to have some of the best beef and lamb in the world, a fact recognised overseas with much of our premium product exported overseas. What remains in Australia covers the range from the best to the worst of what we grow, so a little knowledge on how to pick beef and lamb that delivers on taste and tenderness is a very necessary skill.

The best beef is something found via a description of how it has been produced. It is important not to prime the retailer with what you are looking for as often you will just get the "right" answer. Great beef cannot be described visually, as dark beef can be a sign of a stressed and tough product or of one that has been dry-aged which will be amongst the best you could ever try.

Things you want to hear about your beef

- Aged – like wine, beef improves with age – 21-28 days is optimal
- Hormone free – beyond any health concerns this makes beef tougher
- MSA graded – a system that guarantees you won't get an awful steak – not that it will be great but it won't be terrible
- Cattle breed – British bred is best, Brahman is a worry – living in harsh environments like Brahmans do makes for tougher meat
- Hang method – this can be tenderstretch or Achilles, the latter puts great strain on the loin and butt cuts, making them tougher
- Grass fed or Grain fed – not better than the other, the latter is more flavoursome but can be tougher in dry times of the year or in drought

The best lamb is always sold with the "strip brand" clearly displayed, this is your guarantee that it is the real deal. To make sure your backstrap is the real thing it's actually better to buy it with the fat on, which you can always trim off later. Again, there is a list of what you want to hear.

Things you want to hear about your lamb

- Spring lamb – this lamb is very young and succulent – treat it like you would veal and don't dry it out
- Winter lamb – can be tougher as it is older, and is often sold best if grain fed
- Lamb Breed – this time we want as little Merino as possible – they are better suited to wool growing than meat production
- Hang method – for the same reasons as beef
- Feed – you have more options with lamb – ie as exotic as saltbush, clover and grain fed. Try them all and decide what you like.

One thing that is true of all of these is that there is a huge range of cuts unexplored by most home cooks that offer up amazing value, flavour and tenderness if bought at your butcher, where all your questions are answered. Try the brisket, short ribs, intercostal, skirts or hanging tender from beef, and the breast, neck and skirts of lamb. You will be amazed at just how good these cuts can be.

Cappo Seafood

Underwater gardens of eating by Mike Cappo (Fisheries Ecologist, Australian Institute of Marine Science, Townsville) and Damian Cappo (General Manager, Cappo Brothers Seafood, Glen Osmond Rd)

It takes a pelican's-eye view to appreciate just why SA can provide the most diverse seafood platters in Australia.

The often brown and sparsely covered hinterlands of the three peninsulas hide the luxuriant underwater plant growth that carpets the Gulfs and bays, lines the rocky coasts and stretches out to the underwater reef complexes from the Bight to the South-East. At nearly 5000 square kilometres, the SA seagrass beds are the thickest in the world. Couple them with healthy fringing mangrove stands, wide sand flats and the vast seaweed and kelp forests along the temperate rocky coasts, then you have the sustenance for wild fisheries of unique value.

Thus there is an enormous, readily available range of delectable seafood occurring along climatic gradients: from the near-tropical conditions of the shallow Gulfs to the frigid south-eastern waters bathed by nutrient-rich upwellings. The western king prawns, blue swimmer crabs, calamari squid and yellowfin whiting of the upper gulfs have tropical affinities. The cool limestone reefs produce rock lobster, abalone and octopus in abundance.

In the surface waters, upwellings and currents drive schools of sardines and anchovies on the shelf where the renowned southern bluefin tuna has its seasonal feeding grounds. Indeed, the mighty Leeuwin current brings a flood of juveniles from WA spawning grounds to grow in the rich nurseries of the Gulfs and bays, including the humble tommy ruff and its larger brother the Australian salmon.

Since the 1970s fishing effort in all SA fisheries has been strictly co-managed by industry and government and the clean, clear waters continue to sustain production and support a growing aquaculture industry. The shallowness and proximity of the Gulf fishing grounds allow selective haul netting and hooking of a range of fish - to be landed whole and chilled within hours at processors, thus retaining outstanding colour, freshness and their essential protective skin coating, essential for the discerning local markets.

Seafood variety is available year-round, but seasonal peaks in abundance and condition occur with regular inshore species migrations – such as those of the autumn mullet and garfish, fat winter tommy ruffs, Christmas king prawns and summer snapper and blue swimmer crabs.

There are wonderful tastes and textures available for all palates. The firm, white fillets of garfish and King George whiting suggest tempura batters and crisp white wines, whilst the stronger flavours of grilled Coorong mullet and tommy ruffs beg plenty of rock salt, crusty bread and red wine. Larger species such as bream and pan-sized snapper are mainly cooked whole. Cutlets of large snapper, tuna and yellowtail kingfish are firm and barbecue or grill very well - perfect for outdoor entertaining. Whatever the season or budget, the options are outstanding in SA seafood. Enjoy!

Willunga Farmers Market

Willunga Farmers Market is...
a weekly Market featuring food from the Fleurieu
a vehicle for promoting the produce from the region
a meeting place for locals of the Fleurieu, near and far
an incorporated body
a not-for-profit community event

WHEN:
Every Saturday of the year, rain, hail or shine from 8-12.30pm.
WHERE:
The car park of the Alma Hotel at the entrance to Willunga.
WHO:
- The producers - vegetable growers, dairy farmers, orchardists, livestock, producers, cheese-makers, bakers, cooks, compost makers
- The customers - anyone who enjoys good food, which potentially means everyone. Regular Market shoppers come from the South Coast, Adelaide and the southern suburbs. At peak times up to 5000 shoppers visit the Market the members - currently 1000+ members support the Market and receive discounted shopping & other benefits for an annual fee of $30
- The committee - with members drawn from local producers and Market supporters, the Willunga Farmers Market committee, sets the general direction of the Market.
- Market Manager - Lisa Hall oversees the general management of the Market and is the face of the Market every Saturday.
- The local community who support and champion THEIR Market.

SA oysters

From its humble beginnings, the South Australian Oyster Industry has emerged to be one of the most well-regarded and respected industries of its type in the world. South Australian oyster farmers have revolutionised oyster farming throughout the world using a management system that allows oyster growers to effectively manage their farms and product to avoid storm damage, heat stress, mudworm and to manipulate the oyster to generate meat condition and stop shell growth. The major growing areas include: Ceduna, Smoky Bay, Streaky Bay, Coffin Bay and Cowell (Franklin Harbour).

The unique characteristics of this region which are, a low rainfall, the lack of major river systems and low population density, allows the oysters to be grown in oceanic-driven, nutrient-rich seawater which adds to the unique, clean salty taste. Growers select product for sale based on size, meat weight (meat to shell ratio) and meat appearance. The South Australian oyster season runs from March through to early January.

In early March, the oysters come back from spawn and gradually build up their fat content till about November. Because the water temperature starts to rise during November the oysters then start to go through their reproductive cycle, whereby they convert the fat content to spawn. This event continues through to about mid January when the oysters completely spawn out and then as the water temperature starts to drop, they then come back into condition in early March.

Throughout the season some 45 million oysters are harvested. On weekdays they are graded and packaged in hessian bags, placed in cold stores and transported to Adelaide within 12 hours of harvest, where they are collated and dispatched to markets throughout Australia and overseas.
Recommended Storage Temperatures:
Whole live - 8 days from date of harvest
@ 2 - 5 Degrees Celsius.
Opened oysters - maximum 4 days @
2 - 5 Degrees Celsius.

Industry and Government run "South Australian Shellfish Quality Assurance (QA) Program" (Water Testing Program) compliments the Australian Shellfish Quality Assurance Program, which is AQIS endorsed and based upon USFDA guidelines. Industry based individual grower based HACCP programs supported by the South Australian Oyster Growers Association (SAOGA) and the South Australian Government. Oyster Bob HACCP (QA) based program runs in conjunction with the above programs.

Succulent South Australian Oysters

Oyster Bob
...South Australian Oysters

Contact Bob Simmonds 0428 235 888

restaurant guide

RESTAURANT NAME	ADDRESS	DISTANCE & TIME FROM ADELAIDE	TELEPHONE	FACSIMILE	WEB
Alphutte Restaurant	242-244 Pulteney Street, Adelaide SA 5000	In the City	(08) 8223 4717	(08) 8232 0810	www.alphutte.com.au
Argentinian Bar & Grill	46 Port Road, Hindmarsh SA 5007	3km, 8 minutes	(08) 8340 9331	(08) 8340 9332	www.argentinian.com.au
Beyond India	170 O'Connell Street, North Adelaide	2km, 5 minutes	(08) 8267 3820	(08) 8367 0697	www.beyondindia.net.au
Beyond India	108 Kelly Road, Modbury North	12km, 20 minutes	(08) 8395 2800	(08) 8265 7135	www.beyondindia.net.au
Blanc Seafood & Wine	240 Hutt Street, Adelaide SA 5000	In the City	(08) 8232 11188	(08) 8232 5488	www.blanc.com.au
Blanc Bistro	12-18 Currie Street, Adelaide SA 5000	In the City	(08) 8212 1300	(08) 8212 1155	www.blanc.com.au
Blues Restaurant	Main Goolwa Road, Middleton, SA	1 hour	08 8554 1800	08 8554 2891	www.bluesrestaurant.com.au
Bracegirdles	31 Jetty Road Glenelg	20 minutes	(08) 8294 8482	(08) 8376 9077	www.bracegirdles.com.au
Bracegirdles	389 Greenhill Road Toorak Gardens	10 minutes	(08) 8431 0799	(08) 8376 9077	www.bracegirdles.com.au
Brasserie Moustache	Corner Sedan & Eden Valley Roads, Keyneton 5353	Approx. 80km about 75 minutes	(08) 6564 8388	(08) 8564 8345	www.brasserie-moustache.com.au
Capriccio Restaurant	10 Sussex Street, Glenelg SA 5045	20 minutes	(08) 8295 6453	(08) 8376 2346	www.capriccio.com.au
Chloe's Restaurant	36 College Road, Kent Town SA 5076	1.5km	(08) 8362 2574	(08) 8363 1001	www.chloes.com.au
Cork & Cleaver	2 Bevington Road, Glenunga	10 minutes	(08) 8379 8091	(08) 8338 2984	www.users.bigpond.com/corkandcleaver
Dhaba at The Spice Kitchen	252 Kensington Road, Leabrook SA 5068	10 minutes	(08) 8431 4288	(08) 8331 8661	www.spicekitchen.com.au
Esca Restaurant	Shop 13-15 Marina Pier, Holdfast Shores, Glenelg 5045	20 minutes	(08) 8376 6933	(08) 8376 9655	www.esca.net.au
Juergies Restaurant	Bushman Street, Cnr of Murray Street, Tanunda 5372	70km 1 hour	(08) 8563 3988	(08) 8563 3477	
La Guillotine Restaurant	125 Gouger Street, Adelaide 5000	In the City	(08) 8212 2536	(08) 8212 6171	www.laguillotine.com
Sagarmatha	62-64 Payneham Road, Stepney SA 5069	10 minutes	(08) 363 6291	(08) 8363 6201	www.sagarmatha.com.au
Seasons at the Bay	750 Anzac Highway, Glenelg	10km, 10 minutes	(08) 8294 8228	(08) 8295 3766	www.seasons.net.au
Sevenhill Hotel	Main North Road, Sevenhill	1 hour 25 minutes	(08) 8843 4217	(08) 8843 4177	
Star of Siam	67 Gouger Street, Adelaide	In the City	(08) 8231 3527	(08) 8231 2367	
Sumo Station	172 Pulteney Street, Adelaide SA 5000	2 minutes	(08) 8232 0188 (08) 8232 8477	(08) 8232 8477	www.sumostation.com.au
Sumo Station	Shop 7 Marina Pier, Holdfast Shores Glenelg SA 5045	20 minutes	(08) 8295 5995 (08) 8295 5808	(08) 8295 5808	www.sumostation.com.au
Sumo Station	Shop 7, 117 - 193 The Parade, Norwood SA 5067	5 minutes	(08) 8332 0011	(08) 8332 0011	www.sumostation.com.au
The Greek Mezze	108 Gouger Street Adelaide	In the City	08 8231 3223	08 8231 3117	
The Poplars	Chardonnay Lodge Resort Riddoch Highway, Coonawarra	370km South East 3.5 hours	(08) 8736 3309	(08) 8736 3383	www.chardonnaylodge.com.au
The Treasury	144 King William Street, Adelaide 5000	In the City	(08) 8212 0499	(08) 8212 0599	www.treasurykw.com

restaurant guide

EMAIL	DAYS OPEN	TIMES OPEN	TYPE OF FOOD	CREDIT CARDS	ROOMS FOR PRIVATE FUNCTIONS	BOOKINGS
	Monday - Friday	Lunch from 12pm Dinner from 6pm	International Cuisine with Swiss influences	All major cards accepted	Yes	Advisable, Essential for Friday night
infor@argentinian.com.au	Lunch Mon - Fri Dinner 7 nights	Lunch 12 - 3.30pm Dinner 6pm til late	Steak House	All major cards accepted	Yes	Essential
beyond_India@yahoo.com.au	7 days	Lunch 12 - 3pm Dinner 5pm til late	North, Southern & Regional Indian Cuisine	All major cards accepted	Yes	Advisable
beyond_India@yahoo.com.au	6 days	Tues - Sun Dinner 5pm til late	North, Southern & Regional Indian Cuisine	All major cards accepted	No	Advisable
service@blanc.com.au	6 days	Lunch Mon - Sat 12 - 3pm Dinner Mon - Sat 6pm til late	Seafood	All major cards accepted	No	Dinner bookings only
theblanc1@bigpond.com	7 days	Breakfast 6.30 - 10.30am daily Lunch Mon - Fri 12 - 3pm Dinner Mon - Fri 5.30 - 9.30pm	Modern Australian Seafood	All major cards accepted	No	Dinner bookings only
bluesfood@sa.chariot.net.au	Tues to Sat Lunch & Dinner Sun sometimes, but never Mon!	Lunch 12 - 3pm Dinner 6 till late	Fresh regional, local produce used in an eclectic mix of world cuisine	All major cards accepted	Yes	Bookings preferred to avoid disappointment
susan.bracegirdle1@bigpond.com	7 days	Mon 10am - 6pm Tues, Wed, Thurs, Sun 10am - 9pm Fri & Sat 10am - 10pm	Chocolates/Desserts	Mastercard & Visa	No	Not Required
susan.bracegirdle1@bigpond.com	7 days	Mon 10am - 6pm Tues, Wed, Thurs, Sun 10am - 9pm Fri & Sat 10am - 10pm	Chocolates/Desserts	Mastercard & Visa	No	Not Required
welcome@brasserie-moustache.com.au	Thurs, Fri, Sat, Sun	11am - 11pm	French Bistro Cuisine	All major cards accepted	Yes Up to 8 people	Recommended
franc@capriccio.com.au	Tues to Sat	Lunch Tues to Fri from noon Dinner Tues to Sat from 6pm Sunday by appointment	Italian	All major cards accepted	Yes	Advisable
office@chloes.com.au	Mon to Sat	Lunch Mon to Fri 12 - 2.30pm Dinner Mon to Sat 6 - 9.30pm	Contemporary French	All major cards accepted	Yes	Essential
corkandcleaver@bigpond.com	6 days (closed Sun & public holidays)	Lunch Mon-Fri Dinner Mon-Sat	Steak house and more	All major cards accepted	Yes (3)	Advisable
	7 days	Lunch Tues to Fri 12pm onwards Dinner nightly from 5pm	Regional Indian	All major cards accepted	Yes	Required
info@esca.net.au	7 days	Breakfast 8am Lunch 12pm Dinner 6pm	European	All major cards accepted	Yes	Bookings Essential
labuonavita@ozemail.com.au	Dinner Thurs to Sat Functions available 7 days	6pm til late	International	All major cards accepted	No	Essential
	Tues to Sat	Lunch Thurs & Fri from 12pm Dinner Tues to Sat from 5.45pm	French Cuisine	All major cards accepted	Yes	Bookings Advisable
info@sagarmatha.com.au	Dinner 7 nights	Dinner Mon to Sun from 5.30pm Lunch Wed to Fri from 12pm	Nepalese	All major cards accepted	Yes	Bookings Essential
seasons@bigpond.net.au	6 days	Tues - Sun from 6pm	Mediterranean	All major cards accpeted	Yes	Bookings Preferred
sevenhill@bigpond.com	7 days	Lunch 12 - 2pm Dinner Sun to Thurs 6 - 8pm Fri to Sat 6 - 9pm	Modern Australian	All major cards accepted	Yes	Essential
valee@internode.on.net	Mon to Fri Lunch & Dinner Sat Dinner only	Lunch 12 - 2.30pm Dinner 5.30 - 10pm	Thai	All major cards accepted	No	Recommended
webmaster@sumostation.com.au	Tues to Sun & public holidays (except Mon)	Lunch Tues to Fri 12 - 3pm Dinner Tues to Thurs 6 - 10pm Fri & Sat 6 - 11pm Sun & Public Holidays 6 -10pm	Japanese	All major cards accepted	Yes	Essential
webmaster@sumostation.com.au	7 days	Lunch Thurs to Sat 12 - 3pm Sun & public holidays 12- 5pm Dinner Mon to Thurs 6 - 10pm Fri & Sat 6 - 11pm Sun & public holidays 6 - 10pm	Japanese	All major cards accepted	Yes	Essential
webmaster@sumostation.com.au	7 days	Mon to Wed 11am - 9pm Thurs, Fri & Sat 11am - 10pm Sun 11am - 9pm	Japanese	All major cards accepted	No	Essential
abbsel3@bigpond.com.au	7 days	Breakfast Fri, Sat & Sun Lunch Daily from 11:30am Dinner Daily from 5pm	Traditional Greek	All major cards accepted	Yes	Preferred
enquiries@chardonnaylodge.com.au	7 days	Breakfast 7.30 - 10am Lunch 12 - 2.30pm Dinner 6 - 8.30pm	Regional with international influences	All major cards accepted	Yes	Preferred
info@treasurykw.com	7 days	Breakfast every day of year Lunch Mon to Fri 12 - 3pm Dinner Mon to Sat 6 - 9.30pm	Australian with European & Asian influences	ATM on site	Yes	Preferred

winery guide

WINERY NAME	ADDRESS	DISTANCE & TIME FROM ADELAIDE	TELEPHONE	FACSIMILE	WEB
Amadio Wines	461 Payneham Road, Felixtow SA 5070	8 Kms / 15 minutes	(08) 8365 5988	(08) 8336 2462	www.movingjuice.com.au
Balthazar Barossa	Stonewell Road, Marananga, Barossa Valley	60kms / 1 hour	(08) 8562 2949	(08) 8562 2949	www.balthazarbarossa.com
Cape Jaffa Wines	Limestone Coast Road, Mount Benson via Robe, South Australia 5276	30kms north of Robe / 5kms from Cape Jaffa / 300kms from Adelaide	(08) 8768 5053	(08) 8768 5040	www.capejaffawines.com.au
Ceravolo Estate	St Andrews Estate – Adelaide Plains Office: Suite 16, 172 Glynburn Road, Tranmere 5073 South Australia	30kms / 30 minutes	(08) 8336 4522	(08) 8365 0538	www.ceravolo.com.au
Chain of Ponds	Main Adelaide Road, Gumeracha SA 5233	45kms / 45 minutes	(08) 8389 1415	(08) 8389 1877	www.chainofponds.com.au
Charles Cimicky Wines	Hermonn Thumm Drive, Lyndoch SA 5351	56kms / 1 hour	(08) 8524 4025	(08) 8524 4772	
Currency Creek Estate	Winery Road, Currency Creek, 5214 (Post Office Box 540, Goolwa, 5214)	80kms / 1 hour	(08) 8555 4069	(08) 8555 4100	www.currencycreekwines.com.au
Dennis Wines	Kangarilla Rd, McLaren Vale. SA	45 kms / 40 minutes	(08) 8323 8665	(08) 8323 9121	www.denniswines.com.au
DiGiorgio Family Wines	Riddoch Highway Coonawarra	380kms / 3.5 hours	(08) 8736 3222	(08) 8736 3233	www.digiorgio.com.au
Eldredge Wines	Spring Gully Road, Clare SA	135kms / 1.5 - 2 hours	(08) 8842 3086	(08) 8842 3086	www.eldredge.com.au
Howard Vineyard	Lot 1 Bald Hills Road, Nairne SA 5252	30kms / 25 minutes	(08) 8188 0203	(08) 8388 0623	www.howardvineyard.com
Kilikanoon Wines	Penna Lane, Penwortham via Clare, SA 5453 (PO Box 205 Auburn SA 5451)	130km / 1 hour 35 minutes	(08) 8843 4377	(08) 8843 4246	www.kilikanoon.com.au
Kirrihill Wines	Wendouree Road, Clare SA 5453	140kms / 1 hour 50 minutes	(08) 8842 4087	(08) 8842 4089	www.kirrihillwines.com.au
Langmeil Winery	Cnr Para and Langmeil Rds, Tanunda	60kms / 1 hour	(08) 85632 595	(08) 85 633 622	www.langmeilwinery.com.au
Nepenthe Wines	Jones Road, Balhannah SA 5242	20kms / 25 minutes	(08) 8388 4439	(08) 8398 0488	www.nepenthe.com.au
Parish Hill Wines	Parish Hill Road, Uraidla	18 kms / 30 minutes	(08) 8390 3927	(08) 8390 0394	www.ParishHill.com.au
Parri Estate	Ingoldby Road, McLaren Flat	45kms / 40 minutes	(08) 8383 0462	(08) 8383 0716	www.parriestate.com.au
Red Earth Wines	St Andrews Estate – Adelaide Plains Office: Suite 16, 172 Glynburn Road, Tranmere 5073 South Australia	30kms / 30 minutes	(08) 8336 4522	(08) 8365 0538	www.redearthwines.com.au
Rusticana Wines	Lake Plains Road, Langhorne Creek / part of Newmans Horseradish	85kms / 1 hour	(08) 8537 3086	(08) 85373220	www.rusticanawines.com.au
Tapestry Wines	Olivers Road, McLaren Vale	40kms / 35 minutes	(08) 8323 9196	(08) 8323 9746	www.tapestrywines.com.au
The Poplars Winery	Riddoch Highway, Coonawarra	370kms / 3.5 hours	(08) 8736 3130	(08) 8736 3163	www.chardonnaylodge.com.au
Wirra Wirra Vineyards	McMurtrie Road, McLaren Vale	50kms / 45 minutes	(08) 8323 8414	(08) 8323 8596	www.wirrawirra.com.au

winery guide

EMAIL	DAYS OPEN	TIMES OPEN	WINE GROWING REGION	CREDIT CARDS	ROOMS FOR PRIVATE FUNCTIONS	ACCOMMODATION
info@movingjuice.com.au	Mon – Sat	9am-5.30 pm	Adelaide Hills, Clare Valley, Barossa Valley & McLarenVale	All welcome	No	No
anita@balthazarbarossa.com	See our Website	See our Website	Barossa Valley	Mastercard, Bankcard, Visa	No	No
info@capejaffawines.com.au	Cellar Door Sales & Tasting Open 7 days	10am – 5pm (except Good Friday and Christmas Day)	Mount Benson (Limestone Coast)	All major credit cards	No	No
wine@ceravolo.com.au	By Appointment and Direct Mail	By appointment	Adelaide Plains and Adelaide Hills	All major credit cards	No	No
admin@chainofponds.com.au	7 days Closed Xmas & Good Friday	Mon - Fri 9.30am - 4.30pm Weekends & Public Holidays 10am - 4pm	Adelaide	All major credit cards & Cellar Door Pass	Vineyard Balcony & Cellar	Vineyard Cottage B & B
Cimickywines1@bigpond.com		Mon - Thurs 10am - 4pm or by appointment	Barossa Valley	Visa, Mastercard, AMEX, Diners	No	No
enquiries@currencycreekwines.com.au	7 (except Xmas Day & Good Friday)	10am - 5pm	Currency Creek	Visa, Mastercard, Bankcard, AMEX, Diners	Yes	6 spa villas
dwines@ozemail.com.au	Monday to Friday	10a.m. – 5p.m. Weekends & Public Holidays - 12.00. to 5p.m	McLaren Vale	All major credit cards accepted	Rooms	No
dfw@digiorgio.com.au	7 days, except Good Friday & Christmas Day	10.00am-5.00pm	Coonawarra & Lucindale (Limestone Coast)	All major credit cards accepted	Yes	No
bluechip@eldredge.com.au	7 days	11am - 5pm	Clare Valley	Visa, Mastercard, AMEX	No separate room but private functions available	No
inquiry@howardvineyard.com	7 days	Check website for opening times	Adelaide Hills	Visa, Mastercard, AMEX, Diners	Yes	No
admin@kilikanoon.com.au	Thurs, Fri, Sat, Sun & public holidays	11am to 5pm or by appointment	Clare Valley	Visa, Mastercard, AMEX, Diners	Yes	No
cellardoor@kirrihillwines.com.au	Sunday - Saturday (7 Days)	10am - 4pm	Clare Valley	Bankcard, Visa, MasterCard, Cellar Door Pass	Yes upstairs at Salt n Vines restaurant	No
info@langmeilwinery.com.au	7 days – Closed - Good Friday, Christmas Day	10:30 – 4.30	Barossa Valley	Yes	Yes	No
cellardoor@nepenthe.com.au	7 days	10am till 4pm	Adelaide Hills	All major credit cards	No	No
phwines@tpg.com.au	by appointment	by appointment	Piccadilly Valley, Adelaide Hills	Mastercard & Visa	No	No
cellardoor@parriestate.com.au	7 days except Christmas & Good Friday	11am to 5pm	McLaren Vale & Southern Fleurieu	All major credit cards	Yes large pergola area	No
info@redearthwines.com.au	By Appointment and Direct Mail	By appointment	Adelaide Plains	Visa, Mastercard, AMEX, Diners	No	No
info@rusticanawines.com.au	7 days except Christmas & Good Friday	10am - 5pm	Langhorne Creek	Visa, Mastercard	No	No
cellar@tapestrywines.com.au	7 days a week	11am to 5pm daily	McLaren Vale	All (except Diners)	Yes + a courtyard	No
admin@coonawarrawines.com.au	7 days	Cellar Door Open 9am to 6pm	Coonawarra	All major credit cards	Yes	Yes
info@wirra.com.au	7 Days (except Christmas Day & Good Friday)	Mon-Sat 10.00am-5.00pm Sun 11.00am-5.00pm	McLaren Vale and Adelaide Hills	All major credit cards	Yes	No

index

BEEF

Chargrilled beef fillet (Esca)	67
Chateau Briand (Alphutte)	9
Fillet Steak Poivere (Capricco)	47
Grain-fed T-Bone (The Greek Mezze)	110
Prime rib beef off the bone (Cork & Cleaver)	58
Scotch Fillet Tower (Cork and Cleaver)	59
Steak Tartar (classic) (Cork and Cleaver)	58
Steak Tuohy (Alphutte)	10
Sukiyaki (Sumo)	104
Terra rossa rib eye fillet (The Poplars)	114

CAKES AND PUDDINGS

Hedi's Gleichshuer Cake (Alphutte)	11
Soft centred chocolate pudding (Seasons)	90
Sticky date pudding (Cork and Cleaver)	59

CHEESE

Petit chevre chaud (La Guillotine)	78

CHICKEN AND POULTRY

Balsamic chicken breast (Sevenhill)	93
Charmoula chicken (Seasons)	87
Kaeng-Dang Gai (Star of Siam)	97
Kukhkurako Tihun (Sagarmatha)	83
Larb chicken (Star of Siam)	99
Manchego Chicken (The Argentinian Grill)	15
Mango chicken (Beyond India)	21
Pressed chicken thigh (Esca)	68
Saffron chicken korma (Dhaba)	63
Yakitori (Sumo)	106

CHOCOLATE

Bailey's Seduction (Bracegirdles)	36
Chocolate Affair (Bracegirdles)	35
Chocolate Bomb (Bracegirdles)	37
Hot Chocolate with Chilli (Bracegirdles)	35
Pure Indulgence (Bracegirdles)	34

CUSTARDS AND CREAMS

Blueberry crème brulee (Blues)	32
Crème brulee (La Guillotine)	80
Crème caramel (The Argentinian Grill)	16
Marsala Zabaglione (Esca)	69
The Poplars' jaffa ice cream (The Poplars)	116

DESSERTS

Grand Marnier Parfait (Alphutte)	11
Poached rhubarb with spiced savarin (Chloe's)	54
Wattle seed pavlova (The Poplars)	116
Wild berries and parfait (Juergies)	75

DOUGHS/PASTRIES/TARTS

Loukoumades (The Greek Mezze)	111
Pear tarte tatin with wine ice cream (Blues)	32
Red onion and goat's cheese tartlet (Blues)	30
Sel Roti (Sagarmatha)	82
Tartlettes aux Pommes (Brasserie Moustache)	44
Topless chocolate pastry (Chloe's)	53
Varanasi vegetarian samoosa (Beyond India)	18

DRIED BEANS

Alu Bodi Tamako Takari (Sagarmatha)	84
Cassoulet (Brasserie Moustache)	43
Keyneton Pistou (Brasserie Moustache)	42
Simla Mirch alu channa (Beyond India)	20

DUCK AND GAME

Bug and Beast (Blues)	29
Chargrilled quail (Esca)	68

Do not hesitate to telephone the restaurants if you have any queries regarding the recipes.

index

Duck calvados (The Argentinian Grill)	14
Kleftiko of saltbush goat (The Greek Mezze)	109
Red-roasted duck legs (Treasury)	121
Roasted Gawler River quail (Chloe's)	51
Seared kangaroo (Treasury)	120
Venison pie with potato mash (Juergies)	74

LAMB

Blyth Plains mutton backstrap (Sevenhill)	95
Boneless lamb shank masala (Dhaba)	63
Lamb cutlets (The Argentinian Grill)	14
Lamb Shank tagine (Seasons)	90
Poleko Lamb (Sagarmatha)	84
Rack of lamb (Beyond India)	19

MISCELLANEOUS

Agedashi tofu (Sumo)	106
Dukkah and marinated olive plate (Sevenhill)	92
Good Morning Muesli (Bracegirdles)	57
Tapas Selection (The Argentinian Grill)	15

NOODLES/PASTA

Lasagne of Woodside Edith Ash (Chloe's)	53
Pad Thai (Star of Siam)	99
Penne con Prosciutto (Capriccio)	46
Spaghetti Amatriciana (Capriccio)	48

OFFAL

Cervelle au beurre-noir (La Guillotine)	79
Pan-seared veal kidney with witlof (Treasury)	121

PORK

Artichoke and pork boulangere (Juergies)	75
Pork Fillet and pear salad (The Poplars)	115

PROSCIUTTO

Prosciutto Lunganese (Alphutte)	8

RICE

Chanterelle risotto (Treasury)	118
Kheer-Nepali-style rice pudding (Sagarmatha)	82
Sweet sticky rice with mango (Star of Siam)	100

SALADS

Barramundi and mango salad (Juergies)	73
Garfish, scallop and duck skin salad (Chloe's)	52
Thai prawn salad (Sevenhill)	95

SEAFOOD

Beetroot-cured Atlantic salmon (Treasury)	119
Carpaccio of kingfish and salmon (Blanc)	23
Chawamushi (Sumo)	103
Chilli Bug Tails with Basil Pesto (Blanc)	24
Crevettes a l'ail (La Guillotine)	78
Crispy skin snapper fillet (Blanc)	27
Fish tikka (Beyond India)	21
Garfish Paupiette (The Poplars)	113
Garlic prawns and avocado (Juergies)	74
Grilled Atlantic salmon (Seasons)	89
Grilled Kangarilla marron (Blues)	30
Kangaroo Island yabby (The Greek Mezze)	108
Lemon Myrtle and scallops (The Poplars)	115
Louisiana Crab cakes (Cork and Cleaver)	57
Moules Mariniere (La Guillotine)	79
Mussels Moustache (Brasserie Moustache)	41
Nori-rolled Sushi (Sumo)	104
Oyster duo (Cork and Cleaver)	56
Prawn masala (Beyond India)	20
Prawns with vegetables (Dhaba)	61
Salt and pepper squid (Sevenhill)	94
Seafood Paella (Seasons)	89

Do not hesitate to telephone the restaurants if you have any queries regarding the recipes.

index

Seafood Risotto (Esca)	66
Seared Coorong Mulloway (Blues)	31
Seared salmon and scallops (Blanc)	25
Semolina gnocchi with grilled shellfish (Blanc)	26
Sushi combination (Sumo)	103
Tempura prawns and vegetables (Sumo)	105
Tod-Mon Pla (Star of Siam)	100
Tomato fish curry (Dhaba)	64

SEASONING/PRESERVES

Season's dukkah with Turkish bread (Seasons)	87

SOUPS

Bouillabaisse des Pecheurs (La Guillotine)	77
Duck mulligatawny soup (Dhaba)	64
Kangaroo tail soup (Juergies)	72
Tom-Kha-Gai (Star of Siam)	97
Youvarlakia soup (The Greek Mezze)	109
Zucchini, potato and bacon soup (Sevenhill)	94

VEAL

Osso Bucco Milanese (Capriccio)	49

VEGETABLES

Zucchini flowers stuffed (The Greek Mezze)	111
Misayeko Tarkari (Sagarmatha)	83
Mixed vegetable coconut sambar (Dhaba)	61
Zucchini Flowers (The Argentinian Grill)	13

Telephone the restaurant if you have any queries regarding the recipe.

Ikon. Beautiful range for beautiful kitchens.

Espresso Machine
100% Stainless Steel boiler system
15 bar Italian pump with 5 year warranty
Variable steam control
Advanced dual wall crema system
Filter eject button

Blender
Kinetix blade and bowl system
1.5 litre glass jug
Breville assist lid for one finger leverage removal
1/4 turn blade removal for easy cleaning

Wide Mouth Juicer
25% larger area feed chute for whole fruit and vegetable juicing
Variable speed control for soft fruits
Stainless steel design
Dishwasher safe parts
5 year motor warranty

Grill with Removable Plates
Removable dishwasher safe plates
Bonus flat plate for cooking eggs and pancakes
Grill plate level control for healthy cooking
Quantanium easy clean scratch resistant surface
Variable heat control with steak sear setting

Kettle
Premium quality brushed stainless steel design
1.7 litre capacity
Ergonomic soft grip handle
Cushioned control lid

Toaster
Brushed stainless steel design
Unique 'Lift and Look' feature
Extra wide and deep self centring toasting slots
'Toast Ready' sound alert

www.breville.com.au
The Breville IKON range is available at:
Good guys, Harvey Norman, Retravision and Harris Scarfe.

Breville

Student's
The Economy in Focus 2000/01

Alain Anderton

Causeway Press

Original cover design by Susan and Andrew Allen
Graphics by Chris Collins and Caroline Waring-Collins
Edited by Dave Gray
Photography by Andrew Allen, Dave Gray, Jim Nettleship
Reader Mike Kidson

Acknowledgements

The publisher wishes to thank the following for permission to reproduce copyright material and photographs.
Corel p 4; Office for National Statistics; Photodisc © 2000 Photodisc Inc. pp 9, 10, 11, 12, 14, 17, 21, 26, 27, 28, 30, 43, 44, 53, 55, 71; Rex Features pp 6, 14, 46; Topham Picturepoint pp 5, 31, 51, 71, 73.
Office for National Statistics material is Crown Copyright, reproduced here with the permission of the Controller of Her Majesty's Stationery Office.

Every effort has been made to locate the copyright owners of material in this book. Any errors and omissions brought to the notice of the publisher are regretted and will be credited in subsequent printings.

The author and publisher thank the following for permission to reproduce examination questions.
Edexcel questions reproduced with the permission of London Examinations, a division of Edexcel.
AQA (AEB) examination questions are reproduced with the permission of the Assessment and Qualifications Alliance.
AQA (NEAB) examination questions are reproduced with the permission of the Assessment and Qualifications Alliance.
OCR questions reproduced with the kind permission of Oxford, Cambridge and RSA Examinations.
CCEA questions reproduced from NICCEA GCE Economics examination papers (where appropriate) © 1997, 98, 99, 2000 with the permission of the Northern Ireland Council for the Curriculum, Examinations and Assessment.
The examination boards do not accept any responsibility whatsoever for the accuracy or method of working in the answers given. All suggested examination notes are made by the author. They do not necessarily constitute the only possible solutions and are not provided by the awarding bodies.
'Edexcel, London Examinations accepts no responsibility whatsoever for the accuracy or method of working in the answers given.'
'Oxford, Cambridge and RSA Examinations bears no responsibility for the example answers to questions taken from its past question papers which are contained in this publication.'

British Library Cataloguing in Publication Data
A catalogue record for this book is available from the British Library.

ISBN 1 902796 01 2

Causeway Press Limited
PO Box 13
129 New Court Way
Ormskirk
Lancashire L39 5HP

© Alain Anderton
Ist Impression 2000

Typesetting by Caroline Waring-Collins (Waring Collins Limited), Ormskirk.
Printed and bound by The Alden Press, Osney Mead, Oxford.

Preface

The Student's Economy in Focus is a series of annual publications. It presents some of the main news stories of the year, as well as some of the less well known. The most up to date statistics have been included wherever possible.
   It is intended that the book will be bought by students as a course companion. The book has been written so that it will provide examples, analysis and illustrations for many of the essays and data questions which are set on examination papers. Furthermore, it provides essential information for all types of questions and activities that are undertaken during an Economics course. It is hoped that the book will provide interesting and stimulating background reading material for students and also encourage wider reading.
   The material has been structured into topic areas so that it is easily accessible to students progressing through an Economics course. Each unit finishes with past essay questions from the main awarding bodies as well as a reading list of books commonly available in school and college libraries.
   Teachers and lecturers, too, should find plenty of material for use in the classroom if they so wish. Many of these items would be ideal for classroom discussion. Questions can be added if written work is desired. We hope that the inclusion of the most recent statistics will prove invaluable to students, teachers and lecturers.
   We would welcome your comments about this publication. We hope that you enjoy reading it and that it encourages you to learn more about Economics.

Contents

Unit 1 ECONOMIC SYSTEMS AND THE ECONOMIC PROBLEM — 4
1. Specialisation and the fuel blockade — 4
2. Ethiopia and its production possibility frontier — 4
3. Property rights and hunting — 5
4. Virgin - the market mechanism at work — 5
5. The problems of a free market economy — 6
6. North Korea - the failure of a planned economy — 7
7. Economies in transition — 7

Essay questions and exam notes — 8

Unit 2 PRICES — 9
1. Demand and mobile phones — 9
2. Supply and coffee — 9
3. Coal prices — 10
4. Price elasticity of demand for petrol — 10
5. VAT and sanitary protection — 11
6. OPEC and the price of oil — 11
7. Farming subsidies — 12

Essay questions and exam notes — 13

Unit 3 THE FIRM — 14
1. Racecourses: revenues, costs and profits — 14
2. Ikea: economies of scale — 14
3. C&A - profits and the market — 15
4. Microsoft - a monopoly? — 15
5. Caravans in Hull - external economies of scale — 16
6. Barriers to entry — 16
7. The haulage industry - perfect competition? — 17
8. Games consoles — 18

Essay questions and exam notes — 19

Unit 4 THE FIRM AND MARKET FAILURE — 20
1. Opel and anti-competitive practices — 20
2. Technology and creative destruction — 20
3. Cadbury buys Snapple - a merger — 21
4. Mobile phone auction — 21
5. UK car pricing — 22
6. BT and the local loop — 23
7. The crisis at Rover — 23
8. Diamonds and cartels — 24

Essay questions and exam notes — 25

Unit 5 TRANSPORT AND THE ENVIRONMENT — 26
1. The Kyoto Protocol — 26
2. Regulations and sulphur emissions — 27
3. Polluter pays principle for goods in EU — 27
4. River pollution — 28
5. Incinerators — 29
6. Car use in the UK — 29
7. Bus transport — 30
8. Parking levies and city centre tolls — 31
9. Fuel tax crisis — 31
10. Transatlantic air fares — 32

Essay questions and exam notes — 33

Unit 6 THE PUBLIC SECTOR — 34
1. Taxes as a percentage of GDP — 34
2. Income tax and National Insurance contributions: progressive and regressive taxes — 34
3. EU taxes on earnings — 35
4. Increases in National Health spending — 35
5. Fuel taxes — 36
6. The difficulties of forecasting the PSNCR — 37
7. Japan's public sector debt — 37
8. The mobile phone windfall — 38
9. Efficiency in the NHS — 38
10. Social security spending — 39

Essay questions and exam notes — 40

Unit 7 LABOUR — 41
1. Excess demand for economists — 41
2. Economic activity rates — 41
3. Full employment in Newbury — 42
4. The minimum wage — 42
5. Female wages and the glass ceiling — 43
6. Employment of the disabled — 43
7. The employment market in the South East — 44
8. Earnings differentials between occupations — 45
9. Temporary working — 45
10. Union benefits — 46

Essay questions and exam notes — 47

Unit 8 MONETARY POLICY — 48
1. UK monetary growth — 48
2. Short term and long term interest rates — 48
3. Government spending and monetary policy — 49
4. The millennium bug — 49
5. Monetary policy and exchange rate policy — 50
6. Monetary policy decision making — 50
7. The housing market and monetary policy — 51

Essay questions and exam notes — 52

Unit 9 UNEMPLOYMENT, INFLATION AND INCOME DISTRIBUTION — 53
1. Trends in unemployment — 53
2. Unemployment amongst those aged 50+ — 53
3. The Phillips curve — 54
4. Inflation — 54
5. The Retail Price Index — 55
6. Inflation: goods vs services — 55
7. Child poverty — 55
8. Demand pull inflation — 56
9. Cost push inflation — 56
10. Increasing inequality — 57
11. Relative poverty — 57

Essay questions and exam notes — 58

Unit 10 ECONOMIC RECOVERY AND GROWTH — 59
1. The trade cycle — 59
2. Oil prices and economic growth — 59
3. Underestimating potential economic growth — 60
4. Immigration and growth — 60
5. Deindustrialisation in the textile industry — 61
6. Research and development — 61
7. The hidden economy — 62
8. The Big Mac comparison — 62

Essay questions and exam notes — 63

Unit 11 GOVERNMENT POLICY — 64
1. The goals of government policy — 64
2. The 2000 Budget — 64
3. Unemployment policy — 65
4. Anti-inflationary policy — 65
5. Growth policies — 66
6. The redistribution of income — 66
7. Information and communication technology — 67

Essay questions and exam notes — 68

Unit 12 INTERNATIONAL TRADE AND EXCHANGE RATES — 69
1. The strong pound — 69
2. Export volumes — 69
3. EU and non-EU trade — 70
4. The current account — 70
5. Is a strong pound good for the UK? — 71
6. The balance of payments — 71
7. The problems facing British manufacturing firms — 72
8. The euro and the dollar — 72
9. Should Britain join the euro? — 73

Essay questions and exam notes — 74

Unit 13 DEVELOPMENT ECONOMICS — 75
1. Indicators of development — 75
2. Growth and poverty reduction — 76
3. The Kenyan tea industry — 76
4. Aids — 77
5. Capital flows to the Third World — 77
6. The textile industry in Pakistan and economic growth — 78
7. Population and growth — 78
8. GM crops — 79

Essay questions and exam notes — 80

Unit 1
Economic systems and the economic problem

1 Specialisation and the fuel blockade

In September 2000, the UK almost ground to a halt because of a blockade of fuel depots and refineries by farmers and hauliers protesting at the recent large increases in the price of fuel. The blockades spread across the country within days. Although there were relatively few protesters, tanker drivers refused to cross the picket lines, claiming that they felt intimidated by the protesters. By Monday 11 September, there was no fuel being shipped out to garages and most garages had run dry through panic buying over the weekend. By Thursday 14 September, a number of haulage companies had said that they could no longer guarantee deliveries because they were almost out of fuel. There was general agreement that few cars or lorries would have any fuel left by the following Monday. The economy faced potential collapse if the situation had continued.

The reason why such a problem might be imminent was because of the high degree of specialisation in a modern economy like the UK. Firms and households are not in any sense self-sufficient. They have come to rely upon other firms and households for the production and consumption of nearly all goods and services. For instance, very few households now produce their own vegetables. They rely upon farmers in this country and abroad and a distribution system which gets the produce from the farm to the house. A necessary input for the distribution system is fuel. If supplies of fuel are cut completely, the whole distribution system stops. Fuel is also key to worker mobility. Most workers use private or public transport to get them to work. Some workers, such as community nurses, rely upon their cars to do their jobs. Without fuel, most workers would be forced to stay at home and production would collapse.

The protesters lifted their pickets on Friday 15 September, judging that they could lose the goodwill of the public if the economy experienced collapse as a result of their action. However, it showed the vulnerability of a modern economy to the cutting of an essential raw material in the production process.

2 Ethiopia and its production possibility frontier

During the 1980s, Ethiopia suffered two catastrophes which reduced its productive potential and therefore pushed its production possibility frontier (PPF) back towards to the origin. First, it suffered a series of devastating droughts which considerably reduced output from its agricultural industry. Second, it was engaged in a long running civil war with insurgents from the northern province of Eritrea. In the late 1980s, the Marxist government was toppled and a new government quickly gave Eritrea its independence. With free market reforms, the economy grew at almost 6 per cent per annum between 1992 and 1998. These free market reforms gave incentives for farmers to increase production, whilst industry invested and expanded to take advantage of higher spending.

In 1999-2000, history seemed to be repeating itself. Drought hit the country, reducing agricultural yields. Then the Ethiopian government began a small scale war against its Eritrean neighbour over issues which many in the West felt should have been resolved through peaceful negotiations. The war used up scarce supplies of foreign currency which limited imports. Business confidence fell as did investment. The economy stopped growing. The risk was that the production possibility frontier could start to shift backwards if the war caused too much destruction or if it diverted resources from civilian investment to military spending. As other examples around the world have shown, war can have a devastating impact on the PPF of an economy and it is to be avoided if at all possible.

THE STUDENT'S ECONOMY IN FOCUS 2000/01

3 Property rights and hunting

A market economy can only function if there are clear property rights. This means that who owns what is clearly stated in law, and property can be defended by owners from others who might want to take it or damage it.

Today, there is fierce debate about hunting. The anti-hunting lobby argues that hunting is cruel and harms the welfare of animals, and should be banned. The pro-hunting lobby argues that hunts should be free to continue their activities. They only hunt over land whose owners have given permission to do so and any damage caused to property or crops is paid for.

There are other arguments used by the pro-hunt lobby. It points out that a ban on hunting would lead to a loss of jobs - between 6 000 and 8 000 according to a government report (the Burns Report) published in June 2000. The rural horse economy would be particularly hard hit. In the short term, spending that would have taken place on hunting if a ban were introduced is likely to be diverted to goods and services not provided in local rural communities. The opportunity cost for someone riding in a hunt might be a holiday in the Caribbean or a new sports car. The pro-hunting lobby also argues that hunting keeps down the pest population.

The anti-hunting lobby counters these arguments by saying that in the long term, rural economies will recover. Jobs will be created in new industries. Anyway, 6 000 to 8 000 jobs is insignificant in an economy where nearly 30 million work. As for keeping down pests, the Burns report stated that hunting only kills a fraction of foxes, hares and deer that are killed each year. Most such animals are shot to keep their populations down.

From an economic viewpoint, hunting is perhaps best characterised as a leisure pursuit rather than a means of pest control. The main question, then, is whether landowners have the right to hunt over their land, or allow others to hunt and to kill animals. Should the government, on animal welfare grounds, take away that property right?

4 Virgin - the market mechanism at work

In 2000, two different parts of the Virgin empire announced that they were making changes to their operations in the light of market signals. On the one hand, Virgin announced that it would be converting its 230 Our Price stores into outlets selling its mobile phones and other high technology products, and acting as service centres for online customers. Our Price was originally a joint venture between WH Smith and Virgin but in 1998, Virgin paid £145 million for the 75 per cent stake in the business owned by WH Smith. It has since found it hard to make a profit on a mix of music retailing and mobile telephony. Virgin blamed the move out of music retailing on record companies. Virgin wanted them to give it much better terms for purchase of CDs. If it could lower the price it paid to record companies, Virgin would then be able to make a higher profit, justifying keeping Our Price as a core music retailer. As it was, the record companies refused and Virgin could not see how Our Price could make sufficient profit to justify the resources taken up in the business. Changing the stores to selling mainly mobile phones, with possibly a few CDs, it is hoped would raise profitability. Profits have therefore acted as the signal in the market to change how scarce resources are used.

The second example was Virgin Express. This is a company which operates low cost travel services, mainly between European destinations. In 1999 it reported a loss of £3.4 million for the year. In response, Virgin Express decided to cut two of the routes which had proved unprofitable. These were services between Madrid and Rome and Rome and Barcelona. It also decided to stop flying out of Stansted near London. Virgin Express will transfer the resources used, including aircraft, to more profitable routes including Brussels to Nice and Copenhagen. As with Our Price, profitability determined where scarce resources would be used, with profits acting as both a signal and an incentive to ensure that profitability was maximised.

5 The problems of a free market economy

In 2000, the World Bank held a summit meeting in Prague. As with other summit meetings recently, a number of anti-capitalist protesters travelled to Prague. There were riots and property was damaged. The protests had been even larger the previous year at a World Trade Organisation conference in Seattle. The protesters tended to focus on single issues which, nevertheless, when taken together reflect many of the aspects of the workings of the free market mechanism.

One concern was about the very different pay and working conditions of workers around the world today. In recent years, certain companies have been put under the spotlight. It is argued, for example, that some manufacturers of trainers source part of their output from Third World factories where, by Western standards, low pay and poor working conditions are normal. For instance, an Indonesian worker might work for $2 a day to produce trainers which sell for $120 a pair to the final customer. There are other examples. The majority of the clothes now bought in UK shops are sourced from the Third World because of cheap production costs. Differences in prices and wages are a fundamental characteristic of the free market. They provide signals and incentives for resource allocation to change. If wages in Indonesian shoe factories were the same as in the USA, there would be no incentive for US shoes companies to source their shoes from Indonesia. Equally, given current incomes in Indonesia, paying Indonesian shoe workers the same wage as in the USA would price Indonesian shoes out of the Indonesian market. Many shoe workers in Indonesia only have jobs because their wages are lower than in the USA. Equally, the competitive advantage of shoe factories in the Third World has led to the closure of much of the First World's shoe manufacturing industry.

Another concern of the protesters was the power of large multinational companies. Certain food companies have been criticised for paying low wages to staff, driving out local businesses when setting up new outlets, providing food which can be criticised on environmental grounds, and destroying local cuisine. From a free market viewpoint, they are examples of highly successful businesses. They provide highly affordable products, partly because they keep wage costs down, but also because of their ability to buy in bulk. Their success inevitably means that some small, local competing businesses will see a fall in their trade and will be forced to close. After all, businesses can only survive if they can offer a product that customers want to buy. As for destroying local cuisine, they provide products which children and teenagers around the world seem to enjoy. They do not set out to destroy local cuisine. One of the great strengths of multinational food companies, though, is that they provide a consistency of product which consumers increasingly expect when making any sort of purchase.

A third concern of the protesters was the environment. Capitalism destroys the environment. As with nuclear power or GM crops, it plays with potentially dangerous new technologies. Production itself threatens the world's existence with global warming and the destruction of the ozone layer. There is no doubt amongst free market economists that production can lead to environmental damage. The solution is to identify these problems and ensure that those creating the damage are either forced to stop or to pay for the damage they create. The market mechanism, from a historical viewpoint, does not seem to be any worse from an environmental viewpoint than other economic system. There were environmental disasters in slave owning societies, amongst American Indian tribes and in the planned economies of the former Soviet Union. Getting rid of capitalism is unlikely to solve any environmental problems.

Another focal point of protest was the very diffused nature of the capitalist system. No one seems in charge, whether it be governments, consumers, or even large firms. But then this is the nature of capitalism. Adam Smith in his *Wealth of Nations* published in 1776 explained that capitalism was a way of coordinating the individual decisions of large numbers of individual consumers, workers and firms. For much of the twentieth century, countries such as the Soviet Union and China tried a different way of coordinating the economy through state planning. This, though, ultimately proved a failure because it was impossible to coordinate effectively such a large number of decisions. It also led to severe constraints being imposed on individual freedoms. An irony of the Seattle and Prague protests was that the protesters were free to travel, used petrol produced by some of the multinational companies they were protesting against, ate food which was produced by multinational food giants, and wore clothes which may have been produced by lowly paid Third World workers.

6 North Korea - the failure of a planned economy

Following the Korean war in the early 1950s, North Korea received long term financial aid from the Soviet Union. North Korea created a planned economy and in the 1970s and 1980s, increasingly pursued a policy of self reliance. This meant reducing trade flows between North Korea and other countries, and substituting domestic production for imports wherever possible.

At the end of the 1980s, the Soviet Union broke up. One of the consequences was that it stopped giving aid to allied countries such as North Korea and Cuba. The effect on the North Korean economy was devastating. North Korea had relied upon Soviet imports of oil which it had paid for with exports of manufactured products at very advantageous prices. The collapse of trade deprived North Korea of energy, whilst its industry lost key markets. Production fell by 25 per cent over the 1990s. The situation became critical because North Korean agriculture was deprived of essential fertilisers, reducing crop yields. Floods in 1995 which destroyed part of the crop then led to famine, which continued in the second half of the 1990s. The effects of the prolonged famine were mitigated to some extent by food aid. The North Korean government accepted supplies of food from a variety of sources including western governments.

In 2000, signs that the North Korean government was changing policy became apparent when the North Korean and South Korean heads of state met and had constructive talks. During the late 1990s, North Korea had begun to accept investments of foreign owned capital in its economy. In 2000, Coca Cola made a shipment to North Korea, a landmark in economic relations given that Coca Cola is a symbol of western capitalism for many anti-capitalists. However, investors in North Korea found that many obstacles were continually put in their way to prevent or slow down commercial operations.

In the long term, it is possible that South Korea and North Korea will be reunited. South Korea, which has been one of the success stories of Third World development, is in no rush, though, to achieve this. It fears a collapse of the political system in North Korea which would lead to sudden reunification in the same way that East Germany was reunited with West Germany in 1990. Reunification placed a heavy burden on West German taxpayers in the 1990s because East Germany was poorer than West Germany. In the case of North Korea, its income per capita in 2000 of $714 was just one twelfth that of South Korea. One estimate has put the potential cost for reconstruction of the North Korean economy at $1 000 billion (£666 billion), two and a half times the annual production of the South Korean economy and sixty times that of the North Korean economy. South Korea would like to see the gradual integration of the two economies with South Korean and other foreign firms allowed to invest freely in North Korea. The South Korean government would give aid to North Korea to help rebuild infrastructure such as roads and flood defences. The gap between income per capita could then be reduced over time as North Korea became a mixed economy.

7 Economies in transition

2000 was a good year for the countries of Eastern Europe and the former Soviet Union. Economic growth was positive in almost all countries as Table 1.1 shows. There were two main reasons for this. One was the continued transformation of former planned economies into market economies. Most countries in Eastern Europe are continuing to privatise former state controlled companies. They are encouraging investment from Western companies. Markets are being liberalised to promote greater competition. Firms are being set up to take advantage of the new market freedoms.

The second reason for positive growth was the large devaluation of the Russian rouble in 1998 following a financial crisis. The devaluation of the rouble has made Russian industry much more competitive on international markets. Exports have risen and this has led to higher incomes and hence higher economic growth.

Table 1.1 shows that Eastern countries have paid a heavy price for their transformation. Poland has been the most successful country, achieving a 28 per cent rise in its income (as measured by GDP) compared to its 1989 level. Ukraine, which has been one of the countries least willing to change, has an income only 37 per cent of its 1989 level. Unless it implements large scale market reforms, it is unlikely to grow at the rate of its more reform-orientated neighbours.

	2000 (%)	2000 as % of 1989 GDP
Bulgaria	3.5	70
Czech Republic	2.0	95
Hungary	4.5	104
Poland	5.0	128
Romania	0.5	76
Central & eastern Europe & Baltic States	3.6	100
Kazakhstan	3.5	65
Russia	4.0	59
Ukraine	2.0	37
CIS	3.6	57

Figure 1.1 *Growth in real GDP*
Source: adapted from EBRD.

Reading list

A.G. Anderton, *Economics*, Causeway Press (3rd ed. 2000) pages 1-15, 273-303.
A.G. Anderton, *Economics AS Level*, Causeway Press (2000) pages 1-15, 273-303.
J. Beardshaw *et al*, *Economics: A Student's Guide,* Longman (4th ed. 1998) pages 25-37.
P. Maunder *et al*, *Economics Explained*, Collins Educational (Revised 3rd ed. 2000) pages 3-41.
C. Bamford, editor, *Economics for AS*, Cambridge University Press (2000) pages 18-27.
D. Begg *et al*, *Economics*, McGraw Hill (5th ed. 1997) pages 2-11.
N.M. Healey, 'The progress of transition in Eastern Europe', *Developments in Economics* Vol 13, Causeway Press (1997).

UNIT 1 ECONOMIC SYSTEMS AND THE ECONOMIC PROBLEM

Essay questions

Examine the concept of opportunity cost in terms of:
(a) a decision to drill for oil in an Area of Outstanding Natural Beauty; (50 marks)
(b) a student's decision to continue in education after 'A' levels. (50 marks)
(Edexcel January 1995)

(a) What is the opportunity cost to a student of going to university? (20 marks)
(b) Examine the external costs and benefits of a significant increase in the number of university students. (40 marks)
(c) Examine the economic effects of tuition fees for higher education courses to be paid by students rather than the government. (40 marks)
(Edexcel June 1995)

(a) Outline the main features of command economies such as those which used to exist in Eastern Europe before 1989. (20 marks)
(b) What problems caused many of these economies to place greater emphasis on market forces as a means of allocating resources? (40 marks)
(c) How might this greater reliance on market forces have improved the performance of these economies? (40 marks)
(Edexcel June 1997)

(a) The basic economic problem which confronts every society is scarcity. Explain how, in a market economy, the price mechanism allocates resources between different uses. (12 marks)

(b) Evaluate the arguments for and against a significant reduction in the state provision of health care, which results in an increase in the supply of health care through the market mechanism. (13 marks)
(AQA [AEB] June 1998)

(a) Explain how changes in prices affect the allocation of resources in a market economy. (12 marks)
(b) Evaluate the relative merits of taxation and regulation as methods of reducing the consumption of de-merit goods, such as alcohol and tobacco. (13 marks)
(AQA [AEB] June 1999)

Explain how the market mechanism allocates resources efficiently in a dynamic economy. Discuss how far it is possible to judge whether the system of resource allocation in an economy is fair as well as efficient.
(AQA [NEAB] 1997)

Explain what is meant by an optimum allocation of resources and how it is achieved in a market economy. Discuss how the transfer of the gas, water and electricity industries to private ownership is likely to affect the allocation of resources in the UK.
(AQA [NEAB] 1998)

Describe the main features and functions of an economy. Discuss how the recent economic problems of countries such as Brazil, Japan or Russia might affect the rest of the global economy.
(AQA [NEAB] 1999)

(a) Explain, using economic analysis, why countries in Eastern Europe have made the transition to a market economy. (8)
(b) Discuss why some Eastern European countries have made this transition more successfully and less painfully than others. (12)
(OCR March 1998)

(a) Explain the advantages of the market system relative to the command system. (8)
(b) 'Five former Communist countries from central and eastern Europe (Czech Republic, Estonia, Hungary, Poland and Slovenia) yesterday celebrated having passed the first hurdle on the road towards full membership of the European Union early next century.' (Daily Telegraph, 17th July 1997). Discuss the likely impact of full membership on both the five countries and on the EU as a whole. (12)
(OCR June 1999)

(a) Using a suitable example, explain the concept of 'opportunity cost'. (5)
(b) Discuss how an understanding of opportunity cost might assist in deciding between do-it-yourself house decoration and the employment of specialist decorators. (10)
(c) The government is considering a major public sector investment project to mark the new millennium. Provide an economic evaluation of the factors involved in deciding whether or not to proceed with the project. (10)
(CCEA 1998)

Exam notes

The basic economic problem
Specifications require an understanding of scarcity, choice and opportunity cost. In a world of scarce resources, choices have to be made about what and how to produce, as well as who should receive the resulting output.
Specialisation There are considerable gains to be made if workers and economies specialise. However, one problem with specialisation is that if one link in the chain of production fails, it can have repercussions for the whole of the production process (Box 1).
Production possibility frontiers There are limits to what can be produced in an economy given scarce resources. The productive potential of an economy is shown by its production possibility frontier. Investment in physical or human capital will tend to push the frontier or boundary out. War or natural disasters, as exemplified in Box 2, will tend to pull the frontier inwards.
Types of resources and sectors of the economy There are different types of resources. In economics, they are usually classified as land, labour, capital or entrepreneurship. They are used to produce goods and services in three sectors of the economy: the primary, secondary and tertiary sectors (Box 1).
Markets Markets are one way of allocating resources (Boxes 3 and 4). Markets bring together buyers and sellers who exchange goods, perhaps using barter, but more usually using money. Markets, through the forces of demand and supply, lead to the fixing of prices.

Types of economy Economic systems which rely primarily on markets to allocate resources are called free market economies (Boxes 3 to 5). Resources can also be allocated by government. Economic systems where there is some balance between market allocation and government allocation are called mixed economies. Economies where most resources are allocated by the state are called command or planned economies (Box 6). In recent years, countries in Eastern Europe, the former Soviet Union and China have moved away from being planned economies towards a mixed economy model. Some economies, such as Poland, have seen significant economic benefits from this transition. Others have seen their output fall, mainly because of a mishandling of the transitional process (Box 7).

Unit 2
Prices

1 Demand and mobile phones

By September 2000, mobile phone companies had 34 million customers between them as Figure 2.1 shows. This is over half the population of the UK if each customer were to own only one phone account. In 1990, in contrast, the mobile phone industry was only in its infancy with less than 1 million subscribers. There is a number of reasons why the demand for mobile phones has increased.

First, the price has come down. In 1990, mobile phone subscriptions were paid for almost exclusively by businesses and provided as a work tool and perk for management employees. Charges were so high that few households were prepared to pay the price. Gradually prices fell as Figure 2.2 shows, and as they did so the subscriber base rose. The most significant change to pricing occurred in 1998 when pre-pay services were introduced. Instead of being charged a monthly subscription and being charged for calls in arrears, customers could now pay for phone calls in advance with no subscription. This prevented them from overspending and it allowed many young people to consider acquiring a mobile phone.

Second, average incomes have increased over the period 1990 to 2000. GDP over the period rose 23 per cent. A mobile phone is, for many, a luxury good which they acquire when their incomes increase.

Third, mobile phone technology has improved. The four networks have extended their coverage geographically since 1990. Digital phone networks have been replacing analogue networks giving better reception. New Wap phones introduced in 2000 gave internet and web access.

The country with the highest mobile phone penetration in the world is Finland, with 80 per cent owning a phone. The UK is likely to move rapidly to this position in the next few years driven mainly by lower prices.

Figure 2.1 *Number of mobile phones in the UK per network, millions, September 2000*
Source: adapted from *The Guardian*, 5.10.2000.

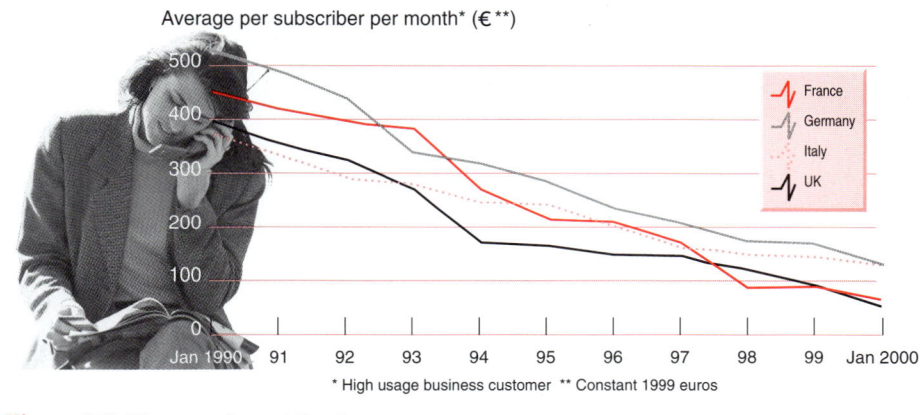

Figure 2.2 *The cost of a mobile phone*
Source: adapted from Analysis Research.

2 Supply and coffee

The Brazilian coffee growing industry is engaged in aggressive expansion. In the late 1990s, farmers planted about 2 billion coffee bushes and were expected to plant 300 million in 2000. It takes time for a coffee bush to grow and start producing coffee beans. However, in 2001, the first 500 million bushes planted in this expansion will come 'on line'. Production is likely to increase from an average 25.6 million bags (of 60 kg) in the 1990s to 35.4 million bags in the first decade of 2000. Other world producers, particularly Vietnam, have also been increasing production aggressively. Analysts predict that 10-15 million bags of coffee are likely to be added to world supply.

Economic theory would predict that increases in world coffee bean production are likely to be caused by rising prices since supply curves are upward sloping. There is some upward pressure in that demand for coffee is increasing worldwide. However, the increase in supply has in recent years outstripped the increase in demand. The result has been falling coffee prices.

So why have countries like Brazil and Vietnam been increasing supply? One reason is that the expansion in Brazil started at a time when coffee prices were rising. Investment decisions in an industry where there is several years between planting and the first coffee harvest are lagged behind actual coffee prices (a situation described by the cobweb model of price determination). Another key reason, though, is that many of the farmers expanding their coffee output are relatively efficient producers with low labour costs. Central American countries like Costa Rica have higher average labour and input costs than in, say, Brazil.

In the long term, coffee prices look set to fall as some countries expand output. This is likely to lead to a shakeout of the least efficient producers. To stay in business, farmers will have to have low costs and be highly efficient.

THE STUDENT'S ECONOMY IN FOCUS 2000/01

UNIT 2 PRICES

3 Coal prices

International coal prices fell in the second half of the 1990s, but in 2000, as Figure 2.3 shows, began to rise again. Partly this was due to strong demand as the world economy grew at a fast rate. Countries like South Korea, for instance, which had seen a sharp downturn in its GDP in 1998 due to the Asian crisis, were recording high growth rates in 2000 as their economies recovered. Partly it was due to falling coal output from China. In the second half of the 1990s, China had exported coal aggressively. But by 2000, it was shutting down some of its smaller unprofitable mines and this led to a downturn in Chinese exports. With demand rising but supply tight, the price of coal increased.

However, there is not a single international price for coal. Most coal is sold under long term contracts at fixed prices. The long term price in the second half of the 1990s tended to be above the spot price - the price for a single purchase for immediate delivery. But in 2000, the situation was reversed. Spot prices exceeded long term contract prices.

Moreover, as Figure 2.3 shows, the price of coal differs depending upon where in the world it will be delivered. Coal for delivery in Europe tends to be more expensive than coal for delivery in Asia. The difference in price represents shipping and other transport costs which can also affect delivery dates. So within the world coal market there are many regional markets, with different prices in each regional market for the same product. There are also different prices for different grades of coal. The regional markets are interlinked though. If prices in, say, the Asian market become very low in relation to prices in the European market, it is going to pay some buyers in Europe to buy in Asia and ship to Europe despite higher transport costs rather than buy in Europe. So prices in the two markets cannot diverge too much.

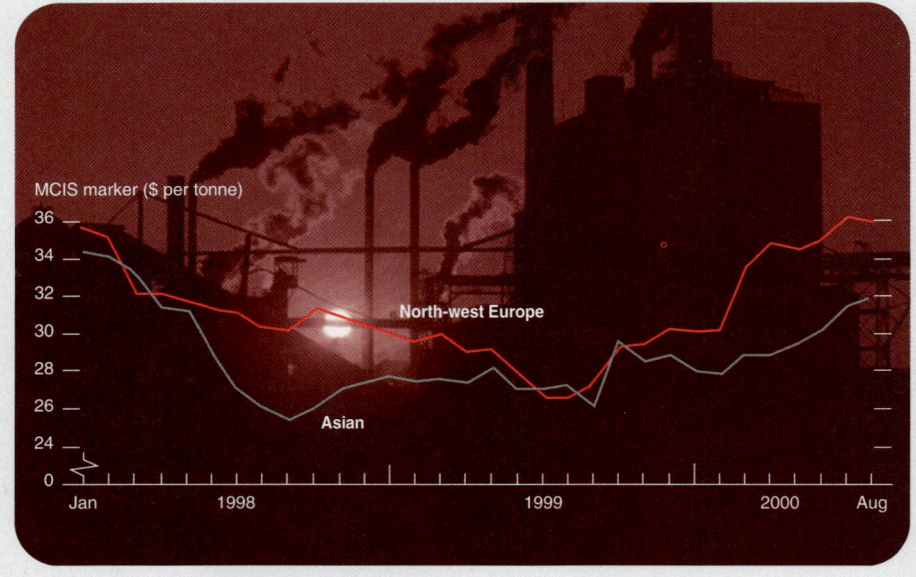

Figure 2.3 *Coal prices*
Source: adapted from McCloskey Coal Information Services.

4 Price elasticity of demand for petrol

In its 1993 Budget, the Conservative government announced that, on environmental grounds, it would be increasing the level of duty on petrol by 3 per cent per annum over and above the rate of inflation for the foreseeable future. This fuel duty escalator would lead to a reduction in the amount of petrol and diesel bought. In turn, this would reduce greenhouse gas emissions which result from the burning of any fossil fuel. It would also help reduce congestion on British roads as fewer miles would be travelled.

However, the government knew at the time that the price elasticity of demand for motor fuel is highly inelastic. Estimates vary, but it is probably around 0.2. This means that the government would need to increase the price of petrol by 100 per cent (i.e. double the price) to achieve a 20 per cent fall in quantity demanded. In the last year in which the fuel escalator was imposed, in 1999, it had been increased to 6 per cent. With an price elasticity of 0.2, this would have led to a 1.2 per cent fall in the quantity bought. It is therefore not a very effective way to reduce the number of miles travelled. What's more, it is very poor at reducing congestion because the tax has to be paid whether the journey is on an uncongested road or a congested one.

Taxing petrol, though, is highly efficient from a tax viewpoint precisely because it does little to alter consumer spending patterns. It can raise large amounts in tax - a 1p rise in duty and VAT yields £540 million in tax. Many believe that governments since 1993, both Conservative and Labour, have continued to increase duties on fuel precisely because small changes in tax can yield large amounts of extra revenue. However, as the fuel protests of 2000 showed, there is a limit as to how much petrol prices can be increased without this becoming extremely unpopular.

5 VAT and sanitary protection

In his 2000 Budget, the Chancellor, Gordon Brown, announced that from 2001 VAT on sanitary towels and tampons would fall from the standard rate of 17.5 per cent to a new 5 per cent rate. The move will cost the government £35 million a year in lost taxes.

Economic theory suggests that a fall in VAT of 12.5 per cent will not necessarily lead to a fall in prices by the same amount. This is because firms along the supply chain could choose to pocket part or all of the fall in tax as extra profit. In the case of sanitary protection, however, the demand is likely to be highly inelastic, i.e. price rises or falls are unlikely to have much effect on quantity demanded. When demand is highly inelastic, economic theory would predict that nearly all of the cut in VAT will be passed on to consumers.

Women's groups and women MPs have been pressing governments for a long time to zero rate sanitary protection products, arguing that they are a necessity for women. As such, they have a low income elasticity of demand. As incomes rise, women spend little extra on sanitary protection products. Spending on these products therefore accounts for a much larger proportion of the budget of low income families than high income families.

The reason why the Chancellor chose to cut the VAT rate to 5 per cent rather than zero per cent was because under EU law, 5 per cent is the lowest rate to which a country can cut VAT on a particular product. This is an example of how the UK's membership of the EU can affect domestic policy decision making. From an EU viewpoint, it would like to see taxes harmonised across the EU, i.e. tax rates would be the same. This is to prevent firms and households shifting their tax burden artificially from country to country to get the lowest rate.

6 OPEC and the price of oil

OPEC, the Organisation of Petroleum Exporting Countries, is an international cartel. Since 1973, it has acted to restrict the supply of oil onto the market, thus raising its price to the benefit of its members.

At the beginning of 1999, oil prices had fallen to around $10 a barrel due to oversupply of the market. OPEC in the late 1990s expected oil prices to be in the $15-$20 a barrel range. It acted to restrict supply by agreeing tougher production quotas amongst member countries. The result was a steady increase in price in 1999 and 2000 to a peak of around $35 a barrel. This was a far greater rise in price than OPEC had intended. What it had not foreseen was that buyers in 1999 had run down stocks of oil expecting prices to fall. In 2000, stocks of refined oil were at relatively low levels. To secure supplies, buyers pushed up prices because in the short term the demand for oil is highly price inelastic. Motorists have no option but to pay higher prices if they want to travel. Equally, firms and households which use oil to heat their premises and homes or run their machinery can't suddenly switch to another fuel. Demand in the Far East also increased as countries such as South Korea and Thailand recovered from the sharp downturns in their economies caused by the Asian crisis of 1997-98.

At $30 a barrel, there will be considerable incentives for users to switch fuels in the long run. They will buy more energy-efficient oil powered machines or switch to other fuels. For this reason, the largest OPEC oil producer, Saudi Arabia, wants to see prices fall back to $20-25 a barrel to discourage users switching fuel. In the long term, a very high price is unlikely to be in the interests of OPEC because the long term price elasticity of demand for oil is likely to be greater than 1.

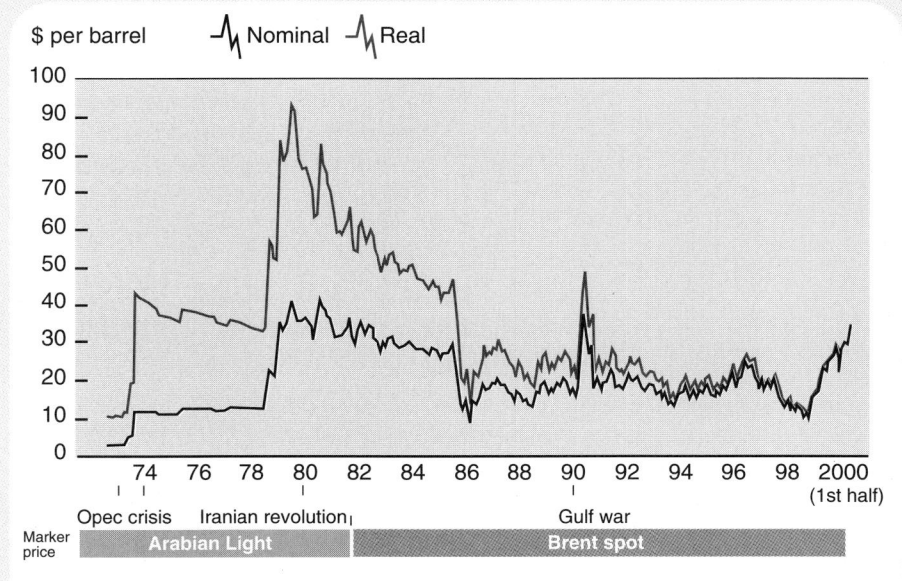

Figure 2.4 *World oil prices*
Source: adapted from Primark Datastream, International Energy Agency.

UNIT 2 PRICES

7 Farming subsidies

In its 2000 review of farm policies, the OECD (Organisation for Economic Co-operation and Development), an economic research body to which all the developed countries subscribe) stated that farming subsidies had increased in the late 1990s as the 'farming crisis' had intensified. In 1999, average aid had risen to 40 per cent of gross farm receipts compared to 31 per cent in 1997 after a decade of slow decline. In money terms, total support reached $361 billion, equivalent to 1.4 per cent of OECD GDP and $360 per capita. Approximately two thirds of this was born by consumers having to pay higher prices for agricultural produce. One third was born by taxpayers paying subsidies to farmers.

The level of aid differed widely between countries. Worst were Japan, Korea, Norway and Switzerland, all of which provided their farmers with at least 65 per cent of gross receipts. EU aid was 49 per cent compared with 38 per cent in 1997 and 44 per cent in 1986-88. Lowest were New Zealand and Australia with 2 and 6 per cent respectively.

The reason for the jump in aid to farmers in the late 1990s was a sharp fall in world agricultural commodity prices. In the UK, this was compounded by the effects of the BSE scandal. Most OECD governments, including the British government, responded to the fall in prices by increasing subsidies to farmers. The BSE scandal in the UK cost the government and taxpayer £4 billion alone, equivalent to £66 per person or £264 for a family of four.

The OECD would like to see farming subsidies abolished. It argues that they create large inefficiencies in the farming sector. Crops are often grown in one place which could be grown far more cheaply elsewhere. Resources which are tied up in agricultural production in, say, Norway, Switzerland or marginal land in Wales or Scotland, could be put to use far more productively in other industries. It would be far better to allow countries like Australia to expand their agricultural exports and for countries like Norway or Switzerland to concentrate on producing other goods and services which they could then sell on world markets to pay for higher agricultural imports.

The OECD also points out that the present farming crisis shows that governments are prepared to increase subsidies to farmers despite many wanting in the long term to reduce subsidies. The danger is that, if farming recovers, there will be strong political pressure on government to maintain subsidies at the levels seen in 1999 and 2000. This ability of farmers, who typically make up a small fraction of the workforce, to manipulate government is one reason why some economists argue that subsidies to any industry should be avoided. Once granted, it becomes politically very difficult to remove them.

Reading list

A.G. Anderton, *Economics*, Causeway Press (3rd ed. 2000) pages 23-77, 135-141.
A.G. Anderton, *Economics AS Level*, Causeway Press (2000) pages 23-77, 135-141.
J. Beardshaw *et al*, *Economics: A Student's Guide*, Longman (4th ed. 1998) pages 104-162.
P. Maunder *et al*, *Economics Explained*, Collins Educational (Revised 3rd ed. 2000) pages 42-95, 159-180.
C. Bamford, editor, *Economics for AS*, Cambridge University Press (2000) pages 28-55.
D. Begg *et al*, *Economics*, McGraw Hill (5th ed. 1997) pages 30-43, 53-67.
R. Ackrill, 'The Common Agricultural Policy', *Developments in Economics* Vol 12, Causeway Press (1996).

Essay questions

(a) Why is demand for Jaguar cars likely to be more price elastic than the demand for electricity? (40 marks)
(b) Using the concept of income elasticity, explain the significance of an increase in real incomes for the suppliers of:
 (i) private health care;
 (ii) bus travel. (60 marks)
(Edexcel June 1997)

'In 1995 real house prices in the UK had fallen back to their 1984 level.'
(a) How might this fall in real house prices be accounted for? (40 marks)
(b) Examine the economic effects of this fall in real house prices. (40 marks)
(c) Explain two measures which a government could take to stimulate the housing market. (20 marks)
(Edexcel June 1997)

The following data relate to the demand for beef in the UK, as estimated by the Ministry of Agriculture, Fisheries and Food.
Price elasticity of demand -0.88
Income elasticity of demand +0.23
Cross elasticity of demand with respect to bacon and ham +1.10
(a) Explain the meaning of these data. (30 marks)
(b) What is the significance of the data for beef producers? (30 marks)
(c) Analyse other factors affecting the demand for meat in the UK. (40 marks)
(Edexcel January 1998)

A national cinema chain has the following information:
(i) the income elasticity of demand for visits to the cinema is + 2.5
(ii) the price elasticity of demand for visits to the cinema is - 2.3
(iii) the cross elasticity of demand for visits to the cinema with respect to the rental payment of pre-recorded video films is + 3.8
(iv) the cross elasticity of demand for visits to the cinema with respect to the price of popcorn sold in the cinema is - 1.0
(a) Examine the significance of each of these figures for the cinema company. (60 marks)

(b) What further economic information would the cinema company require in facing a decision to open more cinemas? Justify your answer. (40 marks)
(Edexcel June 1998)

Nearly £3 billion was spent on subsidising UK farmers in 1997 as part of the EU's Common Agricultural Policy.
(a) How can such subsidies to farmers be justified when far less assistance is available to manufacturing industry? (50 marks)
(b) Examine the likely economic effects of a reform of the Common Agricultural Policy which resulted in a removal of these subsidies. (50 marks)
(Edexcel January 2000)

(a) Explain why both the price elasticity of demand and the price elasticity of supply of primary commodities, such as coffee and copper, are likely to be inelastic in the short run. (12 marks)
(b) Discuss the significance of inelastic demand and supply for the producers and consumers of such commodities. (13 marks)
(AQA [AEB] June 1999)

Explain the relationship between individual demand, market demand and aggregate demand. Analyse how the bonus shares issued by those building societies which converted to banks in 1997 are likely to have affected the demand for individual products and the level of aggregate demand in the economy.
(AQA [NEAB] 1998)

Explain what is meant by the price elasticity of supply and what factors are likely to determine the degree to which products and factors of production are price elastic. Discuss how the price elasticity of the supply of land helps to explain why there are tall buildings in city centres and why new shopping centres are often located on the outskirts of cities. *(AQA [NEAB] 1999)*

(a) The opening of the Channel Tunnel has increased supply in the market for cross-Channel trips. With the aid of a diagram, explain how this will affect travellers on cross-Channel trips. (10)
(b) Analyse and comment upon the factors which are likely to determine the revenue of Eurotunnel, the Channel Tunnel operator. (15)
(OCR June 1997)

The estimated price elasticity of demand for peak period air travel between London and Paris is - 0.8, while at off-peak (weekend) times it is - 2.4.
(a) Explain the difference between the two price elasticity of demand estimates. (10)
(b) Comment upon the business significance of these estimates for airlines and for other providers of transport services between London and Paris. (15)
(OCR March 1998)

(a) Explain the difference between price elasticity of demand and cross elasticity of demand. (10)
(b) Discuss how an understanding of these concepts might be useful to a professional football club in deciding the price of tickets for its matches. (15)
(OCR March 1999)

(a) Describe, with examples, the difference between a normal good and an inferior good. (5)
(b) Explain how a knowledge of cross price elasticities of demand can enable one to distinguish between pairs of goods which are complements and pairs of goods which are substitutes. (10)
(c) What factors may lead economists to suspect that a particular good is a Giffen good? (10)
(CCEA 1997)

Exam notes

Demand Specifications require an understanding of demand and its main determinants such as price and income. Individual and market demand curves and how they shift in response to changes in factors other than price are also required. Box 1 gives as an example the demand for mobile phones.
Supply The determinants of supply, such as price and costs, individual and market supply curves and movements along and shifts in curves need to be understood. Box 2 gives the example of the supply of coffee.
Equilibrium price The forces of supply and demand determine the price of a good. Where demand equals supply, there is equilibrium in the market. If demand exceeds supply, there is excess demand and vice versa. Box 3 gives the example of coal.
Elasticity Specifications require an understanding of elasticity of demand and supply. Elasticity of demand includes price elasticity, income elasticity and cross elasticity. Elastic and inelastic demand with reference to price elasticity need to be known. Box 4 gives the example of motor fuel.
Types of demand and supply Candidates are expected to know the difference between different types of demand and supply, such as derived demand and joint demand, and joint supply and competitive supply. The concepts of substitutes and complements are important too, as is the distinction between normal goods and inferior goods.

Price and indirect taxes Indirect taxes lead to a shift in the supply curve to the left, whilst subsidies push it to the right. Changes in indirect taxes therefore lead to changes in equilibrium price. Box 5 illustrates this with the example of the cut in VAT on sanitary protection products.
Price support schemes Governments or agencies can support prices and incomes in a variety of ways. In agriculture, discussed in Box 7, a wide variety of different support schemes is operated by governments across the world.
Cartels Prices can be manipulated by producers through the creation of cartels. Box 6 gives the example of OPEC.

Unit 3
The firm

1 Racecourses: revenues, costs and profits

Racecourses in the UK face a business problem. They are used only a few days a year for horse racing. For instance, Goodward is used only for a maximum 25 days a year for horse racing. How can a racecourse with revenues from these events cover all its costs and at least break even?

A racecourse has large fixed costs. The land itself is often highly valuable and could be sold off at a large price as building land. The racecourse buildings need maintaining and sometimes replacing and upgrading. Some staff need to be paid all the year round. Variable costs are those costs which occur on race days, such as catering costs, temporary staff and prize money. Revenues come from sources such as ticket monies and sales of merchandise.

In recent years, racecourse owners have attempted to solve their profitability problem by diversifying. One popular route has been to hire the facilities out for hospitality purposes. This may be anything from a wedding reception to a business conference to a corporate party. Ascot racecourse, for instance, in 2000 hosted the annual general meeting of the Waitrose retail group, as well as a party for 5 000 employees to celebrate the merger of the Price Waterhouse and Coopers & Lybrand accounting firms.

Another route has been to develop hotel, gym, sports and leisure facilities on site. Relatively little land is used, but income can be generated either through direct ownership of the facilities or through partnerships with other companies.

The most promising route, however, is through betting. Racecourses can sell the rights to televise races. These rights are mainly used by traditional bookmakers but also increasingly by internet betting companies. For instance, a consortium of 12 racecourses signed up to a £225 million, 10 year television deal in 2000.

All these ways of raising revenue help spread the fixed costs of a racecourse across more activities. Each involves higher variable costs. But the marginal revenue from each individual activity should exceed the marginal cost. Hence, each is profitable and helps offset the losses made on traditional horse racing meetings. The most profitable racecourses are the ones which have diversified and offer a range of leisure opportunities to customers.

2 Ikea: economies of scale

In 2000, Ikea announced that it wanted to open 20 new stores in the UK over the next ten years. The expansion would cost £800 million and create 12 000 jobs. Ikea is the world's biggest furniture retailer. In the UK, it has almost 4 per cent of a highly fragmented market, behind MFI and DFS. However, this 4 per cent market share has been achieved from just 10 stores. At weekends, stores are frequently crowded with long queues at checkouts. The volume of business means that there have been severe problems with stock availability and customer service. Despite this, 20 million shoppers visited an Ikea store in 1999. In that year, sales were £585 million and profits before tax were £110 million. Profit margins (profit as a percentage of cost) were 23 per cent, a very high figure for the furniture trade. Almost certainly, Ikea is earning abnormal profit and this explains why it wants to expand.

The success of Ikea is based on two factors. First, products are seen to be cheap for the quality offered. Second, customers like the designs of the goods sold. Expanding the number of stores will almost certainly increase sales for the group. This, Ikea forecasts, will give Ikea UK even greater purchasing power and allow prices to fall by 20 per cent. This is an example of purchasing economies of scale. The larger the quantity produced, the lower the average cost of buying raw materials and other inputs.

Ikea hopes that expansion will reduce the numbers visiting the 10 existing stores. It admits that overcrowding has put off some potential customers from coming and making purchases. The expansion will almost certainly mean that Ikea becomes the largest furniture retailer in the UK.

3 C&A - profits and the market

In 2000, C&A announced that it would be closing all its 109 stores in the UK with a combined turnover of £500 million a year. C&A is a pan-European retailing company which opened its first UK store in 1922. Its problem was that its UK operations had been losing £1 million a week for some time.

These losses were due to poor sales. C&A had failed to find a clear market niche in the competitive world of clothes retailing in the 1980s and 1990s. It was not a value for money chain like New Look or Matalan. It was not a mass market style store like Gap or Top Shop. Nor could it claim a slightly more upmarket position like Next or Marks & Spencer.

Its problems were compounded when a decision was made in 1995 to centralise buying in two continental European locations - Dusseldorf and Brussels. This helped reduce costs across the group through purchasing economies of scale. But C&A did not have sufficient expertise to match the clothes being bought with the demands of the local market. Sales fell as customers failed to buy what was offered. In 2000, C&A reversed its policy and reintroduced local purchasing, but for UK stores it was too late. Senior management judged that C&A could not be turned around in the UK and hence the closure.

This is an example of the market in operation. If a firm cannot make a profit in the long term, it will be forced out of business. C&A was prepared to continue loss making operations in the short term in the hope that sales would increase. But when it became apparent that this was unlikely, closure was the only option.

4 Microsoft - a monopoly?

In 2000, a US federal judge ruled that Microsoft had acted in an anti-competitive way and ordered the break up of the company. Microsoft immediately appealed against the judgment and it could take years for a final judgment to be made by the Supreme Court of the USA.

Microsoft is a monopoly in that 90 per cent of the world's personal computers use Windows as their operating system. The company also has a large share of the operating systems for computer networks with NT, and is attempting to establish dominance over operating systems for small portable devices like mobile phones with internet access. It is one of the world's most profitable companies.

Microsoft is accused of using its market power in operating systems to control all other commercially produced software. For instance, a key part of the evidence used against Microsoft related to Netscape. This company had produced a web browser before Microsoft realised that the internet would be such a powerful computer tool. In the mid-1990s, Microsoft woke up to the danger that the web could cause to its business. So it produced its browser which initially it gave away free and then incorporated as part of its operating system. It did not allow computer manufacturing companies to buy the Windows operating system without the browser despite the fact that the browser was not a fundamental part of the operating system. In so doing, potentially it could have destroyed much of Netscape's market and ensured the continued dominance of its Windows operating system.

The 'war of the browsers' was just one example of Microsoft acting in an anti-competitive way. Another example related to a computer language called Java. This computer language, produced by Sun, a US company, is designed to allow different computer languages to talk to each other. Microsoft was accused of taking Java and subtly altering it so that Microsoft software written in Java could only be read by other Microsoft software, including the Windows operating system. This defeats the whole point of writing in Java, which is that it is an open industry standard.

The Federal Court ordered that Microsoft be split into two: a company owning the various operating systems, including Windows, and another company owning all the other software including Microsoft Office. Before the split took place, the company was ordered to implement a number of 'conduct remedies'. The most important was that Microsoft would have to disclose the 'source code' of its Windows operating system. This would allow rival software companies to develop programs for use with the Windows operating system on the same terms as Microsoft itself. It would strike at the heart of Microsoft's attempt to control all software development by other companies for Windows and ultimately the internet.

From an economic viewpoint, Microsoft is acting as a classic monopolist. It is earning abnormal profits by charging a high price for its products. It has erected high barriers to entry, for instance by controlling access to its source codes. When threatened by new products, it has attempted either to buy them out or to destroy them by producing its own competing products and linking these with other successful products like Windows or Microsoft Office. The fear of companies like Sun is that Microsoft will come to dominate internet software completely in the same way that it dominates PC operating systems today. This would enable it further to increase profitability, secure in the knowledge that competition was minimal.

5 Caravans in Hull - external economies of scale

External economies of scale occur where average costs of production fall as total output in the industry within which a firm operates rises. External economies of scale tend to be found at a local level. One example is the manufacture of caravans. There are no less than 20 firms manufacturing touring and static caravans in the Hull area. Their combined sales, together with local subcontractors, is £350 million a year and they employ 5 000 workers.

Making a caravan requires a great deal of skilled labour, particularly joiners. Being able to draw upon a pool of skilled workers is one example of an external economy of scale. A caravan firm setting up in, say, Cardiff might have problems recruiting the right sort of labour. In Hull, there is a long tradition of working in the manufacture of caravans.

Another external economy comes from being able to work closely with suppliers. For instance, CEC Plug-In Systems is a firm which makes electrical sockets and wiring harnesses. It is located in Hull and sells half its £7 million production to local caravan makers. By being local, it is able to work more closely with Hull caravan makers, ultimately reducing their costs.

At an even more fundamental level, being in a cluster of similar firms allows caravan makers to share information. In theory, caravan makers compete amongst themselves and therefore should not share information. In practice, it is impossible for one caravan maker to make improvements to design, or use new production techniques, without all the other caravan makers hearing about it and being able to respond. Competition encourages firms to innovate, but equally, close proximity means that any innovation is rapidly diffused within the industry.

Caravan makers gain further in marketing. For instance, Hull has an annual caravan show which is the largest in Europe. Buyers throughout Europe come to the show to see what is on offer. Any UK dealer thinking of selling caravans would first turn to Hull.

Being close together, then, gives caravan manufacturing firms a competitive advantage which they can exploit to reduce costs, innovate and sell more caravans.

6 Barriers to entry

In 2000, the European market for vacuum cleaners was worth £1 billion a year. 70 years ago, one firm dominated the market, Hoover. Indeed many still call vacuum cleaners 'hoovers' and we talk about 'hoovering' carpets. But Hoover today only supplies 10 per cent of the European market and is owned by an Italian company, Candy. It has lost market share to Japanese competitors like Panasonic and other European competitors like Electrolux. All these traditional manufacturers have also suffered from the entry of Dyson into the market, which now has a 20 per cent European market share and 50 per cent UK market share.

The vacuum cleaner market is difficult to enter. There are economies of scale in both production and marketing which favour large companies. James Dyson, founder and owner of the Dyson company, invented the Dyson bagless vacuum cleaner which is based on a different way of picking up dirt than conventional vacuum cleaners with bags. Originally, he offered his invention to several manufacturers including Electrolux, Philips and Black and Decker. They would produce his machine in return for a royalty. They rejected it and so James Dyson decided to go it alone. This was a very bold move because of the high financial cost of entering the market (he initially borrowed £600 000) and because other firms had a strong brand image, which in itself was a barrier to entry. However, between 1993 and 2000, the Dyson company enjoyed considerable growth.

Other vacuum cleaner companies responded by producing their own bagless machines. Hoover adopted a design which was very similar to the patented Dyson technology. In 2000, Dyson took Hoover to court and won a ruling that Hoover had infringed the Dyson patent. This is an example of a firm protecting itself from competition and preserving its monopoly on a technology or product. Hoover's argument was that Dyson technology was based upon technology widely known in the industry before 1993.

However, the granting of a patent on a product presumes that a product or process is innovative and allows the holder of the patent the unique ability in law to use that invention for a fixed period of time. A patent is a powerful barrier to entry whose purpose is to encourage investment and innovation. Hoover planned to appeal against the judgment but it also was attempting to bring out a new bagless machine which it hoped would not fall foul of patent law. James Dyson had successfully preserved his monopoly on cyclonic technology and was able to continue using it to generate high profit margins on his machines.

7 The haulage industry - perfect competition?

The UK haulage industry felt itself to be under threat in 2000. Some firms were going out of business, whilst others had laid up lorries. Overall, profits were wafer thin with larger firms working on profit margins (profits divided by total costs) of at most 2-3 per cent.

Many in the industry put the blame on the government. Fuel is a major cost for any haulage firm and taxes on fuel in the UK were significantly higher than in France, Germany, Italy and the Benelux countries. Road tax licences were also high. Then in 2000 oil prices doubled, leading to further rises in fuel prices. The industry argued that if the government cut road taxes, it would be able better to compete with other EU firms and be able to make a profit.

However, economics would suggest that cuts in fuel duty would do little to help the UK haulage industry. This is because the haulage industry is arguably a perfectly competitive industry. Barriers to entry are low. New entrants can set up in business with their own truck for just £80 000, or even cheaper still, they can rent a truck for £250 a day. These low barriers to entry mean that there is a large number of firms in the industry, nearly all of which are small. There are a few large firms, but they do not have significant cost advantages over smaller firms. It could be argued that larger firms are able to brand their services and therefore the product being sold is not homogeneous. This would make the market monopolistically competitive.

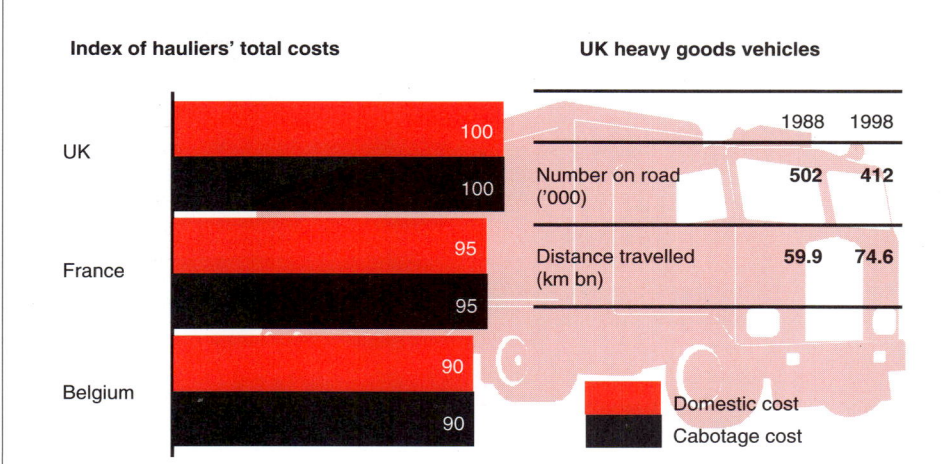

Index of hauliers' total costs

	Domestic cost	Cabotage cost
UK	100	100
France	95	95
Belgium	90	90

UK heavy goods vehicles

	1988	1998
Number on road ('000)	502	412
Distance travelled (km bn)	59.9	74.6

Figure 3.1 *Hauliers' costs and vehicles*
Source: adapted from National Transport Trade Association, BRF.

However, there is fierce price competition and many haulage firms judge that they are price takers; after all, if they were price makers, they could get themselves out of their present problems by raising prices.

Low barriers to entry and positive profits in the past have led to excess capacity in the industry. It is this excess capacity which has led to low prices and low profits or losses. Economic theory would predict that, in the short term, haulage firms will continue in operation so long as they at least cover their variable costs. In the long term, some firms will have to leave the industry. Fewer trucks and fewer firms will reduce supply and thus increase prices.

What about the haulage industry arguments that prices of fuel are too high relative to other EU countries and in absolute terms? First, UK haulage firms don't seem to be at a serious competitive disadvantage to other EU firms. When all costs, including social security taxes on lorry drivers, are taken into account, there is little difference between them. As Figure 3.1 shows, French costs are only 5 per cent lower than those in the UK. More importantly, foreign firms have not rushed into the UK market to exploit cost differences. Only 0.06 per cent of internal UK road haulage by distance travelled is taken by foreign firms (domestic freight carried by foreign firms is called cabotage). If a French firm were to operate in the UK, it too would have to pay the high fuel duties paid by UK hauliers. As for UK firms operating abroad, if a load is taken from London to Milan, the lorry driver can fill up in Calais and Milan with cheaper fuel. British firms pay French petrol taxes when they fill up in France, not English taxes.

Second, if fuel prices were to come down, economic theory would predict that haulage companies would compete amongst themselves and drop their haulage rates. Lower fuel taxes would benefit the customers of haulage firms and not the haulage firms themselves.

In reality, the poor profitability of the industry may not just reflect overcapacity but also be a sign that the industry is changing. In future, with the development of ever more sophisticated logistics systems by large firms like the supermarket chains, it could be that only large haulage firms will be able to survive in much of the market. Only they will have the sophisticated internet links, the capacity and the skills to work closely with large customers. Small haulage firms will see their share of the market reduced, which means in practice that many small firms will have to close down.

UNIT 3 THE FIRM

8 Games consoles

2000 and 2001 will be exciting times in the worldwide games consoles market. The major firms in the industry, Sony, Nintendo and Sega, had launched or were about to launch 128 bit new machines, whilst Microsoft was about to enter the market with its own console. The games console market is oligopolistic, with just three firms in the market in 2000. Barriers to entry are high. The technology in the new generation of machines is complex and requires millions of pounds of investment. It also requires software companies to develop games for these machines. Software companies will not spend money developing games unless there is a mass market for the consoles. Marketing too is a barrier to entry because all the machines are heavily marketed.

Economic theory would suggest that the games consoles firms would avoid price competition in order to maximise profit. In fact, there are two major ways in which the firms compete. First, the companies compete on the technology and capabilities of the machine itself. Sega, for instance, the least successful of the three firms in the late 1990s, gained market share in 1999 and 2000 by being the first to launch a 128 bit machine, Dreamcast. Second, the firms compete on what software is available for each machine. Nintendo, for instance, was able to retain market share against its more popular rival, Sony's Playstation, by having exclusive rights to the Pokemon, Super Mario Brothers and Donkey Kong characters.

As for price competition, companies tend to sell their consoles at roughly the same price as that of their competitors. If one firm lowers its price in a national market, other firms tend to follow. This might suggest that there is no incentive for any firm to ever lower its price. However, pricing tends to be related to the product life cycle. When the new machines were launched in the UK, they were priced at around £300. This is low enough to generate large sales but high enough to enable firms to begin recouping the large fixed costs of launching a new product and to prevent such a large surge of demand that they would be unable to produce enough for the market. By the end of the first year, prices will begin to drop as firms seek to maintain sales. By the time that a new generation of consoles will become shortly available, firms may be selling below the cost of production. They do this because they are able to generate profit from software sales - either directly from their own software or by taking royalties from other software firms which produce software for the machine. In 1999, for instance, half of all revenues for Sony and Nintendo from their Gameboy and Nintendo 64 ranges came from software sales and royalties and only half came from sales of the consoles themselves. So pricing policy on consoles tends to be driven by a view as to what will maximise revenue on both hardware and software.

In the early 1980s, Nintendo was the market leader because of the perceived superiority of the console and its games. In the 1990s, Sony with its Playstation gained market dominance with a new generation of consoles. In 2000, each of the four firms was hoping that it would be the new market leader for the decade with its generation of 128 bit machines. Who will gain market dominance will depend upon customers' votes for the quality of the product on offer rather than on price.

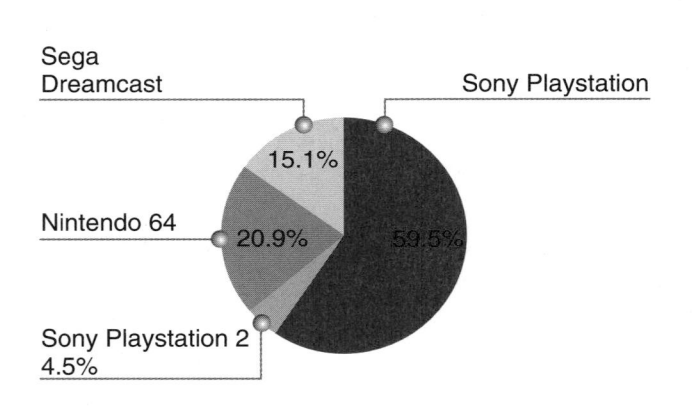

Figure 3.2 *Worldwide game console market share, 2000*
Source: adapted from ING Barings.

- Sega Dreamcast 15.1%
- Sony Playstation 59.5%
- Nintendo 64 20.9%
- Sony Playstation 2 4.5%

Reading list

A.G. Anderton, *Economics*, Causeway Press (3rd ed. 2000) pages 107-118, 304-381.
A.G. Anderton, *Economics AS Level*, Causeway Press (2000) pages 107-118.
J. Beardshaw et al, *Economics: A Student's Guide*, Longman (4th ed. 1998) pages 163-242.
P. Maunder et al, *Economics Explained*, Collins Educational (Revised 3rd ed. 2000) pages 343-418.
C. Bamford, editor, *Economics for AS*, Cambridge University Press (2000) pages 56-72.
D. Begg et al, *Economics*, McGraw Hill (5th ed. 1997) pages 90-160.
R. Stead, 'Profitability and the concentration of industry', *Developments in Economics* Vol 13, Causeway Press (1997).
R. Stead, 'Mergers and acquisitions: an update', *Developments in Economics* Vol 15, Causeway Press (1999).
G. Rhys, 'The motor industry: an economic overview', *Developments in Economics* Vol 15, Causeway Press (1999).
P. Baker, 'Small firms', *Developments in Economics* Vol 16, Causeway Press (2000).

Essay questions

(a) Briefly explain the meaning of the terms 'barriers to entry' and 'barriers to exit'. (30 marks)
(b) How might barriers to entry be expected to affect the way in which markets operate in the real world? Illustrate your answer with relevant examples. (70 marks)
(Edexcel June 1996)

'Soap powder manufacturers operate in an oligopolistic market.'
(a) Explain what is meant by this statement. (20 marks)
(b) What evidence could an economist use to determine the validity of this statement? (20 marks)
(c) How might firms in such a market be expected to compete? (60 marks)
(Edexcel January 1997)

The market for hairdressing in London is monopolistically competitive, the market for soap powder is an oligopoly, and the market for water supply is a monopoly.'
(a) Distinguish the features of these three markets. (40 marks)
(b) Contrast the ways in which suppliers in each of these markets might market their products or services. (60 marks)
(Edexcel June 1997)

(a) Explain what is meant by each of the following:
 (i) price discrimination;
 (ii) non-price competition;
 (iii) marginal cost pricing;
 (iv) limit pricing. (40 marks)
(b) Evaluate the economic implication of one of these price strategies from the points of view of both firms and consumers. (60 marks)
(Edexcel June 1998)

Very few firms have attempted to enter the market for high volume car manufacture, but new entrants into the restaurant market are common.
(a) With reference to these examples, explain why it is more difficult for firms to enter some markets than others. (40 marks)
(b) How might the ease or difficulty of entry affect the marketing strategies and profitability of firms in a market? (60 marks)
(Edexcel January 2000)

Theatres, cross channel ferry operators, the railways and many other businesses charge different prices for supplying very similar, if not identical, services to different groups of consumers.
(a) What are the benefits firms hope to achieve by charging these discriminatory prices? (12 marks)
(b) To what extent do you agree with the view that these policies are against the interest of consumers? (13 marks)
(AQA [AEB] January 1998)

(a) Explain the benefits which are likely to result from an increase in competition between firms in an industry. (12 marks)
(b) The opening of the Channel Tunnel in 1994 resulted in increased competition on the cross-channel route. Discuss the likely impact of the Tunnel upon consumers and the various companies which provide cross-channel services. (13 marks)
(AQA [AEB] June 1998)

Is it necessary or realistic for theories of the firm to assume that firms aim to maximise profits? Discuss whether or not profit maximisation is always in the interests of the individual firm and the national economy.
(AQA [NEAB] 1996)

Explain with examples what is meant by barriers to entry and exit from an industry, and why they are important. In 1990 statistics show that entry and exit of firms was highest in retail and construction and lowest in agriculture and motor manufacturing. Discuss the factors which are likely to have been responsible for this.
(AQA [NEAB] 1997)

(a) Explain, with the aid of a diagram, under what circumstances a loss-making firm might be prepared to continue production in the short run. (10)
(b) Discuss the measures such a firm could take to make normal profits in the long run. (15)
(OCR March 1997)

(a) Explain how large firms can have cost advantages over small firms. (10)
(b) Discuss how small shops are able to compete effectively against large supermarket chains. (15)
(OCR June 1999)

(a) Give a clear definition of the laws of diminishing returns and illustrate this with a suitable example. (5)
(b) Explain how internal economies and diseconomies of scale may influence the shape of a firm's long run average cost curve. (10)
(c) Some economics text books still attribute greater importance to the existence of external economies and diseconomies. Explain why in a modern economy their significance may be much reduced. (10) (CCEA 1998)

Exam notes

Costs and revenues Candidates need to understand different types of costs and how they relate to each other. These include fixed and variable costs (Box 1), short run and long run costs, and marginal, average and total costs. In the short run, firms experience increasing and diminishing returns as their output changes. In the long run, firms experience internal economies and diseconomies of scale (Box 2). They may also enjoy external economies of scale (Box 5). If a firm fails to cover its costs, it may continue trading in the short run, but in the long run it will leave the industry (Box 3).
Perfect competition In perfectly competitive industries (Box 7) there are many firms, none of which is large enough to influence market price. Firms produce homogeneous goods. There is freedom of entry and exit to and from the market. Knowledge is perfect. Firms are price takers and hence the demand curve each firm faces is horizontal. Firms cannot earn abnormal profit in the long run.
Monopolistic competition Only some specifications require an understanding of monopolistic competition. Market conditions are the same as in perfect competition except that firms produce branded (non-homogeneous) goods. The demand curve they face is downward sloping. Customer loyalty, however, is weak and hence individual firms exercise only limited market power. In the long run, firms are unable to earn abnormal profit.
Oligopoly In an oligopoly (Box 8), a few firms dominate output. In the neo-classical model, barriers to entry are high and firms produce branded goods. Market power is such that firms can earn abnormal profit even in the long run.
Monopoly In a monopoly, there is one firm in the market. In a natural monopoly, this is because economies of scale are so large that only one firm can achieve lowest costs. In other types of monopoly, there are other barriers to entry to the market such as legal barriers (Box 6). Monopolies are able to earn abnormal profit because they are free to set a profit maximising price free of competition (Box 4).

Unit 4
The firm and market failure

1 Opel and anti-competitive practices

In September 2000, the European Commission imposed a €43 million (£26.4 million) fine on the Dutch subsidiary of Opel, itself owned by General Motors. Throughout the 1980s and 1990s, the major car companies made it difficult for customers from one country in the EU to buy a car in another country of the EU. This was because they operated a system of price discrimination. The Netherlands was a low price market and hence there was an incentive for French, German and other buyers to purchase their cars in the Netherlands. The European Commission found that Opel Nederland had prevented foreign buyers from buying Opel cars in the Netherlands between September 1996 and January 1998.

The fine was relatively small compared to the €102 million fine imposed on Volkswagen for not allowing foreign buyers, mainly Germans, to buy VW cars in Italy in the mid-1990s.

Car manufacturers are in conflict with EU law because, under common market legislation, any buyer is free to buy goods anywhere in the EU. This is against car manufacturers' interests because they want to price discriminate between national markets in order to maximise profits. Price discrimination only works if the monopolist can prevent customers in a higher price market from buying in a lower price market.

2 Technology and creative destruction

Every major company in the world of ICT (Information and Communications Technology) is looking for the killer application. At present, there is a whole range of devices which provide ICT services. The television provides live entertainment. It can be connected up to a digital box. Video players or DVD players show pre-recorded material. They can also be linked to a games console. There is a variety of audio equipment from CD players to tape decks to amplifiers and speakers. Then there is the PC (personal computer) which can also be used to play games. Equally, it provides internet access. Through the world wide web, information can be called up on the PC. E-mail provides a powerful form of communication which rivals the telephone, the fax and the letter. Mobile phones provide greater flexibility than land line phones and are now coming with WAP technology which connects them to the internet.

The killer application is going to be the device which links most of these together. Already, applications are coming together. For instance, the new generation games consoles have a DVD player and internet connections. Some mobile phones use a slimmed down version of Microsoft Windows, which enables the phone to talk to a computer. Some television sets are being manufactured which have internet capability. There are also very important developments in telecommunications. At the moment, households are linked by narrow band lines to the telephone network. This limits what can be sent down these lines. However, if households were linked with broadband connections, then it would be possible to send, for instance, a film down the line. Broadband connections might make DVD players and video players obsolete. Over the internet, it is already possible to download music which is then recorded on a recordable disk system like MiniDisk.

From an economic viewpoint, there is likely to be one firm which comes to hold a monopoly on one crucial part of the system. At the moment Microsoft, with its Windows operating system, has been the largest winner in ICT developments. It is able to earn large abnormal profits on this and other software products like Microsoft Office. However, it is well aware that it could lose its monopoly power in exactly the same way that IBM, the computer hardware company, saw its monopoly power in the computer market toppled by the coming of the personal computer in the 1970s and 1980s. It is for this reason it has been so aggressive in first developing software to go with its Windows system, then moving into the internet market and attacking the market leader, Netscape, with its own Explorer software, and why it is now moving into the games console market.

This process of creative destruction of well established technologies in the search for the next generation monopoly is an example of dynamic efficiency. Microsoft has defended its monopoly by arguing that it is spending its abnormal profits on developing the software and technologies of tomorrow. Its monopoly on its Windows operating system is therefore to the advantage of customers. Critics argue that it is stifling innovation from other companies through its aggressive tactics.

In 20 years time, there is little doubt that the ICT market will be completely transformed. How it will be transformed and who are the major winners and losers remain to be seen.

UNIT 4 THE FIRM AND MARKET FAILURE

3 Cadbury buys Snapple - a merger

In 2000, Cadbury Schweppes bought the US company, Snapple Beverage. Snapple was founded in 1972 as Unadulterated Food Products. It grew on the back of concerns about unhealthy drinks. Its most famous product, launched in 1978, was Snapple, a carbonated apple drink. In the late 1980s and early 1990s it launched a series of 'new age' drinks, including iced teas and juice-based drinks with names like Mango Madness and Amazin' Grape.

The company was bought in 1994 by Quaker Oats, one of the largest US food producers, for $1.7 billion. At the time, analysts felt that Quaker Oats had overpaid for a company with annual sales of just $700 million. Worse was to come. Quaker planned to market Snapple with its own highly successful Gatorade brand, a sports energy drink. The logic was that Snapple products were mainly sold on the East Coast of the USA and sales could be expanded if it was sold nationwide. The problem was that the two products were sold through different distribution systems. Gatorade was sold mainly through supermarkets and convenience stores. Snapple sold mainly through corner stores and delicatessens. Snapple distributors didn't want to sell Gatorade because it had much lower profit margins. Unable to achieve marketing economies of scale, Quaker launched a disastrous advertising campaign which tried to persuade consumers that being number three in the market behind Coca Cola and Pepsi was good. As Figure 4.1 shows, sales fell between 1995 and 1997.

Quaker Oats finally decided to sell unprofitable Snapple to Triarc, a small US conglomerate, for $300 million. It lost $1.4 billion on the sale. Triarc pulled Snapple round and in 2000 sold it to Cadbury Schweppes for $1.5 billion. Cadbury Schweppes has no plans to integrate Snapple into its other North American operations and will leave management intact.

Snapple provides an example of how mergers and takeovers fail. In theory, a merger or takeover should add value to the combined company. In practice, many fail to do this. One reason is that decisions to merge are made by directors and managers whose rewards may be linked to the size of a company. This gives an inbuilt bias towards expansion. Another problem is that companies often fail to understand the company which they take over. A failure to appreciate the distribution channels used by Snapple, for instance, created difficulties for Quaker Oats. Another problem is the 'herd instinct'. If mergers are taking place in an industry, it is often difficult for management not to join in for fear that they might lose out on a profitable deal.

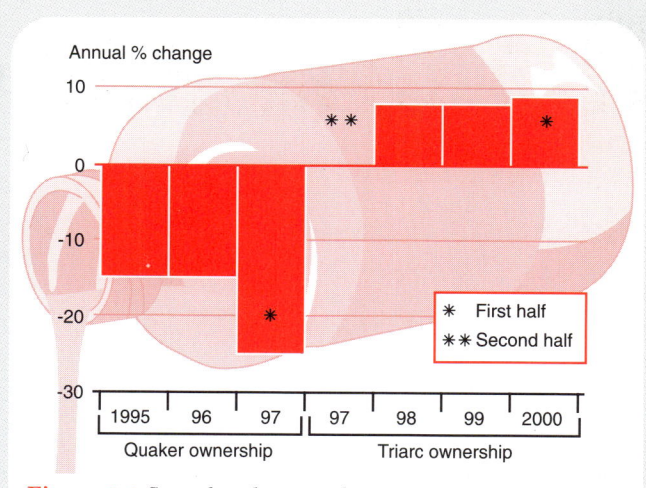

Figure 4.1 *Snapple sales growth*
Source: adapted from company, International Directory of Company Histories.

4 Mobile phone auction

In 2000, the British government auctioned off the rights to next-generation mobile phone licences. There were five licences available. To the surprise of most, the final sum bid totalled £22.5 billion - the equivalent of £375 per person in the UK, or £700 per existing mobile phone subscriber.

Those who favoured the auction method argued that frequency bands are a scarce commodity. An efficient allocation of resources could therefore only be achieved by allowing the market to decide how much it was worth. The £22.5 billion is not 'lost'. It becomes government revenue and will be returned to UK citizens either as lower taxes or as benefits from higher government spending. Moreover, not auctioning the licences would, in all likelihood, have allowed the winning mobile phone companies to earn large abnormal profits. The auction system takes away the monopoly profits from firms, leaving them with just normal profits.

Critics argue that the sums paid for the licences are, in effect, a tax on mobile phones. This tax will have to paid somehow. It could be that mobile phone companies will not have as many resources as before to expand their services. The consequence will be poorer services for customers. There is also a risk that a failure to invest sufficiently in mobile phone technology could put the UK at a competitive disadvantage with countries which have instead opted for a 'beauty contest' approach. This is where mobile phone licences are not awarded to the highest cash bidder but to the companies which promise the most investment and the highest quality service. France has adopted this approach. The other alternative is that the companies will pass on the licence fees in the form of higher charges. Higher prices will reduce the size of the mobile phone market below its optimum level.

The UK and Germany auctioned their mobile phone licences. France awarded them at a fraction of the price in a beauty contest. Over the next 10 years, it will be possible to see which system has produced the highest welfare outcome.

THE STUDENT'S ECONOMY IN FOCUS 2000/01

5 UK car pricing

In April 2000, a long awaited Competition Commission report found that car makers were operating a complex monopoly in the UK and were distorting prices to their own benefit. Car manufacturers, under an EU 'block exemption' to normal competition law, are allowed to sell their cars through an exclusive franchise dealer network. So a Ford dealer, for instance, cannot also sell new Vauxhall cars. The car manufacturers are then able strongly to influence the price at which their dealers sell cars. At worst, a car dealer which consistently goes against a car manufacturer's pricing policies can lose its dealership.

The Competition Commission found that UK new car prices over the previous five years had been 10-12 per cent higher than in similar EU markets. Figure 4.2 shows how prices varied from model to model. Private car buyers were paying about £1 100 too much for the average car, after taking account of discounts, trade-in and finance deals, according to the Commission. Fleet buyers, such are car leasing companies, or companies which buy large numbers of cars each year, or rental companies, on the other hand, were given large discounts of up to 30 per cent of the list price.

The Competition Commission made a number of recommendations which the government endorsed. First, manufacturers can no longer prevent dealers from advertising low prices for new cars. Nor can they refuse to sell to a dealer which is offering low prices. This means they can't pressurise a dealer into selling cars at a higher price to prevent competition.

Second, manufacturers can no longer impose sales targets on dealers and offer incentives based on the numbers of cars a dealer registers in a certain period.

Third, dealers must be given the same terms, including bulk discounts, as fleet buyers. So a dealer who buys 300 cars must be given the same price by the manufacturer as a fleet buyer purchasing 300 cars. Car manufacturers in the UK have traditionally given fleet customers very large discounts, which is one of the reasons why nearly half of all new cars bought are fleet cars. Dealers selling to private customers have not managed to get these discounts, pushing up the final price of the car. The Competition Commission also said that car manufacturers must make available to everyone details of bulk purchase discounts so that pricing is transparent and not secret.

Finally, manufacturers must publish regular figures on the numbers of cars they have pre-registered. This is because in the past, manufacturers have registered some cars (i.e. bought a licence for the car which then fixes its date of sale as new) without having any buyer for them. They do this to increase advertised sales numbers and to be able to claim that a particular model is, say, the third best selling car in the UK in that month. These pre-registered cars are then sold off through the second hand market at a large discount to prices of new cars.

There is little doubt the UK government would have liked to have abolished the exclusive relationship between dealer and manufacturer which is at the heart of the EU block exemption. But this is coming up for renewal in 2002 and there is a reasonable chance that car manufacturers will become subject to normal competition rules. This raises the prospect of, say, supermarkets selling a range of cars from different manufacturers. Supermarkets would be likely to have the buying power to extract large discounts from manufacturers, which they would pass on to consumers in low prices.

The effect of the Competition Commission enquiry was to depress new and used car prices in the UK. Despite companies saying that they would not lower their prices, many began cutting official prices after publication of the report. In October 2000, for instance, Ford cut its list prices by between 5 and 13 per cent. It claimed that the prices consumers would actually pay would remain the same because it also withdrew various incentive schemes. However, it was seen as a sign that prices would fall and that some of the abnormal profit made by manufacturers in the UK would disappear.

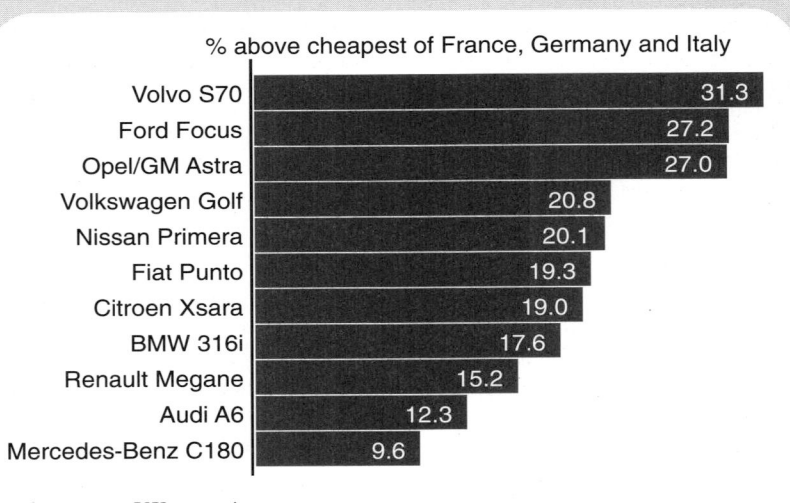

% above cheapest of France, Germany and Italy

Model	%
Volvo S70	31.3
Ford Focus	27.2
Opel/GM Astra	27.0
Volkswagen Golf	20.8
Nissan Primera	20.1
Fiat Punto	19.3
Citroen Xsara	19.0
BMW 316i	17.6
Renault Megane	15.2
Audi A6	12.3
Mercedes-Benz C180	9.6

Figure 4.2 *UK car prices*
Source: adapted from European Commission, Bank of England.

6 BT and the local loop

In the 1980s and 1990s, the UK telecommunications market was slowly opened up to competition. In 2000, the next stage was to break BT's monopoly on the 'local loop', the wires which connect homes and businesses to national and international networks. By July 2001, British Telecom had to have 'unbundled' the local loop, allowing rival companies to use BT local lines. Competing companies could then lease lines from BT in the same way that train operating companies pay a fee to Railtrack for use of the rail network.

Rival companies could just use their new powers to undercut BT on telephone calls. However, this is not the main attraction of unbundling. The most profitable use is likely to be providing new broadband services. By installing DSL (Digital Subscriber Line) equipment at both ends of the local loop, they can offer high speed internet access. Possibly even more important in the short term is that they will be able to offer television pictures over telephone wires. At one end of the loop is the household or business. It will need to install DSL equipment to receive the new facilities. At the other end of the loop is the local telephone exchange.

The deadline of July 2001 is unlikely to be met for two reasons. First, BT is claiming that in most local telephone exchange buildings there is simply not room to put all the equipment needed by all the firms which want to offer the new services. New buildings may be needed, but these will require years to put up. The most crowded telephone exchanges, according to BT, tend to be in city areas. These are just the ones which rival companies most want to target and where it is likely to be most difficult to expand buildings. Second, the Oftel regulator who has set the July 2001 deadline decided that BT and its rivals should sort out between themselves who will get their equipment installed when and where. BT's rivals have complained that BT has failed to agree on anything in negotiations. They point out that it is in BT's interests to delay the opening of the loop for as long as possible.

In September 2000, the regulator stepped in after he was criticised for having been 'captured' by BT. He allocated particular exchanges to companies. However, BT still maintained that it would not be possible to install equipment in many of its most popular exchanges.

The issue shows the importance of strong regulation if dynamic efficiency in the market is to be ensured. It is not in BT's interests to encourage any competition. Given this, many feel that the regulator should have adopted a much stronger stance from the start to break up this monopoly.

7 The crisis at Rover

In an efficient market system, firms producing loss making products in the long term go out of business. Consumer sovereignty, where consumers have the power to choose what they want to buy, leads to an optimal allocation of resources.

However, the process of closure can be very painful as the example of Rover cars illustrates. Rover has a long and troubled history going back to the 1960s when it was formed from a merger of several UK car manufacturing firms. Its UK market share has steadily declined. At the start of 2000, it was only 4 per cent. Rover had been bought by the German company BMW in 1994 from British Aerospace. BMW hoped to use Rover as a new upmarket brand to expand its range of cars. In the late 1990s, it spent £1 billion investing in new plant and new models. However, in early 2000 it decided that however much was invested in Rover, the company could not be turned around. It decided to either sell or close down those parts of Rover that it no longer wanted.

The main problem was the Longbridge plant in Birmingham which was outdated and needed large amounts of new investment. BMW decided to keep the Cowley works in Oxford and launch the new Mini from there. Land Rover, the part of Rover with the best long term future, was sold to Ford for £1.8 billion. BMW didn't want the Rover 25, 45 and new 75 models. Initially, it was in negotiation with a venture capital firm, Alchemy Partners, to acquire Longbridge. Alchemy stated that it saw no future for Rover as a mass manufacturer of cars. Instead, it would concentrate on developing a range of niche upmarket cars branded under the MG badge. There was considerable opposition from Longbridge workers and the government gave little support to the plan.

Negotiations between Alchemy and BMW broke down, leaving the way open for the Phoenix consortium, a group of Midland business people and Rover car dealers, to buy Rover and the Longbridge plant. It paid £10 cash, but received large stocks of unsold Rover cars, the Longbridge site and a £500 million loan repayable in 50 years time or if Rover cars is sold again. In effect, BMW paid Phoenix £500 million to take Rover off its hands.

Phoenix promised to remain a mass manufacturer of cars. However, it faces the same problems that Rover faced unsuccessfully in the past 30 years - how to produce a range of cars which consumers want to buy enough to ensure Rover makes a long term profit. Some believe that it would have been better to let Rover disappear. Resources used by Rover could more efficiently be used elsewhere in the economy. In the short term, though, Birmingham and UK car component manufacturers would have been badly affected.

8 Diamonds and cartels

In 2000, De Beers, the worlds largest diamond producer, announced that it was abandoning the diamond cartel arrangement which it had run since the 1930s. The cartel was a response to market conditions in the 1930s, when diamonds flooded the market and prices collapsed. De Beers, to maintain high prices, set up the London-based central selling organisation (CSO). The company then persuaded all the major diamond producers to sell their diamonds to the CSO, which then sold on the diamonds to gem merchants. To maintain high prices, the CSO had to match supply and demand at the price at which it wanted to sell. When demand was relatively low, as in 1998 (see Figure 4.3), the CSO had to cut supply. In the short term, it did this by stockpiling unsold diamonds. In the slightly longer term, problems of excess supply were solved by persuading diamond producers to cut production.

The decision to abandon the cartel was taken because De Beers found it increasingly difficult to maintain high prices and make a profit in the 1990s. The decade started with the collapse of the Soviet Union and a flood of gems from that area. Then civil wars in Africa, particularly in Angola, led to a further uncontrolled supply onto the market. In 1996, the Argyle mine in Australia, the largest diamond mine by output producing low quality diamonds, announced that it would no longer be selling through the CSO. Then in 1997 and 1998, demand for diamonds fell with the Asian crisis and Japan's continued recession. As a consequence, the CSO's diamond stocks rose from $2.5 billion in 1989 to $5 billion by 1997-98, equivalent to a year's worth of CSO sales.

De Beers was also under threat from competition authorities in the USA and the EU for operating a cartel. De Beers was unable to sell directly to the USA because it has already been investigated for anti-competitive (anti trust) practices. CSO diamond sales to the USA had to go through third parties. De Beers was also fearful that it could be investigated by the EU competition authorities.

So it took the decision to break up the cartel. The CSO would be renamed the Diamond Trading Company (DTC) and it would continue to sell diamonds produced by mines other than those owned by De Beers where it was profitable to do so. De Beers, with 40-50 per cent of world production, would still dominate the market. However, it would not attempt to control world prices in the way that it has done in the past. It also intended to alter its relationship with its customers, the 125 clients who were allowed to buy from the CSO. In future, they will have to agree to pay for some of the marketing costs of diamonds including advertisements carrying the 'A diamond is for ever' slogan. De Beers wants to use marketing to increase demand for diamonds which would help offset price reductions arising from the collapse of the cartel.

Are the decisions in the best interests of consumers? On the one hand, if diamond prices fall, consumers could be argued to be better off. On the other hand, consumers have come to expect diamonds to retain their value over time. A collapse in prices would reduce consumer confidence in diamonds and could lead to them abandoning purchases of diamonds. Because diamonds have an expected value, they have some of the properties of money. A collapse in diamond prices would be like a collapse in the value of money. It isn't immediately obvious that this is in consumers' interests.

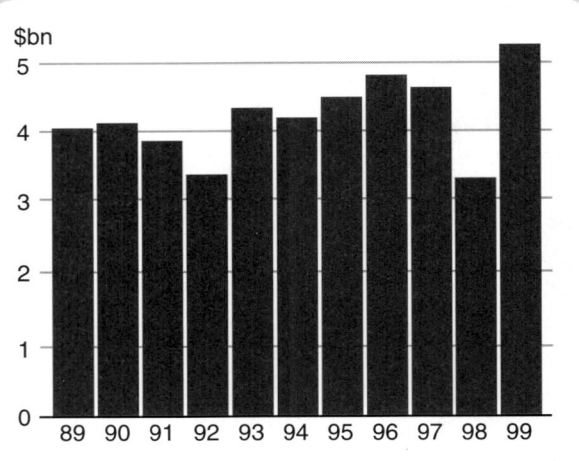

Figure 4.3 *Central selling agency, sales of rough cut diamonds*
Source: adapted from De Beers.

Reading list

A.G. Anderton, *Economics*, Causeway Press (3rd ed. 2000) pages 107-118, 405-441.
A.G. Anderton, *Economics AS Level*, Causeway Press (2000) pages 107-118.
J. Beardshaw et al, *Economics: A Student's Guide*, Longman (4th ed. 1998) pages 208-210, 227-237, 334-351.
P. Maunder et al, *Economics Explained*, Collins Educational (Revised 3rd ed. 2000) pages 453-470.
D. Begg et al, *Economics*, McGraw Hill (5th ed. 1997) pages 240-257, 275-304.
P. Curwen et al, *Understanding the UK Economy*, Macmillan (4th ed. 1997) pages 477-502.
C. Bamford, editor, *Economics for AS*, Cambridge University Press (2000) pages 106-107.
S. Munday, *Markets and Market failure*, Heinemann Educational (2000).
M. Wilkinson, *Equity, Efficiency and Market Failure*, Heinemann Educational (2nd ed. 1997).
D. Parker, 'Regulating the UK's privatised monopolies: theory and practice', *Developments in Economics* Vol 12, Causeway Press (1996).
P. Maunder, 'Competition policy in the UK and EU', *Developments in Economics* Vol 14, Causeway Press (1998).
P. Maunder, 'The regulation of privatised utilities', *Developments in Economics* Vol 15, Causeway Press (1999).

Essay questions

(a) Explain the role of profit in a market economy. (60 marks)
(b) Examine the case for government restrictions on the profits made by privatised firms. (40 marks)
(Edexcel January 1996)

(a) Explain why each of the following is considered to be the result of market failure:
(i) unemployment amongst coal miners in South Wales;
(ii) depletion of fish stocks. (40 marks)
(b) Examine government policies which could be used to rectify each of these examples of market failure. (60 marks)
(Edexcel June 1997)

In September 1995 publishing firms abandoned the Net Book Agreement (NBA) which fixed minimum prices for most books sold in the UK.
Analyse the likely economic effects of the collapse of the NBA for:
(a) the publishing industry; (30 marks)
(b) the retail book trade; (30 marks)
(c) the book buying public. (40 marks)
(Edexcel January 1998)

(a) Explain, and illustrate with examples, the nature of competition in oligopolistic markets. (12 marks)
(b) Discuss the extent to which such competition is in the interest of consumers. (13 marks)
(AQA [AEB] January 1997)

(a) Distinguish carefully between static efficiency and dynamic efficiency. (12 marks)
(b) Discuss the importance of these concepts when the Monopolies and Mergers Commission is carrying out an investigation into the conduct and performance of a dominant firm. (13 marks)
(AQA [AEB] June 1997)

(a) Explain how the regulators (e.g. OFWAT and OFTEL) in the United Kingdom have attempted to prevent the privatised utilities from abusing their monopoly power. (12 marks)
(b) Using examples to support your arguments, assess the strengths and weaknesses of the United Kingdom's approach to regulating privatised industries. (13 marks)
(AQA [AEB] June 1998)

(a) Explain how a firm operating in an oligopolistic market can attempt to increase its market power. (12 marks)
(b) Discuss the various factors the Government is likely to take into account when attempting to assess whether or not a large dominant firm is operating in the public interest. (13 marks)
(AQA [AEB] June 1999)

Explain the relationship between economic efficiency and consumer welfare. Discuss whether, in your view, the deregulation of rail services is likely to have increased or reduced economic welfare.
(AQA [NEAB] 1998)

Explain why monopoly is regarded as undesirable whereas price competition among firms is desirable. Discuss the implications for the UK economy of the increase in the number and influence of global corporations with interests in several markets.
(AQA [NEAB] 1999)

(a) Using examples, explain the difference between internal and external economies of scale. Show how they affect the long-run average costs of a firm. (13)
(b) If there are large benefits from economies of scale why is there so much concern about the existence of monopolies? (12)
(OCR June 1996)

'In 1997, the global telecommunications market was worth about $600 billion yet only about 20% of the market was open to competition. More competition would certainly be expected to lead to an improvement in economic efficiency.' (Adapted from the Financial Times, 14 February 1997.)
(a) Explain the meaning of the term 'economic efficiency'. (10)
(b) Discuss the extent to which more competition always leads to 'an improvement in economic efficiency'. (15)
(OCR June 1998)

(a) With the aid of a diagram, explain how a monopolist might decide on what price to charge for its product. (10)
(b) The price of an official replica football shirt of a top Premier League side increased to £60.00 in 1998, while the production costs were less than £20.00. Discuss the economic argument that the government should intervene to fix a maximum price for Premier League football shirts. (15)
(OCR November 1999)

(a) Outline the main assumptions of the model of perfect competition. (5)
(b) Explain how the short run supply curve of a perfectly competitive industry is derived. (10)
(c) Economists often claim that perfectly competitive industries are more likely to be economically efficient in the long run than other types of industries. Examine the validity of this claim. (10)
(CCEA 1999)

Exam notes

Efficiency Specifications require candidates to be able to define efficiency. They usually specify that candidates know the difference between productive and allocative efficiency, and between static and dynamic efficiency. How markets lead to efficiency is a frequently asked question. Box 7 gives an example of what happens when consumers no longer wish to buy a product in sufficient quantities.

Competition In Economics, there is a presumption that competition leads to economic efficiency, whilst a lack of competition signifies inefficiency. For instance, in the new car market (Box 5), many today are arguing that greater competition would lead to lower prices for the UK consumer. Competition, though, should lead not just to lowest prices but also to greater choice and innovation.

Monopoly Monopoly is considered to lead to inefficiency because profit maximising monopolists raise prices and lower output to customers. However, there may be dynamic efficiency benefits to monopoly such as greater innovation (Box 2) or greater choice. Monopoly profits may also be removed through taxation or licensing (Box 4).

Mergers Specifications usually require candidates to understand the different types of merger and takeover that take place and why they occur. Some economists argue that many mergers fail to lead to greater inefficiency and often lead to a loss of total welfare. Box 3 gives an example.

Anti-competitive practices Specifications require a knowledge of various forms of anti-competitive practices and their implications for economic efficiency. For instance, producers can combine together to restrict output to the market (Boxes 1 and 8). Or firms may price discriminate between markets in an illegal manner (Box 1). Or firms may attempt to keep out competition (Box 6).

Privatised utilities Many privatised utilities are monopolies or are dominant in their market. Specifications expect candidates to have an understanding of the regulatory regimes governing the privatised utilities. Box 6, for instance, gives an example where many feel that the regulatory regime has failed.

Unit 5
Transport and the environment

1 The Kyoto Protocol

In 2000, government representatives met in The Hague in the Netherlands to discuss issues related to the Kyoto Protocol. This was an agreement in 1997 to cut emissions of greenhouse gases. One of the schemes put forward was the Clean Development Mechanism (CDM). This is based on the idea of pollution permits. A rich industrialised country would agree to cut its emissions by, say, 10 per cent. With CDM, it could do this by subsidising energy schemes in the Third World which then lowered greenhouse gas emissions by the equivalent of the 10 per cent. Alternatively, a government of an industrialised country could issue permits to its major greenhouse gas emitters. Permits would restrict emissions to 90 per cent of their former level. Firms would then have two choices. Either they could spend money reducing their emissions directly or they could subsidise Third World energy projects which produced the required fall.

Advocates of the scheme claim two main benefits. First, it will be cheaper to save greenhouse gas emissions in new developments in the Third World than change existing production methods in the First World. The World Bank estimates that it will cost between $5 and $15 a tonne in the Third World but $50 a tonne in the First World. So the First World could save between $35 and $45 a tonne in costs by choosing to reduce greenhouse gas emissions in the Third World. Second, the Third World will benefit from a transfer of technology and is likely to be paid at least some of the savings made by the First World.

Critics worry about how the scheme can be implemented. For instance, how can you be sure that the scheme in the Third World would not have gone ahead anyway if the First World had not given it a subsidy? Will nuclear power and wood-burning projects be included? How can the First World ensure that a few Third World countries which are very good at putting in bids for funds don't obtain all the subsidies? Will the scheme favour richer Third World countries which have a more sophisticated bureaucracy to make claims under the scheme? Will the scheme operate through governments alone, or will it take place as an exchange between a First World firm and a Third World firm?

There are many practical difficulties to implementing CDM. However, pollution control is increasingly likely to be achieved through variations of the tradable permits model because they are capable of reducing the cost of pollution control. With emissions per person highest in the developed world, as Figure 5.1 shows, but emissions growing fastest in the developing world, CDM in theory offers an efficient way of reducing world growth in emissions.

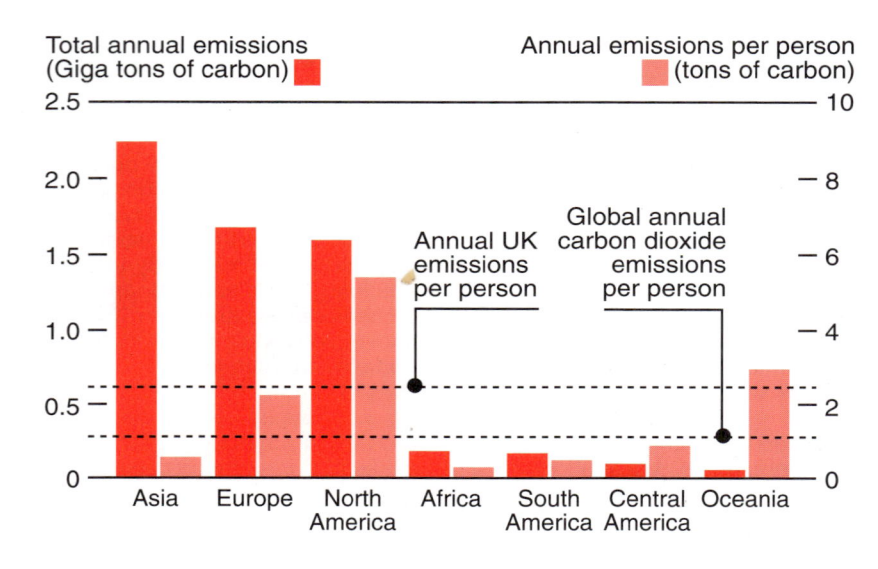

Figure 5.1 *Carbon dioxide emissions from fossil fuels by continent, 1995*
Source: adapted from Royal Commission on Environmental Pollution.

2 Regulations and sulphur emissions

Controlling pollution externalities often gives rise to difficult choices. A good example of this was the controversy concerning the Drax coal-fired power station in Yorkshire in 2000 reported in the press. Emissions from power stations are controlled through regulations in the UK. Each power station is given a maximum level of emissions which it cannot exceed without being fined.

In the 1990s, Drax had been subject to a 100 000 tonne a year sulphur dioxide limit. Sulphur dioxide emissions cause acid rain, where the sulphur dioxide comes down again in very weak acid form with rain. It can then kill trees and forests and damage buildings. Drax was owned by National Power, but in 2000 it was sold to a US-owned group, AES Drax. Shortly before the sale, the Environment Agency responsible for setting regulatory limits on emissions cut the sulphur dioxide limit for Drax to 40 000 tonnes a year.

In June 2000, AES Drax signed an agreement with RJB Mining, the UK's largest coal producer, to supply Drax with 25.5 million tonnes of coal from the nearby Selby colliery over the next 5 years. However, the coal from the Selby colliery contained enough sulphur dioxide to force AES Drax to run the power station at only 70 per cent capacity. It was suggested that the company would have liked to have run it at 90 per cent capacity. However, to do that it would have required a 60 000 tonne a year limit on sulphur dioxide emissions.

The reason why AES Drax was prepared to buy the Selby coal was that the coal was subsidised by the UK government. To preserve jobs in the UK mining industry, the government had given a £100 million support package. However, in 2005, when the contract runs out, AES Drax warned that it would use lower sulphur coal from abroad unless the 40 000 tonne sulphur dioxide limit was raised to 60 000 tonnes. This would lead to exactly the sort of job losses in mining that the government wanted to avoid.

One irony in the situation was that Drax is one of two coal-fired power stations in the UK to be fitted with a 'scrubber', technology which reduces sulphur dioxide emissions. Another irony is that Ratcliffe on Trent in Nottinghamshire, the other UK plant fitted with a scrubber, is half the size of Drax but already has a 60 000 tonne a year sulphur dioxide limit.

This shows some of the problems with controlling emissions through regulation. The limits given to different power stations are too arbitrary and not related to output of electricity and there is no market mechanism through which different power stations can trade pollution allowances to minimise the cost amongst themselves.

Moreover, measures to control pollution often have to be offset against other policy goals. In this case, employment in the coal industry has been judged more important than reductions in emissions because Drax could have used low sulphur imported coal. What is more, Drax might not be operating at all if it weren't for coal subsidies and government imposed limits on the building of new, low emission high efficiency, gas fired power stations.

3 Polluter pays principle for goods in EU

In 2000, the EU announced its long awaited decision about scrap cars. From 2007, car manufacturing companies will have an obligation to take back, free of charge, any car which it has manufactured in the past. Car companies will also have to recycle 80 per cent of car weight by 2006, rising to 85 per cent by 2015. Costs are estimated to run into billions of pounds per year. This would have to be born by car manufacturers unless a government within the EU subsidises the take back of cars within its national boundaries. Car manufacturers say that they will have to pass on the cost to motorists in the form of higher prices for new cars.

In the same year, the EU announced proposals to apply the same principles to electrical products. Manufacturers would be forced to accept back discarded appliances, ranging from toasters to refrigerators to computers to electric trains. The EU is also seeking bans on the use of heavy metals such as lead and mercury in electrical appliances. In 1998, 6 million tonnes of waste electrical and electronic equipment were generated in the EU, representing 4 per cent of municipal waste.

Both of these illustrate the principle of 'polluter pays' which is laid down in the European Union treaty. In economic theory, forcing a firm or household to bear the cost of pollution they create is an example of internalising an externality, i.e. eliminating an externality because it now becomes a private cost to the economic agent that has created it.

Economic theory also suggests that the cost is likely to be born by both the consumer and the producer. Making a car manufacturer bear increased costs is like imposing an indirect tax on a product. The supply curve will shift to the left as a result. How much the producer can pass on of the extra cost in higher prices depends upon the relative elasticities of demand and supply for the good. For instance, if demand is perfectly elastic, the producer will be forced to bear all the cost itself. So manufacturers may not be able to pass on all of the increased costs of recycling to the consumer in higher prices.

UNIT 5 TRANSPORT AND THE ENVIRONMENT

4 River pollution

According to the Environment Agency, 92 per cent of UK rivers and canals were good enough to support fish life in 1999. This was a large improvement on 1990, the year after water privatisation, when 85 per cent of the 25 000 miles of rivers and canals were classified in the top two categories of 'good' and 'fair'. It was an even greater improvement on a century ago when many rivers and canals were heavily polluted due to the discharge of untreated materials straight into the water.

There are two reasons why river pollution has fallen. One is the disappearance of most of the primary and manufacturing industries which caused the pollution. Deindustrialisation in the UK, although it has proved a painful process with millions losing their jobs, has led to a cleaner Britain. The second has been the very heavy investment since privatisation by the water companies to reduce discharges into rivers and canals and into the sea. The investment has been necessary for the UK to comply with strict EU regulations. However, it has also come at a very heavy price because water bills for households and firms have doubled since 1990. A further £15 billion, or £250 per person in the UK, is set to be invested in improvements over the period 2000-2005.

Some have argued that the money has been poorly spent. This is because there has been no account taken of marginal social benefit when allocating investment. Much investment has been taken on the basis of EU regulations which set what might be argued to be arbitrary standards. For instance, improving the water quality of the Aire and Calder rivers in Yorkshire has cost £60 million. Both rivers were heavily polluted in the 19th century and early 20th century by traditional industries such as textiles. From an economic viewpoint, the investment should have gone ahead if the social benefit equalled or exceeded £60 million. However, no attempt was made to quantify the social benefit. Instead, the decision about how much to invest was made on the least cost way of upgrading the rivers to reach the required EU standard. So we don't know whether the social benefit exceeded the social cost and therefore we cannot judge whether households received value for money from their increased water bills.

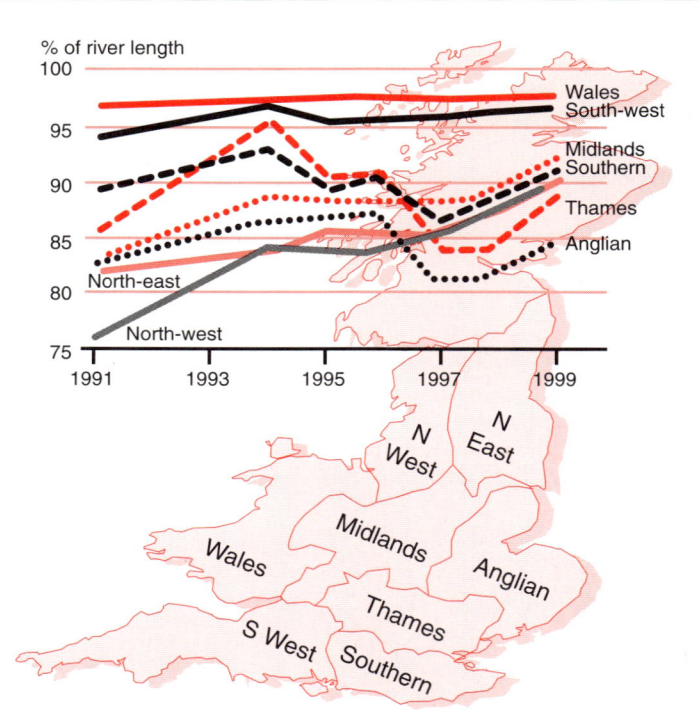

Figure 5.2 *Rivers and canals of good or fair quality in England and Wales*
Source: adapted from The Environmental Agency.

5 Incinerators

Land fill as a method of getting rid of waste is currently unfashionable. It is said to create too many externalities. Scarce land, often in rural areas, is taken up. It creates a nuisance to those living next to the site. Rubbish may have to be transported long distances creating noise and atmospheric pollution. Sites may have problems with emissions of methane gas.

For many years, incineration of waste was seen as a more environmentally friendly solution. Incinerators could be built in centres of population, reducing the distance rubbish had to be transported. There was no need for site after site to be taken up for rubbish disposal, unlike landfill. The incinerator could also generate electricity, reducing the externalities created by conventional electricity generation plants.

However, there has been growing concern about incineration in recent years. First, those living around the incinerator plant suffer noise and other pollution from lorries in the same way that those living around a landfill site suffer. Second, and more importantly, there is now evidence that incinerators may emit dioxins. These are very small particles which are known to be carcinogenic. In 2000, the US Environmental Protection Agency issued a report which suggested that up to 10 per cent of cancers were caused by dioxins. Third, there is a problem about disposal of ash which may be heavily polluted. In 2000, Newcastle-upon-Tyne council workers spent six weeks removing ash which had been used to make paths on an allotment in the city. The ash contained high levels of dioxins as well as heavy metals such as lead, zinc and cadmium.

There is a need to make decisions about disposal because the UK must now conform to European Union regulations which limit the amount of waste that can be deposited in landfill sites. The UK must cut the use of landfill from 85 per cent today to 35 per cent by 2016. Going for an incineration alternative would involve the construction, according to Green groups, of up to 165 incinerators in urban areas across the UK, at a cost of up to £2.8 billion in construction. The government says that it would take 'scores' rather than hundreds. Even so, there is likely to be strong opposition to the building of any incinerators today.

Another alternative is recycling and composting. Scotland has the worst record in Europe on recycling. In the UK, the Isle of Wight has the best record, recycling 41 per cent of household waste. This compares to the best European country, Switzerland, which recycles 52 per cent of household rubbish. Recycling, whilst environmentally friendly, is a very expensive solution. Households have to spend much more time sorting their rubbish and taking it to dumps. Alternatively, council refuse collectors may collect different types of rubbish but the more the rubbish is sorted, the higher the cost of collection.

There is no easy solution to waste disposal. Any changes to current large scale use of landfill are likely to impose higher costs on households. It could then be argued that this will reduce the externalities created by households when disposing of waste. On the other hand, there are some who question whether, in the UK at least, landfill is such a high social cost option as critics claim. A careful consideration of the social costs and benefits is needed to settle this debate.

6 Car use in the UK

The UK, as Figure 5.3 shows, has a poor record on car use from an environmental perspective. 88 per cent of passenger miles travelled are made by car in the UK, compared to an EU average of 82 per cent and 81 per cent for Germany. Italy, with the highest car ownership per head of the population in Europe, has a 76 per cent level of car use. Correspondingly, the UK has a low level of public transport use compared to the EU. Only 11 per cent of journey miles are made by public transport in the UK compared to 15 per cent in the EU.

There is general acceptance that road traffic creates considerable externalities in the form of greenhouse gas emissions, noise pollution and congestion. However, the car has considerable benefits over other modes of transport. In particular, it provides door to door transport and privacy to the traveller. Marginal cost of use is also relatively low because petrol or diesel only accounts for 25 per cent of the cost of running the average car. In contrast, rail and bus users have to pay the full average cost of the journey (less any government subsidy) every time they make a journey.

Improving public transport is unlikely to stem continually growing car use. However, a combination of improved public transport with increased car taxes could reduce this growth in the future.

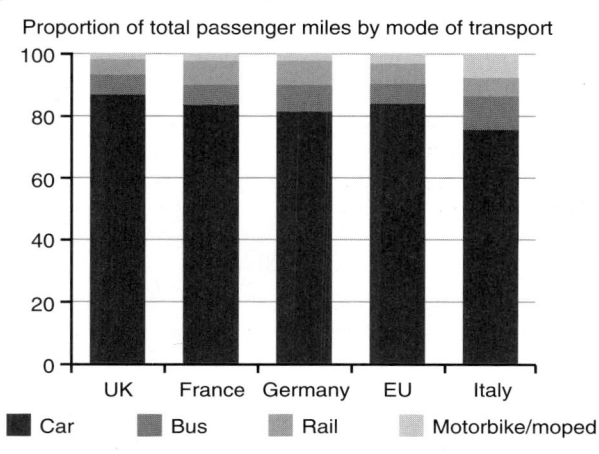

Figure 5.3 *Proportion of total passenger miles by mode of transport*
Source: adapted from Commission for Integrated Transport.

UNIT 5 TRANSPORT AND THE ENVIRONMENT

7 Bus transport

Bus services are as important as rail in the number of passenger kilometres travelled. However, for every one passenger journey by train there are five by bus because bus journeys tend to be much shorter than rail journeys. John Prescott, Minister for Transport, wants buses to be the 'thoroughbred' of public transport. However, bus use outside London is in decline as Figure 5.4 shows whilst the number of kilometres travelled by buses has remained relatively static since the mid-1990s as Figure 5.5 shows.

There is a number of reasons for this. One is the steep rise in fares shown in Figure 5.6. Although the cost of motor transport rose by roughly the same amount over the same period, the retail price index (average prices) only rose 60 per cent. So the cost of transport in general rose nearly twice that of average prices.

Second, incomes rose over the period. Bus travel is arguably an inferior good. As incomes rise, households tend to either buy cars or travel more with the cars they own. So the demand for bus transport is likely to fall over time.

A third problem with buses is the quality of transport offered. There has been heavy investment in new buses by large companies such as Stagecoach and Arriva averaging £500 million a year. However, buses are all too often unreliable in their timing. This is not helped in rush hour traffic by congestion from rising numbers of motor cars and a lack of bus lanes. In the late 1990s, the bus companies were hit by severe shortages of staff, particularly in London, caused by the tightening of the labour market after a prolonged period of growth and falling unemployment.

At the moment, heavy users of buses tend to be those without access to a car - children, the elderly and those on low incomes. If buses are to break out of this limited market, the government will have to make it far more difficult for households to use their cars. Measures such as tolls to enter city centres (see Box 8) or reducing the amount of road space for cars by creating more dedicated bus lanes could see higher income earners taking to the buses.

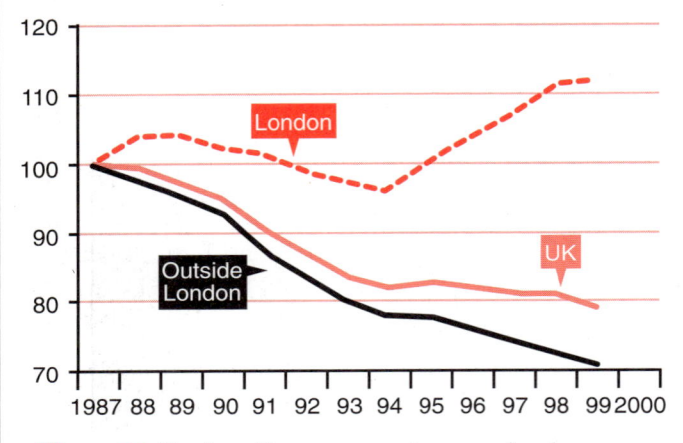

Figure 5.4 *Number of bus passenger journeys, fiscal year 1987-88 = 100*
Source: adapted from DETR.

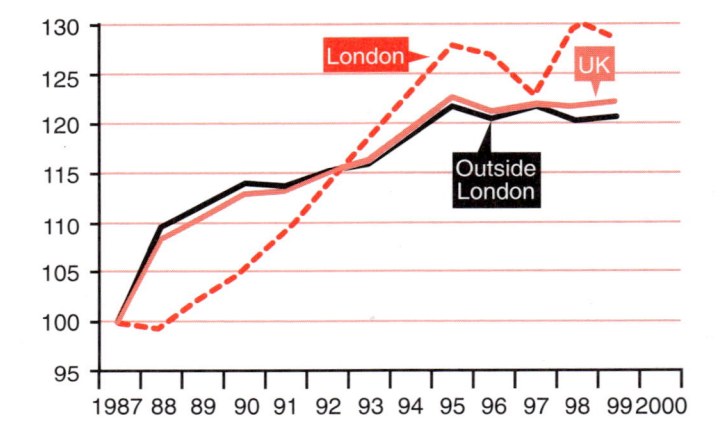

Figure 5.5 *Buses: vehicle kilometres travelled, fiscal year 1987-88 = 100*
Source: adapted from DETR.

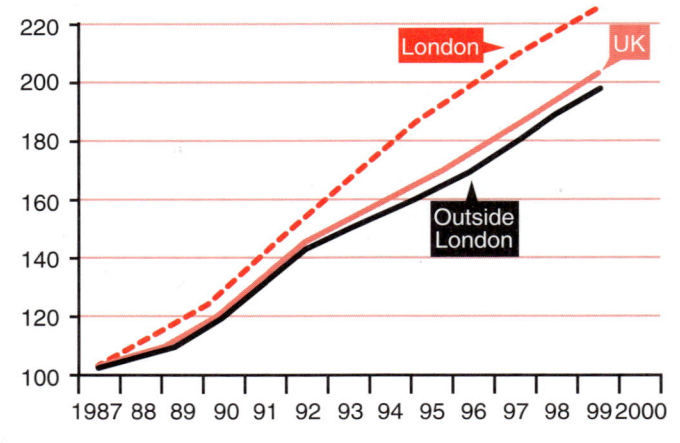

Figure 5.6 *Index of bus fares, fiscal year, 1987-88 = 100*
Source: adapted from DETR.

8 Parking levies and city centre tolls

In 2000, Birmingham City Council abandoned plans to impose a workplace parking levy. This was to be a tax on firms for every car parking space they offered to their employees and possibly their customers. The measure was abandoned after three neighbouring local councils - Coventry, Walsall and Solihull - indicated that they would not implement such measures. Birmingham faced the prospect of businesses moving out of the City to these neighbouring locations.

Birmingham City Council still hopes, though, to be able to impose a toll on all vehicles entering the area inside the city ring road. Similar plans are being studied by a number of cities including London, Edinburgh, Leeds, Bristol and Leicester. Congestion will be reduced in city centres because some motorists will be priced out of the market. This will reduce externalities. Noise and air pollution will be reduced whilst traffic speeds will rise. Those priced off the roads will start car sharing, use public transport or decide that their journey is not necessary.

City centre charges are highly controversial, however. They have been called a 'poll tax on wheels' after the highly unpopular local authority poll tax imposed by the Conservative government in the late 1980s. One objection is that road tolls are inequitable. It is the better off in society who will be able to afford to pay for scarce road space, leaving the poor further disadvantaged. At the moment, everyone, whatever their income, suffers the same traffic delays because of congestion. The toll is also unpopular with retailers in city centres. They fear that consumers will choose to go to out of town shops rather than pay the tolls to take their cars to the city centre. Road hauliers are worried that it will add to their costs and that they will not be able to recoup these in higher prices for their customers. It will be yet another factor to depress profitability in the industry. Finally, road tolls are not even popular with those who will be prepared to pay them and enjoy the benefits of faster journey times. Better off motorists see the road tolls as yet another tax on motoring.

9 Fuel tax crisis

In 2000, the UK economy was on the brink of being brought to a standstill by the picketing of oil refineries and depots. A coalition of self employed road hauliers and farmers, angered by the rise in the price of petrol and diesel fuel due to a doubling in the world price of oil, successfully brought deliveries of oil to a halt throughout the UK.

Environmental groups throughout the crisis claimed that the UK needed higher petrol prices, not lower prices. Between 1993 and 1999, the government imposed a rise in the real cost of petrol at the pumps of between 3 and 6 per cent per year for environmental reasons. This (fuel tax escalator) was abolished in March 2000 by the Chancellor in recognition of the fact that the rises were increasingly unpopular. Abolition did not prevent the fuel strike in September 2000, however, because world oil shortages raised the price of oil from $10 a barrel in 1998 to $35 a barrel in 2000.

The environmental argument is that rises in taxes on fuel discourage its use. Even though the price elasticity of demand for petrol is only 0.2, it still means that a 10 per cent rise in petrol prices will cut petrol consumption by 2 per cent. Assuming no change in engine efficiency, this leads to 2 per cent less kilometres travelled by road than would otherwise have been the case. Estimates put the amount of emissions saved between 1996 and 1999 at between 1 million and 2.5 million tonnes of carbon per year. The UK is committed, under the Kyoto Protocol signed in 1997, to cut its greenhouse gas emissions by 12.5 per cent of its 1990 level of 568 million tonnes by 2008-2012. By 1997 emissions had fallen to 530 million tonnes, 53 per cent of the target reduction. For every fall in 1 million tonnes achieved by higher petrol taxes there is a 1.4 per cent reduction in the 71 million tonnes needed to achieve the Kyoto target.

Environmentalists also point out that rises in fuel tax help ease congestion and reduce the need to build new roads. They also reduce noise pollution.

However, in September 2000 there was widespread public support for the actions of the hauliers and farmers. Voters made it clear that they would prefer lower petrol prices rather than environmental gains. Environmentalists would argue that the motorist creating externalities is unprepared to pay the full social cost of running a car or a lorry. The government, surprised by the public response to the strike, is likely to favour the motorist for the foreseeable future given that there seem few votes in environmentally friendly higher petrol taxes.

UNIT 5 TRANSPORT AND THE ENVIRONMENT

10 Transatlantic air fares

In 2000, transatlantic air flights between the UK and the USA were governed by a restrictive agreement between the governments of the two countries called the Bermuda II treaty. The most restrictive part of the agreement is that only four airlines, two UK companies and two US companies, can fly from Heathrow to the United States. Heathrow is Europe's busiest airport on the transatlantic routes carrying nearly 40 per cent of all passengers to and from the EU to the USA. The agreement therefore gives monopoly powers to the four airlines, British Airways, Virgin Atlantic, American Airlines and United Airlines, on the routes.

Figure 5.7 shows that the airlines use that monopoly power to price discriminate at the expense of Heathrow travellers. A business class traveller from Milan to Los Angeles, for instance, pays one third of the cost of one travelling from Heathrow. Italy has negotiated an 'open skies' policy with the USA which permits any airline to fly between Italy and the USA. The UK in 2000 was only one of four countries in the EU (the others being Greece, Ireland and Spain) not to have liberalised its air space.

The main losers from Bermuda II are passengers wanting to use Heathrow to fly to the USA. They have to pay much higher prices than if there were open competition. However, others losers include airlines which are unable to use the routes. For instance, British Midland has long wanted to operate services but is unable to do so. Its ability to compete is also limited in other ways by Bermuda II. In 2000, for instance, it was ordered by the UK Civil Aviation Authority to abandon plans to offer promotional airfares from Edinburgh, Glasgow and Aberdeen to Washington and Chicago via Manchester on new routes it was to offer in Spring 2001.

The UK and US governments had been negotiating a new treaty for years before 2000. However, competitor airlines claim that UK government policy is strongly influenced by British Airways. It is not in the interests of BA to have any relaxation of Bermuda II because a large proportion of its profits is made on transatlantic routes.

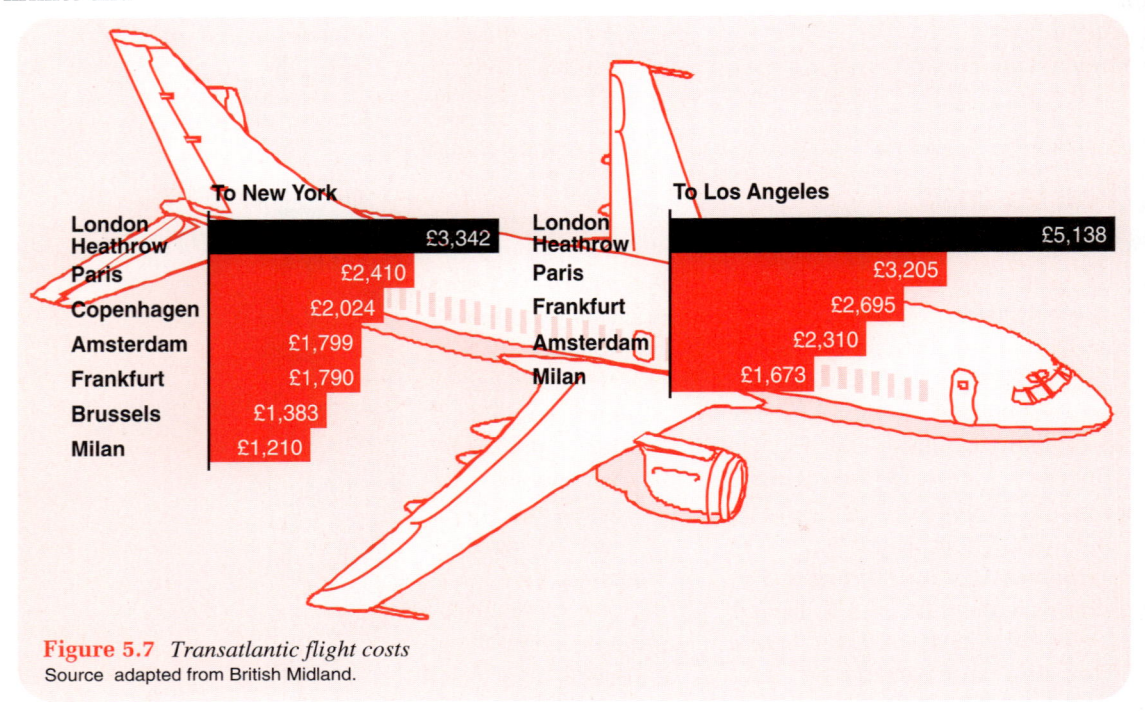

To New York
London Heathrow	£3,342
Paris	£2,410
Copenhagen	£2,024
Amsterdam	£1,799
Frankfurt	£1,790
Brussels	£1,383
Milan	£1,210

To Los Angeles
London Heathrow	£5,138
Paris	£3,205
Frankfurt	£2,695
Amsterdam	£2,310
Milan	£1,673

Figure 5.7 *Transatlantic flight costs*
Source adapted from British Midland.

Reading list

A.G. Anderton, *Economics*, Causeway Press (3rd ed. 2000) pages 119-125, 142-145, 382-387, 458-461.
A.G. Anderton, *Economics AS Level*, Causeway Press (2000) pages 119-125, 142-145.
P. Maunder et al, *Economics Explained*, Collins Educational (Revised 3rd ed. 2000) pages 181-198.
J. Bearshaw et al, *Economics: A student's Guide*, Longman (4th ed. 1998) pages 352-378.
C. Bamford, editor, *Economics for AS*, Cambridge University Press (2000) pages 102-103.
P. Curwen et al, *Understanding the UK Economy*, Macmillan, (4th ed. 1997) pages 509-511.
C. Bamford, *Transport Economics*, Heinemann Educational (2nd ed. 1998).
S. Munday, *Markets and Market Failure*, Heinemann Educational (2000).
D. Burningham and J. Davies, *Green Economics*, Heinemann Educational (2nd ed. 2000).
I. Hodge, *Environmental Economics*, Macmillan (1995).
D. Myers, 'Market failures and government remedies', *Developments in Economics* Vol 12, Causeway Press (1996).
S. Ison, 'Transport', *Developments in Economics* Vol 12, Causeway Press (1996).
R. Kerry Turner, 'Business economics, technological change and the environment', *Developments in Economics* Vol 14, Causeway Press (1998).
C. Nash, 'The integrated transport policy - a critique', *Developments in Economics* Vol. 15, Causeway Press (1999).
D, Myers, 'Green accounting', *Developments in Economics* Vol.16, Causeway Press (2000).

Essay questions

(a) Why might a government wish to reduce sales of cigarettes? (30 marks)
(b) The price elasticity of demand for cigarettes in the UK has been estimated as -0.25. Given this information, what would be the likely economic effects of a substantial increase in the tax on cigarettes? (40 marks)
(c) What would be the likely economic consequences of a complete ban on cigarette advertising? (30 marks)
(Edexcel January 1997)

(a) Explain why the rapid depletion of fish stocks may be considered to be an example of market failure. (40 marks)
(b) Examine the measures which government might take to conserve fish stocks. (60 marks)
(Edexcel January 1998)

In 1997 the EU proposed a ban on all cigarette advertising and sponsorship of sporting and arts events.
(a) Why might the EU wish to impose such a ban? (30 marks)
(b) How might tobacco companies react to the ban? (30 marks)
(c) Evaluate two alternative policies which governments might adopt to reduce tobacco consumption. (40 marks)
(Edexcel June 1999)

(a) Explain why environmental pollution is regarded as a source of market failure. (12 marks)
(b) Evaluate two different policies which a government might implement to reduce pollution. (13 marks)
(AQA [AEB] June 1996)

(a) Explain why the use of cost-benefit analysis is appropriate when assessing whether or not to build a new London Underground line. (12 marks)
(b) Discuss the various problems which are likely to be encountered when using cost-benefit analysis to decide whether or not to build the line. (13 marks)
(AQA [AEB] January 1997)

(a) Explain the main features of cost-benefit analysis. (12 marks)
(b) The Government is considering building a new underground railway line. Discuss the advantages and problems associated with using cost-benefit analysis to decide whether or not the project should be approved. (13 marks)
(AQA [AEB] January 1998)

In what sense are road traffic congestion, and the environmental pollution it produces, economic problems? Discuss what economic measures might be used to alleviate the congestion and pollution resulting from the use and ownership of motor vehicles.
(AQA [NEAB] 1999)

(a) Briefly outline the main benefits of constructing new major roads and motorways. (8)
(b) Comment upon the extent to which all these benefits can be incorporated effectively into a cost-benefit analysis framework. (12) (OCR March 1999)

(a) Explain the economic reasons for the deregulation of local bus services in the UK. (8)
(b) 'The Government believes that regulatory changes to bus services are needed in the future to achieve a better allocation of resources in urban transport.' (G Strang, Transport Secretary, 1997). Discuss this view that greater regulation is now needed. (OCR November 1999)

People who live near football grounds often complain about noise, litter and damage to property on match days.
(a) With the aid of a diagram explain how a divergence between private and social costs can cause market failure. (10)
(b) Discuss the economic policy options that are available to deal with this sort of market failure. (15) (OCR June 1999)

(a) Using suitable examples, explain what is meant by the term 'externalities'. (5)
(b) Explain why most economists believe that the free market will lead to under-provision of public goods and merit goods. (10)
(c) Evaluate the case for the government redistributing income from households with higher incomes to those with lower incomes. (10) (CCEA 1998)

Exam notes

Cost and benefits In economics, economic cost is defined as opportunity cost. Social cost is the opportunity cost to society of an economic activity. Private cost is the opportunity cost to an individual (e.g. person, firm, government) of the activity. Similarly, social benefit is the benefit to society of an economic activity whilst private benefit is the benefit to an individual economic agent (Boxes 1 to 5).
Externalities Externalities exist if there is a difference between net social costs and net private costs. If net social costs exceed net private costs, then a negative externality is said to exist. If, on the other hand, net social benefits exceed net private benefits, a positive externality exists (Boxes 1 to 5).
Cost-benefit analysis This is a technique whereby all costs and benefits of an economic activity are measured and compared to find the rate of return on the project. Included in this is an understanding of the rate of return on a project and the idea that future costs and benefits can be discounted back to the present to give a present value.
Economic efficiency This can be defined as occurring where the marginal social cost of production equals the marginal social benefit. This is equivalent to arguing that economic efficiency occurs when price = marginal cost.
Solutions to environmental problems Economists tend to favour tax solutions as opposed to regulation (Box 2).
Transport Transport is an issue within environmental economics. It can also incorporate many other areas of economics such as demand and supply, competition and monopoly, regulation and government spending (Boxes 6-10).

Unit 6
The public sector

1 Taxes as a percentage of GDP

Taxes as a proportion of GDP are set to remain around 37 per cent to 2004-05 according to government estimates made in its 2000 Budget. The Conservative opposition attacked the government in 2000 for imposing 'stealth taxes'. These are increases in taxes which go largely unnoticed by the taxpayer. For instance, the government in 1999 and 2000 cut the headline rates of income tax. At the same time, though, it removed the married couple's allowance, a tax free sum of money which one person in a couple could earn, and tax relief on mortgage interest payments was finally phased out.

Figure 6.1 would suggest that the tax burden is not increasing.

However, in absolute terms, more is being paid in tax because incomes are rising at over 2.5 per cent per annum. The Conservative opposition would like to see taxes being cut in absolute terms and therefore for taxes as a proportion of GDP to fall over time. The opportunity cost of this will either be an increase in government borrowing or a cut in the growth of public spending.

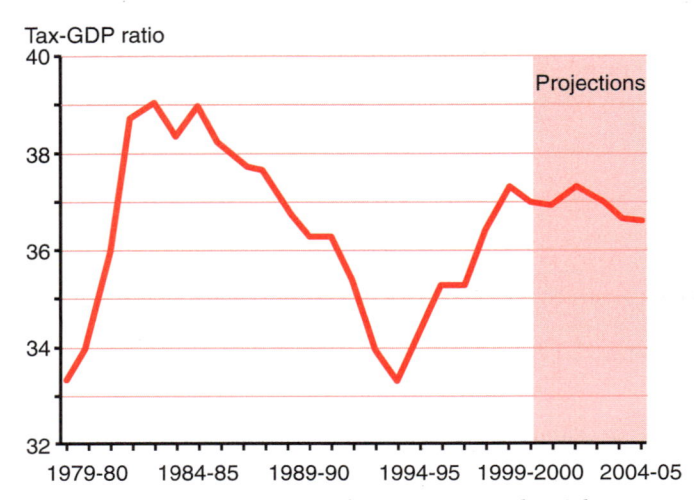

Figure 6.1 *Tax as a percentage of GDP (net tax and social security contributions)*
Source: adapted from HM Treasury.

2 Income tax and National Insurance contributions: progressive and regressive taxes

Table 6.1 shows the amount and percentages paid in income tax and employees' National Insurance contributions by an employed single person with no other tax allowances.

Income tax is a progressive tax. For instance, a single person pays 10.5 per cent of gross income on £10 000 of income. This rises to 17.4 per cent on £25 000 and 36.3 per cent on £190 000.

Employees' National Insurance contributions are progressive too over part of the income range for individuals. However, any income over approximately £30 000 a year is free of employee National Insurance contributions. This means that the tax becomes regressive on incomes over this amount. For instance, those earning £40 000 a year pay 6 per cent in National Insurance contributions, whilst those on £190 000 a year pay only 1.3 per cent.

Overall, the combined burden of income tax and employees' National Insurance contributions is progressive. The progressive nature of income tax outweighs the regressive nature of employees' National Insurance contributions on income over £30 000. So, for instance, a single worker earning £10 000 a year pays 16.6 per cent in income tax and National Insurance compared to 25.8 per cent for a worker on £25 000 a year and 37.5 per cent for a worker on £190 000.

Gross income (£)	Income tax paid (£)	National Insurance contributions (£)	Income tax as a percentage of gross income	National Insurance contributions as a percentage of gross income	Income tax and National Insurance contributions as a percentage of gross income
10 000	1 053	605	10.5	6.0	16.6
25 000	4 353	2 105	17.4	8.4	25.8
40 000	8 952	2 386	22.4	6.0	28.3
55 000	14 952	2 386	27.2	4.3	31.5
70 000	20 952	2 386	29.9	3.4	33.3
100 000	32 952	2 386	33.0	2.4	35.3
190 000	68 952	2 386	36.3	1.3	37.5

Table 6.1 *Income tax and Employees' National Insurance contributions as a percentage of gross income: single person 2000-2001[1]*
1. Assuming the taxpayer's only allowance is the personal allowance.
Source: adapted from PricewaterhouseCoopers.

UNIT 6 THE PUBLIC SECTOR

3 EU taxes on earnings

Figure 6.2 shows wide disparities in direct taxes on average earnings between countries of the EU. It ranges from over 40 per cent in Belgium to less than 20 per cent in Ireland. These figures do not show the overall tax burden because governments also levy taxes on businesses and on spending.

However, the figures are significant if direct taxes influence incentives to work. One criticism made of many European states is that incentives to work are low because direct taxes are too high. On this argument, the high growth in employment and fall in unemployment seen in the UK in the 1990s was partly caused by its low direct tax regime. The failure of many other EU countries to see any growth in employment whilst unemployment rose reflected their high direct tax regimes.

Direct taxes are only one influence upon levels of employment and unemployment. There is also considerable controversy about whether direct taxes do influence incentives to work. However, Figure 6.2 could be used by supply side economists to support their theories.

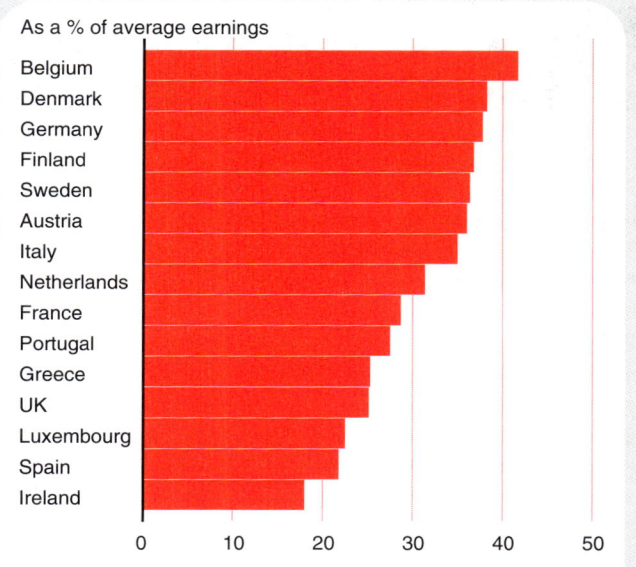

Figure 6.2 *EU tax and social security deductions, 1999*
Source: adapted from William M Mercer.

4 Increases in National Health spending

The state of the National Health Service was a key political issue in 2000. In response to this, the government announced in July 2000 a new set of public spending plans for 2000-04 which included historically high rates of increase of spending on the NHS. As Figure 6.3 shows, health care spending did not increase by 6-8 per cent per year over four years at any time during the 1980s or 1990s. Early in the year, the Prime Minister had stated that he wanted to see NHS spending rise to the average for the EU, which is about 8 per cent of GDP. At present, the UK only spends around 6 per cent of GDP on health care.

The Conservative opposition at the time wanted to see greater use made of private health care. It would like more people to take out private health insurance to add to the total resources for health care in the UK. However, there are possibly two main reasons why voters prefer to see a strengthened NHS rather than more private health care. First, voters recognise that health care is a merit good. Private health care is too expensive for many to afford. Certainly, few of the growing numbers of old people could afford comprehensive private health care plans. There is a fear that a strengthened private health care system would lead to less priority being given to public health care systems. The result could be worse treatment for the most vulnerable - for children, the elderly and those on low incomes. Second, many voters see access to health care as an issue of equality. They do not see health care as being the same as a car or a holiday, where the better off can afford more expensive goods and services. Instead, many believe that the same quality of health care should be available to everyone, irrespective of income. Raising spending on the NHS is shown by opinion polls to be popular with voters even though they know that an alternative could be cuts in tax.

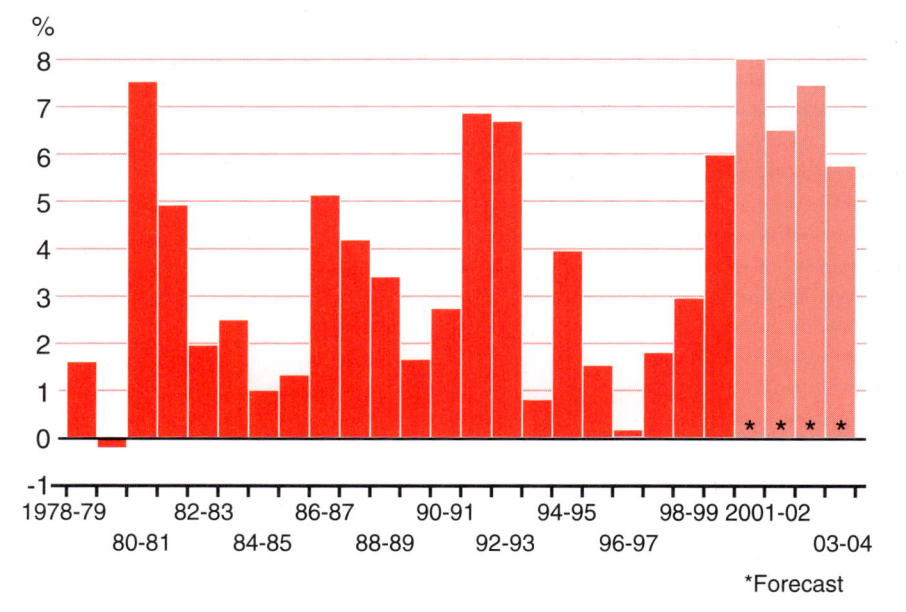

Figure 6.3 *NHS spending: real percentage change[1]*
1. Assuming 2.5 per cent annual inflation for 2000-2004.
Source: adapted from IFS.

*Forecast

THE STUDENT'S ECONOMY IN FOCUS 2000/01

35

5 Fuel taxes

In September 2000, there was a taxpayers' revolt over high fuel taxes. Road hauliers and farmers blocked oil refineries and depots and almost brought the economy to a standstill before calling off their protests. Opinion polls showed that the vast majority of the general public supported their demands for cuts in fuel taxes.

One of the ironies of the situation was that the large rise in petrol prices in 2000 was not caused by the government at all but by a doubling of crude oil prices. However, the government benefited by an estimated annual £2 billion from higher prices because any price increase imposed by oil suppliers is then taxed at 17.5 per cent through VAT. The oil price rise also followed years of large increases in duties on fuel which, as Figure 6.4 shows, increased tax revenues from £15 billion in 1993 to £26 billion in 1999.

The government was caught by surprise by the protest. It argued that it could not change tax policy between budgets to cope with short term changes in oil prices which were probably unsustainable anyway. If oil prices fell sharply, motorists would not expect the government to claw back lost VAT through increasing fuel taxes. Anyway, on environmental grounds, high petrol prices were desirable. Cutting fuel taxes could lead to more miles travelled, greater congestion and more greenhouse gas emissions.

However, the signs of the tax revolt were easy to see with hindsight. In 1999 and 2000, the haulage industry had lobbied the government hard for a reduction in the taxes it paid. By 2000, as Figure 6.5 shows, taxes on fuel were high compared to other EU countries. Moreover, petrol prices had risen far more than average prices as Figure 6.6 shows during the 1990s. Hauliers also complained that in the UK, little difference was made in tax between petrol and diesel, whereas in many European countries, diesel was significantly less taxed than petrol.

Ultimately the government was caught out because taxpayers felt that the fuel taxes they paid were not certain. One of Adam Smith's canons of taxation is that taxpayers should know in advance how much tax they will pay so that they can budget for it. Equally, taxes need to be seen as fair or equitable. Motorists, particularly hauliers, felt that the government had placed too great a burden of tax on them. As for farmers, the fuel protest was part of a wider campaign to win larger government subsidies to compensate them for the falls in the free market price of much of what they produced. The fact that it was rising oil prices that caused the final problem was not an issue which motorists wished to understand. As they saw it, the government could reduce petrol prices by reducing tax. With a buoyant economy in 2000 producing larger than expected tax revenues for the government, they also saw no reason why the government should not use some of this unexpected surplus to help them out. However, cutting fuel taxes is not cheap. A 3p a litre cut in tax would cost an estimated £1.0 billion - £1.5 billion. Reducing petrol prices to their December 1999 level would have cost £2 - £3 billion. The government was reluctant to lose this tax revenue because it judged there were higher priorities for public sector finances.

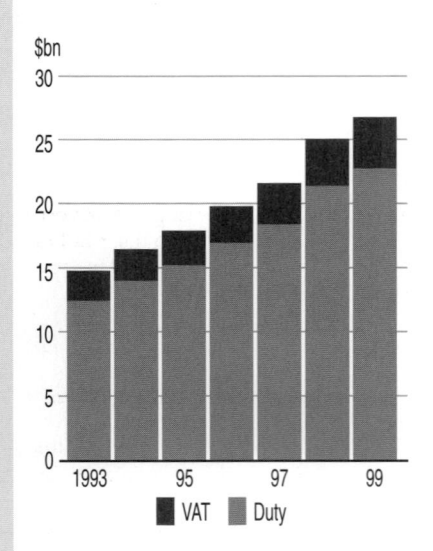

Figure 6.4 *Tax revenue from expenditure on fuel*
Source: adapted from HM Treasury, Merrill Lynch.

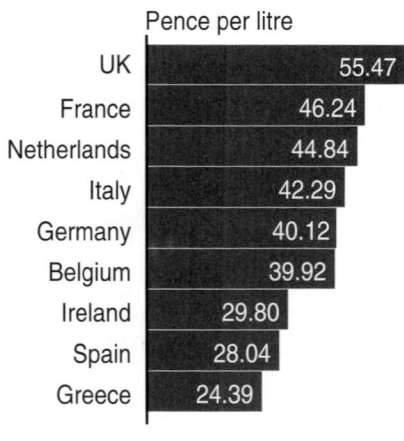

Figure 6.5 *Fuel taxes (duties plus VAT) on unleaded petrol, pence per litre*
Source: adapted from HM Customs.

Country	Pence per litre
UK	55.47
France	46.24
Netherlands	44.84
Italy	42.29
Germany	40.12
Belgium	39.92
Ireland	29.80
Spain	28.04
Greece	24.39

Figure 6.6 *Price of unleaded petrol compared with average prices*
Source: adapted from IFS.

6 The difficulties of forecasting the PSNCR

The PSNCR is the Public Sector Net Cash Requirement, a measure of the difference between government spending and government receipts, the most important of which is taxes. Figure 6.7 shows the outcomes for the PSNCR in 1998 and 1999 and then two forecasts for 2000-05. One forecast was the official Treasury forecast made in July 2000, whilst the other was a forecast made by Goldman Sachs, an independent firm of City analysts. The differences between the two forecasts are considerable. For instance, in 2004-05, Goldman Sachs predicted a budget surplus of £3 billion, whilst the Treasury predicted a deficit of £13 billion.

This £16 billion difference is very large in absolute terms. However, it is very small in comparison with the size of government spending and tax receipts. For instance, in the fiscal year 1999-2000, government spending was £341 billion whilst tax receipts before windfall receipts were £334 billion. The result was a deficit of £7 billion. The deficit was therefore just 2 per cent of government spending. Very small changes in percentage terms in government spending and taxation can lead to very large changes in the PSNCR.

Since 1997, the year Gordon Brown became Chancellor, the Treasury has been very conservative in its estimates of tax receipts. Partly, this is because the Treasury has been too cautious in its predictions of economic growth and falls in unemployment. The higher the rate of growth and the lower the level of unemployment, the higher is likely to be tax revenues. Government departments have also failed to spend to the limit of their budgets. The result is that government spending tends to be lower than forecast. Overall, budget deficits have tended to be overestimated and budget surpluses underestimated by the Treasury. The Goldman Sachs predictions shown in Figure 6.7 are therefore probably more realistic than the Treasury predictions.

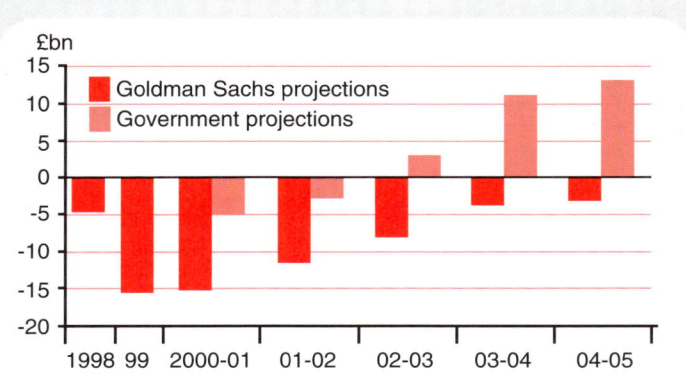

Figure 6.7 *Government borrowing (including windfall tax receipts and associated spending)*
* Negative numbers indicate a surplus.
Source: adapted from HM Treasury, Goldman Sachs.

7 Japan's public sector debt

Japan experienced a prolonged period of recession in the 1990s. At times, it appeared that the economy was in recovery, but then it quickly fell back. The result was that the miracle economy of the post-war period saw almost no real economic growth in the 1990s. To stop the economy slipping further into recession, the Japanese government adopted traditional Keynesian demand management techniques, spending large amounts on public works and creating significant budget deficits year after year. A budget deficit adds to the government debt (or the National Debt as it is called in the UK). Figure 6.8 shows how this debt has grown over time as a percentage of GDP.

The UK's National Debt in the 1990s too had increased from 28 per cent of GDP in 1991-92 to a peak of 44.1 per cent in 1996-97 due to the recession of 1990-92. However, fast economic growth combined with rises in tax rates and the introduction of new taxes saw the Debt fall to under 40 per cent by 2000-01. Continued budget surpluses could see the National Debt fall back to under 30 per cent of GDP over the next decade.

In the EU, the level of debt to GDP set under the Maastricht Treaty as a maximum for euro zone countries was 40 per cent. This is because high levels of debt can become unsustainable and lead to defaults on borrowing. Figure 6.9 shows that in 2000, the ratio of debt to tax revenues in Japan was over 1 500 per cent. This was far worse than other countries in their most difficult fiscal years.

In the next decade, two factors will help reduce Japan's debt burden. The first is high economic growth which will raise tax revenues and enable the government to cut its public works spending. Ideally, the government would run yearly budget surpluses. The second is relatively high inflation. Rising prices will reduce the real value of debt.

The worst scenario is that the Japanese economy fails to grow or grows at very low rates and there is deflation, i.e. a fall in average prices. This will raise the real value of the debt which is then also increasingly yearly because the government is continuing to run budget deficits.

A default on its debt by the Japanese government is almost unthinkable. However, Figures 6.8 and 6.9 show that it is a possibility. Faced with default, the Japanese government could print the money, a traditional way of financing high debt levels, but this would lead to inflation and devalue the savings of a rapidly ageing population. Alternatively, it could cut its spending and raise taxes, but this will reduce aggregate demand. If recovery is fragile, this is likely to be enough to send the economy back into recession.

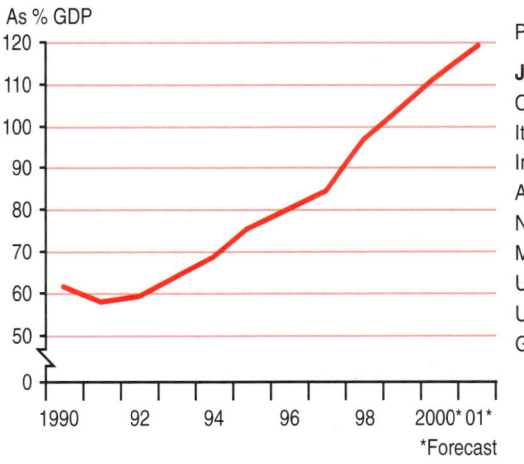

Figure 6.8 *Japan: government debt*
Source: adapted from American Enterprise Institute, OECD.

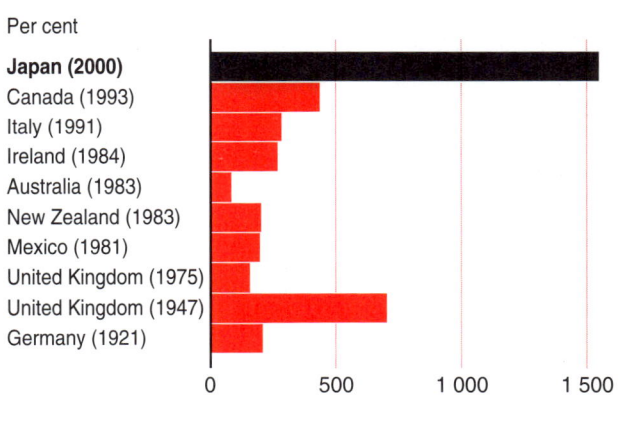

Figure 6.9 *Peak debt/tax revenue ratios*
Source: adapted from American Enterprise Institute, OECD.

UNIT 6 THE PUBLIC SECTOR

8 The mobile phone windfall

In 2000, government finances received a windfall payment of £22.5 billion from the auction of mobile phone licences. The amount raised was totally unexpected. Many expected the outcome to be between £5 and £10 billion.

The money raised could have been used in a variety of ways - to increase government spending, cut taxes or pay back government debts or some combination of these. The Chancellor immediately announced that the £22.5 billion would be used solely to repay debt. This option, though, has implications for government spending and taxes. With interest rates at around 5 per cent, the debt repayment will save around £1 billion a year in interest payments. This is £1 billion which can be used again to reduce debt, increase spending or reduce taxes.

9 Efficiency in the NHS

In 2000, the government increased funding for the NHS in real terms. However, it made clear that it wanted fundamental reforms in the way that the NHS was run. In particular, it wanted wide variations in health standards across the UK eliminated.

One variation is in the cost of performing operations. Figure 6.10 shows just how different costs can be between different NHS Trusts. For instance, a primary knee replacement can cost anything between £489 and £11 922, with an average of £4 326. Sometimes, there are sound economic reasons why the cost of operations differ. Some hospital departments specialise in treating patients with particularly serious problems. As a result, their costs per patient tend to be higher. Often, though, there are no apparent reasons for differences in costs. One hospital is more expensive than another not because it deals with difficult cases or its outcomes are better, but simply because it is not following best practice.

In Leicester, for instance, there are two teaching hospitals in the City dealing with very similar patients. Department of Health performance tables in 2000 showed that the Royal Infirmary had lower costs because it spent £158 per bed per day and often got people out of hospital faster. Three quarters of people who suffered a broken hip had left hospital within a month at the Royal Infirmary compared to just one quarter at the other hospital, Leicester General. At Leicester General, hospital beds cost £178 per day, £20 more than at the Royal Infirmary. The result was that each bed cost £7 300 more a year at Leicester General.

The government is keen for National Health Trusts to take a critical look at their costings compared to other Trusts. In theory, Trusts should be seeking to lower their costs to those of the most cost efficient Trusts in the UK, i.e. they should be seeking to secure productive efficiency. They can do this by changing the way in which they are run. Of course, the government does not wish cost cutting to be associated with poorer treatment. The Department of Health also publishes performance tables on clinical outcomes. The performance tables, though, can provide clear indications of when a Trust is giving good value for money or poor value for money.

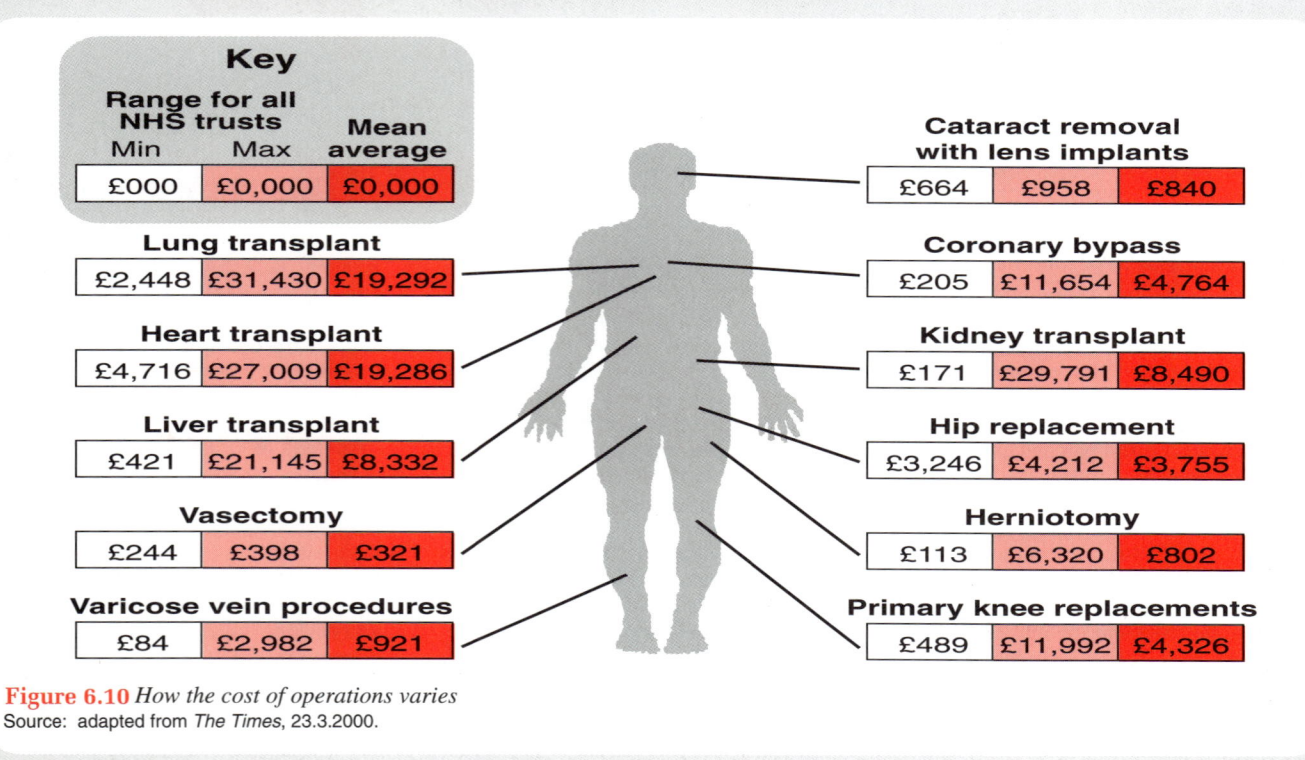

Key

Range for all NHS trusts: Min | Max | Mean average
£000 | £0,000 | £0,000

Operation	Min	Max	Mean
Lung transplant	£2,448	£31,430	£19,292
Heart transplant	£4,716	£27,009	£19,286
Liver transplant	£421	£21,145	£8,332
Vasectomy	£244	£398	£321
Varicose vein procedures	£84	£2,982	£921
Cataract removal with lens implants	£664	£958	£840
Coronary bypass	£205	£11,654	£4,764
Kidney transplant	£171	£29,791	£8,490
Hip replacement	£3,246	£4,212	£3,755
Herniotomy	£113	£6,320	£802
Primary knee replacements	£489	£11,992	£4,326

Figure 6.10 *How the cost of operations varies*
Source: adapted from *The Times*, 23.3.2000.

10 Social security spending

Social security spending in the second half of the 1990s remained broadly stable in real terms as Figure 6.11 shows. Disaggregating the total shows in Figure 6.12 that whilst there were small increases in spending on the elderly and those with health problems, this was roughly balanced by a fall in spending on unemployment arising from the fall in unemployment over the period.

There are growing pressures for the government to increase substantially its spending on the elderly. First, there has been a small but growing increase in the population aged 65 and over, particularly concentrated in the 75 plus age range. So demographics alone has been pushing up spending. Second, those aged 75 and over for the most part live almost entirely on state benefits. So the fastest growing group of pensioners is also the group most dependent on the state for care. Third, the state old age pension has, since 1981, only been linked to the increase in average prices. State pensioners over that time have seen no increase in their standard of living despite the fact that average incomes have increased by two thirds. This growing inequality has become increasingly unacceptable to state pensioners and also to many future pensioners who can see that they too will be poor if they have no other means of support in old age.

Government policy in 2000 was to resist large increases in the state old age pension but to provide large targeted increases in means tested benefits to the poorest pensioners. Government policy is driven by the desire to reduce inequality but also to keep spending on benefits down. An across the board large increase in state pensions would be very costly since the elderly account for nearly half of all benefit spending. On the other hand, better off pensioners argue that they paid a lifetime of National Insurance contributions to secure a state pension which, compared to average earnings, is becoming smaller every year. There is therefore a conflict between the distribution of income today, where workers wish to minimise the taxes they pay, and the distribution of income over time where workers want to ensure that the taxes they pay to fund their state pension give them a good return when they come to retire.

In the rest of the EU, state pensions tend to be much higher because states often provide the main pension for retired workers. There is far less of a tradition of workers taking out pensions with their employers or of personal pensions where individuals save for their retirement. This is one of the reasons why social protection benefits are higher in the EU on average than in the UK, as Figure 6.13 shows.

Figure 6.11 *Real growth in social security benefits*
Source: adapted from *Social Trends*, Office for National Statistics.

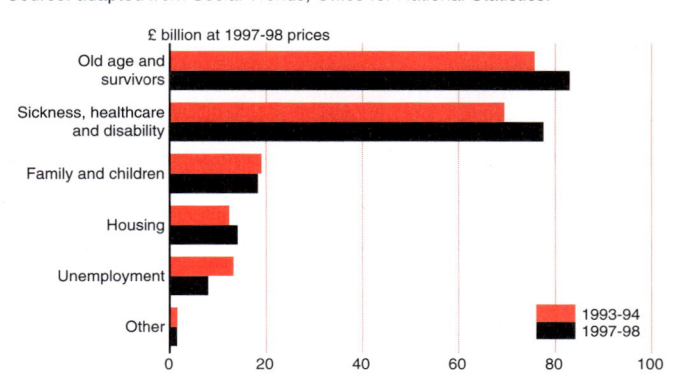

Figure 6.12 *Expenditure on social protection benefits in real terms: by function 1993-94 and 1997-98*
Source: adapted from *Social Trends*, Office for National Statistics.

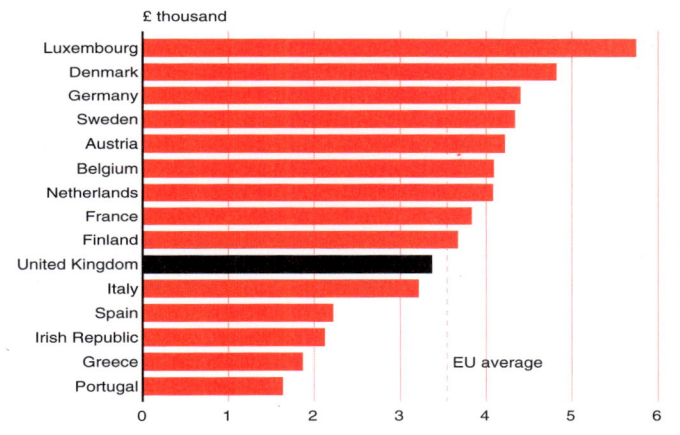

Figure 6.13 *Expenditure on social protection benefits per head: EU comparison, 1996*
Source: adapted from *Social Trends*, Office for National Statistics.

Reading list

A.G. Anderton, *Economics*, Causeway Press (3rd ed. 2000) pages 126-134, 528-543.
A.G. Anderton, *Economics AS Level*, Causeway Press (2000) pages 126-134.
J. Beardshaw et al., *Economics: A Student's Guide*, Longman (4th ed. 1998) pages 68-78.
P. Maunder et al, *Economics Explained*, Collins Educational (Revised 3rd ed. 2000) pages 121-137, 199-218, 486-497.
C. Bamford, editor, *Economics for AS*, Cambridge University Press (2000) pages 82-87, 100-102
D. Begg et al, *Economics*, McGraw Hill (5th ed. 1997) pages 261-274.
P. Curwen et al, *Understanding the UK Economy*, Macmillan (4th ed. 1997) pages 166-204.
A. Palmer, 'The economics of taxation', *Developments in Economics* Vol 11, Causeway Press (1995).
A. Dilnot, 'Background to the Budget', *Developments in Economics* Vol 14, Causeway Press (1998).
M.J. Powell, 'The economic case for social security reform', *Developments in Economics* Vol 15, Causeway Press (1999).
D.K. Whynes, 'UK health care: re-organisation and rationing', *Developments in Economics* Vol 16, Causeway Press (2000).

UNIT 6 THE PUBLIC SECTOR

Essay questions

(a) Outline the main characteristics of a free market economy. (20 marks)
(b) What are the main advantages of market forces as a means of allocating resources? (30 marks)
(c) Examine the problems which might arise if health care and education were provided solely by market forces. (50 marks)
(Edexcel June 1996)

(a) What economic arguments can be used to justify government intervention in the market for health care? (60 marks)
(b) Examine the problems which face governments when they provide or finance health care. (40 marks)
(Edexcel January 1997)

'The National Lottery is disguised taxation; it redistributes from the poor to the rich; it undermines thrift and hard work.'
(T. Congdon, The Times, 15 March 1996)
(a) Discuss each of these three propositions. (60 marks)
(b) Outline some further impacts of the existence of the National Lottery in the UK. (40 marks)
(Edexcel June 1998)

In his first Budget in July 1997, Mr Gordon Brown forecast a PSBR of 5.4 billion in 1998-99 (excluding the windfall tax on privatised utilities). This contrasts with a PSBR of £45 billion in 1992-93.
(a) Discuss the economic significance of the PSBR in the UK. (50 marks)
(b) Analyse the factors which might result in a reduction in the PSBR. (50 marks)
(Edexcel June 1998)

In most countries the role of the state in the economy has been reduced in recent years.
(a) Analyse the factors which might explain this trend. (50 marks)
(b) Examine the likely economic implications of an increase in the proportion of health care and education provided by the private sector. (50 marks)
(Edexcel June 1999)

(a) Why do governments levy taxes? (12 marks)
(b) Discuss the view that the United Kingdom government should further reduce the burden of direct taxation and recover the lost revenue by imposing substantial increases in indirect taxation. (13 marks)
(AQA [AEB] June 1995)

Compare the characteristics and purpose of direct and indirect taxes. Discuss the factors which may affect whether an increase in the tax per unit on products such as beer, cigarettes and petrol will be paid mainly by the consumer.
(AQA [NEAB] 1998)

Outline the major functions of taxation. Discuss to what extent, if any, the economic effects of an indirect tax differ from those of a direct tax.
(AQA [NEAB] 1999)

(a) Using examples, describe the economic characteristics of public goods. (10)
(b) Why does the government provide
(i) defence,
(ii) education? (15)
(OCR June 1995)

(a) Distinguish between private, public and merit goods. (10)
(b) In 1987, the UK Government abandoned its policy of providing free eye examinations for all patients. Use economic theory to discuss the likely effects of this policy decision. (15)
(OCR November 1997)

Traditionally, university education in the UK has been subsidised, with tuition fees paid by the state.
(a) Explain why university education in the UK is regarded as a merit good. (10)
(b) Discuss the likely economic effects on the market for university education of requiring students to pay £1 000 a year towards tuition fees. (15)
(OCR March 1999)

(a) Outline why education and health care are both regarded as 'merit goods'. (5)
(b) Explain the various methods by which governments may encourage the production and consumption of merit goods. (10)
(c) 'Increasing spending on the National Health Service is not necessarily the best way of improving the health of the nation.' Discuss the validity of this claim. (10)
(CCEA 1999)

Exam notes

Public spending Specifications require an understanding of the difference between public and merit goods. Public goods have the qualities of non-rivalry and non-excludability. Merit goods, such as health care (Boxes 4 and 9) and education, are those which would be underprovided by the market mechanism and which create positive externalities. Recent trends in public spending should be known, together with an understanding of the factors determining those trends.
Taxation The distinction between direct and indirect taxes, and progressive, regressive and proportional taxes (Boxes 2 and 3) should be known. What constitutes a 'good' tax should be understood (Box 5), which includes a knowledge of Adam Smith's canons of taxation. The effects of tax on the economy, such as changing incentives to work or changing shopping patterns (Box 3), should be appreciated. The main taxes in the UK together with recent trends in tax revenues (Box 1) are also required.
Government borrowing Specifications require candidates to understand government borrowing (Box 6) and why levels of government borrowing might be important (Box 7). It should be noted that candidates often confuse government borrowing with a deficit on the current account on the balance of payments. The two are different.
Efficiency and equity Governments provide goods and services often because it is more efficient for them to be financed through taxation than through the market mechanism (Box 4). However, governments also use their spending and taxation powers to produce a more equitable distribution of resources between households and individuals (Boxes 4, 5 and 10).

Unit 7
Labour

1 Excess demand for economists

In the late 1990s, the UK government faced a recruitment crisis for economists. Demand for economists from government departments had risen by 40 per cent over the 1989 level. This was because government departments had recognised that they needed the skills and knowledge of professional economists in decision making. Over the same period, the numbers of Economics graduates from British universities, particularly with post-graduate qualifications, had shrunk. At undergraduate level, students had increasingly opted to read Business Studies rather than Economics. At post-graduate level, better Economics graduates had been lured away from further study by high paying jobs, particularly in the City of London. The result was that by 2000, there were hardly any British born post-graduate students on Economics courses.

In a market situation, wages will rise where demand is greater than supply. In the private sector, starting salaries for economists had certainly risen substantially in the 1990s. However, the civil service is bound by pay scales which fail to differentiate between different groups of workers. In 2000, a graduate economist could expect to start on a salary of £19 000 a year, or £21 500 if they held a post-graduate qualification. This was not enough for the civil service to recruit sufficient economists.

It was therefore decided to increase the supply of potential economists by recruiting abroad. So graduates from Australia, New Zealand, Spain and even Ethiopia have been offered jobs on three year contracts. Wages for economists in these countries are below those in the UK and hence there is financial incentive for economists to move to the UK. Working for the civil service will also give them high quality job experience for their later careers.

2 Economic activity rates

Figure 7.1 shows that economic activity rates since 1971 have been rising for women but falling for men. The activity rate is the proportion of those in the relevant age group who are either in work or are officially unemployed (as defined by the ILO measure, i.e. those actively seeking work).

There is a number of reasons for this. First, real wage rates have been rising over time. The higher the real wage rate, the greater the incentive to work, as non-paid work activities, such as staying at home to bring up children, become relatively more expensive. Moreover, Figure 7.2 shows that women's earnings have been rising at a faster rate than those of men. In 1970, average women's earnings were 55 per cent of men's earnings. By 1999, this was 73 per cent. Hence, there has been a greater incentive over time for women without jobs to go out to work than men. This helps partially to explain the difference in the change of male and female activity rates over time.

A second factor affecting activity rates has been education. A growing proportion of 16-25 year olds have chosen to stay in full-time education. This depresses the activity rates of workers aged 16-60 or 65. The participation of females in post 16 education has risen at a faster rate than males since 1971. This has acted as a drag on the growth in the overall female activity rate, but has not been large enough to cause it to fall.

A third factor affecting activity rates has been early retirement. In 1999, 92 per cent of males aged 35-49 were economically active compared to 77 per cent of females. However, only 73 per cent of males were economically active in the 50-65 age group compared to 65 per cent of women aged 50-59. The activity rate for males aged 50-65 has been falling over time, but for women aged 50-59 it has been rising. These statistics show that it is increasingly common for men to take early retirement, particularly after the age of 60. There are women taking early retirement too. But first, the official retirement age for women is 60 anyway, and second, more women who are not economically active take a job in their 50s than become economically inactive through early retirement.

A number of other factors may also have played a part in encouraging women to enter the workforce. Discrimination against women has fallen over time, although evidence suggests it still exists. The invention of labour saving machines, such as microwave ovens and automatic washing machines, and the increasing availability of ready to cook meals have reduced the amount of time needed to complete housework. There is also a growing trend for men to stay at home and for the female partner to be the main breadwinner, although absolute numbers are still very small.

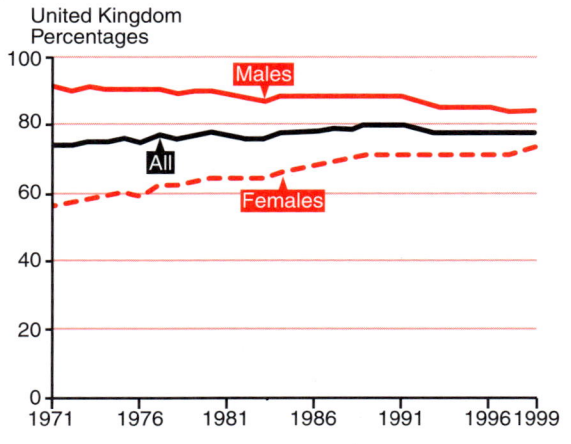

Figure 7.1 *Economic activity rates by gender*
Source: adapted from *Social Trends*, Office for National Statistics.

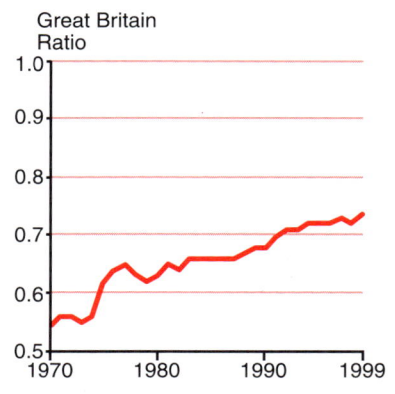

Figure 7.2 *Weekly earnings gender differential*
Source: adapted from *Social Trends*, Office for National Statistics.

THE STUDENT'S ECONOMY IN FOCUS 2000/01

UNIT 7 LABOUR

3 Full employment in Newbury?

Newbury in Berkshire in 2000 had one of the UK's lowest unemployment rates at 1 per cent compared to a national average of 4 per cent. The town is situated near to the M4 and the motorway between London and Bristol links an area which has a high concentration of new technology firms. Newbury's prosperity is built upon one company, Vodafone, which has its headquarters in the town. The mobile phone company has seen enormous expansion during the 1990s which has been reflected in an increasing number of jobs at its headquarters. However, many other employers in the town have expanded too and increased their demand for workers.

This increase in demand for workers has led not just to low unemployment but also to relatively high wages. Supermarkets, for instance, are paying twice the minimum wage for shelf stackers. Permanent administration jobs for moderately skilled staff with some experience start at £13 000.

Firms, though, are reluctant to push wages up too high because otherwise their operations would become uncompetitive. As it is, there is a trickle of firms leaving Newbury to relocate in areas where the labour market is less tight. Vodafone itself, the largest employer with 3 500 jobs in Newbury, has set up offices elsewhere to cope with the continued expansion of its business rather than further expand its headquarters. So firms are limiting increases in the demand for labour in Newbury.

They are also trying to limit the wages they pay to new workers taken on. Economic theory suggests that the supply curve for labour is upward sloping. Some administration workers, for instance, would be prepared to work for £8 000 a year. Others would need a wage of £10 000 a year to persuade them to take on a job. The marginal worker is the worker who is only prepared to work for the wage rate that is finally set, say £13 000. One way in which some firms attempt to limit wages in Newbury is by offering existing staff bonuses if they introduce new staff to the company. Vodafone, for instance, offers bonuses of between £200 and £2 000 according to the seniority of the position, to staff who recruit friends to vacant positions. Another way is to offer perks which staff value more than the monetary cost to the company of offering them. Vodafone, for instance, offers share options, mobile phones, free travel to work, a pension scheme and special deals on purchases of cars, televisions, hi-fi equipment, sports clubs, food outlets and clothes shops for many employees. Perks are also a vital tool in retaining staff and encouraging staff loyalty, essential in an area where the labour market is so tight.

With unemployment continuing to fall nationally, it could be that in five years time most areas of the country will be experiencing the same level of full employment as Newbury enjoys today. This is not inconceivable given that unemployment was very low for 25 years between 1945 and 1970 in the UK. If this happens, firms will have to adjust their recruitment policies to prevent excess demand leading to large increases in wage rates which would inevitably lead to inflation and then to deflationary policies by the government and the Bank of England.

4 The minimum wage

The minimum wage was introduced in 1999 at £3.60 an hour for workers over the age of 21. Figure 7.3 shows how this affected the distribution of gross hourly earnings. After the introduction, there was a clear bunching of workers around the £3.60 an hour level. The numbers earning less than the minimum wage have fallen. It is still legal to pay less than the minimum wage so long as workers are aged 21 or less.

Some predicted that there would be upward pressure on wages at above the £3.60 an hour level in order to maintain wage differentials. Workers who, for instance, earned £3.60 an hour before the introduction of the minimum wage in a factory where other workers earned £3.20, might have demanded a wage increase to say, £4.00. However, there is no obvious evidence from Figure 7.3 that there was a substantial increase in wages over and above the 5 per cent average rise that was recorded for the year.

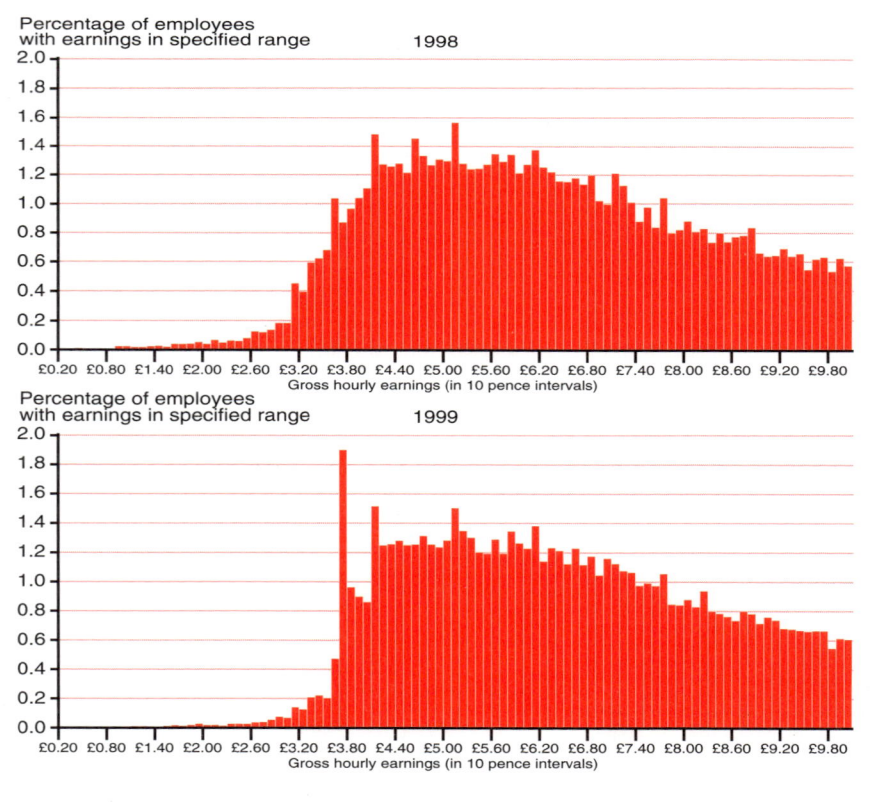

Figure 7.3 *Distribution of gross hourly earnings: Great Britain, April 1998 and 1999.*
Source: adapted from *Labour Market Trends*, Office for National Statistics

UNIT 7 LABOUR

5 Female wages and the glass ceiling

Female workers often complain there is a 'glass ceiling' put in the way of their careers. As men are promoted, women find it difficult to keep up due to discrimination in the work place. Table 7.1 would certainly at first suggest that women face a problem. In 1999, only 11 per cent of women workers were managers and administrators compared to 19 per cent for men. The gap between men and women also has not narrowed between 1991 and 1999.

However, Table 7.1 also shows that there is a significant difference in the occupations which men and women choose. Women are particularly concentrated in clerical and secretarial work, personal and protective services and selling. Women are far more likely to be secretaries, nurses, health care assistants or shop assistants than males. In contrast, males are far more likely to be found on the shop floor in manufacturing industry as plant and machine operatives, or in craft trades such as carpentry, plumbing or bricklaying.

These very different patterns of employment are likely to give rise to differences in average pay and in career structures for men and women. It could be argued that the reasons why men and women choose particular careers is because of discrimination and prejudice in the first place. How many male school leavers become secretaries or nurses for instance? Or how many female school leavers look for or get jobs as bricklayers or machine tool operators?

There is evidence, for instance from the work of industrial tribunals, that there is discrimination against women seeking promotion. A glass ceiling exists, but the extent to which it exists is likely to be affected by the very different professions that men and women choose in the first place.

United Kingdom	Males 1991	Males 1999	Females 1991	Females 1999
Managers and administrators	16	19	8	11
Professional	10	11	8	10
Associate professional and technical	8	9	10	11
Clerical and secretarial	8	8	29	26
Craft and related	21	17	4	2
Personal and protective services	7	8	14	17
Selling	6	6	12	12
Plant and machine operatives	15	15	5	4
Other occupations	8	8	10	8
All employees (=100%) (millions)	11.8	12.4	10.1	10.8

Table 7.1 *Employees by gender and occupation, 1991 and 1999*
Source: adapted from *Social Trends*, Office for National Statistics.

6 Employment of the disabled

Table 7.2 shows the position of the 6.8 million people defined as disabled in the workforce compared to all workers. Economic theory would suggest that, in a completely free market, disabled people will find it more difficult to get a job than the average worker. This is because the marginal revenue product, the output, of the average disabled worker is likely to be lower than for the average worker. Equally, the cost of employing a disabled worker is likely to be on average higher because the employer may have to make modifications to the workplace to accommodate the needs of the disabled worker. So at any given wage, fewer disabled workers are likely to be employed compared to the average worker.

Table 7.2 would support these conclusions. Only 46.4 per cent of the disabled are in work compared to 80.7 per cent for workers who are not disabled. Unemployment rates for disabled workers are higher than for workers who are not disabled. The long term unemployment rate for disabled workers is almost twice that of workers who are not disabled. There is also a far larger proportion of economically inactive disabled people who would like a job if it were available. 16.7 per cent of disabled people are not actively seeking work and are therefore not classified as unemployed. However, they would like to work. This compares to 4.1 per cent for workers who are not disabled.

Equal opportunities legislation has helped the disabled in the workplace. Employers are under pressure to take on disabled workers. Equally, legislation makes it more difficult for employers to make workers redundant if they become disabled. However, Table 7.2 would suggest that there is widespread discrimination in the workplace against the disabled. Employers believe that the marginal revenue product is lower and the cost of employment is higher for disabled workers than is actually the case. Legislation is not helping the disabled sufficiently to combat this discrimination.

	Men Disabled	Men Not disabled	Women Disabled	Women Not disabled	All Disabled	All Not disabled
Economically active	55.2	91.0	47.8	78.1	51.7	84.9
In employment	49.0	86.0	43.5	74.7	46.4	80.7
Working full time	43.1	79.5	22.4	43.0	33.2	62.1
Working part time	5.9	6.5	21.1	31.8	13.1	18.5
ILO unemployed	6.2	4.9	4.4	3.4	5.3	4.2
ILO unemployed for less than 1 year	3.3	3.4	3.3	2.8	3.3	3.1
ILO unemployed for at least 1 year	2.9	1.5	1.1	0.6	2.0	1.1
ILO unemployment rate	11.3	5.4	9.1	4.3	10.3	5.0
Economically inactive	44.8	9.0	52.2	21.9	48.3	15.1
Wants job	16.8	2.4	16.7	6.0	16.7	4.1
Does not want job	28.0	6.6	35.5	15.8	31.6	11.0
All people of working age (=100%)(millions)	**3.5**	**15.5**	**3.2**	**14.1**	**6.8**	**29.5**

Table 7.2 *Economic activity status of working age people according to whether they are disabled, by sex; United Kingdom 2000, not seasonally adjusted*
Source: adapted from *Labour Market Trends*, Office for National Statistics.

UNIT 7 LABOUR

7 The employment market in the South East

The South East of England is the region of the UK with the lowest unemployment rate as Figure 7.4 shows. It also has the highest average wage. There is a number of reasons for this.

One is that the level of human capital is on average higher in the South East than the rest of the UK. Figure 7.5 shows that the South East has a higher proportion of its workforce with higher education qualifications than the Great Britain average. Equally, a greater proportion of its workforce has its A levels or their equivalent as highest qualification. At the other end of the scale, fewer workers have no qualifications. Qualifications and human capital enhance the productivity of workers and raise their marginal revenue product. Hence, on average, employers are willing to pay better qualified workers higher pay.

Another linked factor is the type of job found in the South East compared to the average for Great Britain. Figure 7.6 shows that there is a larger percentage of jobs in the highest paid occupations in the South East. These are managers and administrators, professional workers and associate professional and technical workers. The South East has a smaller proportion of its workers employed in manufacturing industry and hence has fewer plant and machine operatives. Manufacturing industry has shrunk over the past thirty years due to its relative uncompetitiveness and increases in wages in manufacturing have tended to fall behind increases in those in services, which account for a larger proportion of output and jobs in the South East than the national average.

With unemployment below the national average, wages rose faster in 1999 in the South East than the average for the whole economy. In a tight labour market, the South East could continue to pull away from the rest of the economy, increasing the north-south divide which many see as undesirable.

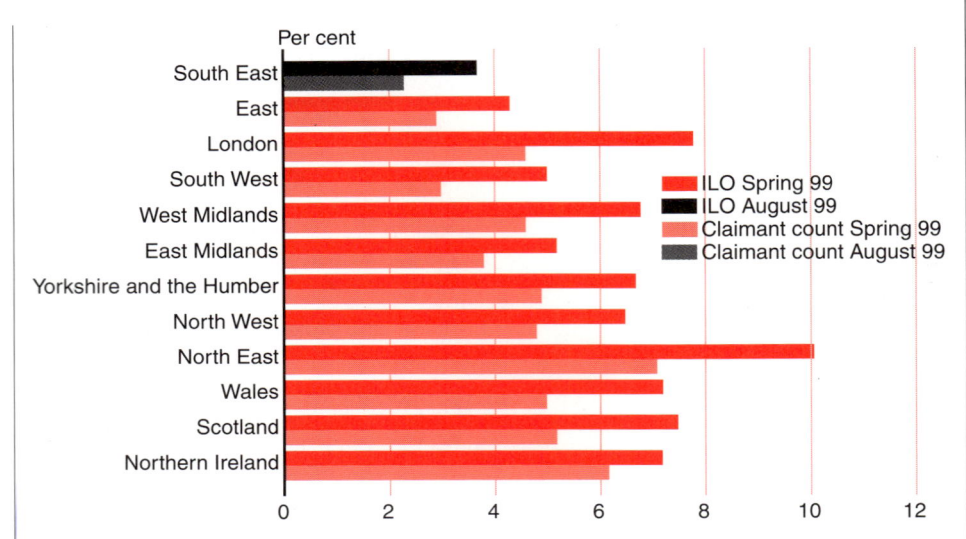

Figure 7.4 *Unemployment rates by region: United Kingdom, seasonally adjusted*
Source: adapted from *Labour Market Trends*, Office for National Statistics.

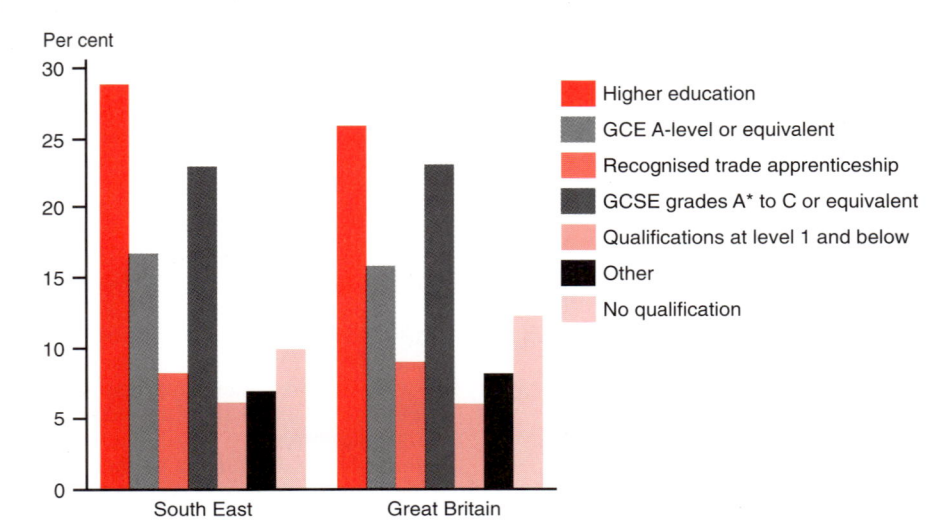

Figure 7.5 *Highest qualification of those economically active of working age, March-May 1999*
Source: adapted from *Labour Market Trends*, Office for National Statistics.

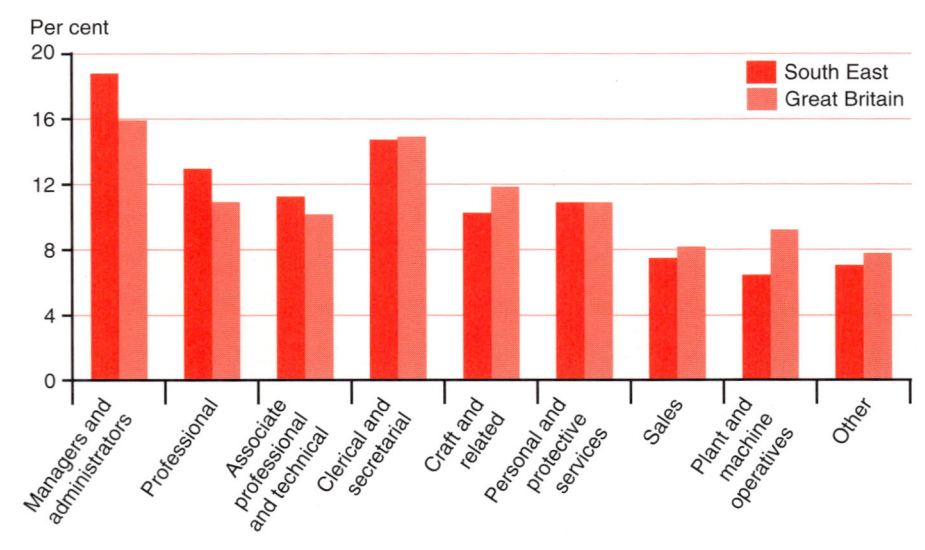

Figure 7.6 *Employment by occupation, March-May 1999*
Source: adapted from *Labour Market Trends*, Office for National Statistics.

THE STUDENT'S ECONOMY IN FOCUS 2000/01

UNIT 7 LABOUR

8 Earnings differentials between occupations

Figure 7.7 shows levels of earning differentials between occupations. Those with the highest levels of human capital, as measured by qualifications, tend to earn the most. For instance, secondary school teachers tend to be slightly better qualified on average than primary school teachers and both groups have higher average qualifications than nurses. Those with few or no qualifications tend to earn the least, such as waiters and cleaners.

Qualifications are not the only reason which accounts for wage differentials. Postal workers, for instance, tend not to be better qualified than, say, sales assistants. However, postal workers are strongly unionised, which arguably enables them to earn above the wage earned by sales assistants, who tend not to belong to trade unions.

Figure 7.7 also shows that women are less well paid than men in every occupation. The higher the average pay, the higher tends to be the gap between male and female workers. For instance, female waitresses earn on average 94 per cent of the pay of male waiters. However, female treasury and company financial managers earn on average only 66 per cent of the earnings of their male counterparts.

The difference in male and female wages is due to a number of factors. One key factor is difference in work experience between the sexes. Women on average have fewer years of work experience than men because some women take time out of their careers to bring up children at home. This time out also affects levels of training between the sexes. Women are also more likely to enter jobs which are less well paid. For instance, nurses are predominantly women, whereas chartered accountants are predominantly men. Discrimination against women must also play a part in earnings differentials.

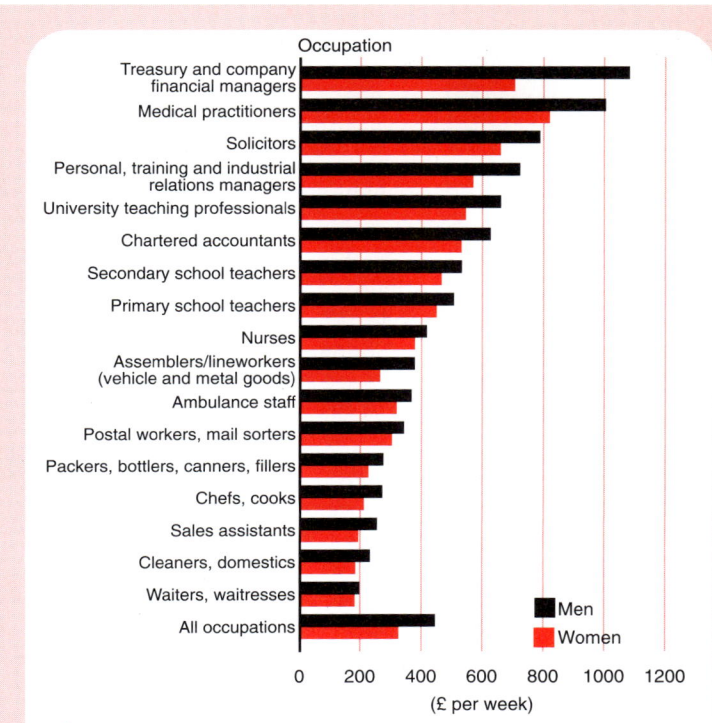

Figure 7.7 *Average full-time gross weekly earnings by occupation: Great Britain, April 1999*
Source: adapted from *Labour Market Trends*, Office for National Statistics.

9 Temporary working

Figure 7.8 shows that temporary working increased over the 1990s in the UK. It can be argued that this pattern reflects changes in unemployment. In 1990-92, the UK experienced a prolonged recession which raised claimant count unemployment from 1.5 million to 3 million. In a recession, firms will be reluctant to take on permanent workers for fear that trading conditions will worsen. Hence, temporary working is likely to rise. However, as unemployment fell during the 1990s, firms became more willing to take on permanent employees. Workers also might have been less willing to take on temporary work.

However, another interpretation of the figures is that labour markets have become more flexible. Instead of workers holding permanent jobs for life, workers are increasingly moving from job to job as the demand for labour changes. Supply side economists tend to argue that flexibility of labour leads to higher economic growth because workers can be attracted into the most productive occupations whilst unemployment is lower than it would be if labour were inflexible. However, if temporary work is an indication of labour market flexibility, Figure 7.8 indicates that the UK labour market became less flexible from 1997 onwards, possibly because of the cumulative effect of the fall in unemployment since 1993.

Another interpretation is that the UK is nearing the point of full employment. As the example of Newbury (see Box 3) shows, in a full employment economy workers are able to pick and choose jobs. They then are prepared to be flexible because losing a job or resigning from a job does not mean that they worker will become unemployed. Instead, the worker will be immediately able to start in a new job of their choosing. In these conditions, an economy where most jobs are permanent can also be an economy where labour markets are highly flexible.

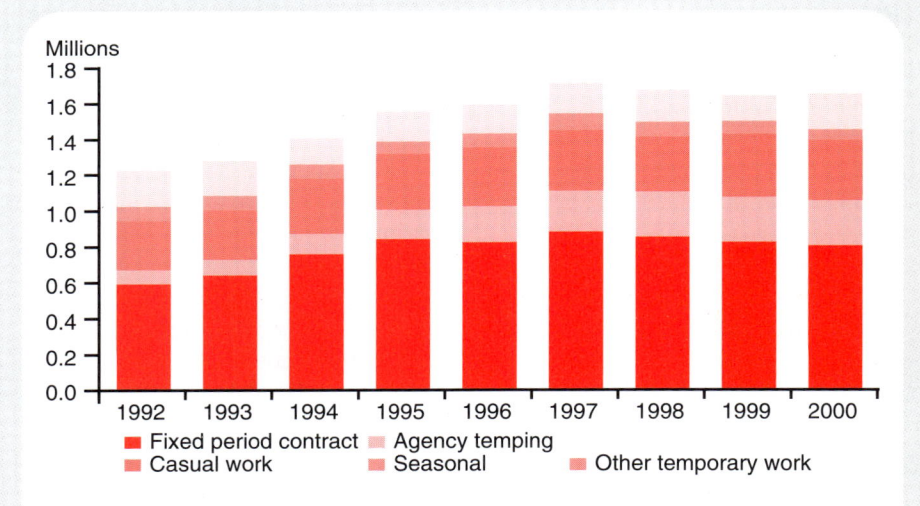

Figure 7.8 *Temporary employees, United Kingdom 1992-2000*
Source: adapted from *Labour Market Trends*, Office for National Statistics.

THE STUDENT'S ECONOMY IN FOCUS 2000/01

45

10 Union benefits

Economic theory suggests that unions act to increase wages and other benefits for their members, but this leads to a reduction in the demand for labour by employers. Figure 7.9 would tend to support the view that unions help increase benefits for members. It shows that work entitlements for non-managerial female employees are considerably better in workplaces which recognise unions (i.e. are prepared to negotiate with unions) than those which don't. For instance, 51 per cent of unionised workplaces give parental leave compared to 22 per cent of non-unionised workplaces. 28 per cent give term-time only contracts compared to 12 per cent of non-unionised workplaces.

The evidence must be treated with caution. About 35 per cent of female workers are union members. Female union members tend to be concentrated in large workplaces and in the public sector. Large private sector firms and the public sector are more likely to give better benefits to their employees anyway. However, these factors do not explain away fully the difference in benefits shown in Figure 7.9.

As for trade unions creating unemployment, some economists argue that the continued fall in unemployment since 1993 has been the result of legislation largely passed in the 1980s which severely reduced the legal powers of trade unions to strike and to organise in the workplace. The percentage of wages set through collective bargaining has fallen from 70 per cent in 1980s to 35 per cent in 1998. Only 18 per cent of young workers aged 18 to 29 were union members in 1999 compared to an average for all workers of 30 per cent. These falls have led to a more flexible labour force, it is argued. Employers are able to employ more temporary staff to fill vacancies, helping to resist upward pressure on wages from permanent staff. They are also less likely to be faced by unions threatening to take strike action if pay levels are not raised. This again has led to firms being able to pay lower wages to staff than would otherwise have been the case. Lower wages mean that the demand for labour is higher and hence unemployment is lower.

Trade unions would argue that their activities do not cause unemployment. The demand for labour in the whole economy is wage inelastic. Hence, rises in wages achieved by trade unions lead to very little fall in the quantity demanded of labour.

Figure 7.9 *Entitlements for non-managerial female employees, % of workplaces*
Source: adapted from Centre for Economic Performance.

Entitlement	Firms not recognising unions	Firms recognising unions
Switch from full-time to part-time employment	42	64
Perental leave	22	51
Job sharing schemes	15	50
Term-time only contracts	12	28
Working at or from home in normal working hours	11	17
Workplace nursery or nursery linked with workplace	2	7
Financial help/subsidy to parents for child care	3	5

Reading list

A.G. Anderton, *Economics*, Causeway Press (3rd ed. 2000) pages 82-83, 462-518.
A.G. Anderton, *Economics AS Level*, Causeway Press (2000) pages 82-83.
J. Bearshaw et al, *Economics: A Student's Guide,* Longman (4th ed. 1998) pages 243-271.
P. Maunder et al, *Economics Explained*, Collins Educational (Revised 3rd ed. 2000) pages 224-231, 419-437.
D. Begg et al, *Economics*, McGraw Hill, (5th ed. 1997) pages 163-197.
P. Curwen et al, *Understanding the UK Economy*, Macmillan, (4th ed. 1997) pages 366-400.
C. Bamford, editor, *Economics for AS*, Heinemann Educational (2000) pages 52-53, 88-89.
L. Simpson and I. Paterson, *The UK Labour Market*, Heinemann Educational (2nd ed. 1998).
P. Nolan, 'Trade unions and British economic performance, *Developments in Economics* Vol 11, Causeway Press (1995).
A. Palmer, 'Changes in Labour force participation - are women taking men's jobs?', *Developments in Economics* Vol 13, Causeway Press (1997).
B. Thomas, 'Flexible labour markets', *Developments in Economics* Vol 14, Causeway Press (1998).
P. Nolan and G. Slater, 'Employee relations, labour market change and economic performance', *Developments in Economics* Vol 16, Causeway Press (2000).

Essay questions

In 1992 average male earnings in the UK were £295.90 per week whereas average female earnings were £211.30 per week.

How might this difference in male and female earnings be explained?
(Edexcel January 1996)

(a) Explain why the average salary of a secretary is less than the average salary of a solicitor. (12 marks)
(b) Discuss the importance of wage differentials for the efficient functioning of a market economy. (13 marks)
(AQA [AEB] November 1995)

(a) Explain why there has been an increase in the proportion of the working population employed in the service sector in the United Kingdom. (12 marks)
(b) Discuss the economic significance of this change in the pattern of employment. (13 marks)
(AQA [AEB] June 1996)

(a) What are the main factors which account for differences in wage rates? (12 marks)
(b) Discuss the view that the main reason why the average earnings of women remain below those of men is discrimination in the labour market. (13 marks)
(AQA [AEB] January 1998)

According to a recent survey (A Clark and A Oswald, *Economic Review*, November 1993), trade unions would prefer an increase in their members' wages with employment held constant, to an increase in employment with wages held constant. Does this, in your view, give a realistic and comprehensive picture of the objectives of trade unions? Discuss the possible reasons for the decline of more than 10 per cent in the proportion of the workforce who are members of trade unions since 1980.
(AQA [NEAB] 1996)

What factors determine wages in economic theory? Does this explanation adequately account for the relative pay of teachers, Members of Parliament and directors of large companies? (AQA [NEAB] 1997)

In 1998 public sector pay increased by about 2.5 per cent while private sector pay grew by about 6 per cent. Outline the marginal productivity theory of wage determination and discuss whether it provides a convincing explanation of the differences in the above pay increases.
(AQA [NEAB] 1999)

(a) Explain, with an example, the difference between transfer earnings and economic rent. (8)
(b) Discuss why different amounts of economic rent are earned in different occupations, such as headteachers and school cleaners. (12) (OCR November 1999)

Governments in many countries are facing the problem of an ageing population - tough decisions have to be made about how any system of state-provided retirement pensions should be paid for.
(a) Explain why many governments provide retirement pensions. (8)
(b) Discuss how governments can deal with the problems that an ageing population could create for a system of state-provided pensions. (12)
(OCR June 1999)

In 1998, a report recommended that a minimum wage for the U.K. should be set at £3.60 an hour. This compared with an average wage of £3.20 an hour throughout much of the hotel and catering industry.
(a) Using a diagram, explain the impact upon the labour market of the hotel and catering industry. (10)
(b) Discuss how an individual firm in the hotel and catering industry might react to the introduction of the proposed minimum wage. (15) (OCR November 1999)

(a) Using examples, distinguish between the geographical mobility and the occupational mobility of labour. (5)
(b) With the aid of demand and supply analysis, examine why skilled workers tend to be paid more than unskilled workers. Explain why this is not always the case. (10)
(c) Critically examine the view that, as we move into the new millennium, there is little useful role for trade unions in the UK economy. (10)
(CCEA 1999)

Exam notes

The demand for labour Labour is a derived demand from the demand for goods and services. It is determined by the value placed by employers on the last worker employed, called the marginal revenue product of labour (Box 6). In turn, this value is determined by factors such as the qualifications of workers (Boxes 7 and 8) and their ability to influence the profitability and growth of the firm.
The supply of labour Within the national labour market, there is a national supply of labour, a supply of labour to each occupation, industry or region and an individual supply. Supply is determined by a number of factors including population, the cost of living, demand from other occupations and levels of pay (Boxes 2, 3 and 7).
The equilibrium wage rate Wages are determined by the forces of demand and supply in a competitive market (Boxes 7 and 8). If wages levels in an occupation are too low, there will be excess demand (Box 1); if too high, there will be excess supply. Some workers suffer from discrimination in the workplace which will lower their wages (Boxes 2, 5 and 6).
Labour market flexibility Trade unions (Box 10) represent an imperfection in the labour market, making it less flexible. The weaker the power of trade unions, the greater the flexibility of the market. However, trade unions may bring about a more equitable distribution of income and they may also lead to greater efficiency in markets where there is a monopsonist (a single buyer of labour). Minimum wages too make labour markets less flexible and efficient. However, they are usually introduced to bring about greater equity (Box 4). A number of factors affect labour market flexibility including the mix of permanent to temporary work (Box 9).

Unit 8
Monetary policy

1. UK monetary growth

Monetarists argue that increases in the money supply (M) over and above the real rate of growth (PT) in an economy are likely to lead to inflation. As Figure 8.1 shows, the rate of growth of the money supply increased slightly in the late 1980s. This was accompanied by a rise in the rate of inflation. The sharp fall in the rate of growth of the money supply, from a peak of 19 per cent year on year in the last quarter of 1989 for M4 to a low of 2.3 per cent in the second quarter of 1993, was accompanied by a sharp fall in the inflation rate. Since then, there has been little correlation between the rate of increase of the money supply and the rate of inflation. Some economists argue that this is because, at low rates of inflation, there is not a perfect correlation between M and P. Slightly above average increases in M arise because there is an increase in the demand for money and V, the velocity of circulation, falls as a result. However, most economists would agree that high rates of inflation upwards of 10 per cent per annum will be associated with higher rates of increase of the money supply.

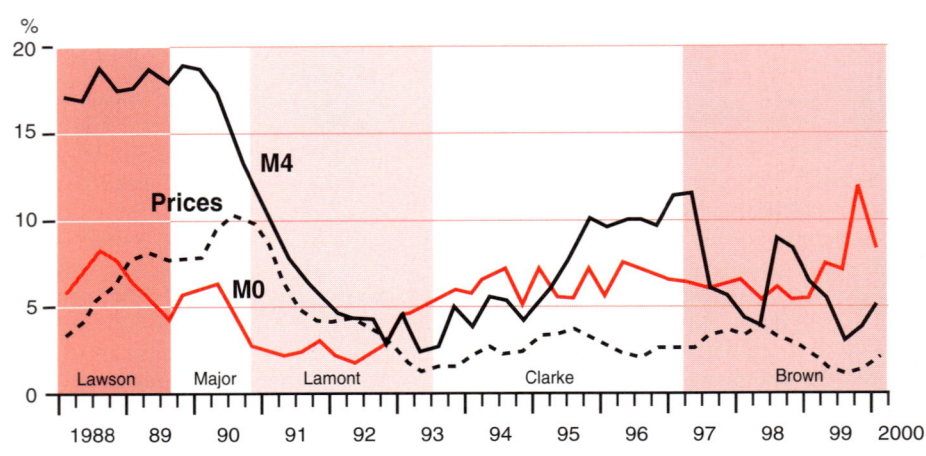

Figure 8.1 *Money supply (M0 and M4 seasonally adjusted) and prices (RPI), % change over previous year*
Source: adapted from *Economic Trends*, Office for National Statistics.

2. Short term and long term interest rates

Bank base rate is the rate of interest around which the major banks in the UK set all their interest rates. Savers are offered rates of interest below bank base rate, whilst borrowers are charged above base rate. When bank base rates change, so too do most of the interest rates set by banks to their customers, such as mortgage rates.

The level of bank base rate is determined by the Bank of England. Since the 1980s, changes in bank base rates have been the main way in which government has influenced aggregate demand and, in particular, the rate of inflation. When, as in the late 1980s, the mid-1990s and 1997-98, inflationary pressures began to build up, interest rates were increased. This helped reduce spending and hence aggregate demand. In turn, this reduced the rate of growth of prices. When inflationary pressures fell, as in the early 1990s, in 1996 and in 1999, the Bank of England cut interest rates and allowed high growth in aggregate demand.

Long term interest rates, such as the market rate of interest on British Government 20 year securities, are not fixed directly by the Bank of England. Market forces determine these rates of interest. However, long term interest rates do tend to move with bank base rates. Higher short term interest rates tend to make borrowers and lenders believe that long term interest rates will be higher in the future and vice versa.

Long term interest rates should normally be above short term interest rates. Longer term savers should receive a premium for locking their money away for a long time or taking a greater risk that the second hand value of a financial asset like a government bond could go down substantially if long term interest rates rise. In 1998-2000, however, short term interest rates were above long term interest rates. This may have been because savers and borrowers expected short term interest rates to fall in the near future. With inflation at around 2.5 per cent, real short term interest rates were relatively high at the time. Long term interest rates in Europe and the USA were also lower than in the UK. With savings being internationally mobile, there is a tendency for long term interest rates worldwide to converge.

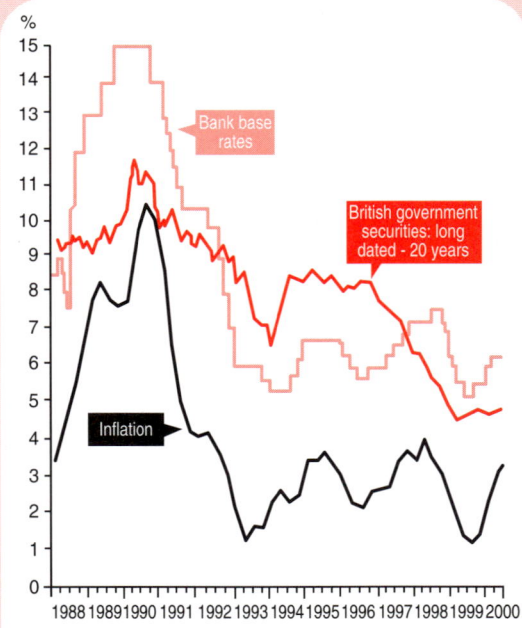

Figure 8.2 *UK interest rates*
Source: adapted from *Economic Trends*, *Annual Abstract of Statistics*, Office for National Statistics.

UNIT 8 MONETARY POLICY

3 Government spending and monetary policy

In his March 2000 Budget, the Chancellor of the Exchequer announced sizable increases in government spending, particularly on health, education and transport. Government spending is one of the components of aggregate demand. A rise in government spending, all other things being equal, is likely to raise aggregate demand. Keynesian economists would indeed argue that there will be a multiplier effect, with every £1 of extra government spending generating further spending in the rest of the economy.

However, an increase in aggregate demand will put pressure on prices. If the increase in government spending is large enough, the inflation rate will rise. To prevent this from happening, the Bank of England would have to raise interest rates to reduce other spending in the economy.

In its August 2000 Inflation Report, the Bank of England pointed out that some of the increase in government spending would be financed by falls in social security spending arising from lower than expected unemployment. Debt interest repayments would also fall because the government was predicting a budget surplus which would enable it to repay debt. However, overall the measures would 'make a small addition to overall demand growth'. It is unlikely that the Bank of England would therefore want to raise interest rates solely because of this increased government spending. However, if the spending were larger than predicted, the Bank of England may be forced to raise interest rates.

In general, to maintain stable prices, the looser the fiscal policy, the tighter must be monetary policy. Put another way, the higher the government contribution to aggregate demand, the lower must be the contribution of the private sector to maintain stable inflation rates. To reduce aggregate demand from the private sector, the Bank of England has to impose a tighter monetary policy regime.

4 The millennium bug

The turning of the clock from 23.59 on the 31 December 1999 to 00.00 on 1 January 2000 had been well prepared for by industry. Thousands of workers were on hand to sort out potential problems arising from the millennium bug - the problem that many computer programs had been written in such a way that they would turn the clock back and not forward from 99 to 00.

The financial sector too suffered from fears that its systems would be thrown into chaos. One fear was that the millennium bug might disrupt the flow of funds from bank to bank. For instance, the bug might prevent the automatic repayment of a loan from Bank A to Bank B. Bank B would then be short of funds which it would then have to borrow from Bank C, perhaps at higher rates of interest. Or Bank B may have promised a loan to client D which it was then unable to make and was forced to pay compensation to client D for failure to execute the loan contract. Banks responded to this threat by increasing the amount of short term funds they kept. This increased the demand for short term loans and as a consequence increased their price, the rate of interest. Figure 8.3 shows how the interest rate differential between three month interbank deposits (loans between banks repayable in three months time) and repo interest rates (equivalent to the interest paid on money borrowed and lent for just 24 hours) increased sharply in October and November 1999.

The millennium bug also forced the banks to carry more cash. There was a fear that some cash machines might not work, prompting a run on other cash machines as customers panicked. Panic withdrawing of cash could also occur if banks lost computer-held records of customer accounts. Perhaps more importantly, there was an expectation that bank customers would withdraw more money than usual to spend on millennium night. Figure 8.4 shows this millennium spike in M0, the amount of notes and coins in the economy. The figures have been seasonally adjusted to smooth out the customer rise in demand for cash during the Christmas period.

Figure 8.3 *Interest rate spread between 3 month interbank deposits and repo interest rates (per cent, 5 day moving average)*
Source: adapted from Reuters.

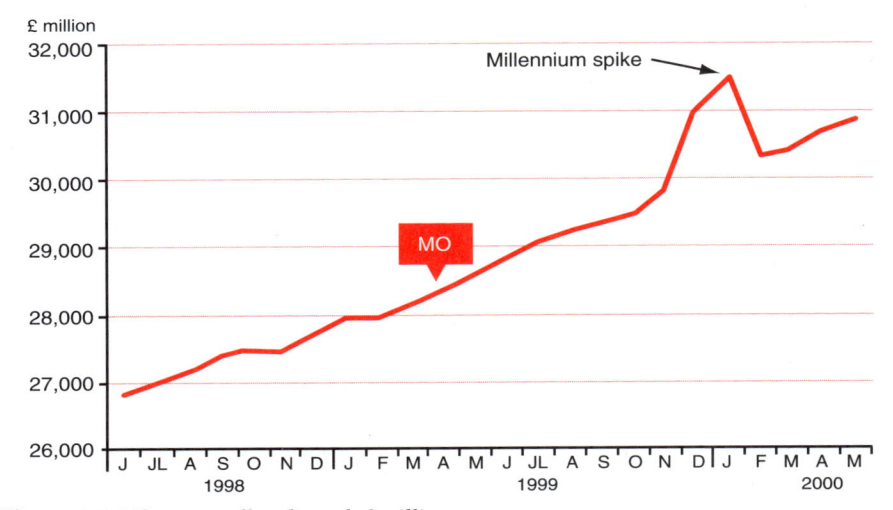

Figure 8.4 *M0, seasonally adjusted, £ million*
Source: adapted from *Economic Trends*, Office for National Statistics.

UNIT 8 MONETARY POLICY

5 Monetary policy and exchange rate policy

Monetary policy and exchange rate policy are interlinked. A tight monetary policy where interest rates are high is likely, all other things being equal, to increase the value of the domestic currency against other currencies and vice versa. So a government wanting high interest rates to curb inflation is most unlikely at the same time to achieve a low value of its currency to boost exports.

In 2000, the value of the pound continued to be high against the euro. However, it fell in value against the US dollar. Interest rates may have played a part in this. Figure 8.5 shows interest rate differentials between 3 month sterling deposit accounts and those denominated in $US and deutschmarks (a proxy for the euro). In 1999 and 2000, the US central bank, the Federal Reserve Bank, pushed up short term interest rates in the USA at a faster rate than the Bank of England was doing in the UK. Both were afraid that inflation might rise if growth in aggregate demand was not curtailed. The result was that the interest rate differential between sterling deposits and dollar deposits fell from being positive to being negative. Economic theory would suggest that a change in interest rate differentials, all other things being equal, will lead to a change in exchange rates as funds flow into the country with the improved interest rate differential.

Against the euro, as Figure 8.6 shows, the pound remained strong and even increased in value despite a falling interest rate differential - the opposite of what might be expected. However, the value of the euro became weaker in 1999 and 2000 partly because a variety of factors made the dollar stronger (see unit 12). Interest differentials between the pound and the euro were not the most important factor which was setting the exchange rate between the two currencies.

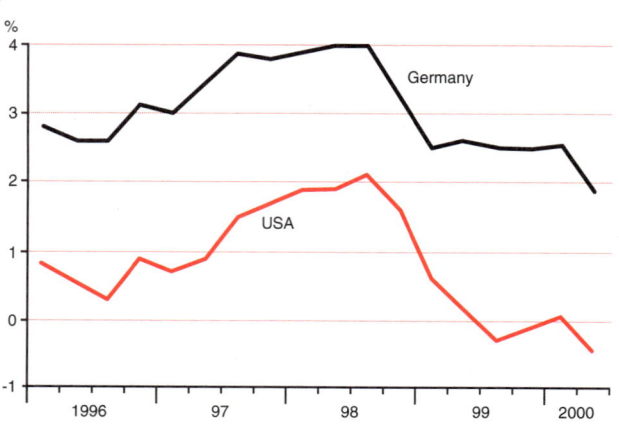

Figure 8.5 *Spread between UK interest rates and US and German interest rates[1]*
1. Three month deposit rates.
Source: adapted from *Financial Statistics*, Office for National Statistics

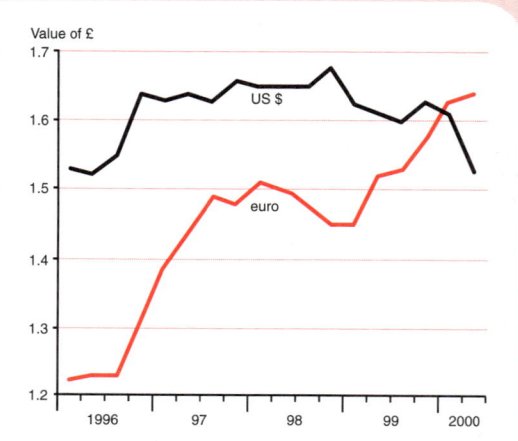

Figure 8.6 *Exchange rate of pound against the US$ and the euro*
Source: adapted from *Economic Trends*, Office for National Statistics

6 Monetary policy decision making

Between August 1999 and February 2000, the Monetary Policy Committee (MPC) of the Bank of England raised the repo rate, and hence bank base rates, from 5 per cent to 6 per cent. This represented a tightening of monetary policy. Why did it choose to do this?

One factor was the relatively strong growth of the economy at the time. As Figure 8.7 shows, the Bank of England had pushed up interest rates from late 1996 and kept them high to late 1998 to dampen the strong growth in the economy at the time which was threatening to raise the inflation rate. It was widely expected that the economy would fall into a recession in 1998 due to this tight monetary policy. Instead, the growth rate fell but remained positive. By the third quarter of 1999, economic growth had increased and by the fourth quarter was above the long term trend rate for the UK economy. The MPC became anxious that this strong growth would raise inflationary pressures. Hence it pushed up interest rates. Strong growth in GDP continued in 2000 and there seemed little likelihood that there would be substantial falls in interest rates. Indeed, some economists on the MPC wanted to increase interest rates even more to further tighten monetary policy and dampen the economy.

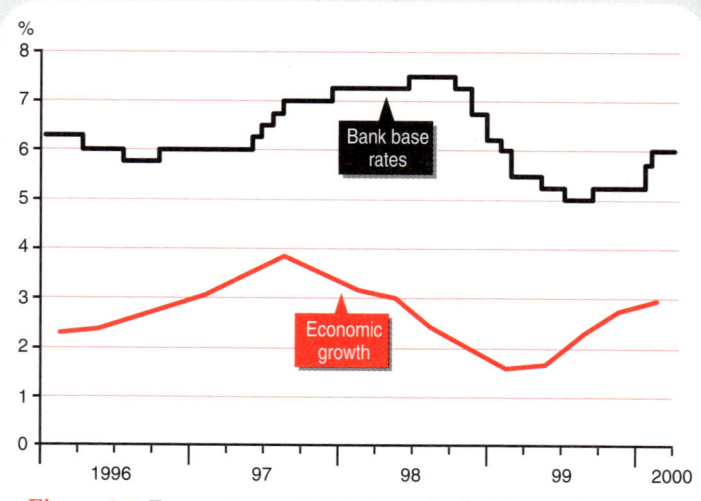

Figure 8.7 *Economic growth (% change in GDP at market prices) and bank base rates*
Source: adapted from *Economic Trends*, Office for National Statistics

7 The housing market and monetary policy

The housing market can be a cause of inflation. First, the construction of new housing accounts forms around 15 per cent of total investment in the economy, which in itself contributes around 19 per cent of GDP at market prices. Consumer spending on housing services (imputed rents) accounts for around 8 per cent of total consumption, which in itself accounts for two thirds of GDP at market prices. In addition, spending on goods such as furniture and carpets, which are closely related to turnover in the housing market account, forms another 6 per cent of consumption. So any upturn in the housing market contributes directly to an increase in aggregate demand, which in turn can lead to higher inflation rates.

Second, housing represents approximately half of household wealth. When house prices rise sharply, household wealth increases sharply too, which increases the willingness of households to spend and take on debt. Hence aggregate demand is likely to rise.

Third, when people move house, they may borrow more money through a mortgage than they need to pay for the house. This difference between the amount needed and the mortgage is called mortgage equity withdrawal (MEW). When consumer confidence is low, as in a recession, MEW is often negative. Households put their own savings into a house purchase to limit the size of a mortgage because they are worried about whether they will be able to afford the repayments. In a boom, though, with consumer confidence high, MEW is likely to be positive. In the housing boom of the second half of the 1980s, MEW was common and helped stoke the Lawson boom. MEW became positive again in the late 1990s as house price inflation increased.

The state of the housing market is one of the key indicators the Bank of England Monetary Policy Committee considers when deciding whether to change interest rates. The strong growth of house prices in 1999 was a factor in influencing the Bank's decision to raise interest rates from 5 per cent in August 1999 to 6 per cent by February 2000. Equally, the slowdown in house prices in 2000 helped influence the Bank's decision to maintain interest rates at 6 per cent for most of the rest of 2000.

When considering the state of the housing market, the Monetary Policy Committee has data about recent house price increases. For instance, both the Nationwide Building Society and the Halifax bank publish an index of house prices based on the price of houses for which they have extended mortgages. Figure 8.8 shows the sharp rise in house prices in 1999 and the slowdown in 2000. Figure 8.8 also shows that house prices are correlated with the number of houses bought and sold (as measured by the number of legal purchase documents delivered to land registration offices). When the number of houses bought and sold increases, this is likely to be caused by an increase in demand for houses, which in turn accounts for the rise in the price of houses.

The Monetary Policy Committee also has access to advance indicators of changes in house prices. For instance, the number of net reservations for new houses (buyers signing contracts of intention to buy new houses typically not yet completed) is closely correlated to particulars delivered as Figure 8.9 shows. There is typically a 3-5 month time lag between signing a reservation and final completion of the sale. So the number of net reservations in one month gives an indication of what is likely to happen to house prices in 3-5 months time. As Figure 8.9 shows, the downturn in the number of net reservations at the end of 1999 correctly predicted the fall in growth in house prices in the first half of 2000.

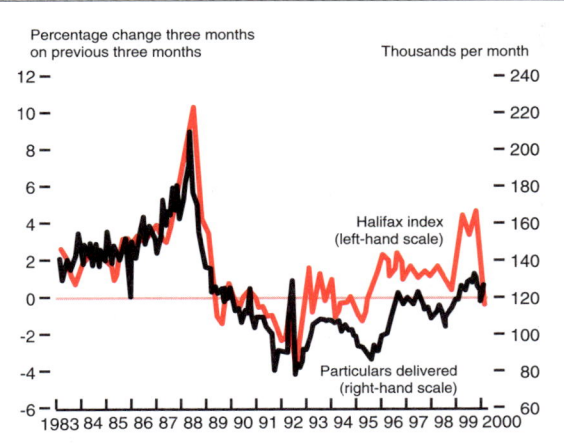

Figure 8.8 *Particulars delivered and house price inflation*
Source: adapted from Bank of England, *Inflation Report* August 2000.

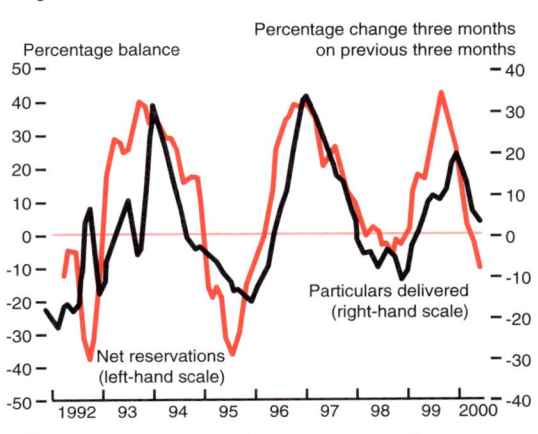

Figure 8.9 *Net reservations and particulars delivered*
Source: adapted from Bank of England, *Inflation Report* August 2000.

Reading list

A.G. Anderton, *Economics*, Causeway Press (3rd ed. 2000) pages 241-247, 552-580, 611-612, 626-629.
A.G. Anderton, *Economics AS Level*, Causeway Press (2000) pages 241-247.
J. Beardshaw et al, *Economics: A Student's Guide*, Longman (4th ed. 1998) pages 465-510.
P. Maunder et al, *Economics Explained*, Collins Educational (Revised 3rd ed. 2000) pages 389-321, 471-485.
D. Begg et al, *Economics*, McGraw Hill (5th ed. 1997) pages 367-398.
P. Curwen et al, *Understanding the UK Economy*, Macmillan (4th ed. 1997) pages 525-544.
C. Bamford, editor, *Economics for AS*, Cambridge University Press (2000) pages 154-155, 158-161.
D. Heathfield and M. Russell, *Inflation and UK Monetary Policy*, Heinemann Educational (3rd ed. 1999).
D. Gowland, 'Interest rates', *Development in Economics* Vol 12, Causeway Press (1996).
G. Dawson, 'The Bank of England', *Developments in Economics* Vol 14 Causway Press (1998).
M. Schmidt, 'The German Bundesbank: instruments and policy', *Developments in Economics* Vol 14, Causeway Press (1998).
K. Pilbeam, 'International capital markets', *Developments in Economics* Vol 16, Causeway Press (2000).

UNIT 8 MONETARY POLICY

Essay questions

(a) What is meant by the money supply? (20 marks)
(b) Why might a government wish to control the money supply? (40 marks)
(c) Why is tight control of the money supply difficult to achieve? (40 marks)
(Edexcel January 1995)

Assume that there has been a substantial increase in the rate of a country's money supply. Analyse what impact this might have on the level of economic activity and on the price level.
(Edexcel January 1995)

The broad measure of money supply increased at a rate of 12 per cent per annum in the UK in 1997.
(a) Outline the factors which might have led to this growth in the money supply. (30 marks)
(b) Why might the UK government be concerned about such an increase in the money supply? (40 marks)
(c) How might the existence of European Monetary Union affect the conduct of monetary policy in the UK? (30 marks)
(Edexcel June 1999)

(a) How can the government influence the level of interest rates? (12 marks)
(b) Discuss the likely effects of a significant increase in interest rates upon the rate of inflation. (13 marks)
(AQA [AEB] June 1995)

(a) What determines the rate of growth of the money supply? (12 marks)
(b) Why has the Bank of England often found it difficult to achieve the targets which it has set for the rate of monetary growth? (13 marks)
(AQA [AEB] January 1997)

(a) How does the Bank of England attempt to influence interest rates? (12 marks)
(b) Discuss the role of monetary policy in controlling inflation. (13 marks)
(AQA [AEB] January 1998)

What factors determine the rate of interest in an economy? Are relatively high interest rates necessary and desirable for achieving a low inflation rate?
(AQA [NEAB] 1997)

Explain briefly what is meant by money and why it is necessary to have different measures of the money supply such as M0 and M4. Discuss the relationship between inflation in the economy and the supply of money.
(AQA [NEAB] 1998)

What economic factors determine the level of interest rates in the economy? Discuss how changes in interest rates affect the components of aggregate demand in the economy.
(AQA [NEAB] 1999)

(a) What is the PSBR and what may cause it to increase over time? (8)
(b) Discuss how the government might fund a growth in the PSBR and the likely impact of such funding on the economy. (12)
(OCR March 1997)

(a) Explain the functions of money and how these might be affected by high rates of inflation. (8)
(b) Analyse and comment upon how a change in the money supply might affect the rate of inflation in an economy. (12)
(OCR November 1997)

Banks and other financial institutions create money, whilst one of the roles performed by the Bank of England is responsibility for monetary control.
(a) Explain how financial institutions create money. (8)
(b) Discuss the extent to which the Bank of England has been successful in its attempt to control the growth of the UK's money supply. (12)
(OCR November 1999)

(a) Briefly outline the main functions of money. (5)
(b) Distinguish between nominal and real interest rates and explain how, in theory, interest rates are determined in a free market economy. (10)
(c) Discuss the wisdom of the Chancellor of the Exchequer's decision of May 1997 to hand over control of interest rates to the Bank of England. (10)
(CCEA 1999)

Exam notes

Money supply definitions Recent questions have tended to avoid asking for explanations of what is money and money supply definitions. However, these topics are still on some specifications. Money is any asset which performs the four functions of money - a medium of exchange, a unit of account, a store of wealth and a standard for deferred payment. The money supply in the UK is officially calculated in two main ways: M0 and M4.
Money creation, demand for money, the City Examiners also may expect an understanding of how money is created through the banking system, as well as topics such as the demand for money, the role of the Bank of England and the function of capital markets. The millennium (Box 4) provides an example of how the demand for money can change and how this can affect interest rates.

Interest rates Questions sometimes ask why there are different interest rates in the economy. Examiners may also ask how interest rates are determined (Box 2).
Monetary policy Most questions now concentrate on monetary policy: its objectives, implementation and effects on the real economy, the exchange rate and inflation. There are two main objectives of monetary policy at present. These are the control of inflation and the maintenance of growth in the UK. The Bank of England implements monetary policy through short term interest rate control (Box 2). Fixing short term interest rates influences other interest rates in the economy such as government bond yields. It also influences the rate of growth of the money supply; the higher the rate of interest, the lower is likely to be the growth of the money supply.

Trends in money supply growth are discussed in Box 1. However, policy making can only be as good as the data available to policy makers and the Monetary Policy Committee has to rely on a range of often conflicting evidence when coming to their decisions (Boxes 6 and 7).
Links Monetary policy is often linked to other areas of the syllabus. For instance, fiscal policy cannot operate independently of monetary policy (Box 3). Equally exchange rate policy and monetary policy are interlinked (Box 5). Monetary policy can also be linked to individual markets such as the housing market (Box 7). Questions also frequently ask about how monetary policy can affect the key macroeconomic variables of inflation and unemployment (units 9 and 11) and the current balance (unit 12).

Unit 9
Unemployment, inflation and income distribution

1 Trends in unemployment

Unemployment in the UK fell steadily between 1993, when it peaked on a claimant count basis at 3 million, and 2000, when it stood at 1.1 million. This fall in unemployment in part reflects a fall in cyclical unemployment. The economy went into deep recession between 1990 and 1992 which led to a doubling of unemployment. Unemployment reached a peak of 2.9 million (on an ILO count) in 1992 and 1993. Since then unemployment has continued to fall to a low of 1.7 million by the year 2000.

The continued fall in unemployment could be argued to be a fall in structural unemployment. Regional economies, such as the North West, which performed poorly in the 1960s, 1970s and 1980s because of the contraction of mining and manufacturing, performed better in the 1990s as new, particularly service, industries moved in. Older unemployed workers with outdated skills have left the workforce through retirement and been replaced with young workers who have more skills and are more geographically mobile. Government expenditure on education and training helped produce this better educated and more mobile labour force.

Figure 9.1 shows that the ILO count has fallen less fast than the claimant count. Partly, this is because a variety of government measures, including the New Deal, have shaken out workers who claim benefits for unemployment but who had no intention of taking a job. Partly it is because many, particularly female workers, don't claim benefits but do look for work when employment opportunities arise. They do not appear on the claimant count as unemployed. However, they appear on the ILO count because it is a survey which counts those actively seeking work as unemployed whether or not they are claiming benefits for being unemployed.

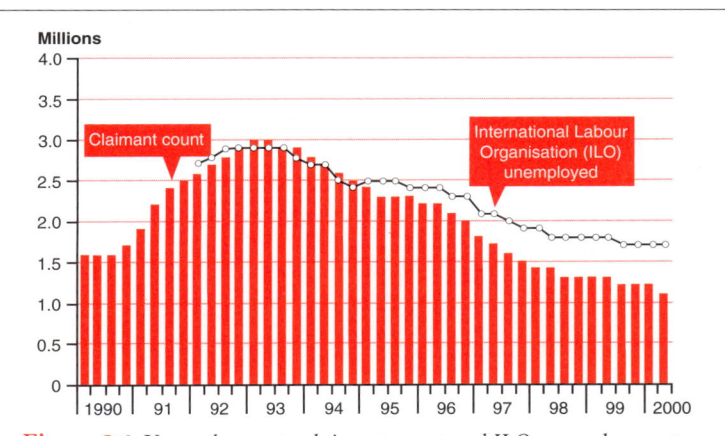

Figure 9.1 *Unemployment: claimant count and ILO unemployment, seasonally adjusted*
Source: adapted from *Economic Trends*; *Economic Trends Annual Supplement*, Office for National Statistics.

2 Unemployment amongst those aged 50+

Those aged 50+ in the population of working age (defined as men aged 50-64 and women 50-59) are less likely to be working than the average worker, but equally they are less likely to be unemployed. Table 9.1 shows that the activity rate (i.e. the proportion of the age group either in work or seeking work) of the over 50s is 69.4 per cent compared to 79.1 per cent for the whole population of working age. Many older workers, particularly males aged 60-65, have taken early retirement and therefore are no longer in work. However, older workers had an unemployment rate of 4.0 per cent compared to 5.7 per cent for all workers. Partly this is because early retirement is sometimes an alternative to unemployment for older workers who lose their jobs. Partly it is because the unemployment rates of young workers aged 16-24 are particularly high and this helps increase the average for all workers.

Older workers though, once they become unemployed, often find it difficult to find a new job. Hence, the proportions who are unemployed for 12-24 months and more than 24 months are higher than for all workers. There is a variety of possible explanations for this. One is that older workers tend to be paid more than younger workers. Employers may therefore prefer to employ younger workers to keep their costs down. Some older workers do not have the job specific skills required for current vacancies because they have worked all their lives in industries which today are shrinking. Coal miners, steel workers or ship builders are examples of workers who over the past 30 years have had difficulty getting new work. There is also widespread discrimination against older workers by employers who perceive that older workers are less flexible and less productive than young workers.

	Activity rate %	Unemployment rate (ILO) %	Proportion (%) of workers in age group unemployed for 12-24 months	24 months +
Over 50s	69.4	4.0	13.6	27.4
All workers	79.1	5.7	11.4	15.2

Table 9.1 *Activity rates and unemployment rates of older workers, February to April 2000, seasonally adjusted*
Source: adapted from *Labour Market Trends*, Office for National Statistics.

UNIT 9 UNEMPLOYMENT, INFLATION AND INCOME DISTRIBUTION

3 The Phillips curve

The Phillips curve shows the relationship between inflation and unemployment. A.W. Phillips argued in his original article in 1958 that high unemployment was associated with low inflation and vice versa. Figure 9.2 shows that this inverse relationship was broadly true in the 1980s and the first half of the 1990s.

Figure 9.2 also shows how the Phillips curve has shifted since the mid-1960s. The original Phillips curve, which ran through the points shown by the years 1963 to 1967, has shifted to the right. According to Milton Friedman, the shift to the right has been caused by a rise in inflationary expectations. The higher workers and firms expect inflation to be, the further to the right will be the short run Phillips curve.

The data suggest that inflationary expectations in the first half of the 1980s were higher than in the second half of the 1980s and early 1990s. Since 1994, the short run Phillips curve seems to have been shifting back towards its origin. Each year unemployment has fallen with little or no change in inflation.

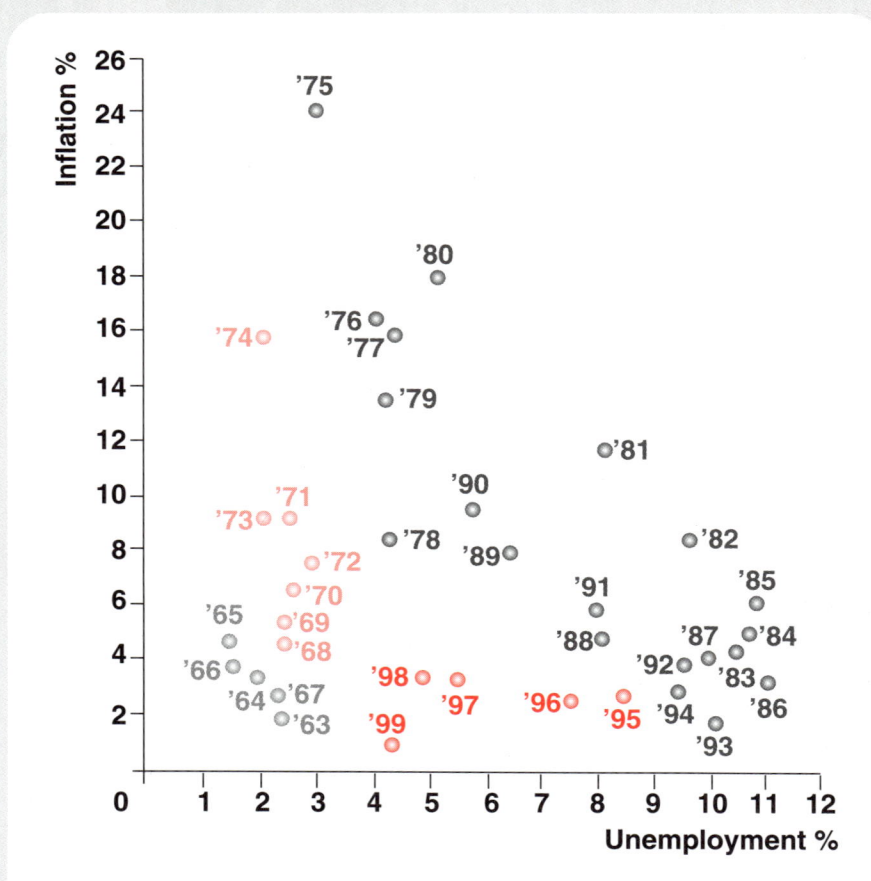

Figure 9.2 *Phillips curve data, 1963-99*
Source: adapted from *Economic Trends*; Office for National Statistics.

This is good for the British economy because lower rates of unemployment can be achieved for any given rate of inflation.

4 Inflation

Inflation, as measured by the RPIX (the Retail Price Index excluding mortgage interest payments), fluctuated broadly in the 2.0-3.5 per cent range between 1995 and 2000. Figure 9.3 shows the forecast for inflation made by the Bank of England in August 2000. The Bank of England no longer gives a single forecast. Instead, it gives a range within which it thinks inflation will lie in the future. The forecast says that there is a 90 per cent chance that inflation will be in the 1.5 to 3.9 per cent range. The central forecast is that inflation will rise slightly in 2001 and 2002 to exceed a little the target 2.5 per cent rate set by the government.

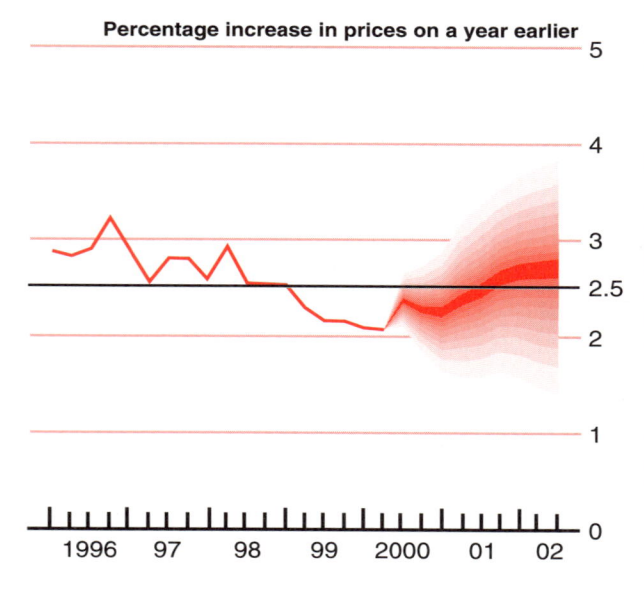

Figure 9.3 *Inflation (RPIX projection), August 2000*
Source: adapted from *Inflation Report*, Bank of England.

Note: The bands indicate the relative likelihood of an inflation outcome. The darkest band includes the central (single most likely) projection and covers 10% of the probability. Each successive pair of bands is drawn to cover a further 10% of probabilities until 90% of the probability distribution is covered. The bands widen as the time horizon is extended, indicating increasing uncertainty about outcomes.

UNIT 9 UNEMPLOYMENT, INFLATION AND INCOME DISTRIBUTION

5 The Retail Price Index

The Retail Price Index is an average of all prices in the economy. It is far too costly to collect all prices at a point in time. Instead, statisticians collect prices of a sample of goods and services.

The goods and services chosen to be sampled represent current spending patterns. When spending patterns change, so too does the composition of the Retail Price Index. For instance, in 2000, women's leggings, admission fees at bingo halls, luncheon meat, custard powder and tinned ravioli were removed from the basket of goods making up the RPI. They were replaced by women's shorts, charges at ten pin bowling alleys, broccoli, prepacked salads and takeaway pizzas.

Prices for each item in the index are collected in different regions of the country and in different types of retail outlet. In 2000, for the first time, prices for selected items including books and toys were collected from internet sites. The weighting of the internet prices in the total index was just 0.05 per cent, representing the very small proportion of internet spending to total spending in the economy.

6 Inflation: goods vs services

The increase in prices of services was much higher than the increase in prices of goods in 1998 and 1999 as Figure 9.4 shows. The prices of services is heavily determined by wage rates in the UK. With wages increasing at 4-6 per cent over the period, it is perhaps not surprising that inflation in services was around 3-4 per cent.

In contrast, the prices of goods are much more determined by material costs, which are in turn to some extent determined by the cost of imports of goods. In 1998 and 1999, the pound was very high in value and this helped reduce import prices. Low inflation for goods and a strong pound have also forced manufacturing firms to find ways of cutting their material costs in order to remain competitive in their industries. Productivity growth, historically higher in the production of goods compared to services, has also helped reduce the rate of price rises for goods.

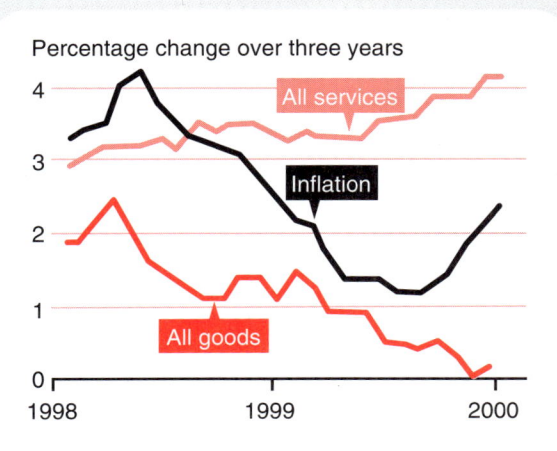

Figure 9.4 *Inflation for goods and services*
Source: adapted from Office for National Statistics, Datastream.

7 Child poverty

Research by the Joseph Rowntree Foundation (*Child Poverty and its Consequences*, March 1999) found that 4.3 million children, one third of all children in Britain, were living in households with below half average income in 1995/96. In 1968, only 1.3 million children lived in households with below half average income. So the incidence of relative poverty amongst children has increased over time despite rising average real incomes.

In absolute terms, the picture is slightly different. 55 per cent of children in 1968 lived in households with the same real income as half the average income in 1995/96. So the percentage of children in absolute poverty, as defined by half the average income in 1995/96, fell from 55 per cent to 33 per cent. However, almost of this fall, from 55 per cent to 36 per cent, occurred between 1968 and 1979. Since 1979, despite a rise of one third in average real household income, the fall in the number of children in households with half the 1995/96 real average income has been just 3 per cent.

This suggests that children have suffered considerably from the policies pursued mainly by the Conservative government of the 1980s, which redistributed income from the poor to the rich. It also suggests that child poverty can be reduced, as it was in the 1960s and 1970s, by an appropriate mix of policies designed to raise the incomes of the poorest households with children.

THE STUDENT'S ECONOMY IN FOCUS 2000/01

UNIT 9 UNEMPLOYMENT, INFLATION AND INCOME DISTRIBUTION

8 Demand pull inflation

The early 1990s saw a deep recession in the UK with falling inflation as demand-pull pressures eased. The recovery of 1992-94 was followed by a very mild slowdown in economic growth in 1995 which helped moderate rising inflation. Faster economic growth in 1996-98 led again to a moderate rise in demand-pull inflation. It was this rise which led the Bank of England to raise interest rates in 1997 and 1998 to slow the economy and reduce demand pressures. It was successful in doing this. Growth in the economy in the second half of 1998 and first half of 1999 fell, although a widely expected mild recession (negative growth for at least two quarters) failed to materialise. The rate of inflation too fell and enabled the Bank of England to cut interest rates again from October 1998. When economic growth began to increase again in the third quarter of 1999, the Bank of England began to increase interest rates again to control the recovery and prevent inflation from rising.

Figure 9.5 shows that in the mid-1990s, it was exports which were fuelling economic growth. With a weak pound at the time, exporters were finding it easy to find markets for their products. However, the strong pound from 1998 onwards saw export growth fall and even in one quarter become negative. In late 1999 and 2000, export growth resumed as exporters adjusted to a high pound.

Consumption growth was relatively high between 1996 and 2000, averaging 4 per cent per annum. This helped fuel inflationary pressures during the period.

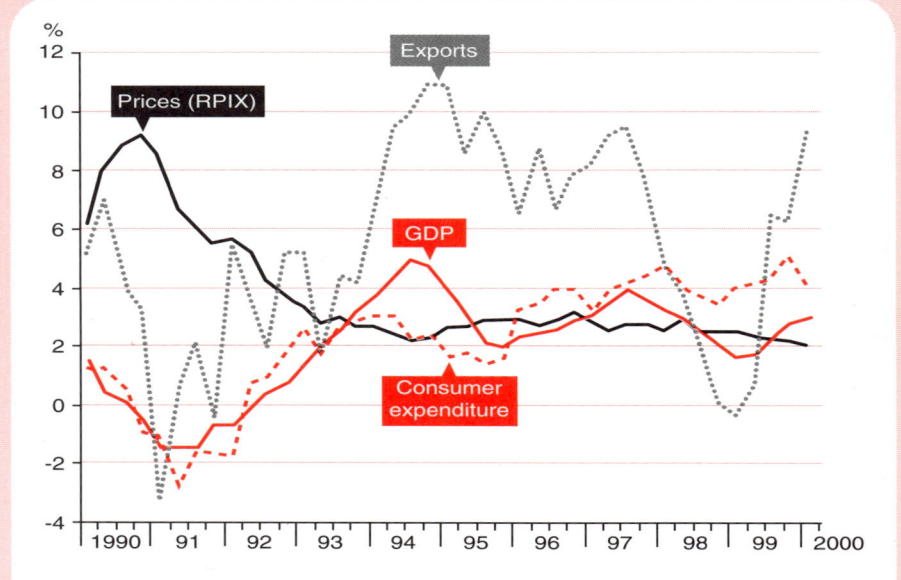

Figure 9.5 *Prices (RPIX), GDP, consumer expenditure and exports: annual percentage change*
Source: adapted from *Economic Trends*, Office for National Statistics.

9 Cost push inflation

Cost push inflation is caused by increases in costs feeding through to increases in retail prices. Figure 9.6 shows how the most important costs, earnings and import prices, changed between 1990 and 2000. The link between earnings and inflation can be seen during this period. Increases in average earnings tend to be a little above increases in prices. So when the rate of increase of average earnings accelerates, so too does the rate of inflation. This is because earnings are the largest element in costs for businesses on average.

Import prices too are important. The fall in import prices between 1996 and 1998 helped reduce inflationary pressures. However, import price inflation became positive again in 1999. The sharp rise in the price of oil in 2000 contributed to a significant rise in imported inflation.

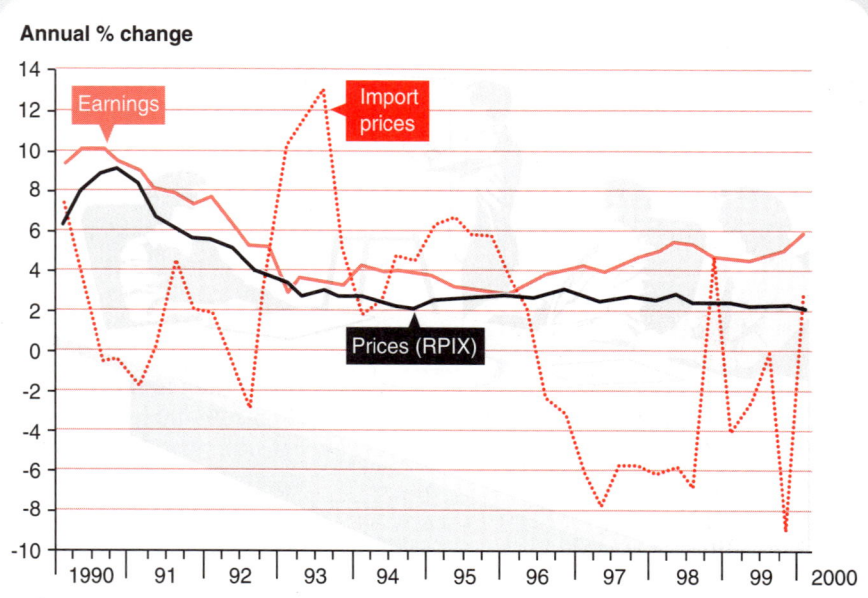

Figure 9.6 *Prices (RPIX), earnings and import prices: annual percentage change*
Source: adapted from *Economic Trends*, Office for National Statistics.

10 Increasing inequality

Figure 9.7 shows that inequality of income continued to increase in the 1990s. The number of households with an income at below 40 per cent of the average income (judged by the Joseph Rowntree Foundation to be on 'very low incomes') increased from less than 2 million in 1979/80 to 8 million in 1990/91 and then, having fallen a little, climbed back to over 8 million by 1997/98.

Figure 9.7 is an indicator of increased relative rather than absolute poverty. Between 1979 and 1998, real average household incomes increased. However, the increases in income disproportionately favoured the better off at the expense of the poorest in society.

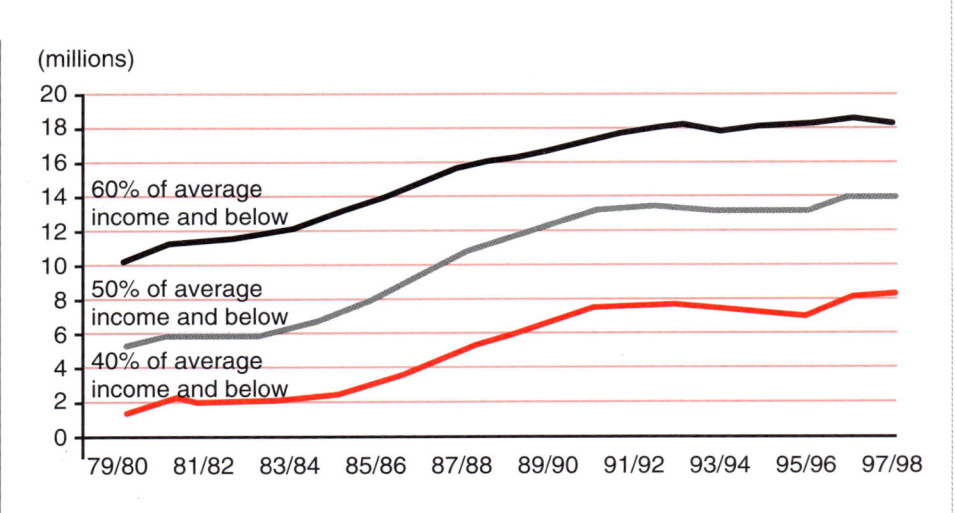

Figure 9.7 *Numbers of households on low incomes (after housing costs)*
Source: Joseph Rowntree Foundation, *Monitoring Poverty and Social Exclusion*, 1999.

11 Relative poverty

In 2000, the Joseph Rowntree Foundation published a report (*Poverty and Social Exclusion in Britain*) which suggested that inequalities were widening. The researchers undertook a large scale survey to establish a checklist of household items and activities that a majority of people considered to be necessities that everyone should be 'able to afford and which they should not have to do without'. For instance, the majority of respondents said that homes should be adequately heated, free from damp and in a decent state of decoration. Fridges, telephones and carpets were considered essentials. Being able to afford to visit friends and family, attend weddings or funerals or have celebrations on special occasions were also considered necessities. Ownership of a dishwasher, a mobile phone, internet access or satellite television were not considered to be necessities by over 90 per cent of respondents.

The researchers then interviewed individuals to find out whether they were able to afford or owned these necessities. They found on the basis of survey evidence that, for instance, 9.5 million people lived in housing which was inadequate. 8 million people could not afford one or more essential household goods such as a fridge or a telephone. 7.5 million were too poor to engage in social activities such as attending weddings or funerals.

Overall, 26 per cent of the population lacked two or more necessities and had low incomes. This definition of poverty applied to 71 per cent of unemployed people and 61 per cent of long-term sick and disabled people who lived in households where no one was in paid work. The rate for lone parents with one child was 62 per cent.

This survey is the latest in a series of surveys which the Joseph Rowntree Foundation has conducted using this methodology. Over time, the surveys have shown that between 1983 and 1990 the number of households living in poverty grew from 14 per cent to 21 per cent. By 1999, this had increased to 24 per cent. Without government measures to shift income and opportunities back to the poor, a significant minority of individuals will continue to live in relative poverty in the UK.

Reading list

A.G. Anderton, *Economics*, Causeway Press (3rd ed. 2000) pages 151-155, 180-190, 564-569, 581-618.
A.G. Anderton, *Economics AS Level*, Causeway Press (2000) pages 151-155, 180-190.
J. Beardshaw et al., *Economics: A Student's Guide*, Longman (4th ed. 1998) pages 621-656.
P. Maunder et al, *Economics Explained*, Collins Educational (Revised 3rd ed. 2000) pages 138-153, 219-280, 262-263, 474-478, 481-483.
D. Begg, *Economics*, McGraw Hill (5th ed. 1997) pages 442-479.
P. Curwen et al, *Understanding the UK Economy*, Macmillan (4th ed. 1997) pages 325-365, 421-444.
C. Bamford, editor, *Economics for AS*, Cambridge University Press (2000) pages 122-125, 130-133.
D. Heathfield and M. Russell, *Inflation and UK Monetary Policy*, Heinemann Educational (3rd ed. 1999).
A. Clark, R. Layard and M. Rubin, *UK Unemployment*, Heinemann Educational (3rd ed. 1997).
L. Simpson and I. Patterson, *The UK Labour Market*, Heinemann Educational (2nd ed. 1998).
J. Hudson, 'Inflation', *Developments in Economics* Vol 13, Causeway Press (1997).
D. Brooksbank, 'Unemployment policies and the New Deal', *Developments in Economics* Vol 16, Causeway Press (2000).

UNIT 9 UNEMPLOYMENT, INFLATION AND INCOME DISTRIBUTION

Essay questions

(a) Examine the economic costs of unemployment to society. (40 marks)
(b) Compare employment subsidies and reduced unemployment benefits as methods of reducing unemployment. (60 marks)
(Edexcel January 1998)

In 1991 the UK rate of inflation was 5.9 per cent and unemployment was 8.8 per cent. By June 1998 both inflation (2.8 per cent) and unemployment (4.8 per cent) had fallen significantly.
(a) Examine the costs associated with (i) inflation and (ii) unemployment. (50 marks)
(b) To what extent are policies designed to reduce the rate of inflation also appropriate for reducing unemployment? (50 marks)
(Edexcel June 1999)

(a) Monetarist and supply side economists believe that an economy has a natural rate of unemployment.
  (i) What is the natural rate of unemployment? (5 marks)
  (ii) What factors determine whether the natural rate of unemployment in an economy is likely to be high or low? (7 marks)
(b) Assess the significance of the 'natural rate of unemployment hypothesis' for the conduct of economic policy. (13 marks)
(AQA [AEB] November 1995)

(a) Explain the various costs of inflation. (12 marks)
(b) Discuss the proposition that, if the economy is to prosper in the long run, the main objective of government economic policy should be to control inflation. (13 marks)
(AQA [AEB] June 1998)

(a) Explain how the system of taxation in the United Kingdom affects the distribution of income. (12 marks)
(b) Discuss the advantages and disadvantages of increased expenditure on means-tested benefits as a way of relieving poverty in the United Kingdom. (13 marks)
(AQA [AEB] June 1999)

Briefly outline the factors which determine the distribution of income among individuals in the UK and suggest reasons why the gap between rich and poor has widened over the last decade. Discuss the measures a government might take to alleviate the causes and consequences of poverty.
(AQA [NEAB] 1996)

"Despite the moves towards a more flexible labour market in the UK, over one-third of claimants have been without a job for a year or longer." (*The Independent,* 5 October 1995.) Explain how unemployment may be defined and measured. Discuss the possible reasons for UK long-term unemployment and the policy measures which might be used to reduce it.
(AQA [NEAB] 1996)

How have the characteristics of the workforce and the unemployed in the UK changed in recent years? What are the implications of these changes for policies to deal with unemployment?
(AQA [NEAB] 1997)

Explain how unemployment may be measured. Discuss the possible effects on unemployment in the long-run and the short-run of increasing government expenditure on education and training.
(AQA [NEAB] 1998)

Explain why inflation is seen a major problem for an economy. Discuss whether it is possible to reduce inflation without increasing unemployment.
(AQA [NEAB] 1999)

(a) Outline the main types of unemployment which may exist in an economy. (5)
(b) Explain why it is important to try to determine the main causes of unemployment in an economy. (10)
(c) Examine the arguments for and against reducing the standard retirement age in the UK for males and females to 60 years. (10)
(CCEA 1998)

Exam notes

Examination questions in this area cover a wide range of issues and are often linked with government policy (discussed in unit 11).
Unemployment Specifications may require an understanding of the causes, costs and consequences of unemployment (Boxes 1 and 2).
Inflation Similarly, knowledge is required of the causes, costs and consequences of inflation (Boxes 4, 5, 6, 8 and 9).
Income distribution An understanding of differences in income between individuals, households and regions is needed as well as their causes and consequences (Boxes 7, 10 and 11).
Recent economic history Questions may expect candidates to have knowledge of recent economic history and in particular of recent inflation and unemployment trends (Boxes 1 and 4).
The Phillips curve The interaction between inflation and unemployment, summarised by the Phillips curve (Box 3), suggests that the natural rate of unemployment has been falling in the late 1990s because unemployment has been falling without increasing the rate of inflation.

Unit 10
Economic recovery and growth

1 The trade cycle

In the post-war era, the UK has tended to experience trade cycles with 5 year amplitudes. This means that the economy goes from boom to boom every 5 years and boom to bust every 2½ years.

Recessions in the 1950s and 1960s tended to be very mild. They were characterised by a fall in the rate of growth of GDP rather than the more severe recessions of 1974-76, 1980-82 and 1990-92 when GDP fell in absolute terms. The mid-1980s arguably saw a very mild recession in 1984 when the rate of growth fell from around 4 per cent back to 1 per cent. The mid-1990s too saw a mild downturn, with growth rates falling back in 1994 and 1995 as Figure 10.1 shows. This did not prevent unemployment from continuing to fall, however.

In 1997, the economy bounced back and continued to grow at rates above the long term trend rate of 2½ per cent into 1998. The Bank of England became concerned that the economy was overheating. Inflation seemed to be rising and unemployment continued to fall. It therefore pushed up interest rates. This was successful in reducing the growth rate, which fell to a low of 1.6 per cent in the first quarter of 1999. This was the 'soft landing' which the government had hoped for. The economy then recovered quickly and by the first quarter of 2000 was growing at 3 per cent per annum, above the trend rate.

The two mild downturns in 1994-95 and 1998-99 were characteristic of the mild recessions seen in the 1950s and the first half of the 1960s, a period of low inflation and low unemployment with relatively sustained growth. If the UK could continue on this course, its economic performance in the new millennium would be better than that achieved in the 1970s and 1980s.

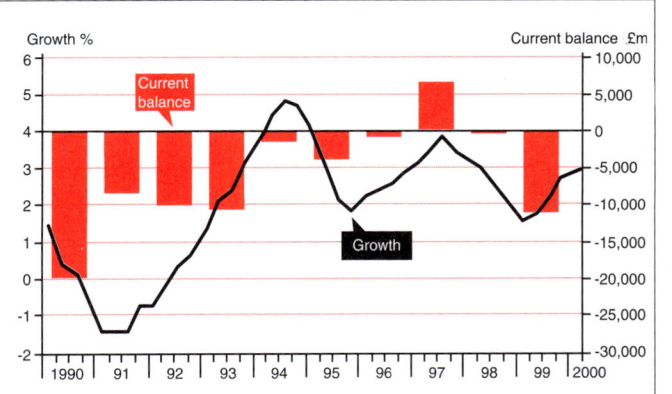

Figure 10.1 *Growth and the current balance, 1990-2000*
Source: adapted from *Economic Trends*, Office for National Statistics.

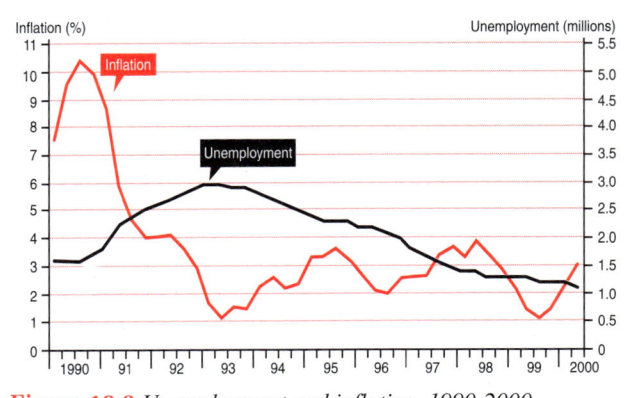

Figure 10.2 *Unemployment and inflation, 1990-2000*
Source: adapted from *Economic Trends*, Office for National Statistics.

2 Oil prices and economic growth

In 2000, crude oil prices rose to over $30 a barrel, from a low of $10 a barrel at the start of 1999 and around $15 for much of the 1990s. An increase of this size is likely to have an impact on economic growth.

One effect is a transfer of resources from oil consuming countries to oil producing countries. For instance, the IMF, in an estimate made in 2000, suggested that a sustained $5 increase in the price of crude oil above $25 a barrel would raise the net oil imports of high-income countries by about $40 billion, or 0.2 per cent of GDP. This means that GDP in developed countries as a whole would be 0.2 per cent lower than it would otherwise have been because spending power was being transferred to other oil producing countries. Some countries would be worse affected than others. The UK, with sizeable oil production in the North Sea, would suffer less than, say, Germany with little or no oil production. The USA would suffer because it is not self-sufficient in oil production and has by far the largest per capita oil consumption in the world as Figure 10.3 shows.

If oil prices remained significantly over $15 a barrel for a long period of time, then there would be an incentive to scrap oil consuming machines before the end of their useful life and replace them with technology which used other fuels. This would be a major cost and the scrapping of oil powered machinery would represent a one-off inward shift of the production possibility frontier of an economy.

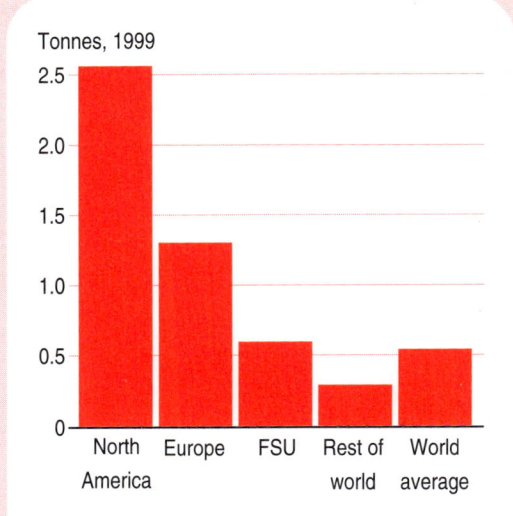

Figure 10.3 *Oil consumption per head*
Source: adapted from IMF WEO, BP, Primark Datastream.

THE STUDENT'S ECONOMY IN FOCUS 2000/01

3 Underestimating potential economic growth

The long term average growth rate for the UK economy is approximately 2.5 per cent per annum. Between 1994 and 1999, a period which included two mild slowdowns, the economy grew at an average 3 per cent.

Both the Treasury and the Bank of England assume that growth above 2.5 per cent is potentially inflationary. When it exceeds this level, the Bank of England tends to raise interest rates to reduce growth in GDP.

However, there are some economists who believe that the UK economy could grow at 3-4 per cent without triggering inflation. The reason is that investment in new technologies linked to information and communication technology (ICT) is transforming productivity. In the United States, growth averaged 3.4 per cent between 1994-99 compared to a long term average of 2.5 per cent. The Federal Reserve Bank, the central bank of the USA, has become convinced that the potential growth rate of the economy is now higher than 2.5 per cent because of new technology. Like the UK, the USA in the second half of the 1990s has seen unemployment fall to rates not seen since the 1960s. Incomes have been rising fast and yet inflation has been subdued.

Investment in new technologies has been growing. Real investment in the USA in general capital equipment has been growing at less than 10 per cent per annum in recent years. However, business investment in computers has been growing at 45 per cent per annum. Investment in software has been growing at 25 per cent, whilst investment in communications equipment has been growing at 20 per cent. The share of ICT capital in total capital has risen from 10 to 15 per cent. It is this which is increasing labour productivity and enabling the economy to grow at a faster rate. Some economists believe that ICT investment in the UK is comparable to that in the USA. Therefore the monetary authorities should allow the economy to grow at a faster rate without constantly restraining it by putting up interest rates.

4 Immigration and growth

Economic growth arises from an increase in the quantity or quality of the factors of production. For instance, information and communication technology, an improved type of capital, is revolutionising many aspects of production and allowing more to be produced with the same amount of land and labour.

Economic growth in western Europe has averaged 3-4 per cent since 1945, but in many countries this could fall considerably over the next 50 years. This is because Europe's population is ageing. The numbers retiring from the workforce are exceeding the numbers entering the workforce. The result is that the workforce will shrink in size. Fewer workers means less output and hence acts as a constraint on economic growth.

The UK is one of the countries least affected by this change. In Italy, the population as a whole will soon begin to shrink because fewer babies are being born than old people are dying. In Japan, the worst affected industrial country, the population will shrink from 127.6 million in 2010 to 100.5 million in 2050 on current trends.

One solution to this long term problem is immigration. Figure 10.4 shows just how many migrants will be needed per year between 2000 and 2050 to maintain at a constant level the total population, the working population and the ratio of 15-65s to the retired. In the UK, keeping the population constant would require net migration of 53 000 per year. Today, immigration is around 150 000 a year. Half of these are accepted for permanent settlement, whilst half are on temporary work permits and for the most part will go back to their country of origin. Emigration is around 90 000. So net migration is around 60 000 per year, just enough to keep the population constant. But this is not enough to keep the working population constant. For that, the UK would need net inward migration of 125 000 per year. To keep the ratio of workers to the retired constant, given the growing bulge of pensioners, the UK would need net inward migration of 1.2 million per year. This is a totally unacceptable figure from a political viewpoint.

In 2000, the government announced that it would make it easier for those with skills in short supply to come to work in the UK on a temporary basis. With the economy growing rapidly, skills shortages were becoming apparent and there was a fear that they would constrain Britain's growth. Preference would be given to workers with high levels of skills, for instance in the ICT sector.

Figure 10.4 also shows that other EU countries are likely to suffer more from an ageing population than the UK. Italy and Germany are particularly badly affected by the worsening ratio of pensioners to workers. Immigration could be a solution to this problem if there were more political will to accept that migration has always been a feature of human societies and economies.

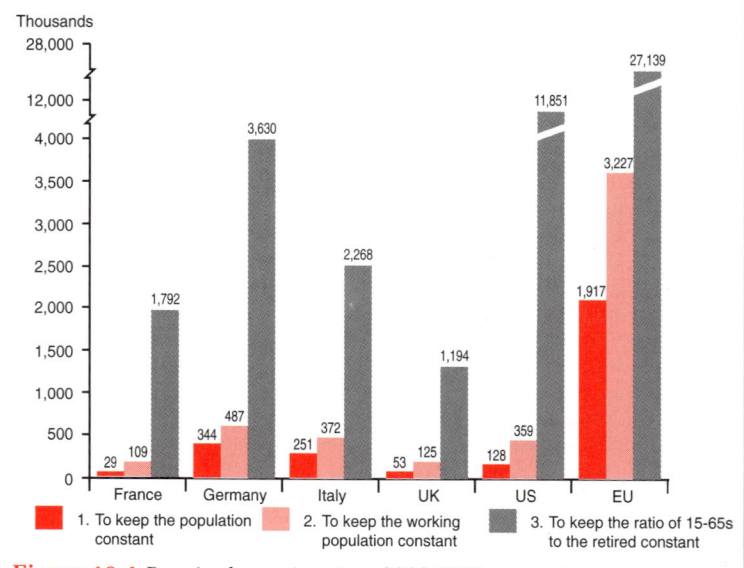

Figure 10.4 Required net migration, 2000-2050, annual average
Source: adapted from UN population division.

Thousands

Country	1. To keep the population constant	2. To keep the working population constant	3. To keep the ratio of 15-65s to the retired constant
France	29	109	1,792
Germany	344	487	3,630
Italy	251	372	2,268
UK	53	125	1,194
US	128	359	11,851
EU	1,917	3,227	27,139

5 Deindustrialisation in the textile industry

In 2000, Coats Viyella, the largest textile company in the UK, announced that it would be selling all its operations apart from its global thread operations and its Jaeger and Viyella retail brands. Coats Viyella was the latest victim in Marks and Spencer's decision to source more of its products overseas rather than from British factories. M&S had come under severe pressure in the late 1990s from disappointing sales and profits figures. Sourcing from overseas allowed M&S to cut its costs. In the short term, it was able to benefit from a strong pound. Over the long term, it could take advantage of cheap labour in the Third World where wages per hour are in pence rather than pounds.

The decision by Coats Viyella was the latest in a long line of sales, downsizing and closures by UK textile companies. At the end of the last century, for instance, textiles were the single largest export for the UK and the country's mills produced 80 per cent of the world's cotton cloth. Today, the industry is small in comparison. Deindustrialisation really began to hit in the 1960s. Figure 10.5 shows how, even in the 1990s, the industry continued to decline and employment fell.

The story of the textile industry is a classic example of the benefits and losses from the exploitation of comparative advantage. Textiles are, typically, a labour intensive, low technology product. Their production is ideally suited to low income countries with relatively little physical capital and, by western standards, a poorly educated workforce. Acceptable quality products can be produced and sold to the rich industrialised countries of the world at a lower price than they would cost to make in these countries.

Countries like the UK, though, are best advised to see the demise of their textile industries in the long term. In the short term, closures like Coats Viyella cause unemployment and lower GDP. In the long term, though, the scarce resources used in textile manufacture in the UK can be better put to use producing higher added value products. Workers on average gain because they can get higher paid jobs, whilst consumers gain from lower textile prices.

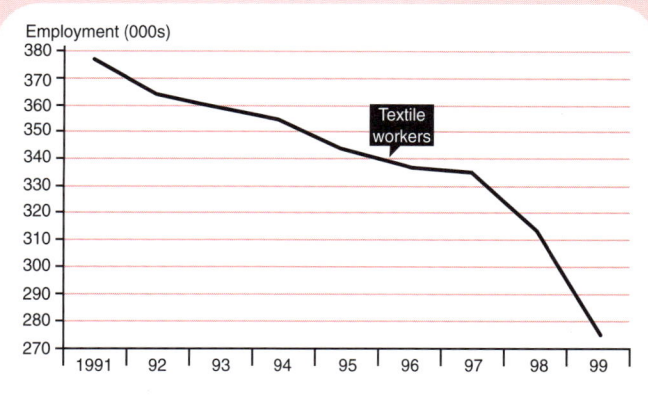

Figure 10.5 *Employment in the UK textiles industry, at June each year*

6 Research and development

Research and development plays a vital role in economic development. R&D enables new products to come to market and transforms existing production techniques. In a global economy, the results of research and development can flow through to other countries, for instance by the leasing of copyright or patents. However, firms and countries which make technological breakthroughs tend to benefit more than others because they are able to exploit the R&D first, giving them a competitive advantage.

Figure 10.6 shows the level of spending on R&D as a percentage of GDP for the G7 group of countries. Japan and the United States have the highest levels of spending, with Italy and Canada at the bottom. The United States spends twice as much as a percentage of GDP on R&D as Italy. Figure 10.7 shows how the most important part of R&D spending, that by businesses, has changed since 1966. Disappointingly, over the 1990s the level of expenditure by businesses on R&D has remained constant in real terms at a time when real income has been rising.

R&D is only one factor amongst many which determine the growth rate of an economy. However, the high levels of R&D spending in Japan and the USA are likely to have give their industries a competitive advantage in areas such as information and communication technology and biotechnology. The UK's failure to spend more on R&D could be one reason why its growth performance has been so poor over the past 50 years.

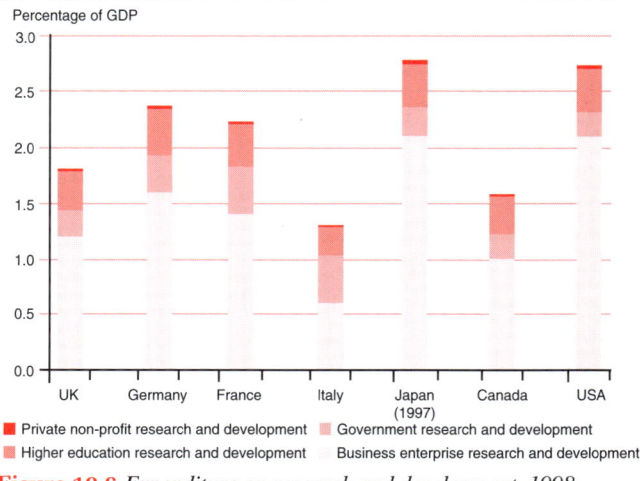

Figure 10.6 *Expenditure on research and development, 1998*
Source: adapted from *Economic Trends*, 2000, Office for National Statistics.

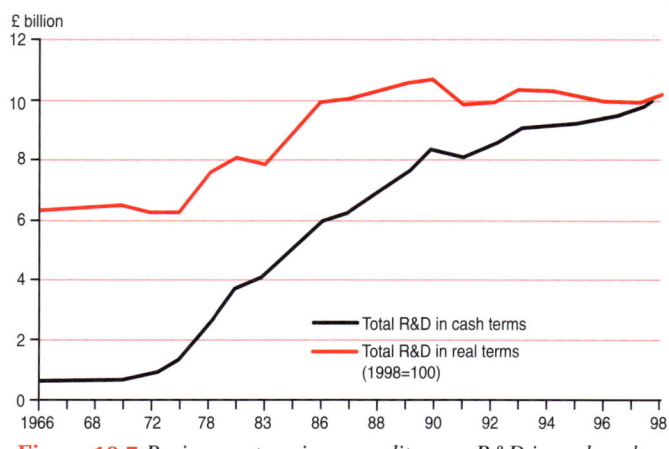

Figure 10.7 *Business enterprise expenditure on R&D in cash and real terms*
Source: adapted from *Economic Trends*, 2000, Office for National Statistics.

UNIT 10 ECONOMIC RECOVERY AND GROWTH

7 The hidden economy

In 1999, the government announced that it was launching an enquiry into the hidden economy. This is the part of the economy where output goes unrecorded because workers are not declaring income or sales, and where benefits are claimed fraudulently. The size of the hidden economy is disputed, but many estimates put it at between 4 and 8 per cent of GDP.

Government is concerned about the size of the hidden economy because of the tax revenues it loses. For instance, self-employed workers may evade paying income tax and National Insurance contributions. They may also have a turnover large enough to pay VAT on their sales. A European Commission report in 1998 estimated that undeclared income in the UK was worth between £58 billion and £108 billion a year. If taxed at just 10 per cent, this represents a loss of revenue for the government of between £5.8 billion and £10.8 billion. Customs and Excise estimate that goods to the value of £66 billion escape VAT each year. Again, if taxed at just 10 per cent, this represents a loss of revenue of £6.6 billion.

As for benefits, many claim benefits fraudulently because they are also earning. One way of estimating the amount of fraud is to consider the difference between the numbers receiving benefits and the numbers declaring they receive benefit in government surveys. Two surveys in particular, the Labour Force Survey used to calculate the ILO measure of unemployment, and the Family Resources Survey used to measure household spending and income, show a large disparity between the benefits given and claimed. Table 10.1 shows, for instance, there are 17 per cent fewer people who actually claim Family Credit than admit it when asked by the Labour Force Survey. Part of the mismatch may be a genuine lack of knowledge about what benefits are received by claimants. However, some must be because claimants don't want to admit to receiving a benefit when asked by an official government survey for fear of being detected.

The Department of Social Security estimates that around 9 per cent of benefits are fraudulently claimed. In addition, another 10 per cent is suspected fraud but difficult to prove. Given that the government spent £94 billion on benefits in 1998/99, eradicating the 9 per cent of fraud would save the taxpayer £8.5 billion.

Some taxpayers benefit from the hidden economy because they are able to employ workers or buy goods and services at a lower price than they would if the hidden economy didn't exist. However, other taxpayers who have no contact with the hidden economy have to pay higher taxes or receive worse public services than they would otherwise. The hidden economy therefore acts as a Robin Hood mechanism, transferring income from one group to another in a democratically unaccountable way.

%	Labour Force Survey	Family Resources Survey
Family credit	-17	-23
Income support	-27	-13
Housing benefit	-36	-6
Retirement pension	-5	n/a
JSA	-23	n/a
Child benefit	-8	-14

Table 10.1 *Under-count of claimants*
Source: adapted from *Labour Market Trends*, September 1999, Office for National Statistics.

8 The Big Mac comparison

There are many ways of comparing living standards between countries. Economists tend to use GDP per head at purchasing power parities (i.e. national output divided by the number of inhabitants and adjusted for the cost of living in the country). There are simpler calculations. One is to compare the cost of an item which is commonly available in most countries. Table 10.2 gives one such item, a McDonald's Big Mac. It comes from a survey by UBS Warburg of living standards in 58 of the world's cities. Table 10.2 shows how long the average worker in a city has to work to buy a Big Mac. In Tokyo, it is 9 minutes. In London, it is 18 minutes whilst in Nairobi it is 178 minutes.

The difference in times needed to buy a Big Mac arises for two reasons. One is that, at market exchange rates, workers are paid different amounts in different cities on average. For instance, average salaries are very high in Tokyo and New York. At the bottom of the 58 city league were Nairobi, Jakarta and Bombay, with average earnings of 3-6 per cent of those at the top.

The other reason is that the cost of a Big Mac differs from city to city. The cost of a Big Mac acts as a proxy for the general cost of living. The survey found that the cost of goods in general was highest in Tokyo, London and New York.

Overall, the survey found that London ranked 23rd in the standard of living league. Wages in London were only moderate compared to other cities. However, the cost of living was relatively high, particularly due to the cost of accommodation and of public transport. The rent on an unfurnished three room apartment, for instance, was the highest in the world, whilst tickets on the London Underground were expensive compared to most other cities.

Working time required to buy a Big Mac	
Tokyo	9 minutes
Hong Kong	9 minutes
New York	12 minutes
London	18 minutes
Nairobi	178 minutes

Table 10.2 *The cost of a Big Mac*
Source: adapted from *Prices and Earnings around the Globe*, 2000, UBS Warburg.

UNIT 10 ECONOMIC RECOVERY AND GROWTH

Reading list

A.G. Anderton, *Economics*, Causeway Press (3rd ed. 2000) pages 151-179, 619-625.
A.G. Anderton, *Economics AS Level*, Causeway Press (2000) pages 151-179.
J. Beardshaw et al., *Economics: A Student's Guide*, Longman (4th ed. 1998) pages 657-667.
P. Maunder et al, *Economics Explained*, Collins Educational (Revised 3rd ed. 2000) pages 241-258, 531-547.
D. Begg et al, *Economics*, McGraw Hill (5th ed. 1997) pages 503-527.
P. Curwen et al, *Understanding the UK Economy*, Macmillan (4th ed. 1997) pages 45-109.
C. Bamford, editor, *Economics for AS*, Cambridge University Press (2000) pages 121-122, 134-135, 160.
S.Grant, *Economic Growth and Business Cycles*, Heinemann Educational (1999).
S. Bazen and T. Thirlwall, *Industrialization and Deindustrialization*, Heinemann Educational (3rd ed. 1997).
D. Coates, 'UK economic underperformance: causes and cures', *Developments in Economics* Vol 11, Causeway Press (1995).
I. Stone, 'Inward investment into the UK', *Developments in Economics* Vol 14, Causeway Press (1998).

Essay questions

(a) What do economists understand by the term 'recession'? (20 marks)
(b) Using economic analysis, explain how a recession in the UK economy might affect each of the following:
 (i) the construction industry; (40 marks)
 (ii) the food retailing industry. (40 marks) (Edexcel June 1994)

(a) Should economic growth be an objective of macroeconomic policy? (40 marks)
(b) In what ways might a faster rate of economic growth be achieved in the long run? (60 marks)
 (Edexcel June 1994)

(a) Examine the benefits of economic growth. (30 marks)
(b) In what circumstances might economic growth lead to a decrease in economic welfare? (70 marks) (Edexcel June 1995)

(a) How might supply side policies help to increase a country's rate of economic growth? (50 marks)
(b) Analyse the factors which might result in a reduction in the PSBR. (50 marks) (Edexcel June 1998)

(a) Why do economies periodically experience a recession? (12 marks)
(b) Discuss the extent to which it is possible for governments to reduce the severity of recessions which are experienced by the economy. (13 marks)
 (AQA [AEB] January 1997)

"Conventional GDP statistics fail to show real economic well-being." (Headline, the *Financial Times*, 28 September 1995.) Explain what is meant by GDP and briefly outline how it is measured. Discuss the drawbacks of GDP per head as an indicator of living standards and suggest what improvements might be made to produce a more accurate measure.
 (AQA [NEAB] 1996)

Outline the main factors responsible for productivity growth in firms. Discuss the main effects on industry of the spread of information technology in recent years. (AQA [NEAB] 1998)

Explain the main features and causes of the business cycle and how its different stages may be identified. Discuss how the business cycle might affect a garage selling new cars compared with a garage specialising in car repairs. (AQA [NEAB] 1998)

In 1994, the USA had a Gross National Product (at factor cost) nearly 30 times that of Switzerland, when both were expressed in US dollars, using the exchange rate on 31.12.94.
(a) Explain the meaning of GNP at factor cost. (8)
(b) How far might the above information be useful in attempting to compare living standards between the USA and Switzerland in 1994? (12) (OCR June 1997)

(a) Describe the extent of de-industrialisation in the UK at the present time. (8)
(b) To what extent is de-industrialisation an inevitable feature of any mature economy? (12) (OCR March 1998)

(a) Define deindustrialisation and explain the view that any definition should be universal and cause-free. (8)
(b) Discuss the view that, on balance, the British experience of deindustrialisation has been positive. (12) (OCR March 1999)

(a) Explain the problems that the Office for National Statistics would encounter estimating the GDP of the UK economy. (8)
(b) Even if there were an accurate measure of GDP, discuss how useful this would be in making comparisons of living standards between countries. (12)
 (OCR November 1999)

Exam notes

National income Different specifications have different requirements concerning knowledge of national income definitions. However, it is useful for any examination to understand what is meant by GDP and how national income can be measured in three ways through income, output or expenditure. Reasons why national income statistics do not necessarily reflect the actual level of output, for instance because of the hidden economy (Box 7), should also be known.
The trade cycle Some questions focus on the trade cycle (Box 1) and its different phases. For instance, a question might ask for an understanding of recession or recovery.
Growth Many questions focus on the causes of economic growth. Factors such as increases in productivity (Box 3), innovation (Box 6) and labour supply (Box 4) are significant. Some factors can lead to a fall in the rate of growth. For instance, a significant rise in oil prices might harm growth rates in developed countries (Box 2). Equally, changes in comparative advantage, which in a developed country could lead to deindustrialisation, may harm economic growth (Box 5). It is often helpful in answers to make links with government policies to promote growth (see unit 11), particularly supply side policies.
Living standards National income is often seen as a measure of living standards. However, questions frequently focus on why this can only be a crude measure and what other factors are important in measuring living standards (Box 8).

Unit 11
Government policy

1 The goals of government policy

The government has four main macroeconomic goals. The most important short term goal is the control of inflation. Since 1997, the government has set the Bank of England a target of 2.5 per cent which it has been successful at achieving. The measure of inflation which is targeted is the RPIX, the Retail Price Index, but excluding the effect of interest rate changes. This is because the Bank of England uses interest rates to manipulate aggregate demand and thus the rate of inflation.

The second macroeconomic goal of government policy is to achieve low unemployment. In the 1950s and 1960s, the goal was to achieve full employment, with unemployment levels at a few hundred thousand. In the mid-1970s, this was abandoned because it became clear that policies to reduce unemployment, such as increasing government spending or reducing interest rates, caused higher inflation. Since 1993, however, unemployment has been falling without increasing inflation. With claimant count unemployment in 2000 at 1.1 million and still falling, it is unclear at what level of unemployment the Phillips curve trade off (inflation for unemployment) will reappear.

The third macroeconomic goal of government policy is to achieve high growth. The long term average rate of growth for the UK economy is around 2.5 per cent. However, in the six years between 1994 and 1999 the economy grew at an average 3 per cent per annum. Some economists believe that changes in productivity linked to information and communication technologies will allow the economy to grow at a faster rate than 2.5 per cent without causing inflation.

The last major policy goal is to achieve a balance on the external account. Over time, this means that the current balance should be equal to zero. Higher economic growth in recent years has been linked with low inflation and falling unemployment. In 2000, there were clear signs that the current account was falling into significant deficit. In the long term, this cannot continue and is likely to be corrected by a fall in what in 2000 was a high value of the pound against the euro.

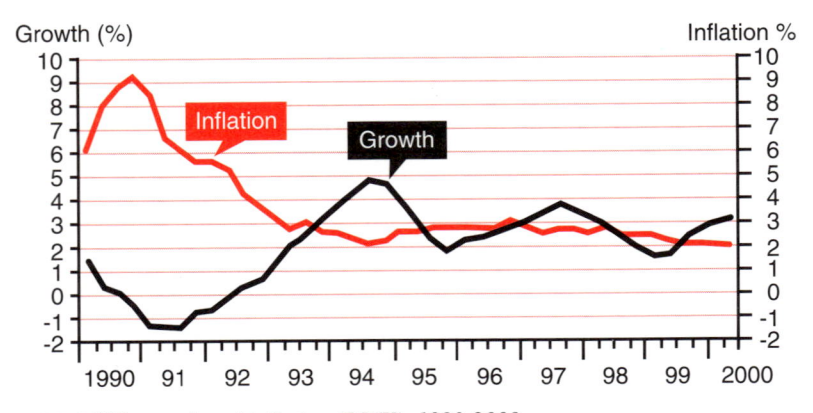

Figure 11.1 *UK growth and inflation (RPIX), 1990-2000*
Source: adapted from *Economic Trends*, Annual Supplement and *Monthly Digest of Statistics*, Office for National Statistics.

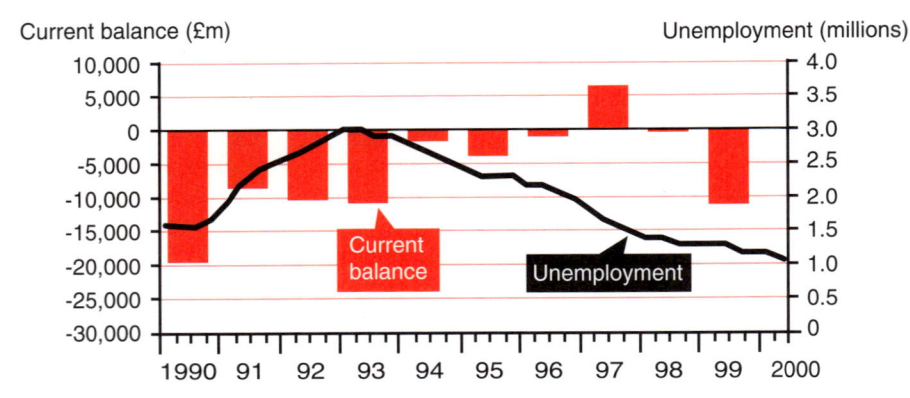

Figure 11.2 *UK unemployment (claimant count) and the current balance, 1990-2000*
Source: adapted from *Economic Trends*, Annual Supplement and *Monthly Digest of Statistics*, Office for National Statistics.

2 The 2000 Budget

The March 2000 Budget saw public sector finances in a very sound position. The economy had grown at a faster rate in 1999-2000 than predicted and unemployment was still falling. In consequence, tax revenues were buoyant and there was predicted to be a budget surplus.

The Chancellor, Gordon Brown, chose to allocate a major part of this to spending on the health service. Over the period 2000 to 2004, spending on the NHS was to rise by 35 per cent in real terms. This was double the rate at which real spending on the NHS had grown in the post-war era. Spending on education and public transport was also increased.

The Chancellor chose not to make major tax cuts. Indirect taxes such as duties on fuel and tobacco were increased in line with inflation. Increased revenues from these sources were offset by a 1p cut in the basic rate of income tax, announced in the 1999 Budget, and a cut from 20p to 10p in the lower rate of income tax.

Overall, the impact of the 2000 Budget was expected to be deflationary in 2000-2001 and 2001-2002, but give a boost to GDP thereafter because of higher spending on the health service.

3 Unemployment policy

Government has been relying on supply side policies to bring about a reduction in unemployment. However, it could be argued that at least some of the fall in unemployment and rise in employment could be attributed to successful demand management policies. The UK has seen rising real incomes since 1991, the longest period of sustained growth since the 1960s. Most importantly for consumer and business confidence, there is every indication that growth will remain positive over the next few years.

There is a number of supply side policies which the government is pursuing to further reduce unemployment. The New Deal is giving advice and training to workers under 25 and over 50, the two main groups with above average unemployment. The government has made it harder for workers to receive benefits and refuse to look for employment. It has also increased incentives for those only able to get low paid jobs to join the labour force by cutting taxes and National Insurance contributions for the low paid and introducing more generous welfare benefits.

The success of government policy can be seen from the fact that the claimant count measure of unemployment has fallen from 2.9 million in 1993 to 1.1 million in 2000. The ILO measure, though, shows only a fall from 3 million to 1.7 million. One reason for the difference is the success of the government's policy of making it more difficult for the unemployed to claim benefit. It also reflects the growth in the workforce. As unemployment falls, many who were not seeking work begin to look for work. For instance, the number of those in jobs (either as employees or the self employed) grew from 22.7 million in 1993 to 26.7 million in 1999, a rise of 3.9 million. But the claimant count unemployment fell only by 1.8 million and the ILO count fell 1.3 million over the same period. Many of those who are now in work were not registered as unemployed over this period. Women in particular fall into the group of people not able to claim benefit but who take work when it is easily available. Indeed, the government has increased incentives for single parent mothers and fathers to go to work by increasing their in-work benefits.

There are still several million people who could join the labour force if they were given the right incentives and the right training, including women bringing up children and the over 50s who have taken some form of early retirement. If the economy is to continue to expand without inflation rising, these people must be brought into the workforce as well as getting more people off the unemployment claimant count registers.

4 Anti-inflationary policy

The government, in 1997, gave the responsibility of controlling inflation to the Bank of England. It was made independent of government and is free to pursue monetary policy in whatever way it thinks best. However, the government sets the Bank of England an inflation target, currently 2.5 per cent as measured by the RPIX.

Since 1997, the Bank of England has made frequent small changes to the rate of interest as Figure 11.3 shows. If it thinks that inflation is likely to rise above 2.5 per cent, it increases interest rates. This affects inflation through a fall in aggregate demand from what it would otherwise have been. If inflation is likely to be below 2.5 per cent, the Bank of England tends to cut interest rates to allow higher economic growth.

The control of inflation since 1997 has been been made easier by the high value of the pound against other EU currencies, now measured by the euro. Around 60 per cent of UK trade is now with other EU countries. The high pound has made it hard particularly for UK manufacturing companies to maintain export sales. This has had a depressing effect on exports, part of aggregate demand. Equally, it has made it easier for EU firms to export to the UK. Higher imports depress aggregate demand too. One of the reasons why the pound has been high is because UK interest rates have been higher than EU interest rates. UK manufacturing industry on the whole would like to see UK interest rates fall to bring about a sharp fall in the value of the pound against the euro. This, though, would add to inflationary pressures.

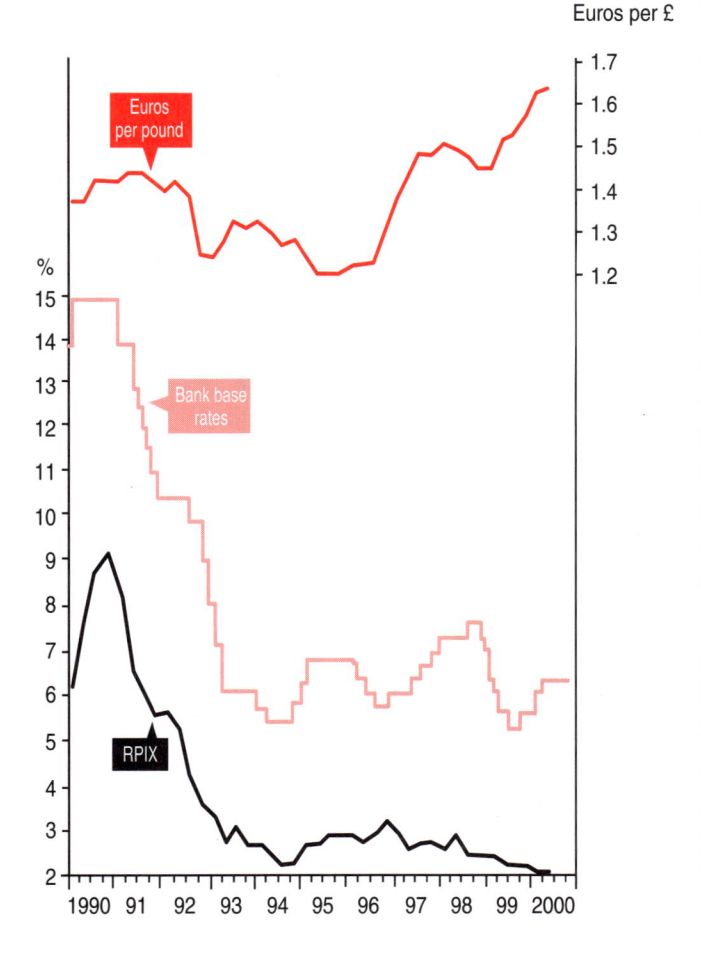

Figure 11.3 *Inflation, interest rates and the value of the pound*
Source: adapted from *Economic Trends*, Office for National Statistics.

UNIT 11 GOVERNMENT POLICY

5 Growth policies

Economic growth is caused by a complex mix of factors which increase either the quality or the quantity of the factors of production. The government has a large number of supply side policies designed to improve the competitiveness and performance of the economy.

In terms of labour, it is encouraging more people to take jobs, thus increasing the size of the labour force. Continued growth, and the absence of boom and bust policies, has led to a steady increase particularly in the number of women joining the labour force. The official unemployed have been given help with advice and training. Incentives to work have been improved by reducing taxes and increasing benefits for the low paid. In 2000, the government also announced that it would be making it easier for immigrant workers with scarce skills to obtain work permits to stay in the UK. In the longer term, the government has placed great emphasis on education and training as the way to raise the skills level of the workforce and reduce the productivity gap that exists between the UK and the rest of the EU. For instance, in education it has set targets for schools to achieve examination and test results. Higher education continues to expand.

Government is encouraging firms to invest in physical capital. It provides grants and other incentives to firms relocating to areas of deprivation. It is also encouraging urban regeneration through partnerships with private industry. In its 1999 and 2000 Budgets, it cut corporation tax rates on small businesses, allowing them to retain more profit for investment.

It also wants to encourage entrepreneurship. In its 2000 Budget, for instance, the government cut rates of capital gains tax for entrepreneurs selling their businesses. This is to prevent individuals being discouraged from establishing businesses knowing that much of the proceeds of any sale would be subject to tax.

6 The redistribution of income

Table 11.1 shows how the government redistributed income between different types of household in 1997/98. Original income is income before any tax has been deducted and benefits added. Original income includes wages and salaries, self employment income, private and occupational pensions and interest and dividends on savings.

Disposable income is income after direct taxes (income tax, National Insurance contributions, council tax and water charges) have been taken away and state benefits (such as retirement pensions and child benefit) have been added. Post-tax income is disposable income minus indirect taxes (such as VAT and excise duties).

Different types of household tend to earn different amounts. For instance, single parent households only average an original income of £4 943 compared to single adult non-retired households of £13 793. This is because many single parents do not have a job, many only work part-time and those with full-time jobs are often low paid. In contrast, the large majority of single non-retired adults are in full time work and many are upwardly mobile. Two adult non-retired households with no children earned on average £27 241 compared to £30 047 for two adult households with two children. Whilst the presence of children in a household may mean that one partner is not in paid work, adults in households with children have a higher average age than two adult households with no children. Older workers tend to be paid more than younger workers and hence the small difference in original income.

Direct taxes and benefits tend to be linked to earnings and age. The higher the earnings of a household, the more they are likely to pay in direct tax and the less they receive in benefits. For instance, a one adult pensioner household with an average original income of £3 219 saw its income rise by 122 per cent, mainly because of the payment of the state old age pension. In contrast, the two adult with two children household lost 17 per cent of its income in direct taxes minus benefits.

Having children in a household also tends to reduce the amount of tax minus benefits taken. Single parents saw their original income increase 90 per cent, whilst two adult with three or more children households saw their original income fall by 6 per cent compared to 17 per cent for two adult with one or two children households.

The amount of indirect taxes paid tends to be weakly linked to the level of disposable income. For instance, the one adult retired household with a disposable income of £7 132 pays 17 per cent of disposable income in indirect taxes. In contrast, the three or more adult household with no children and an income of £30 628 paid 21 per cent in indirect taxes.

	Retired households		Non-retired households								
	1 adult	2 or more adults	1 adult	2 adults	3 or more adults	1 adult with children	2 adults with 1 child	2 adults with 2 children	2 adults with 3 or more children	3 or more adults with children	All households
Number of households in the population (Thousands)	3 477	2 787	3 692	4 909	2 283	1 453	1 887	2 249	882	937	24 556
Average per household (£ per year)											
Original income	3 219	9 693	13 793	27 241	35 439	4 943	28 337	30 047	24 437	31 721	19 680
Disposable income	7 132	14 100	12 183	22 699	30 628	9 408	23 646	24 934	23 007	28 604	18 402
Post-tax income	5 893	11 035	9 775	18 270	24 214	7 164	18 989	20 219	18 409	21 721	14 685

Table 11.1 *Average income of households before and after taxes and benefits, 1997-98*
Source: adapted from *Annual Abstract of Statistics*, Office for National Statistics.

7 Information and communication technology

The US Federal Reserve Bank believes that the potential growth rate of the US economy has risen recently by 1 per cent because of productivity gains due to investment in ICT (information and communication technology) - everything from computers, to the internet and the web, to microchips used in machinery and appliances. The UK government wants to see productivity levels in the UK rise too and part of its policy to achieve this is to promote ICT. There is a variety of ways of doing this.

For instance, since the 1990s, ICT has been a compulsory part of the school curriculum, producing a generation of future workers who will have some familiarity with ICT. In the field of industrial training, the government has pumped money into the ICT sector through Training and Enterprise Councils and through further and higher education establishments.

In its 2000 Budget, the government set a target of encouraging 1 million small companies to go online by allowing them to write off 100 per cent of the cost of computer hardware and internet technology purchases against tax in the year of purchase rather than the existing 25 per cent per year.

The government, through its regulator OFTEL, forced British Telecom to relinquish its monopoly on the 'local loop' from 2001. The local loop is the connection from trunk lines on the telephone network (the equivalent of main roads) to individual homes and businesses (the equivalent of side streets). Other companies will be allowed to install equipment in telephone exchanges owned by British Telecom. The aim is to encourage competition in broad band access to homes and businesses. Broad band access is needed to allow much faster internet and web connections which again will stimulate the ICT revolution.

To tackle the shortage of skilled workers in ICT, the government in 2000 announced that it would make it easier for foreign workers with shortage skills to obtain work permits to work in the UK.

The government is also supportive of the development of e-commerce. As Figure 11.4 shows, e-commerce in 1998 accounted for only a fraction of GDP, but is forecast to rise to a small but significant level in 2002. ICT applications have the potential to give the UK a competitive advantage over other countries slower to implement change. As the Chancellor said in his 2000 Budget speech, 'I want to make Britain the best environment for e-commerce and catch up with America as swiftly as possible'.

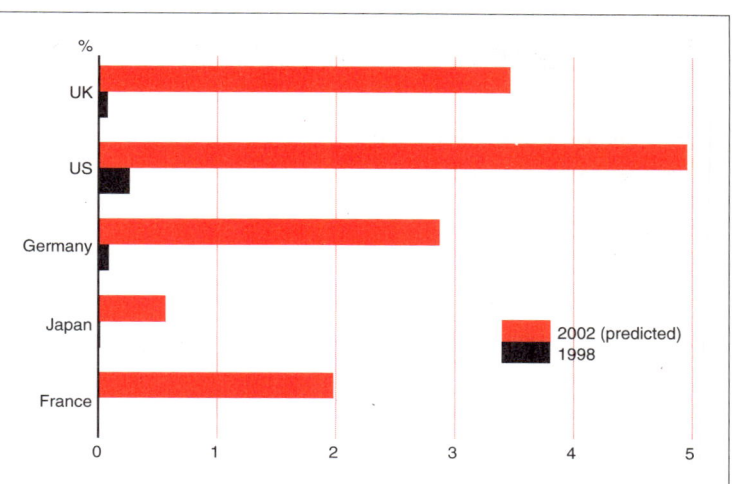

Figure 11.4 *E-Commerce as a proportion of GDP*
Source: adapted from International Data Corporation, OECD.

Reading list

A.G. Anderton, *Economics*, Causeway Press (3rd ed. 2000) pages 234-257, 544-551, 596-603, 611-629.

A.G. Anderton, *Economics AS Level*, Causeway Press (2000) pages 234-257.

J. Beardshaw et al,, *Economics: A Student's Guide*, Longman (4th ed. 1998) pages 603-620.

P. Maunder et al, *Economics Explained*, Collins Educational (Revised 3rd ed. 2000) pages 486-497, 540-543.

D. Begg et al, *Economics*, McGraw Hill (5th ed. 1997) pages 352-364, 400-418.

P. Curwen et al, *Understanding the UK Economy*, Macmillan (4th ed. 1997) pages 522-542.

C. Bamford, editor, *Economics for AS*, Cambridge University Press (2000) pages 118-128, 152-161.

D. Smith, *UK Current Economic Policy*, Heinemann Educational (2nd ed. 1999).

N. Healy and M. Cook, *Supply Side Economics*, Heinemann Educational (3rd ed. 1996).

David. J. Brooksbank, 'Unemployment Policies and the New Deal', *Developments in Economics* Vol 16, Causeway Press (2000).

UNIT 11 GOVERNMENT POLICY

Essay questions

(a) Explain how supply side policies might be used to:
 (i) reduce the level of unemployment;
 (ii) increase the rate of economic growth. (70 marks)
(b) To what extent have supply side policies been effective in achieving these aims in the UK? (30 marks)
(Edexcel June 1996)

Analyse the likely impact of (i) a decrease in income tax rates and (ii) increases in interest rates on:
(a) aggregate demand; (50 marks)
(b) aggregate supply. (50 marks)
(Edexcel January 1997)

(a) Why might a country wish to restrain inflationary pressures? (40 marks)
(b) Examine the policies which a member country of the European Union might use in an attempt to prevent an increase in the domestic rate of inflation. (60 marks)
(Edexcel June 1997)

In the November 1996 Budget the UK government announced it planned to limit general government expenditure to just under £315 bn for the next financial year.
(a) Explain why a government might wish to prevent a large increase in government expenditure. (50 marks)
(b) Examine the likely economic effects of limiting the growth of government expenditure. (50 marks)
(Edexcel January 1998)

(a) Which two objectives of UK government macro economic policy do you consider to be important at the start of the twenty-first century? Justify your answer. (50 marks)
(b) To what extent do your chosen objectives conflict with one another? (50 marks)
(Edexcel January 2000)

A report published by the Rowntree Trust in 1995 concluded that the gap between the rich and the poor in the United Kingdom has increased since 1979.

(a) How might the government use fiscal policy to reduce inequalities in income and wealth? (12 marks)
(b) Discuss the impact of such policies upon both the pattern and the level of economic activity. (13 marks)
(AQA [AEB] June 1996)

(a) Describe and explain the main changes in the rate of inflation which have occurred in the United Kingdom during the last ten years. (12 marks)
(b) Evaluate the various policies which the Government has adopted in order to control inflation during this time. (13 marks)
(AQA [AEB] January 1997)

(a) Explain the various causes of poverty in the United Kingdom. (12 marks)
(b) Discuss the view that the introduction of a national minimum wage will make an important contribution to relieving poverty in the United Kingdom. (13 marks)
(AQA [AEB] June 1997)

(a) Explain the policies that governments might adopt if they wish to increase the flexibility of their labour markets. (12 marks)
(b) 'Inflexible labour markets are often said to be the cause of high unemployment and low growth in Europe.' Assess the contribution a more flexible labour market can make to improving the performance of an economy. (13 marks)
(AQA [AEB] June 1999)

Outline the functions of the different forms of taxation used in the UK and suggest why the Conservative and Labour parties seem to regard raising taxation on incomes as undesirable. Discuss the micro and macro economic consequences of reducing income taxes and explain whether or not you feel this policy is justified.
(AQA [NEAB] 1997)

Explain what is meant by a flexible labour market. Discuss whether or not flexible labour markets are in the interests of both the economy as a whole and the individual worker.
(AQA [NEAB] 1998)

Briefly outline the determinants of aggregate supply and aggregate demand in the economy. Discuss how measures to alleviate unemployment in both the long-term and short-term are likely to affect the levels of aggregate demand and aggregate supply.
(AQA [NEAB] 1999)

(a) Explain how an increase in government spending can result in a greater change in the equilibrium level of national income. (10)
(b) A government is faced with an unacceptably high level of unemployment, but does not wish to increase its overall expenditure. Discuss alternative policies for reducing unemployment. (10)
(OCR June 1998)

(a) Explain the main determinants of the level of consumption expenditure in an economy. (6)
(b) Suppose a government wishes to reduce the level of consumption expenditure in order to reduce inflationary pressures in an economy. Explain how fiscal policy might be used in order to achieve this objective, and comment upon how effective such a policy may be in reducing inflation. (14)
(OCR June 1999)

(a) Explain the difference between a goal and an instrument in macroeconomic policy making. (5)
(b) Explain how increases in aggregate supply have reduced rates of inflation in the UK over the past ten years. (10)
(c) 'Now that the UK government has clearly got inflation under control, it is time to start boosting the economy by stimulating aggregate demand.' Discuss the validity of this claim. (10)
(CCEA 2000)

Exam notes

A considerable number of exam questions are set on this area of the specification. However, it should be noted that a successful answer inevitably involves a good understanding of other areas of the specification, particularly government spending and taxation (see unit 6 and Box 2 in this unit), inflation, unemployment and income distribution (see unit 9), economic recovery and growth (see unit 10) and international trade and exchange rates (see unit 12), as well as monetary policy (see unit 8) and exchange rate policy (see unit 12). Specifications tend to cover the following areas.

The objectives of government policy These are to control inflation and unemployment, secure an external balance on the balance of payments, promote high economic growth and achieve a desirable distribution of income and wealth (Box 1).
Unemployment policy This includes the use of demand management techniques as well as supply side policies. Demand management includes the effects of changes in government borrowing, the exchange rate and interest rates (Box 3).
Inflation policy Similarly, demand management and supply side policies need to be understood. Particularly important today is the role of monetary policy to control demand (Box 4). Occasionally, though, reference is still made to incomes policies.
Growth policies The management of the trade cycle is sometimes asked, but these use of supply side policies to promote economic growth is a frequent question (Box 5). The role of ICT in promoting growth could be a source of future questions (Box 7).
Income distribution Questions are asked about how income can be redistributed and the effect of such policies on other economic variables such as unemployment (Box 6).

Unit 12
International trade and exchange rates

1 The strong pound

The value of the pound has fluctuated sharply in the 1990s. **A strong pound 1990-92** At the start of the decade, the government had entered the Exchange Rate Mechanism (ERM) of the European Monetary Union at what commentators judged to be too high a rate.

A weak pound 1992-1995 In September 1992, on 'Black Wednesday', speculators forced the pound out of the ERM and its value fell 17 per cent between 1992 and and the first quarter of 1996 on a trade weighted basis.

A strong pound 1996-2000 The value of the pound then started to climb again against the euro and the Japanese yen, but changed little against the US dollar. By the second quarter of 2000, the pound was up 34 per cent against the first quarter 1996 value of the euro and 29 per cent up on a trade weighted basis. Against the dollar it had risen 10 per cent by the fourth quarter of 1998, but then fell back in 2000 to equal its 1996 value. Against the Japanese yen, it appreciated 43 per cent between the first quarter of 1996 and the third quarter of 1998, but then had fallen back to its first quarter 1996 value by 2000.

Figure 12.1 *Trade weighted index*
Source: adapted from *Economic Trends*, Office for National Statistics.

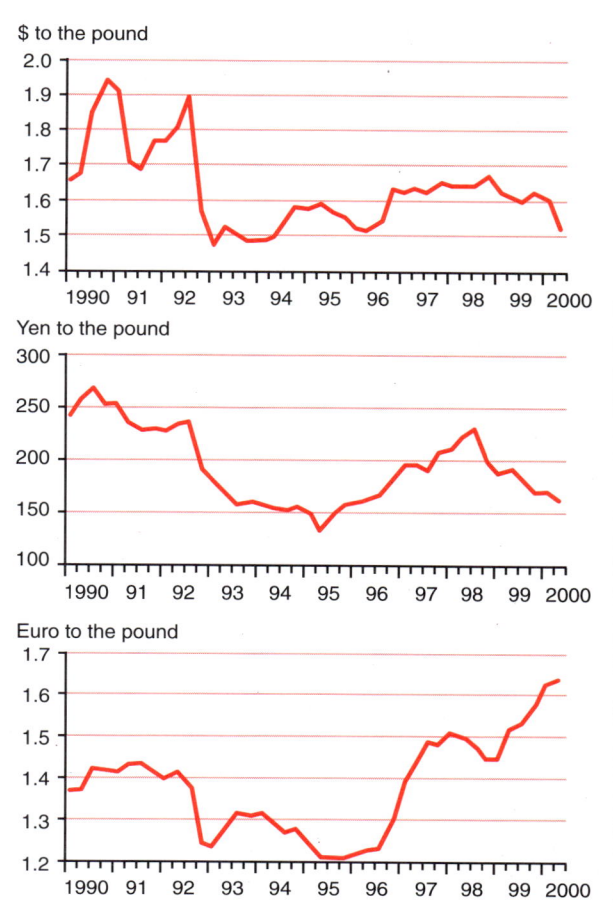

Figure 12.2 *Sterling exchange rates*
Source: adapted from *Economic Trends*, Office for National Statistics.

2 Export volumes

Economic theory would suggest that a weak pound would make importers less competitive but would give a competitive advantage to UK exporters. Equally, a strong pound should harm exporters but benefit importers.

Box 1 explained that the pound was weak between Black Wednesday in September 1992 and 1995. Figure 12.3 shows that between the fourth quarter of 1992 and the last quarter of 1995, export volumes of goods (the number of goods being sold) increased 26 per cent. In contrast, import volumes increased only 13 per cent. This data would tend to support economic theory.

The pound then appreciated sharply. On a trade weighted basis, the pound increased in value by 26 per cent between the first quarter of 1996 and the first quarter of 1998 and remained high through 1999 and 2000. Between the first quarter of 1988 and the first quarter of 2000, export volumes rose 13 per cent, whilst import volumes rose 18 per cent. Again this would tend to support economic theory.

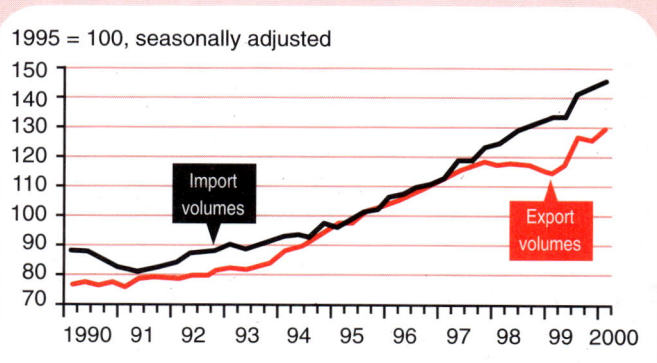

Figure 12.3 *Export and import volumes, seasonally adjusted*
Source: adapted from *Economic Trends*, Office for National Statistics.

THE STUDENT'S ECONOMY IN FOCUS 2000/01

UNIT 12 INTERNATIONAL TRADE AND EXCHANGE RATES

3 EU and non-EU trade

Box 2 explained that overall export and import volume data would support the theory that a weak pound benefits exporters, whilst a strong pound reduces export volumes from they would otherwise have been. The reverse is true for imports. However, Figures 12.4 and 12.5 would seem to indicate the reverse. They show export and import volumes divided between EU and non-EU trade. In 1998, nearly 60 per cent of UK trade in goods was with other EU countries and only 40 per cent with non-EU economies. In 1998, only 15 per cent of the UK's trade was with the USA and just 2 per cent with Japan. The pound against the euro is therefore by far the most important exchange rate for the UK.

With the pound strong against the euro in 1998-2000, it might be expected that exports to the EU would stagnate whilst imports would surge ahead. In contrast, with the pound stable against the US dollar, or even falling as in 2000, exports to the non-EU area should have risen whilst import growth should have been sluggish. But Figure 12.4 shows that export volumes to non-EU countries fell in 1998 although they grew strongly from the start of 1999. Equally, Figure 12.5 shows that growth in EU imports to the UK have lagged behind non-EU imports - the reverse of what might be expected.

Two factors can help explain this contradictory data. First, non-EU exports were severely affected by the Asian crisis in 1998. Countries such as South Korea, Indonesia and Malaysia saw a sharp downturn in their economies due to problems with their financial systems. This severely reduced demand for imports to the region including from the UK. By 1999, these economies were recovering quickly and hence there was a sharp rise in exports to the region. It should be noted too that there was above average growth in the EU in 1999 which would have helped UK exports in that year. Even so, overall export growth to the EU between 1998 and 2000 was sluggish.

As for imports, a much larger proportion of non-EU trade is accounted for by raw materials than with EU trade. Despite a slowdown in the UK economy in 1998-99, demand remained strong for raw materials. The Asian crisis led to sharp falls in the value of affected currencies and gave them a competitive advantage to export to the UK. Finally, many EU exporters chose to keep their sterling prices the same as the pound appreciated and benefit not by selling more but by increasing their profit margins. One example of this was the motor trade. Motor vehicle manufacturers producing cars on the Continent saw profits surge on UK car sales as the euro fell. The UK became known in the trade as 'treasure island' as prices of cars at market exchange rates became some of the highest in Europe. High prices increased the value of EU imports but did little for import volumes.

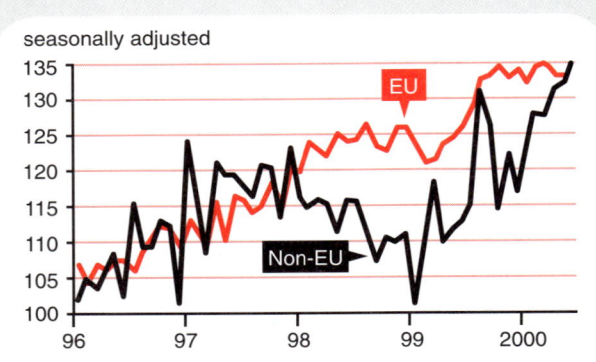

Figure 12.4 *Export volumes to EU and non-EU countries (excluding oil and erratics)*
Source: adapted from *Economic Trends August 2000*, Office for National Statistics.

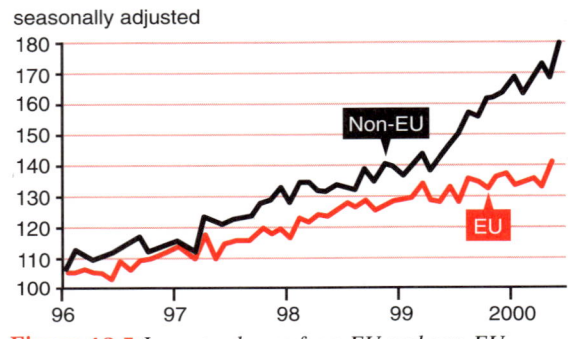

Figure 12.5 *Import volumes from EU and non-EU countries (excluding oil and erratics)*
Source: adapted from *Economic Trends August 2000*, Office for National Statistics.

4 The current account

Between 1996 and 2000, the value of the pound appreciated against currencies in the euro zone, the currency used for most of Britain's trade. Economic theory would predict that the current balance would at first improve and then deteriorate - the J curve effect. Figure 12.6 would give some support to this. The balance of trade in goods improved in 1997 before seriously deteriorating in 1998. The balance in traded services (which does not include other invisibles such as investment income) stagnated between 1997 and 1999.

Figure 12.6 also shows that the UK has a permanent imbalance in total trade in goods and services. The current balance was only in surplus in 1997 because of a positive balance in net investment income. Equally, the current balance would have been in greater deficit during the rest of the period from 1992 if there had not been a net investment income surplus.

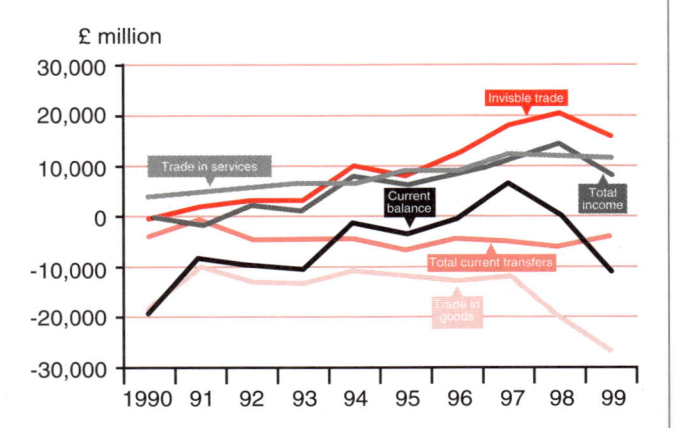

Figure 12.6 *Balance of trade in goods and services and the current balance*
Source: adapted from *Economic Trends Annual Supplement*, *Monthly Digest of Statistics*, Office for National Statistics.

5 Is a strong pound good for the UK?

The main advantage of a strong pound for the UK should be that imports are cheap. This raises living standards because consumers can buy more with their money. It also helps keep inflation low. However, it could be argued that the strong pound in 1998-2000 gave little benefit to consumers. First, the pound was only strong against the euro and EU firms have tended to maintain their £ sterling prices constant in order to increase their profit margins (see Box 7). Second, the pound has not been particularly strong against the US dollar. In fact, in 2000 the pound began to fall in value against the dollar. Many of the UK's raw material imports are priced in US dollars. So a strong pound against the euro has not benefited UK firms using imported raw materials and in 2000 they saw their prices rise.

The main disadvantage of a strong pound is that it makes UK exports less competitive. UK firms exporting to Europe have been forced to drop their £ sterling prices to remain competitive. This has cut their profit margins. Some firms have lost export contracts and this has led to less output and fewer jobs than would otherwise have been the case. The strong pound against the euro combined with a stable or falling US$ exchange rate, though, will have encouraged UK firms to increase their exports to non-EU countries at the expense of EU orders. However, UK exporters have been hard hit by the strength of the pound against the euro because 60 per cent of UK trade is with the EU.

6 The balance of payments

The balance of payments account for 1999 is shown in Table 12.1. Like most years of the 1990s, the current account was in deficit, amounting to £10 981 million or 1.2 per cent of GDP at market prices. The balance on trade in goods (the balance of trade) was negative, whilst the balance of trade in services was positive. Overall, the balance of trade in goods and services was negative, which has been typical of the 1990s.

There was a net inflow of funds on the capital account which was needed to offset the negative balance on the current account. However, £7 182 million, two thirds of the current account deficit, remained unaccounted for and was recorded as net errors and omissions. The current account deficit could therefore have been much smaller than was stated.

Trade in goods		
Export of goods	165 667	
Import of goods	192 434	
Balance of trade in goods		- 26 767
Trade in services		
Export of services	63 982	
Import of services	52 444	
Balance of trade in services		11 538
Balance of trade in goods and services		-15 229
Income		
Credits	109 099	
Debits	100 767	
Balance		8 332
Current transfers		
Credits	18 278	
Debits	22 362	
Balance		- 4 084
Current balance		-10 981
Capital account		
Credits	1 178	
Debits	740	
Balance		438
Financial account		
Credits	108 472	
Debits	117 566	
Balance		-9 094
Net errors and omissions		7 182
		0

Table 12.1 *The balance of payments 1999 (£m)*
Source: adapted from *Economic Trends*, Office for National Statistics.

UNIT 12 INTERNATIONAL TRADE AND EXCHANGE RATES

7 The problems facing British manufacturing firms

British manufacturing firms have been hard hit by the strong pound. They faced two choices when the value of the pound increased by one third between 1996 and 2000. On the one hand, they could have chosen to keep their prices constant in pounds sterling and allow their euro prices to rise. On the other hand, they could have kept their euro prices the same but allowed the amount they received in pounds sterling to fall by one third. Alternatively, they could, as many did, have adopted some combination of the two strategies.

The result of reducing prices in pounds sterling to minimise the rise in euro prices of goods has been a sharp fall in profits for UK manufacturing. Figure 12.7 shows the fall in profit margins on export sales. In contrast, profit margins on domestic sales have remained relatively steady, indicating that other EU manufacturers are choosing to increase their profit margins on UK sales rather than compete on price.

Figure 12.8 shows that manufacturers have also been forced to increase their productivity to remain profitable in the export market. In 1998 and 1999, productivity gains were high despite a slow down in the domestic UK economy.

Finally, Figure 12.9 shows that the strong pound has affected overall growth in manufactures. The weak pound between late 1992 and 1995 saw strong growth in manufacturing. Since 1995, however, manufacturing output has hardly increased.

In the long term, manufacturing companies cannot continue in business with profit margins of 5 per cent. This doesn't give them enough profit to reinvest in the business and provide a return to shareholders. Without a weaker pound or much higher productivity, firms which are selling to the rest of the EU now will fall out of the market, leading to job losses and lower GDP.

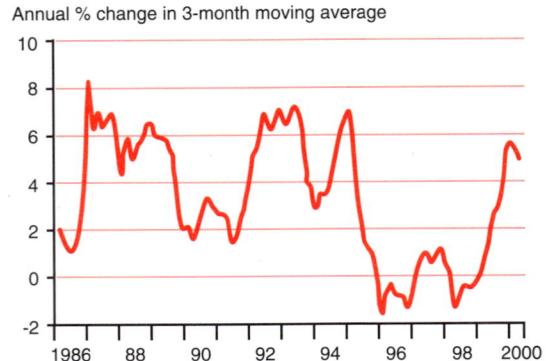

Figure 12.8 *UK manufacturing productivity*
Source: adapted from Primark Datastream, NIESR.

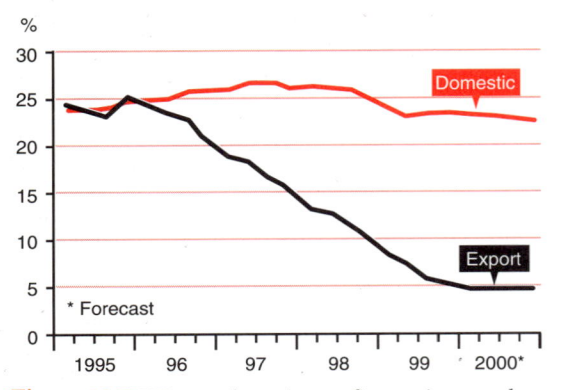

Figure 12.7 *UK manufacturing profit margins on sales*
Source: adapted from Primark Datastream, NIESR.

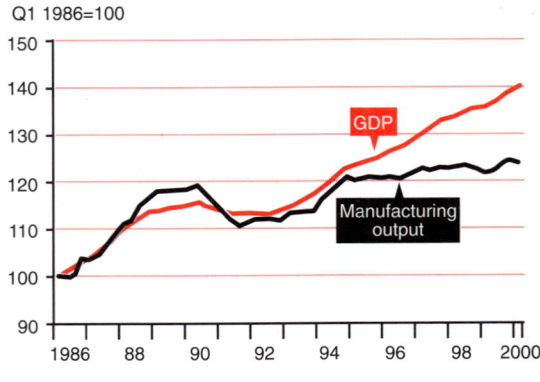

Figure 12.9 *UK GDP and manufacturing output*
Source: adapted from Primark Datastream, NIESR.

8 The euro and the dollar

Between the start of 1999 and September 2000, the euro lost one quarter of its value against the US dollar. Many commentators said this was a reflection of the weakness of the euro. Some, however, argued that it reflected the strength of the dollar.

One key factor which has been forcing up the price of the dollar has been strong economic growth in the USA which was estimated at nearly 5 per cent in 2000 compared to under 3 per cent for the euro zone.

Strong economic growth can undermine a currency's value. For instance, the strong growth which occurred during the Lawson boom of the late 1980s in the UK was accompanied by large increases in imports and rising inflation. The large increase in imports increased the supply of pounds onto foreign exchange markets whilst rising inflation undermined the international competitiveness of British industry.

The current strong growth in the USA, though, whilst seeing a rise in imports, is not producing inflation. Indeed, it is being accompanied by strong growth in productivity which is helping to keep US firms internationally competitive. Moreover, strong growth means that profits are high in the USA and investment is increasing. Some of the finance for this investment is coming from abroad, attracted by higher rates of return than in slower growing Europe. Net inflows of financial capital into the USA from Europe are helping to push up the dollar and depress the euro.

However, it is likely that markets have pushed the dollar up to unsustainable levels in the long run. Foreign exchange speculators tend to act as a 'herd' because it is easier to make money if everyone is acting as if the value of dollar can only go up. At some point, the market will turn and the dollar could find itself losing much of its value against the euro.

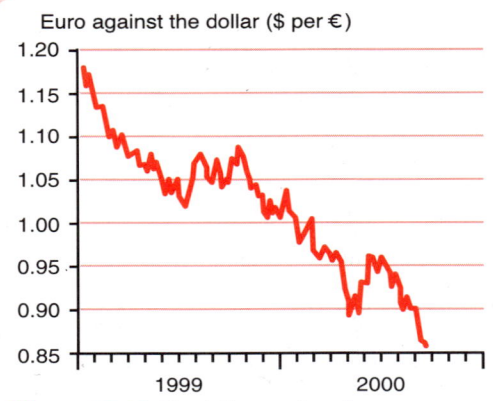

Figure 12.10 *The dollar against the euro*
Source: adapted from Primark Datastream, ABN Amro, Chicago Mercantile Exchange.

9 Should Britain join the euro?

Opinion polls in 2000 showed that a majority of British adults did not want to join the euro. The arguments against are simple.

- Voters do not wish to go through a process of change. There are transition costs in any change. Consumers and workers will suffer because they will have to learn to think about transactions in a new currency. More hard hit will be business which will have to update software, change counter tills and vending machines and reprint price lists. These one-off costs will run into billions of pounds.
- Joining the euro will further increase the powers of the EU and diminish the powers of national government. Many voters have a deep mistrust of the EU, fuelled by a press which is mostly anti-EU. This is an issue of sovereignty and who is most competent to run the economy.
- Few voters understand the serious economic argument that monetary unions are not necessarily good for all regions within the union. Inevitably, the central bank of a monetary union has to set a monetary policy which it believes is in the best interests of the majority of the population. However, it may be inappropriate for some regions. For instance, in 2000 Ireland was enjoying what some argued was an unsustainable boom, with above average inflation. Interest rates in Ireland would probably have been much higher to counter the inflation threat if Ireland had had independent control of its monetary policy. Within a UK context, it is often argued that a tight monetary policy which is appropriate for a booming London and the South East is harmful to areas such as Wales or Northern Ireland where there is above average unemployment.
- If the monetary union were to collapse, there would be large transition costs back to national currencies.
- The exchange rate at which the UK enters the euro is crucial. The very high value of the pound in 1998-2000 against the euro would be the wrong exchange rate to use, according to most exporting businesses. This high exchange rate is likely to lead to large current account deficits. So a much lower exchange rate is needed.
- Many argue that the UK doesn't need to be part of the euro-zone to benefit from it. For instance, although foreign businesses complained about the high value of the pound, the UK in 1999 saw record levels of inward investment. So long as the pound doesn't fluctuate wildly against the euro, the UK can get the benefits without membership.

Those arguing in favour of the joining the euro say that any potential drawbacks are outweighed by the benefits.

- Individuals and firms will not have to pay fees and commissions to exchange UK currency for EU currencies. This reduces costs and encourages trade.
- Exchange rate uncertainty will be abolished with the area which accounts for 60 per cent of our foreign trade. Importers and exports will know how much they will be charged when dealing with, say, French firms. This too will reduce costs and encourage trade.
- Consumers should benefit because there will be greater price transparency. Firms will find it more difficult to segment markets in Europe and charge higher prices for goods in, say, the UK than in Belgium.
- Monetary union is a further step towards creating a single market in Europe. Single markets, like the United States, allow firms to exploit economies of scale and this reduces prices to consumers.
- By staying out of monetary union, the UK is losing its ability to influence how the EU is run and how the EU should develop. This is against the long term interests of the UK.
- If the UK should stay out of the euro, then presumably the anti-euro lobby might argue that Scotland, Wales or Northern Ireland should have their own currencies too. They would also presumably agree that it is against the interests of many individual states in the USA, like California (the 6th largest economy in the world by GDP), to stay within the US dollar monetary union.

Overall, perhaps, the main argument of the anti-euro lobby is a political one, centred around the issue of sovereignty and who should control British affairs. On economic grounds, there are strong arguments both for and against entry. All economists would agree that the exchange rate at which the UK enters will be crucial to whether the UK benefits or suffers in the short term from entry. They also agree that the UK should be at roughly the same point in the trade cycle as Europe to prevent the European Central Bank from setting interest rates which are either too high or too low for the best interests of the UK. In the long term, with the euro-zone being such an important trading partner for the UK, it could be argued that it is difficult to see how the UK could stay out of monetary union, just as it would be difficult to see how California could benefit from being out of the US dollar zone.

Reading list

A. G. Anderton, *Economics*, Causeway Press (3rd ed. 2000) pages 84, 87-94, 258-272, 630-678.
A. G. Anderton, *Economics AS Level*, Causeway Press (2000) pages 84, 87-94, 258-272.
J. Beardshaw et al,, *Economics: A Student's Guide*, Longman (4th ed. 1998) pages 537-602.
P. Maunder et al, *Economics Explained*, Collins Educational (Revised 3rd ed. 2000) pages 96-120, 498-514.
D. Begg et al, *Economics*, McGraw Hill, (5th ed. 1997) pages 542-591.
C. Bamford, editor, *Economics for AS*, Cambridge University Press (2000), pages 154-155, 158-161.
P. Curwen et al, *Understanding the UK Economy*, Macmillan (4th ed. 1997) pages 208-320.
B. Hill, *The European Union*, Heinemann Educational (3rd ed. 1998).
S. Goodman, *The European Union*, Macmillan (3rd ed. 1996).
E.J. Pentecost, 'The modern approach to exchange rate determination and UK exchange rate policy', *Developments in Economics* Vol 12, Causeway Press (1996).
R. Ackrill, 'Economic and monetary union', *Developments in Economics* Vol 13, Causeway Press (1997).
B. Ingham and Osama Abu Shair, 'The World Trade Organisation', *Developments in Economics* Vol 14, Causeway Press (1998).
Nigel M. Healey, 'Britain and the euro', *Developments in Economics* Vol 15, Causeway Press (1999).
R. Ackrill, 'EU enlargement', *Developments in Economics* Vol 16, Causeway Press (2000).

UNIT 12 INTERNATIONAL TRADE AND EXCHANGE RATES

Essay questions

Assume that the UK joins a monetary union with a single European currency. Examine the likely economic effects of this on:
(a) the UK's pattern of trade; (30 marks)
(b) EU consumers and producers; (40 marks)
(c) UK macroeconomic management. (30 marks)
(Edexcel June 1997)

'There are strong arguments both for and against floating exchange rates around the world. However, these arguments should not be confused with the debate about a single European currency.'
(a) Explain the economic issues involved in the debate on the desirability of floating exchange rates. (60 marks)
(b) Evaluate the economic arguments for a single European currency. (40 marks)
(Edexcel January 1998)

Between 1990 and 1996 the value of the UK's exports of goods rose by about 63% and the value of its imports of goods rose by about 48%.
(a) Analyse the factors which might have contributed to these increases in (i) the value of the UK's exports and (ii) the value of its imports. (60 marks)
(b) How might this increase in the value of the UK's exports have affected the level of economic activity? (40 marks)
(Edexcel June 1998)

(a) Examine the costs and benefits for firms and consumers of a country being part of a free trade area. (60 marks)
(b) What might be the economic advantages and disadvantages for a member of the European Union which does not join the European Monetary Union? (40 marks)
(Edexcel June 1998)

Between 1995 and 1997 the effective exchange rate of the pound sterling appreciated by 20%.
(a) What factors might explain this increase in the value of the pound? (40 marks)
(b) Examine the likely effects of this increase in the value of the pound on the UK economy. (60 marks)
(Edexcel January 2000)

(a) Explain how changes in the external value of the pound (the exchange rate) affect the volume and value of United Kingdom exports. (12 marks)
(b) Discuss other factors which influence the sales of United Kingdom products in overseas markets. (13 marks)
(AQA [AEB] June 1996)

(a) How can the Bank of England influence the value of the pound on the foreign exchange market? (12 marks)
(b) Discuss the reasons why the Bank of England might wish to influence the external value of the pound. (13 marks)
(AQA [AEB] June 1997)

Outline the arguments for and against European monetary union. Explain how the creation of a single currency and a European Central Bank could affect monetary policy in the UK.
(AQA [NEAB] 1996)

Outline the theory of comparative advantage. Discuss to what extent the increasing level of foreign investment in the UK can be explained by the theory of comparative advantage.
(AQA [NEAB] 1997)

Explain what is meant by the proposed economic and monetary union of the members of the EU. Discuss the factors which the Government ought to take into account in reaching a decision on whether or when to join the monetary union.
(AQA [NEAB] 1998)

Explain what is meant by a strong pound and what determines the strength of the pound. Discuss whether or not it is in the UK's interest to have a strong pound.
(AQA [NEAB] 1999)

(a) Describe how the UK's recent experience of deindustrialisation compares with that of other countries. (10)
(b) Discuss the impact of the UK's membership of the European Community/Union on manufacturing industry in the UK. (10)
(OCR March 1997)

(a) Explain the term 'economic integration'. (8)
(b) Discuss how economists might analyse the effects of economic integration upon the economies of Europe. (12)
(OCR June 1997)

(a) Using relevant European examples, distinguish between a customs union and an economic union. (8)
(b) Assess the arguments for and against the UK becoming part of the Economic and Monetary Union (EMU). (12)
(OCR June 1998)

(a) Explain what is meant by 'the convergence criteria' for Economic and Monetary Union (EMU). (8)
(b) Assess the economic advantages and disadvantages of EMU. (12)
(OCR March 1999)

(a) Describe what the balance of payments accounts show. (5)
(b) Explain why the balance of payments on current account may be in deficit, even though the overall balance of payments must always balance. (10)
(c) Explain why a fall in the exchange rate may not be successful in tackling a currency account deficit. (10)
(CCEA 1998)

Exam notes

International trade is an area which is always covered on examination papers.
Comparative advantage The theory of comparative advantage states that countries will find it beneficial to trade so long as the opportunity cost of production of goods and services between countries differs.
The balance of payments The balance of payments account (Box 6) is split into two: the current account which shows export and imports, and the capital account which shows flows of money for investment and saving. Trends in the current account are shown in Box 4. Essay questions tend to ask how government policy can affect the balance of payments (see unit 11).
Exchange rates Changes in exchange rates (Boxes 1 and 8) have an impact on exports and imports (Boxes 2 and 3). In turn these have an effect on the broader economy (Boxes 5 and 7). Exchange rate systems, the determinants of exchange rates and their impact on the economy are all part of Advanced level specifications.
The European Union The key question today for the UK is whether or not to join the European Monetary Union (Box 9). Other topics which are set for examinations include the Common Agricultural Policy (see unit 2), competition policy (see unit 4) and the single market.

Unit 13
Development economics

1 Indicators of development

Third World countries show a number of common characteristics, although countries and regions are very different from each other in economic terms. What Third World countries all share is a per capita income level which is well below that of rich industrialised First World countries such as the United States or the UK. Figure 13.1 shows that a significant minority of the Third World population lives on less than $1 a day. Poverty is greatest in Sub-Saharan Africa where nearly 50 per cent of people live at this level. This proportion has changed little over the period 1987-1998. In Latin America and the Caribbean the proportion has even increased. Figure 13.2 shows the numbers living on less than $1 a day in 1998. Over one third live in South Asia, mainly in India, Pakistan and Bangladesh, with approximately 20 per cent living in Sub-Saharan African and another 20 per cent living in East Asia.

Poverty is associated with high levels of infant mortality. Figure 13.3 shows that Sub-Saharan Africa again on this indicator is a very poor region, followed closely by South Asia. Life expectancy too is a good indicator of development. Figure 13.4 and Table 13.1 show selected countries and how life expectancy has changed between 1980 and 1997. For countries like Oman and Bangladesh, there has been a considerable improvement in life expectancy over the period. However, life expectancy has actually declined in some countries. The break up of the Soviet Union in the early 1990s and poorly managed transitions to market economies led to a sharp decline in income in the region. Kazakhstan saw a 40 per cent drop in its GDP in the 1990s and this may help to explain the fall in life expectancy. As for the four Sub-Saharan African countries, all saw low levels of growth in the 1980s and 1990s, with rapidly rising populations. All have suffered greatly from the Aids epidemic which tends to kill young people. Uganda and Rwanda have also seen civil war, which has reduced living standards.

	(years) 1980	1997
Oman	60	73
Bangladesh	48	58
Indonesia	55	65
Bolivia	52	61
Honduras	60	69
Yemen, Rep. of	49	54
Russian Federation	67	67
Kazakhstan	67	65
Zimbabwe	55	52
Uganda	48	42
Rwanda	46	40
Zambia	50	43

Table 13.1 *Life expectancy at birth*
Source: adapted from World Bank.

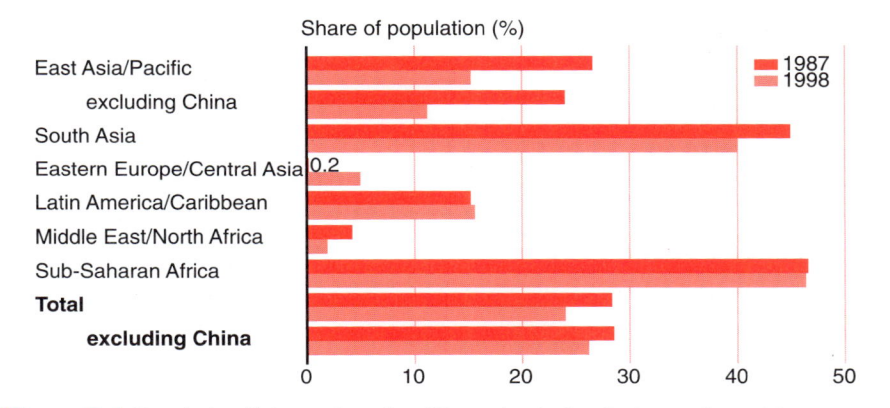

Figure 13.1 *Population living on less than $1 per day in developing and transition economies*
Source: adapted from World Bank, WTO.

Figure 13.2 *Number of people living on less than $1 a day, 1998*
Source: adapted from World Bank.

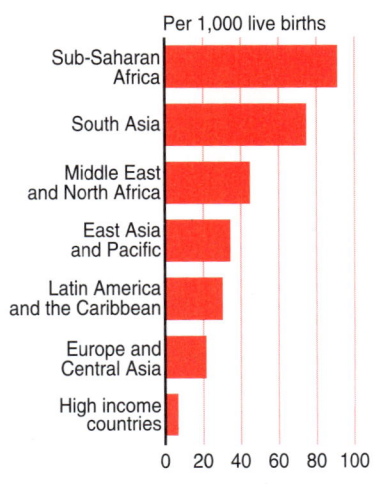

Figure 13.3 *Infant mortality rates, 1998*
Source: adapted from World Bank.

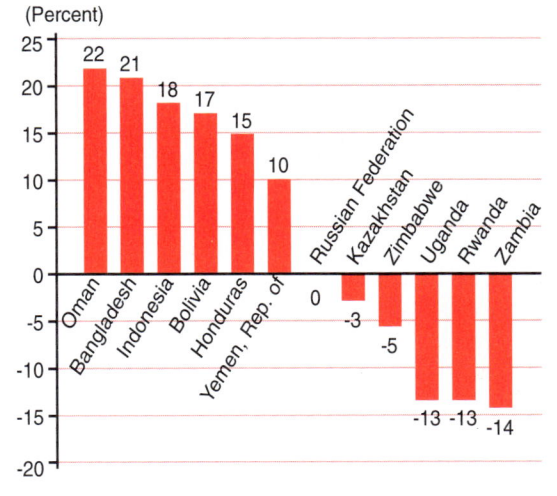

Figure 13.4 *Change in life expectancy, 1980-97*
Source: adapted from World Bank.

THE STUDENT'S ECONOMY IN FOCUS 2000/01

2 Growth and poverty reduction

Economic growth and development are not the same. Economic growth is the change in the productive potential of an economy. It tends to be measured by the long run average change in GDP. Development is about a wide range of issues which includes average incomes. However, it also includes levels of education, income distribution and poverty levels, the environment and political systems.

Changes in GDP act as a broad indication of changes in development. Figure 13.5, for instance, shows that the higher the rate of growth, the greater the level of poverty reduction. The statistics are taken from the period 1988-97 and poverty is measured as the number of people below $1 a day at purchasing power parity values.

However, development can take place without there being corresponding changes in GDP. Figure 13.6, for instance, shows that there is a correlation in Third World urban areas between GDP per capita and access to safe water. Some countries with very low incomes have achieved very high rates of access to safe water, whilst others with higher incomes have relatively low levels of access to safe water.

In general, the higher the GDP per capita of a country, the more is able to be spent on health, education, sanitation and the environment. Rich, industrialised countries tend to have less polluted environments than poorer Third World countries. Almost all young people in First World countries are in school or other education at least to the age of 16, whereas many Third World countries struggle to provide universal primary education. Women in First World countries have some degree of equality with men. In Third World countries, women frequently are denied education and in some countries are restricted in both the social sphere and in the world of paid work. Finally, First World countries are all democracies where citizens enjoy considerable political freedoms. Certain Third World countries are dictatorships, where civil rights are restricted and where there is widespread corruption.

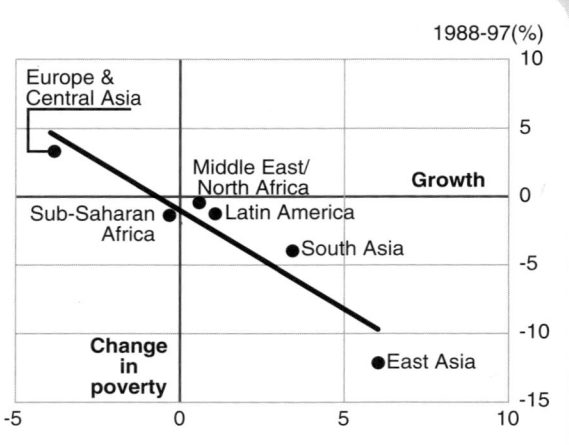

Figure 13.5 *Growth and poverty reduction, by region*
Source: adapted from World Bank, WTO.

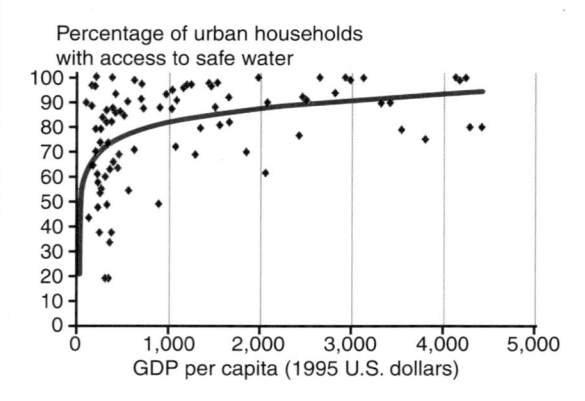

Figure 13.6 *Access to safe water in urban areas and GDP per capita*
Source: adapted from World Bank, WTO.

3 The Kenyan tea industry

Tea is an important crop for Kenya. It accounts for one third of the country's export earnings and it employs 350 000 farmers. The crop's success is partly due to the creation of the Kenya Tea Development Authority (KTDA) in 1964.

This is a marketing board, typical of many found in Third World countries. Unlike some marketing boards, there is no obligation on the part of farmers to sell their tea crop to the KTDA. In 2000, the KTDA only handled 60 per cent of the Kenyan tea crop. The role of the KTDA is to buy tea from farmers, process it in one of 45 tea factories and then sell it on either to the domestic market or more likely to international markets.

When first set up, farmers received 97 per cent of the auction price of tea sold by the KTDA. By selling through the KTDA, small farmers could cut out middlemen and sell directly onto international markets. By 1999, however, farmers were only getting 64 per cent of the auction price of tea. An audit carried out on the KTDA's operations stated that the organisation suffered from 'poor and dishonest corporate governance'. Officials were both inefficient and corrupt. Waste was too high, tendering processes failed to achieve highest prices and officials of the organisation lined their own pockets through bribes and backhanders.

Corruption and inefficiency is a major problem throughout the world, but is particularly prevalent in Third World countries. Because government is often weak, or is itself totally based on corruption, state and other officials are able to siphon off funds to their own advantage. This subverts the workings of the market mechanism and leads to economic inefficiency. By reducing the amount that went to Kenyan tea farmers, the KTDA reduced incentives for Kenyan tea farmers to expand their production. It also reduced the amount available for reinvestment in the industry. This cost both exports and jobs.

In 2000, the KTDA was partially liberalised. Each of its 45 tea factories is to be put into the hands of directors elected by the farmers which they served. The overall board of the KTDA is also to be elected directly by farmers. Investment for individual factories will now have to be sought from the private sector rather than government.

In the long term, many, particularly small, farmers need the services of a marketing board. It is no co-incidence that in the First World, agricultural co-operatives are very common, where individual farmers pool resources to buy equipment or market their products. However, the marketing board needs to be a highly efficient organisation which returns as much as possible to its members, the farmers, and keeps its costs to a minimum.

UNIT 13 DEVELOPMENT ECONOMICS

4 Aids

The Aids virus has had a devastating effect on many countries in Sub-Saharan Africa. Two thirds of the world's 36 million HIV/Aids cases are now thought to be in the region. Figure 13.7 shows that, whilst HIV infections have been limited in industrialised countries, in Sub-Saharan Africa the number of new cases continues to rise.

Aids is not just a devastating illness for its victims. It is also crippling to economies where it is prevalent. Aids tends to be a disease of the young. Young adults can catch Aids through sexual contact. Babies can be born with the HIV virus from their infected parents. For developing countries, young adults often represent expensive human capital which is only just beginning to create goods and services when the illness arrives. Developing countries can ill afford to spend limited resources on education when a significant percentage of those trained to be teachers, nurses or skilled agriculturalists die in their 20s. Countries most affected will soon experience skill shortages which will limit their ability to develop and grow.

As for children, Figure 13.8 shows how significant Aids can be in causing child mortality. In Botswana, 64 per cent of children who die under the age of 5 die from Aids. Children also suffer when one or both of their parents die from Aids. In 2000, there were an estimated 13 million children orphaned by Aids in the world. Orphaned children are more likely to be malnourished and illiterate.

In the First World, Aids has been contained through awareness. In Sub-Saharan Africa, governments have tended to ignore the problem. What is more, in First World countries, Aids victims have been able to fight the virus with a $15 000 a year cocktail of expensive drugs which has prolonged life. These drugs are prohibitively expensive for any Third World citizen. Drug companies have offered to sell the drugs to Third World patients at a fraction of the price. But even if the cost were just $100 a year, this would be too expensive for the majority of Aids victims in Africa. Moreover, distributing the drugs and following a strict dosage regime requires a sophisticated health service and patients who understand the need to take pills daily. Neither is present in poorer countries. African victims suffer not just from Aids but from the poverty in which they live.

At present, there is no let up in the spread of Aids within the Third World. It is a crucial factor in future economic development.

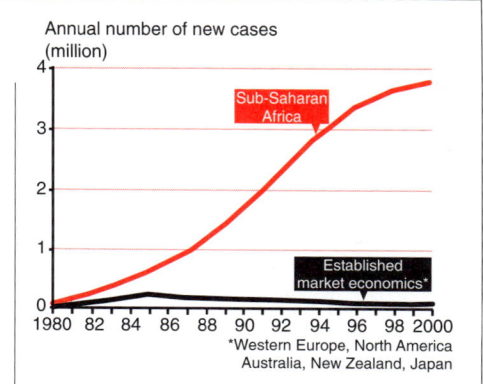

Figure 13.7 *HIV infections*
Source: adapted from UNAids.

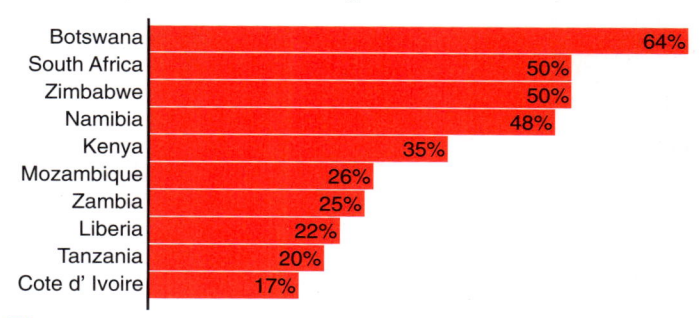

Figure 13.8 *Aids and child mortality, under five child mortality due to aids projected for 2000-05*
Source: adapted from UN Population Division, 1999.

Botswana 64%
South Africa 50%
Zimbabwe 50%
Namibia 48%
Kenya 35%
Mozambique 26%
Zambia 25%
Liberia 22%
Tanzania 20%
Cote d' Ivoire 17%

5 Capital flows to the Third World

Net capital flows to the Third World (the difference between flows into Third World countries and flows out to First World countries) boomed in the mid-1990s as Figure 13.9 shows. However, they halved over the period 1996-99. The main fall was in portfolio investment. This includes purchases of shares through stock exchanges and acquisitions of up to 10 per cent of the equity capital of a company.

Most Third World countries were relatively unaffected by these changes. This is because portfolio investment and loans were concentrated in a handful of countries in Asia, such as China, South Korea, Indonesia, the Philippines, Thailand and Malaysia. The fall was due to the Asian crisis, when a number of these countries suffered problems caused by over-borrowing. Not surprisingly, supplies of financial capital to the region fell sharply.

Despite the Asian crisis, capital inflows to the Third World are seen as desirable. One reason is that they add to the GDP of a country, enabling it to spend more. Figure 13.10 shows gross capital market flows added over 2.5 per cent to the GDP of developing countries in 1999. The money can be used in a variety of ways. In the past, loans to African countries have been used wastefully on armaments or consumption for the ruling elite. The result is that the recipient country is left with debts which it finds difficult to repay.

However, the money can be used for investment, increasing the productive potential of the economy. Foreign direct investment, where First World companies establish factories or buy up Third World companies, is likely to lead to such investment. Technology is often transferred to the Third World. Jobs are created and local suppliers spring up. Much foreign direct investment has gone to Pacific Asian countries, helping these economies to grow at rates of 5-10 per cent per annum in the 1980s and 1990s. Africa has had relatively little foreign direct investment. This is one reason why economic growth rates for the continent have been disappointing over the past 20 years.

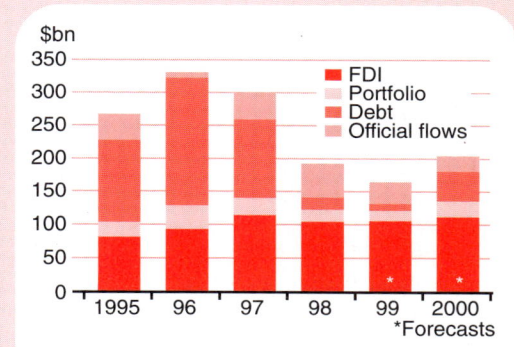

Figure 13.9 *Net capital inflows to Third World countries*
Source: adapted from Primark Datastream, IIF, Goldman Sachs, Euromoney, IMF, World Bank.

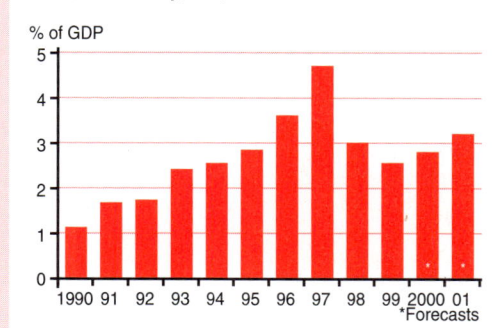

Figure 13.10 *Capital market flows as a percentage of Third World GDP*
Source: adapted from Primark Datastream, IIF, Goldman Sachs, Euromoney, IMF, World Bank.

UNIT 13 DEVELOPMENT ECONOMICS

6 The textile industry in Pakistan and economic growth

In the late 1990s, Pakistan's textile industry enjoyed considerable growth as Table 13.2 shows. Textiles is an industry which is ideally suited to relatively poor Third World countries like Pakistan. Technology is simple, whilst low labour costs give firms a comparative advantage on world markets.

A number of factors has helped growth in the textile industry in Pakistan. The government has identified the industry as a high growth industry in a 'Vision-2005' plan. Textile firms have found it easy to obtain loans from banks. Firms have also shown confidence in their industry by reinvesting profits in new equipment and factories. International competitiveness in 2000 was further helped by a 6.6 per cent devaluation of the Pakistani currency, the Rupee. Labour is very cheap by international standards. Raw cotton too is relatively cheap, produced mainly within the country.

Vision-2005 sees the textile industry expanding exports from $6.4 billion in 1999 to $14 billion by 2005. However, the plan recognises that this might be optimistic and gives two other forecasts of $10 billion and $7 billion. Certain factors will determine which of these proves correct. First, raw cotton prices in 1999 were very low due to a bumper harvest. Exports of $14 billion would require a considerable expansion of raw cotton production. The danger is that raw cotton prices will rise substantially, reducing profitability in the textile industry and cutting both sales and investment. Second, Pakistan will soon have to remove barriers to trade for imported textiles under its World Trade Organisation (WTO) obligations. This could hit output and profitability and reduce investment needed for higher exports. Third, Pakistan is coming up against trade barriers put up by other countries. For instance, in 2000, the country had used up more than 70 per cent of its quota of exports of men's T-shirts to the USA in the first 8 months of the year. On the other hand, the industry has been reluctant to move into manufacture of higher value products. For instance, in 2000 Pakistani firms used up virtually none of its US quota for ladies' skirts.

The textile industry is important for Pakistan. In 2000, it accounted for two thirds of all export earnings. It is a major producer and employer. Pakistani cotton growers depend on the industry for their markets. Doubling exports by 2005 would result in economic growth and a rise in employment. With extra export income, the country would be in a better position to pay its foreign debts and import machinery and technology, and economic development would be promoted.

($m)	Jul-Apr 1998-99	Jul-Apr 1999-2000*	Growth (%)
Textiles			
Cotton yarn	764.7	878.6	14.9
Cotton fabrics	906.1	899.4	-0.7
Knitwear	591.1	698.6	18.2
Bed wear	486.8	569.7	17.0
Readymade garments	529.2	621.3	17.4
Synthetic textiles	326.2	362.4	11.1

Major contributor to additional export earnings
Jul-Apr, 1999-2000*

	Net change ($m)	Contribution (%)	% share in total exports
Additional exports	619.3	100.0	100.0
Textile manufacturers	480.5	77.6	65.0
Other manufacturers	113.3	18.3	14.0
Primary commodities	72.5	11.7	12.8
Others	-47.0	-7.6	8.2

*Provisional

Table 13.2 *Pakistan textile exports*
Source: adapted from FBS Islamabad, EA Wing.

7 Population and growth

The population of the First World is almost static, whilst the population of the Third World is growing. As Figure 13.11 shows, by 2050 the world's population is likely to be between 7.5 and 10.5 million.

A country's population growth has a considerable impact on its economic development. Figure 13.12 shows how Ghana's population is projected to increase from 19.7 million in 1999 to 36.9 million in 2025, almost a doubling of the population. In comparison, the UK will see its population grow by less than 5 per cent, whilst Italy's population is projected to fall by 13 per cent.

Ghana's population grew by 5.4 per cent per annum in the 1980s and 3.1 per cent per annum in the 1990s. Its real GDP grew by 3 per cent in the 1980s and 4.2 per cent in the 1990s. These growth rates compare well with, say, the UK which grew at an average 2.5 per cent per annum over the two decades. However, GDP per capita in Ghana fell in the 1980s because the population growth outstripped the economic growth rate. In the 1990s, the real GDP per capita growth rate was only 1.1 per cent per annum.

High population growth resulting from an increase in births initially acts as a drag on resources. Children need feeding, clothing and education. They might be put to work as young as five but they are unlikely to be very productive till they reach their teens. Then, high population growth puts pressure on the capital of an economy. Unless the economy is growing fast, there is unlikely to be sufficient physical capital to employ the young people entering the job market. The result is high levels of official unemployment. People have to survive and so they create jobs in the informal economy. But these jobs may not be productive, with the consequence that workers earn very low wages. At worst, wages may not be enough to feed, clothe and shelter workers and their families.

For instance, in Ghana, the infant mortality rate per thousand live births was 66 in 1997 compared to 6 in the UK. 23 per cent of adult males and 43 per cent of females were illiterate. Average life expectancy was 58 for males and 62 for females compared to 75 for males in the UK and 80 for females. 27 per cent of children under the age of 5 were malnourished in Ghana compared to 0 per cent in the UK.

Population control, it is argued, is essential if incomes per capita are to be raised quickly. Certainly, large increases in population place stress on the scarce resources available for development to a Third World country.

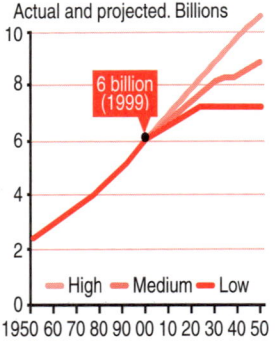

Figure 13.11 *Projected world population*
Source: adapted from *World Population Prospects*, United Nations.

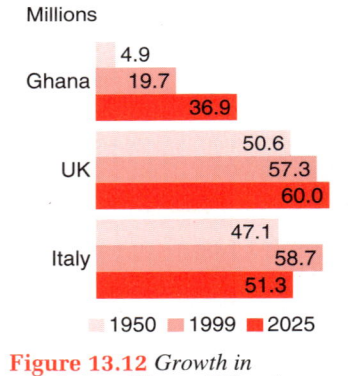

Ghana: 4.9 / 19.7 / 36.9
UK: 50.6 / 57.3 / 60.0
Italy: 47.1 / 58.7 / 51.3
1950 / 1999 / 2025

Figure 13.12 *Growth in population: Ghana, UK and Italy*
Source: adapted from *World Population Prospects*, United Nations.

8 GM crops

GM (genetically modified) crops have been rejected as unsafe by the majority of European consumers. In the United States and Canada, where GM crops were increasingly being planted in the late 1990s, problems with exporting to the EU and protests from environmental groups meant that the acreage planted with GM crops dropped in 1999 and 2000.

The large agro-chemical companies such as Monsanto that have spent billions of dollars and twenty years of research developing GM seeds have been dismayed by the reaction. However, it was always part of their marketing plan that GM seeds would not just lead to lower costs of agricultural production in the First World, but that they would transform the food supply situation in the Third World. By tailoring seed to local Third World environments, farmers could plant crops which would be resistant to pests and diseases. GM crops could also be produced which increased the nutritional content of the crop.

One example of this food modification was 'golden rice'. Vitamin A deficiency is common in the Third World because diets are not varied enough. The result is that millions of children each year are killed or blinded through lack of Vitamin A. Golden rice, unveiled in 1999, provides a neat solution. It is a genetically modified rice strain which contains beta-carotene, a yellow compound which the body converts to Vitamin A. The name 'Golden' comes from the yellow colour of the rice.

Critics of GM foods for use in the Third World put forward a number of arguments. One is that GM food may not be safe to eat and that putting GM crops into the field may lead to jumping of species, with super weeds being created or non-GM species being wiped out by GM affected plants. These are the arguments used against First World planting of GM crops. However, there are additional arguments against the use of GM crops in the Third World. First, there is a fear that it will produce much more monoculture. Instead of farmers producing a range of crops, much of which they will consume themselves, they will choose to specialise, growing just wheat, for example. This will narrow their diet, producing problems like Vitamin A deficiency, and make them more susceptible to sudden crop failures. Second, GM crops are likely to reduce bio-diversity in agricultural systems where strains of crops have been grown for hundreds if not thousands of years because they suit local conditions. Third, Third World farmers will become dependent on First World multinational agri-businesses for seed. Profits will be sucked out of the impoverished Third World farmer and given to the rich First World shareholder.

Supporters of GM crops point out that they are developed to solve existing problems. Millions of children have Vitamin A deficiency because farmers don't grow a sufficient variety of crops today. Golden Rice could solve this problem at a stroke in the same way that vitamins were put into bread in the UK during the Second World War to solve the threat of vitamin deficiency. As for bio-diversity, it is inevitable that farming in the Third World will concentrate on fewer and fewer strains of plant in exactly the same way that this has happened in the First World. Saying that Peruvian farmers should use the strain of wheat that their ancestors have used for hundreds of generations merely condemns them to eternal poverty. The anti-GM lobby is not suggesting, for instance, that UK farmers should use strains of wheat commonly used in 1066. As for profits, Third World farmers will not buy GM seed unless they increase their profitability. Agro-chemical companies can only make sales if their seed has advantages over other varieties.

In 2000, it looked as if the anti-GM lobby would win out. Many believe, however, that this will condemn Third World populations to many more years of unnecessary malnourishment.

Reading list

A.G. Anderton, *Economics*, Causeway Press (3rd ed. 2000), pages 679-727.

J. Beardshaw *et al.*, *Economics: A Student's Guide*, Longman (4th ed. 1998) pages 667-675.

P. Maunder *et al*, *Economics Explained*, Collins Educational (Revised 3rd ed. 2000) pages 515-530.

D. Begg *et al*, *Economics*, McGraw Hill (5th ed. 1997) pages 592-605.

D. Coleman and F. Nixson, *Economics of Change in Less Developed Countries*, Philip Allan (3rd ed. 1995).

G. Rees and C. Smith, *Economic Development*, Macmillan (2nd ed. 1998).

M Todaro, *Economic Development*, Addison Wesley Longman (7th ed. 2000).

World Bank, *World Development Report* (Annual publication).

F. Nixson, *Development Economics*, Heinemann Educational (2nd ed. 2000).

F. Nixson, 'The newly industrialising economies of Asia', *Developments in Economics* Vol 12, Causeway Press (1996).

B. Evers and F. Nixson, 'International institutions and global poverty', *Developments in Economics* Vol 13, Causeway Press (1997).

F. Nixson, 'The Asian financial crisis', *Developments in Economics* Vol 15, Causeway Press (1999).

UNIT 13 DEVELOPMENT ECONOMICS

Essay questions

'A rise in oil prices benefits oil producing nations in the short run but causes serious economic problems to oil consuming nations. However, in the long run everybody is worse off.' Examine the meaning and validity of these statements.
(Edexcel January 1994)

Examine the factors that could determine either: the level of investment in the motor car industry in the UK by both domestic and foreign firms; or: the aggregate level of investment in a country of your choice. (Edexcel June 1994)

According to the 1993 World Bank Development Report, the GNP per capita in 1991 was $100 in Tanzania whereas in the UK it was estimated to have been $16 550. To what extent does it follow that economic welfare in the UK was 165 times greater in 1991 than in Tanzania?
(Edexcel January 1996)

(a) Outline the main economic problems faced by poor developing countries such as those in Africa and Asia. (8 marks)
(b) Critically assess the various ways in which the richer countries of the world can try to help the governments of the poor countries to improve the standard of living of their people. (17 marks)
(AQA [AEB] June 1994)

In what sense may under-population or over-population be regarded as an economic problem? How can economics contribute to the solution of population problems?
(AQA [NEAB] 1997)

How do the economic characteristics of developing economies differ from those of mature economies? Discuss how and why the structure of economic activity in an economy changes over time as economies mature. (AQA [NEAB] 1997)

Explain whether measures of national income per head also accurately measure the quality of life in an economy. What might be the effects of the exploitation of the mineral and timber resources of some Third World countries on the national income per head and the quality of life in those countries and the rest of the world? (AQA [NEAB] 1998)

Outline the main factors which impede the development of the world's poorest nations. Discuss what in your view are the economic policies which might best overcome the problems of the less developed economies. (AQA [NEAB] 1999)

(a) Describe the forms that foreign aid can take. (6)
(b) Discuss the view that for developing countries foreign aid can cause more problems than it solves. (14)   (OCR June 1998)

(a) How does the heavy reliance on agriculture in some developing economies cause problems for them? (8)
(b) Discuss whether these problems mean that development policy should concentrate only on the manufacturing sector. (12)
(OCR March 1999)

(a) Compare GDP per capita and the Human Development Index as alternative measures of development. (8)
(b) Discuss whether economic development and economic growth necessarily occur together. (12)   (OCR June 1999)

(a) Outline the main economic differences between developed countries, newly industrialised countries (NICs), and less developed countries (LDCs). (5)
(b) Illustrate how both developed countries and LDCs can gain from trade with one another. (10)
(c) Some organisations are suggesting that, at the start of the new millennium, all foreign debts of LDCs should be cancelled. Evaluate this idea as a possible strategy for aiding the development of such countries. (10)
(CCEA 1999)

Exam notes

Development Three quarters of the world's population live in the Third World. Development economics considers how Third World countries can grow in a sustainable way, first to relieve absolute poverty (Box 1), and then to relieve relative poverty in relation to First World countries.
Characteristics of developing countries Some questions focus on the characteristics of developing countries, such as low income per capita (Box 1), low levels of education, lack of availability of medical care and low life expectancies (Box 2).
Growth Many examination questions focus on the issue of growth and how it can be achieved.

These questions are much easier to answer if the candidate can remember that the causes of growth for the UK are broadly the same as the causes of growth for Third World countries. Growth comes about when the quantity or quality of the factors of production are increased or they are used more efficiently (Boxes 3 and 6). Factors such as the Aids epidemic can limit growth (Box 4).
Population Population growth is much higher in many developing countries than in the industrialised countries of the world. This presents problems relating to issues such as education spending and unemployment and growth in per capita income (Box 7).

Foreign investment and aid Examination questions may distinguish between investment and aid flows. Some developing countries have grown very fast over the past twenty years, partly because they have received large amounts of foreign investment (Box 5)
The physical and working environment Not all growth is sustainable. There is a growing recognition that environmental, human and social considerations need to be taken into account when discussing whether there has been genuine economic development (Box 8).